Environmental Law in Italy

Environmental Law in Italy

Second Edition

Stefano Grassi
Marcello Cecchetti
Alessandro Andronio
Antonio Borzì
Gianni Taddei
Andrea L. Davis

This book was originally published as a monograph in the International Encyclopaedia of Laws/Environmental Law.

Founding Editor: Roger Blanpain
General Editor: Frank Hendrickx
Volume Editor: Kurt Deketelaere

Wolters Kluwer

Published by:
Kluwer Law International B.V.
PO Box 316
2400 AH Alphen aan den Rijn
The Netherlands
E-mail: international-sales@wolterskluwer.com
Website: lrus.wolterskluwer.com

Sold and distributed in North, Central and South America by:
Wolters Kluwer Legal & Regulatory U.S.
7201 McKinney Circle
Frederick, MD 21704
United States of America
Email: customer.service@wolterskluwer.com

Sold and distributed in all other countries by:
Air Business Subscriptions
Rockwood House
Haywards Heath
West Sussex
RH16 3DH
United Kingdom
Email: international-customerservice@wolterskluwer.com

Printed on acid-free paper

ISBN 978-94-035-1325-6

e-Book: ISBN 978-94-035-1361-4
web-PDF: ISBN 978-94-035-1392-8

Printed in the United Kingdom.

The Authors

Stefano Grassi, born in Florence on 5 December 1945. Classical studies, followed by a law degree from the University of Florence, Italy with a thesis on constitutional justice under the direction of Professor Paolo Barile. He was a professor of public law, constitutional law, parliamentary law and regional law at the Universities of Sassari, Cagliari, Pisa. He was a Professor of constitutional law and environmental law at the Faculty of Law of the University of Florence and Director of the Observatory of Environmental Protection Legislation (O.Le.A.) of Ceradi-Luiss Guido Carli in Rome. He is a member of the scientific committee of *Gazzetta Ambiente* (environmental law review). He is on the editorial board of the magazine *Rivista Quadrimestrale di Diritto dell'Ambiente*, and the magazine *Italian Papers on Federalism*. He is also a practising attorney and is a member of the Bar of Florence.

Marcello Cecchetti, born in Rome on 2 May 1965. Classical studies, followed by a degree in law from the University of Florence, Italy with a thesis in tax law. He has been a lecturer on public law, Faculty of Law, University of Florence and is currently a professor of public law at the University of Sassari, Italy. He has taught numerous law courses at a postgraduate level and has taught environmental law at the University Luiss Guido Carli in Rome. He is a research coordinator for the Observatory of Environmental Protection Legislation (O.Le.A.) of Ceradi-Luiss Guido Carli, directed by Professor Stefano Grassi. He was head of the Legislative Office of the Ministry of the Environment and the Protection of the Territory and the Sea from 2014 to 2018. He is also a practising attorney and is a member of the Bar of Florence.

The Authors

Alessandro Andronio, born in Rome on 21 August 1969. Classical studies, followed by a law degree from the University of Florence, with a thesis in philosophy of law. He is a judge of the Court of Cassation, and has obtained a Ph.D. from the University of Florence in public law. He was an assistant at the Constitutional Court. He has taught environmental law and has taught numerous law courses at a postgraduate level.

Antonio Borzì, born in Nocera Terinese (Catanzaro) on 16 January 1976. He has a law degree from the University of Florence, with a thesis on constitutional law. He is a research doctorate in constitutional law. He received a research grant for constitutional law, and currently is an official of the Regulatory Authority for Energy Networks and the Environment. He has previously worked at the Ministry of the Environment and the Protection of the Territory and the Sea, the Environmental Department of the Region of Calabria and the Regional Environmental Protection Agency of Calabria.

Gianni Taddei, born in Rome on 8 April 1955. He pursued classical studies, followed by a law degree from the University of Florence, with a thesis on constitutional law. He was a lecturer on constitutional law and environmental law with the Faculty of Law at the University of Florence. He is also a practicing attorney and is a member of the Bar of Florence.

The Authors

Andrea L. Davis, born in Boston, Massachusetts (U.S.A.) on 25 October 1954. She obtained a degree in political science and comparative literature from Wellesley College, followed by a law degree from Harvard Law School. She is an American lawyer with an international law practice based in Florence, Italy.

The Authors

Glossary

L. legge (Law): ordinary law representing a source of a general nature, or residual competence, as it regulates all subjects that have not been specifically reserved by the Constitution or by constitutional laws to other sources.

Laws are an expression of the legislative function which Article 70 of the Constitution attributes collectively to the two chambers of Parliament.

The phases of the proceedings that lead to the approval of a law and its entry into effect are: initiative, discussion, examination and voting, promulgation and publication.

Initiative consists of the exercise by determined subjects of their power to submit draft laws to Parliament; this right rests with the government, to each member of the two chambers, and to the organs and entities having this right in accordance with constitutional law (CNEL, *Consiglio nazionale dell'economia e del lavoro*: national economic and labour council; electoral body; regional councils; municipalities).

The second phase of the proceedings takes place within Parliament and involves the examination, discussion and vote of the draft law.

The law must be promulgated within thirty days of Parliamentary approval and is the responsibility of the President of the Republic. The law must be published in the Official Gazette and inserted in the Official Collection of normative acts of the Italian Republic (*Raccolta ufficiale degli atti normativi della Repubblica italiana*) immediately after its promulgation, and in any event no later than thirty days from the same.

The law enters into effect the fifteenth day subsequent to its publication, unless the same law establishes a different term.

D.l. decreto legge (Law Decree): temporary provision having the force of law that the government can adopt in extraordinary cases of necessity and urgency. It is approved by the Council of Ministers, issued by the Head of the Government and published in the Official Gazette, upon which it immediately enters into effect.

The government must transmit the law decree the same day that it is issued to the Chambers of Parliament so that it can be converted into law; even if the Parliament is not in session, it is specially convened and must meet within five days.

The conversion into law must take place within sixty days from the publication of the law decree, otherwise the decree loses its effect retroactively to the date it was adopted. Only the Chambers of Parliament can regulate juridical relationships by means of laws based on unconverted decrees.

Glossary

Legislative Decree. decreto legislativo (Legislative Decree): act having the force of law that the government adopts upon an express delegating law of the Parliament. Such delegating law must indicate the object of the delegation, the term within which the government must exercise the delegated legislative function, and the legal principles and guidelines that the government must respect in preparing the new regime.

Violation of the limits of the delegating law constitutes an indirect violation of Article 76 of the Constitution, the ascertainment of which is the jurisdiction of the Constitutional Court.

The legislative decree is adopted by the Council of Ministers and issued by the President of the Republic in the form of a *decreto del Presidente della Repubblica* (decree of the President of the Republic) (*see* below); it is published in the Official Gazette and enters into effect the fifteenth day subsequent to the date of publication, unless the same decree provides for a different term.

DM decreto ministeriale (Ministerial Decree): formal act with which regulations and administrative acts are adopted by individual ministries. The regulations must specify in their titles that they are regulations, and are adopted after the opinion of the Council of State has been received; they are submitted to the review of and registration by the Court of Auditors and published in the Official Gazette.

The power of the ministries to regulate can only be exercised in matters for which the ministries or subordinate authorities are competent, and on the basis of a law that expressly confers such power (Article 17, paragraph 3, Law No. 400/1988).

Ministerial regulations cannot contain norms that conflict with the regulations issued by the government.

DPCM decreto del Presidente del Consiglio dei Ministri (decree of the President of the Council of Ministers): formal act with which regulations and administrative acts are adopted by the President of Council of Ministers. This corresponds to DMs.

DPR decreto del Presidente della Repubblica (decree of the President of the Republic): formal act promulgating the acts having the effect of law (Law Decrees and Legislative Decrees) and governmental regulations (listed in Law No. 13/1991). After the entry into effect of Law No. 400/1988, such formula only refers to governmental regulations, in that with respect to law decrees and delegated decrees only the formula of d.l. and d.lgs. are used (*see supra*).

RD regio decreto (decree of the king): this corresponds to decrees of the President of the Republic and refers to decrees of the king issued prior to 1944, when Italy was governed by a monarchy. In 1944, the last king retired to private life, but the monarchy did not formally end until 1946 when a popular referendum was approved in favour of a Republic. In the present volume, RD's are cited exclusively for acts having the force of law presently in effect.

LR legge regionale (Regional Law): regional laws are laws that are promulgated by the regions. They are an expression of primary normative function and are connected with State laws on the basis of the principle of competence. Regional laws cannot refer to subject matters for which the State has exclusive legislative power (listed in Article 117, paragraph II of the Constitution). With respect to certain subject matters (listed in Article 117, paragraph III of the Constitution), regional laws must comply with fundamental principles determined by State legislation. Regional laws can regard all other subject matters. Similar to State laws, all regional laws must respect constitutional principles, as well as limits established by European Union (EU) laws and international obligations (for regions having special charters, the subject matters over which they have legislative power are specified in their charters).

Environmental Code – TUA (*Testo Unico Ambientale*), also referred to as the Uniform Text, refers to Legislative Decree No. 152 of 2006.

Glossary

Preface

This volume describes Italy's legislative regime on environmental protection, updated through 31 December 2018.

The description of the legal system and the social-economic characteristics of the Italian situation are limited to summary considerations, with some references to the most common issues of constitutional law and prospects of institutional reform already in course.

The description of the regulation of the individual sectors considers the most recent laws implementing EU regulations and directives, which constitute the backbone of the legal system regarding environmental protection. Given recent innovations, the individual chapters almost always illustrate the regime that was in effect up until recently, which it is still essential to know for the proper application of the most recent laws.

The volume is the result of the common work of all of the authors. The introduction and chapters on general law, zoning and land-use planning, and juridical action of individuals were prepared by Stefano Grassi, who directed the entire project. The chapters on water pollution, air pollution, noise pollution, radiation, land reclamation, waste management and landscape were prepared by Antonio Borzì; the chapters on major accident risks and noise pollution were prepared by Marcello Cecchetti; the chapter on water resource management and soil conservation was prepared jointly by Antonio Borzì and Marcello Cecchetti; the chapters on protected areas, biodiversity, wetlands, sea protection and mining activity, as well as environmental crimes were prepared by Alessandro Andronio, and the chapter on liability questions was prepared by Gianni Taddei. The preparation of the English text, which involved the general coordination and revision of the entire volume, was done by Andrea L. Davis.

Table of Contents

Table of Contents

List of Abbreviations

ACAP	Conservation of Albatrosses and Petrels
ACCOBAMS	Agreement on the Conservation of Cetaceans in the Black sea, Mediterranean Sea and contiguous Atlantic Area
AEWA	African-Eurasian Migratory Waterbird Agreement
AIA	Integrated Environmental Authorization *(Autorizzazione integrata ambientale)*
ANCI	National Association of Italian Municipalities (*Associazione Nazionale Comuni Italiani*)
APAT	National Environmental Protection and Technical Services Agency
ARPA	Regional Environmental Protection Agencies (*Agenzie regionali di protezione dell'ambiente*)
ARERA	Authority for Energy, Networks and the Environment
ASCOBANS	Conservation of Small Cetaceans in the Baltic and North Seas
ATO	Optimal Territorial Area (*Area Territoriale Ottimale*)
AUA	Single Environmental Authorization (*Autorizzazione Unica Ambientale*)
CDU	Certificate of Urban Planning Destination
CIPE	Inter-ministerial Committee for Economic Planning
COBAT	National Used Batteries Consortium
CONAI	National Packaging Consortium
CONOE	Oils and Vegetable and Animal Fats
COOU	Consortium for the Collection, Management and Processing of Used Oils
CSC	Threshold Concentrations of Contamination
CSR	Threshold Concentrations of Risk
DPCM	Department of the Presidency of the Council of Ministers
DPEF	Economic and Financial Programming Document

List of Abbreviations

DPR	Decree of the President of the Republic (*decreto del Presidente della Repubblica*)
DM	Ministerial Decree (*decreto ministeriale*)
EC	European Community
ECJ	European Court of Justice
EEC	European Economic Community
EIA	Environmental Impact Assessment (*valutazione di impatto ambientale*)
EMAS	Eco-Management and Audit System
EQS	Environmental Quality Standards
EUROBATS	Agreement on the Conservation of Populations of European Bats
GDP	Gross Domestic Product
ICNIRP	International Committee for Protection against Non-Ionizing Radiation
IEA	Integrated Environmental Authorization *(Autorizzazione integrata ambientale)*
INFS	National Wildlife Institute
IPPC	Integrated Pollution Prevention and Control
ISPRA	National Institute for Environmental Protection and Research (*Istituto Superiore per la protezione e la ricerca ambientale*)
ISTAT	National Institute for Statistics
MATTM	Ministry of the Environment, Land and Sea
MEDWET	Mediterranean Wetlands programme
MISE	Emergency Security Measures
MUD	Single Environmental Statement Form
NO_x	Nitric Oxide
OECD	Organisation for Economic Co-operation and Development
OGM	Genetically Modified Organism
MISO	Operative Security Measures
PAI	Hydrogeological Plan
POLIECO	National Consortium for the Recycling of Polyethylene Wastes
RAEE	Waste from Electrical and Electronic Equipment
SAC	Special Areas of Conservation
SCAS	Chemical state of ground water
SCENIHR	Scientific Commission on Emerging and Newly Identified Health Risks
SCI	Sites of Community Importance

SEA	Strategic Environmental Assessment
SECA	Ecological State of Waterways
SEL	Ecological State of Lakes
SISTRI	System for Checking the Traceability of Waste
SO_2	Sulphur Dioxide
SPA	Special Protection Areas
TFEU	Treaty on the Functioning of the European Union
TEU	Treaty of the European Union
TUA	Environmental Code (*Testo Unico Ambientale*)
UNESCO	United Nations Educational, Scientific and Cultural Organization
UNLA	National Union for the Fight Against Illiteracy
VIS	Health impact assessment (*valutazione di impatto sanitario*)
VDS	Health damage assessment (*valutazione del danno sanitario*)
VOC	Volatile Organic Compounds
ZPS (Italian abbreviation)	Special Protection Areas
ZSC (Italian abbreviation)	Special Conservation Areas

List of Abbreviations

General Introduction

by *Stefano Grassi*

§1. General Information

I. Geography and Population

1. The Republic of Italy reached a population of 60.5 million inhabitants in 2018 (of whom 8.4% – 5.6 million – are foreigners). Its geographical territory covers a surface area of 302,073 km^2; the population density is approximately 200 inhabitants per km^2 (Source 2018: National Institute for Statistics – ISTAT).

The Italian territory consists of a peninsula that spreads vertically for approximately 1,200 km from north to south, with a coastline of approximately 8,000 km along the Mediterranean Sea, of which 67% is fit for public swimming. The peninsula's land frontiers consist of the broad mountain chain of the Alps. In addition to minor islands located along its coastline, two large islands also constitute part of the Italian territory: Sicily, located south of the peninsula, and Sardinia, located west between the Tyrrhenian and Sardinian Seas.

More than one-third of the country is mountainous (35.2%). In addition to the Alps, the Apennine mountain chain crosses the entire peninsula from north to south, and Italy's two principal islands have notable mountains as well. The rest of the country is predominantly hilly (41.6%), and only 23.2% is flat, largely surrounding the principal rivers Po, Adige, Tiber, Arno, and so on.

Land use is as follows: (a) artificially modelled territories 4.73%; (b) agricultural lands 51.90%; (c) woodlands and semi-natural environments 42.06%; (d) wetlands 0.23%; and bodies of water 1.08%.

2. Mineral resources (carbon, hydrocarbons, etc.) are limited. There are numerous water resources, but they are distributed in an unequal manner. Italy's most important river, the Po, runs through the North, close behind the Alpine valley region which also has lakes of considerable dimensions. The river Tevere runs through Tuscany, Umbria and Lazio, the river Arno runs through Tuscany, the other rivers present in the rest of the peninsula are torrential in nature and normally have modest flows, and there are many lakes of different dimensions in the other regions of the peninsula.

3. The climate changes noticeably throughout the various parts of the peninsula: continental and rainy in the North; variable and influenced by the ocean in the South. The climate also differs among the regions that face the Tyrrhenian Sea (which is wider and more open as compared to the Mediterranean's other marine areas), or the Adriatic Sea (which is more closed with shallower depths and is negatively influenced by the fact that it receives water from the Po and other important rivers in the North).

Italy has numerous areas of important environmental value: approximately 10% of the territory is included in protected natural areas (distributed in twenty-five national parks and numerous regional parks) and many other parts of the country, including cities, constitute important elements of its cultural and landscape heritage (40% of the worldwide artistic heritage is currently in Italy, and forty-seven cities and sites are included in the list maintained by United Nations Educational, Scientific and Cultural Organization (UNESCO)).

II. Legal and Political Structure

4. The Italian State was constituted during the second-half of the eighteenth century. Since its conception (1861), the Kingdom of Italy had a form of parliamentary government. After the First World War, the monarchy was unable to impede the rise of the totalitarian regime of the fascist party.

After the Second World War, fascism was defeated and the Italians, by means of a referendum held on 2 June 1946, decided to definitively close the monarchical era and create the Republic of Italy. A Constitutional Assembly under a proportional electoral system was elected on the same date; it approved a written Constitution which entered into effect on 1 January 1948 and which is still in force today.

5. The principles on which the Italian Constitution is based include both the liberal principles of a State of Law (e.g., the principle of separation of powers), and the democratic principles of a social State (e.g., a guarantee of well-being for its citizens, with specific regard to its workforce). The unalienable rights of man are recognized and guaranteed in the first part of the Constitution, together with all of the other civil and political freedoms (personal liberty, freedom of domicile, freedom of circulation, freedom to assemble, freedom of association, religious freedom, freedom to manifest opinion, freedom to join political parties, freedom to vote, etc.). Economic and social rights are also guaranteed (right to work, right to fair remuneration, right to health, rights of the family and of minors, rights relating to public order, right to a fair division of taxes). The right of self-defence and access to the legal system are also guaranteed. The judiciary is independent and constitutes an autonomous branch with respect to all other State powers, in particular, the executive branch (the government) and Parliament.

The fundamental rights of man are recognized and guaranteed for all individuals. Social rights are guaranteed, not only for Italian citizens but also for European citizens as well as foreigners in certain circumstances.

The right to a healthy environment and consequently a certain quality of life can be placed among social rights. Such right is not expressly stated in the Constitution.

Constitutional case law identifies it, however, as a fundamental concept embodied in certain constitutional principles. Constitutional law No. 3 of 2001 introduced 'protection of the environment and the ecosystem' among the matters reserved to the State's exclusive legislative power, thus, recognizing the constitutional value of the environment as a specific objective for which the State is responsible.

6. The Republic of Italy is a parliamentary republic having two houses (the Chamber of Deputies and the Senate of the Republic), which are responsible for exercising the legislative function and which have control power over the government and its political course. Legislative initiative is normally taken by members of Parliament (as individuals or as parliamentary groups) as well as, in a prevalent measure, by the government. Proposed laws can also be presented directly by the electoral body (50,000 electors) or by regional councils (organs representing the regions that comprise the Republic), but this possibility is rarely used. The same text of each law must be approved by both the Chamber of Deputies and by the Senate of the Republic.

Parliamentary commissions play an important role in legislative proceedings, as they must examine all draft laws and, in many cases, can directly approve them. The two houses may also perform investigations: parliamentary investigative commissions can exercise the same powers as the judiciary in order to acquire necessary information. The Parliament approves an annual budget and authorizes the ratification of international treaties. The houses can promulgate laws revising the Constitution by means of two votes taken at a distance of three months, which must be approved by a qualified majority (minorities can, however, request that such laws be subject to a popular referendum in order to impede their entry into effect).

7. The government must have the confidence of the majority in Parliament. It is composed of the President of the Council of Ministers, the various ministers, and the Council of Ministers itself. The President of the Council of Ministers is responsible for the government's general policies and for maintaining the cohesiveness of administrative and political direction by promoting and coordinating the activity of the different ministers.

The government's principal decisions are adopted collegially (its programme, the budget, foreign policy, draft laws and acts having the force of law, etc.). The single ministers, in addition to their joint responsibility in the Council of Ministers, are individually responsible for their own ministries. Currently, the various ministries have been organized in accordance with a traditional hierarchical model.

The most recent legislation introduced coordination instruments among the various administrative sectors of the State's central administration, and agencies and independent authorities have been authorized to perform administrative functions in sectors in which it is indispensable that the rights of citizens be guaranteed in an impartial manner and with specific technical skill. This is the case, for example, of environmental rights, where the Ministry of the Environment is presently assisted by National Institute for Environmental Protection and Research (*Istituto Superiore per la protezione e la ricerca ambientale* – ISPRA). The intent of the reform is to make the government more efficient in performing those public services that in general the State and public entities must guarantee to citizens. There is also a tendency to distinguish, more decisively than in the past, the policy-setting role that rests with the political power from the role of managing services which rests with the bureaucratic bodies operating under the political power's guidance.

The President of the Republic is elected by the Chamber of Deputies and by the Senate of the Republic united in a common assembly, with the participation of some representatives of the regional administrations. A qualified majority is required for the election of the president, and it is essential that he or she be independent from the parliamentary majority. The President of the Republic remains in office for a period (seven years) that is longer than the duration of the houses (five years) that elect him or her for the same reason.

8. The President of the Republic is the Head of the State and represents the nation as a whole. The powers of the President of the Republic are those aimed at guaranteeing the proper functioning and independence of the State's constitutional bodies. The acts of the President of the Republic are countersigned by the President of the Council of Ministers or by the minister proposing a specific act. In the majority of cases, the countersignature of a minister implies the latter's assumption of responsibility for the act being promulgated, whereas with respect to certain acts for which the president is responsible (e.g., messages to Parliament, appointment of the government, dissolution of the Parliament, etc.), the countersignature by a minister assumes the value of a guarantee of the legitimacy of the president's act.

9. The Italian Republic is a unitary State, but it recognizes and promotes local autonomies. The Republic's territory is, in fact, divided into territorial districts made up of regions (twenty). Each region includes a certain number of provinces (approximately ninety, to which twelve metropolitan cities and the capital city of Rome must be added). Each province encompasses various local municipalities (more than 8,000).

The regions enjoy the greatest autonomy. In accordance with Law No. 3 of 2001, which revised the Italian Constitution, regions currently have legislative power in all matters not reserved to the exclusive legislative power of the central State (Article 117 of the Constitution). Specifically, the central State has exclusive legislative power for the matters listed in Article 117, second paragraph of the Constitution (foreign policy, domestic security, currency regulation and monetary and economic policies, inclusive of antitrust legislation, the organization of the various bodies of the Italian Republic, the provisions of the Criminal Code and Civil Code, the objectives and principles of the social State, as well as the determination of the essential levels of civil and social rights and protection of the environment, the ecosystem and cultural heritage). The regions have legislative power in matters that are very important for local economic development (land use control, health, infrastructures, etc., listed in detail in Article 117, third paragraph of the Constitution); in these matters, regional laws must comply with the fundamental principles determined by State legislation.

The regions have legislative power in all other matters not mentioned in the second and third paragraphs of Article 117, and the State is not required to determine the relative fundamental principles (Article 117, fourth paragraph): these sectors are equally important for the economy and the environment (industry, commerce, crafts, transportation and local public works and services). The State intervenes in many of these sectors when there is the need for economic and social uniformity (e.g., antitrust matters or the coordination of public finances – *see also* Article 120 of the Italian Constitution).

Regional laws are only enforceable within the territory of each region and must comply both with the limits imposed by the Constitution and the restrictions deriving from European law on the environment and the ecosystem, and to ensure 'essential levels' of social and civil rights, placing a significant limit on all regional laws (which contain substantially similar and often homogeneous regulations with respect to the principles dictated by the central State).

Administrative activity is attributed to minor local entities (municipalities, provinces and metropolitan cities). In the case of need for uniformity, however, it can be carried out by the regions or by the State. The attribution of administrative functions occurs on the basis of principles of subsidiarity, differentiation and adequacy (*see* the Constitutional Court, Judgments No. 303 of 2003; No. 6 of 2004; No. 7 of 2016; No. 252 of 2016; and No. 86 of 2017).

The regions have limited financial autonomy. The regions participate in a marginal manner in the functions of the central State (e.g., regional councils can propose draft laws to Parliament and can propose referendums in favour of abrogating national laws; a limited number of regional representatives participate in the election of the President of the Republic; and the principal acts of the government that refer to matters of regional interest are only approved after consultation with representatives of the regional governments). The regions also play an important role in defining regulations and performing administrative functions that regard environmental protection, but the State maintains full responsibility both for determining levels of protection and for compliance with relevant EU and international obligations.

10. Municipalities, provinces and metropolitan cities are territorial entities, provided for by the Constitution (Article 114 of the Italian Constitution et seq.), whose autonomous powers are defined by a general law of the State. Until 1990, the laws regarding the organization of the municipalities and provinces were strictly based on a Napoleonic model (subdivision of the national territory into administrative units organized according to a uniform model, capable of implementing the decisions of the central government in peripheral areas). Today, according to the 1948 Constitution and the law that finally implemented the relative constitutional provision (Law No. 142/1990, and in Consolidated Law No. 267 of 10 August), the municipalities and provinces must be a direct expression of the territorial community that they govern, and they must enjoy statutory autonomy (with the possibility of limited differences in their respective organizations. The metropolitan cities were created by Law No. 56 of 2014 and some significant changes were made with respect to the organization of the provinces).

Municipalities carry out administrative functions, but functions that require coordination and uniformity are attributed to higher levels of government (provinces, metropolitan cities, the regions and the State).

The major part of the administrative activities of the municipalities and provinces regard matters of regional competence. The regional laws, therefore, establish the manner in which the administrative functions of the municipalities and provinces are performed, and for the major part the regions themselves carry out their administrative activity by utilizing the offices of the municipalities and provinces. Many of the administrative functions in environmental matters are, thus, delegated to provincial and municipal organizations (in particular, with respect to environmental monitoring and waste management).

11. All of Italy's public administrations are subject to controls of legitimacy. The laws of Parliament, acts of the government having the force of law and regional laws can be annulled by the Constitutional Court if they conflict with constitutional principles. The Constitutional Court, consisting of fifteen judges (chosen from among the country's most prestigious judges and university professors) also adjudicates with respect to conflicts of competence among the constitutional organs of the State and between the State and the regions. In addition, the Constitutional Court adjudicates accusations against the President of the Republic for acts of contempt with respect to the Constitution or for treason.

The acts of government and all acts of the public administration requiring public expenditure are subject to the control of the Court of Auditors and administrative courts (Council of State and Regional Administrative Tribunals).

12. The entire Italian constitutional system is founded on principles of representative democracy. The Constitution also provides for forms of direct democracy, allowing electors to propose referendums to abrogate laws approved by Parliament, as well as to propose draft laws to the houses. The right to vote is granted to all citizens, both men and women, who have reached the age of majority and, with respect to local elections, is extended to European citizens as well as to foreigners who have been residents for a certain number of years. For more than forty years, all of the Republic's representative bodies (Parliament, Regional Councils, Provincial and Municipal Councils, etc.) were elected using a rigorous proportional method. This guaranteed the presence of a plurality of political parties that the Constitution recognizes as free associations, thus, allowing citizens to contribute by democratic means in determining national policies.

Major modifications to the electoral system were introduced subsequent to proposals for referendums that were made in the early 1990s. In 1993, the electoral system became a mixed system, with 75% of the seats in both the Chamber of Deputies and in the Senate of the Republic assigned using the majority method (with single member constituencies), and 25% of the seats assigned using a proportional system. In 2005, the electoral system underwent a further reform, with the introduction of a proportional system with some threshold levels and a majority premium to the party coalition that achieves the best electoral result (the premium guarantees that the winning coalition obtains 55% of the seats in the Chamber of Deputies; in the Senate, the majority premium is made on a regional basis – there are twenty different regional constituencies – and consequently, a coalition can only obtain an ample majority if it wins in all of the regions). Such electoral system was repealed by the

Constitutional Court (judgment No. 1 of 2014), because it attributed a majority premium independently from whether the winning party reached a minimum threshold of votes. The subsequent Law No. 52 of 2015, which established such threshold to be 40%, was also annulled by the Constitutional Court in Judgment No. 35 of 2017. At present, Law No. 165 of 2017 is in force, which introduced a 'mixed' electoral system (one-third of the seats of both the Chamber of Deputies and the Senate are assigned using a 'first-past-the-post' majority, whereas the other two-thirds of the Chamber of Deputies and the Senate are assigned using a proportional method, corrected by an entry threshold).

The electoral system for regional councils is established by the electoral law of the individual regions (in accordance with Article 122 of the Constitution), in compliance with the fundamental principles established by State legislation. In most cases, a proportional system is used with a majority premium to be attributed to the coalition that presents the candidate for the Presidency of the region.

The mayors of the municipalities are chosen by direct elections (with a two-round proportional system). The presidents of the provinces are elected by the mayors and councillors of the municipalities that are included in the provincial territory.

13. The frequent modification of the electoral system is the cause and effect of a strong evolution of the entire Italian political system which, starting from 1989, is no longer conditioned by the balance between a rightist block and a leftist block; instead, it is recognized that Italy must position itself among the States guiding the EU by means of an adequate organizational structure. This is one of the reasons why significant modifications of its institutional structure have recently been studied and implemented. Among others, such modifications have helped develop a process of modernization and simplification of administrative procedures that play a decisive role in the environmental regulatory framework. Among many others, the following laws deserve particular mention: Law No. 241 of 1990 on administrative proceedings, as well as Laws No. 59 of 1997 and No. 127 of 1997, which initiated a complex process of reform of the central as well as regional and local administrations. The most significant reform was implemented by the revision of Title V of the Constitution (Law No. 3 of 18 October 2001 which amended the Constitution). Such reform established that administrative functions must be performed at the level of government that is the closest to citizens (the municipal level), attributing higher levels of government (provinces, regions and the State) with functions that are incompatible with smaller territorial dimensions or which require uniform application. Subsequent legislative practice and the case law of the Constitutional Court have reserved the major part of significant administrative functions to the central State. Administrative functions in environmental matters are carried out based on State law, which establishes standards for uniform protection throughout the national territory.

The system was evolving towards forms of federalism, with the expectancy of new instruments for financial autonomy granted to regions and minor territorial entities. Delegation Law No. 42 of 5 May 2009 moved in this direction, but the Italian Government did not fully implement such reform.

14. Italy's participation in the EU constitutes a decisive reference point not only for the entire Italian constitutional system, but, above all, with respect to Italy's implementation of the environmental policies prepared and approved by the EU's political organs. Italy has been part of the European Economic Community (EEC) since its institution (1957 Treaty of Rome) and is the State of the EU (the Single European Act of 1988, the Maastricht Treaty of 1992, the Lisbon Treaty of 2007) that more than any other was promoting strong integration among the Member States.

Italy's participation in the EU is consistent with a fundamental characteristic of the constitution system: international openness, set forth in Article 10 of the Constitution (according to which the Italian legal system conforms to the generally accepted norms of international law), Article 11 of the Constitution (in which the Republic accepts limits on its sovereignty to achieve social justice and peace among all people), and Article 117, first paragraph of the Constitution (which subjects national and regional legislation to compliance with international obligations and community law).

This allows norms and principles of international and EU law on environmental protection to be implemented in the Italian legal system.

Both Italy as well as the EU have adhered to the international conventions promoted by the United Nations (UN) (starting from the principles of the Conferences of Stockholm in 1972, Rio in 1992, Johannesburg in 2002, through the recent Paris Agreement of 2015), linking themselves to the broad development that environmental law has had in the context of international law (with the development – among many principles – of those aimed at defining a unitary concept of the environment; identifying environmental resources as the common heritage of humanity; introducing the need to preserve and develop environmental equilibriums to protect the rights of future generations).

15. First the European Community (EC), and then the EU, implemented environmental protection action programmes, which indicate increasingly advanced objectives and guidelines. The first programmes were approved in the 1970s, when the EC Treaties had not yet introduced European competence on environmental policy (environmental goals and standards were introduced as implementation of competence in matters of antitrust, to ensure a level playing field among companies in bearing the technological costs for environmentally friendly production techniques). The first two programmes can be cited (1973–1977 and 1977–1981), which affirmed the principles of prevention and 'the polluter pays', implemented by the first community directives on environmental protection in matters regarding waste, toxic and hazardous waste, fuels, hazardous substances in water and air quality).

With the Third Programme (1982–1986), the EC established an organic policy for environmental protection, which led both to the adoption of important directives (on the risks of major accidents, emissions from industrial plants, on environmental impact assessments (EIAs)), as well as the inclusion in the EC Treaty of a Title containing the principles and objectives for environmental protections (Articles 130R, 130S, 130T – *see* Single European Act of 1988).

The need to integrate environmental protection with other EC policies inspired the Fourth Programme (1987–1992), and concluded with the express attribution to the EU of competence in matters of 'environmental policy' and the explicit inclusion in the European Treaties and Regulations of the precautionary principle (Treaty of Maastricht of 1992 – Article 2 and Articles 171–173).

In the subsequent programmes, the EU emphasized the need to balance environmental protection with the needs of economic development (Fifth Programme, 1993–2000), stating, in the subsequent layout of the Sixth Programme (2000–2020), the co-responsibility of public authorities, entrepreneurs and citizens to implement the principle of integration, with an indication of strategic issues in the areas of greatest environmental significance.

The Seventh General Action Programme of the EU approved by Decision 1386–2013 of the European Parliament and of the Council, identified the priority objectives to be pursued within the period of 2013, specifying the measures to be taken to achieve such goals.

16. The opening of the European legal system led to the implementation in the Italian legal system of an environmental constitution, contained in the law of the EU (consolidated in the current treaties: Treaty on European Union – TEU – and Treaty on the Functioning of the European Union – TFEU – both defined by the Lisbon Treaty of 13 December 2007).

The TEU states that the Union 'shall work for the sustainable development of Europe based … on a high level of protection and improvement of the quality of the environment' (Article 3, paragraph 3, TEU); promote 'scientific and technological advance', 'solidarity between generations', 'sustainable development of the Earth' (Article 3, paragraphs 3 and 5, TEU); and the use of its competence 'is governed by the principles of subsidiarity and proportionality' (Article 5, TEU).

The TFEU establishes the concurrent competence of the EU in environmental matters and affirms the fundamental principle of integration ('environmental protection requirements must be integrated in the definition and implementation of the union's policies and activities, in particular with a view to promoting sustainable development' (Article 11, TFEU); objectives are established for environmental policy (repeating the pursuit of 'a high level of protection … taking into account the diversity of situations in the various regions of the Union'; and the principles to implement in order to achieve those results are specified, basing their achievement 'on the precautionary principle and on the principles that preventive action should be taken, that environmental damage should as a priority be rectified at source and that the polluter should pay' (Article 191, paragraph 2, TFEU).

The criteria to determine environmental policy are also indicated (Article 191, paragraph 3, TFEU, – according to which environmental policy must consider 'available scientific and technical data; environmental conditions in the various regions of the Union; the potential benefits and costs of action or lack of action; the economic and social development of the Union as a whole and the balanced development of its regions'), also referring to the principle of subsidiarity (which was affirmed as a principle for the first time as a criteria for the assumption of responsibility for environmental policy – *see* Article 174 of the EC Treaty, introduced by the Single European Act – was transformed into the fundamental principal for all national policies – *see* Article 5, TEU) and the possibility of more stringent protective measures by the Member States (Article 193, TFEU).

17. On the basis of the action programmes, there has been an intense development of the European regulations and directives, which today cover all sectors of the environmental regime. It is a regulatory body of significant quantitative and qualitative dimensions (there are more than 1,000 regulatory acts), to which all Member States of the union must adapt (in practice, it is the broadest uniform regime at the international level). The European Commission can initiate infringement procedures against Member States that do not comply in a timely manner with European law. The Court of Justice of the EU decides conflicts that arise from these procedures and ensures uniformity in the interpretation of European law.

The legislative acts of the EU are binding (*see* Article 288 of TFEU). The regulations (legislative acts having a general content) and decisions (regulatory acts referring to specific cases) are immediately enforceable (*self-executing*) and must be applied both by citizens as well as by the administrations and courts of the Member States (Article 288, paragraph 2, TFE. The European regulations prevail over Italian law in the case of conflict, and in such case the courts do not apply Italian law and the European legislation is directly applicable). Directives bind the Member States to achieve the results for which they were issued within predetermined timeframes. The Member States have discretion to choose the form and methods to implement the principles and objectives established by directives (Article 288, paragraph 3, TFEU. The provisions of some directives are particularly detailed and contain express prohibitions, so that, upon the expiration of the deadline for their implementation, they become directly enforceable, in the same manner as regulations).

18. Periodically (in principle every year), the Italian Parliament verifies the Italian Republic's compliance with the obligations deriving from its membership in the EU. Law No. 234 of 2012 provides that Parliament approve an annual 'European Delegation Law' (which delegates the government to implement European Directives through the adoption of delegated decrees having the force of law or through regulator acts), and a 'European law' (in which Italian laws that conflict with European law are modified and measures are approved aimed at overcoming infringement procedures initiated by the European Commission).

After a lengthy period of delay, Italy has implemented almost all of the EC and EU directives and regulations relating to the environment: the principal provisions emanating from the EC/EU, therefore, constitute the reference point of the entire environmental protection regime in force in the Italian legal system.

In the case of delays in adapting to European law, the European Commission can initiate an infringement procedure and can also adopt sanctions (Italy has been subject to various procedures. The most significant still underway regard the protection of water from pollution and urban wastewater; ambient air quality, the waste emergency and landfills; and infringement of the Habitats Directive for protection areas for avifauna).

III. Economic Characteristics

A. General Characteristics

19. Italy is one of the seven most economically advanced countries in the world. Its development began starting from the end of the Second World War and has reached high levels over the past two decades, both in the industrial sector and in the service industry.

Its territory is densely populated. Approximately 39 million Italians live in the North and Centre of the country (specifically, according to ISTAT 2018, 27,213,382 in the north and 11,600,675 in the centre, of whom 15.5 million live in the Po Valley) and more than 20 million live in the south (specifically 20,619,697 according to ISTAT 2018). Only approximately forty cities have more than 100,000 inhabitants, and only some metropolitan cities (Turin, Milan, Bologna, Florence, Naples, Bari, Catania, Palermo) and the capital city of Rome have a population that exceeds 1 million inhabitants. There are highly accentuated economic and cultural differences between the wealthy regions in the north and the less developed regions in the south. This is due to both economic characteristics and services relating to schools, housing and social protection in general; analogous differences can be seen with respect to environmental protection.

The presence of strong immigration is felt both in the south and in the industrial areas of the north (which does not, however, reach the levels of immigration in Germany or France). This constitutes an important new phenomenon for Italy, which was a country with a strong flow of emigrants up until only a few decades ago.

20. The Italian economic system, especially in the past, developed due to public intervention, represented in large part by State-owned companies. During the past few years, a process of privatization has been initiated, accompanied by adoption of severe measures to reduce the public deficit and inflation. This process was also begun in order to comply with the levels of State ownership established by the EC in the 1992 Treaty of Maastricht. Italy, whose economy is strongly conditioned by the trend of the world economy, is still affected by the financial crisis that occurred during 2008, and its growth (as in many European countries) has not yet returned to the levels of the past decades. The equilibrium of public finance and an adequate reaction to the most crucial phases of the crisis is also due to the modifications made to internal economic structures over the course of the past two decades: the decrease of interest rates; tax incentives for specific productive sectors; the privatization of companies that were largely publicly held; and the expansion, including with respect to levels of exportation, of high quality economic districts.

Industry and agriculture, although they continue to be significant sectors of the economy, have lost economic importance over the past few years. More than 70% of the Gross Domestic Product (GDP) originates from the service sector (banks, tourism, transportation and insurance).

Major industries are prevalently located in the North and in the central regions (where there are large companies in the service sector as well). There is a prevalence of micro businesses both in the service and in the industrial sectors in Southern Italy. Mid-size industrial companies are spread throughout the north-east. The major part of the facilities considered to be subject to major accident risk are in Lombardy, Piemonte, Veneto and Emilia-Romagna. Petrochemical centres are also located in the other regions (including Sicily, Sardinia and Basilicata).

B. Economic Instruments for the Environment

21. Among the inspirational principles behind Italian environmental policy is certainly the principle of appreciating the economic value of its environmental heritage. The Fifth Action Programme of the EC also affirms:

> in as much as it is difficult to express in monetary terms the value of a large part of the environmental heritage and one must abstain from setting a price for resources that are particularly valuable or rare, the mechanisms for determining the value of prices and accounting instruments are an essential element of sustainable development. The attribution of an economic value to environmental resources can induce economic subjects to consider environmental impact in their decision-making regarding investments or consumption.

The Seventh Programme of the EU specifies:

> an appropriate combination of policy tools would assist economic actors and consumers to gain a better understanding of the environmental impact of their activities and to manage it. Such policy tools consist, among others, in economic incentives, market tools, information requirements, as well as measures and instruments that engage stakeholders at various levels, as a supplement to legislative frameworks.

22. From a legal standpoint, the principle of environmental economics is translated in terms of responsibility: the polluter pays. Such formulation leads to measures intended to internalize environmental costs by means of direct regulatory instruments ('command and control'), economic instruments (among which the various forms of environmental taxation) and instruments based on the application of various forms of *ex post* compensation for damage caused to the environment.

Environmental policy must, therefore, be accompanied by public expenditure policies geared towards favouring environmental protection by means of economic instruments aimed at motivating actions that favour the environment, or which at least create a basis for avoiding or compensating environmental damage.

Italy's public expenditure for the environment is difficult to identify, because notwithstanding the presence of the Ministry of the Environment (the complete name is the Ministry of the Environment, Land Protection and Protection of the Sea – *Ministero dell'Ambiente, della tutela del Territorio e del Mare* – MATT, hereinafter the Ministry of the Environment), allocations are distributed among the individual objectives of the various expense items of at least eleven different ministries. In addition, there are the actual expenses incurred by the regions and by minor local entities (municipalities and provinces), which are paid for using funds specifically transferred by the State.

23. The State's financial undertaking is fairly modest and has tended to diminish over the past few years, notwithstanding the exponential increase of environmental problems and emergencies.

24. Noticeably greater are expenditures made by the regions (using funds that are transferred by the State), due in part to the quantity of functions attributed to them. Such overall expenditure largely refers to water cleanup and the management of water resources, which together constitute 50% of the total amount. Soil and nature conservation together represent approximately one-third of the total expenditure; waste disposal corresponds to approximately 10% of the expenditure; and environmental policy instruments account for 5%. Allocations by the regions for atmospheric cleanup and environmental information, by contrast, appear to be scarce. The resources designated for development of the activities of the National Environmental Protection Agency (ISPRA) and those of the Regional Environmental Protection Agencies (i.e., *Agenzie regionali di protezione dell'ambiente* or ARPA) also appear to be fairly modest to date.

A significant item to be added to those mentioned above consists of the expenses that must be sustained by the Department of Civil Defence in the event of environmental disasters caused by natural catastrophes.

25. The following ministries or departments allocate funds in environmental matters: the Ministry of Agricultural, Food and Forestry Policies; the Ministry of Health, the Ministry of Infrastructure and Transport; the Ministry of the Interior, the Ministry of Fine Arts and Cultural Activities; the Ministry of Education, University and Research; and the Ministry of Foreign Affairs.

26. Investments in environmental matters have, however, created a system of ecological industries and ecological service companies (eco-industries and ecoservices). This is a sector that is still undergoing a period of adjustment and depends in large part on industries in other countries, above all, with respect to aspects regarding technological know-how. The labour sector in eco-industries is in continuous expansion, however, and new professions are emerging.

27. The economic instruments utilized by the Italian legislator in the environmental sector primarily consist of taxes and tariffs. Within certain limits, taxes and tariffs are the price to be paid for the pollution or consumption of a natural resource. Consequently, the costs and damages inflicted on society as a whole are internalized in individual cost-benefit calculations. Taxes and tariffs can serve as incentives or yield, or both.

The following are the principal forms of environmental taxation in Italy:

Waste pollution:

- Tariff for urban waste management (Article 238 of Legislative Decree No. 152 of 3 April 2006).
- Tax assessed on waste sent to dump sites (Article 3, paragraphs 24 et seq., Law No. 549, 28 December 1995).

– Provincial tax for environmental protection (Article 19, Legislative Decree No. 504 of 30 December 1992).

Air quality:

– Regional tax on noise emissions produced by civil aircraft (Article 90, Law No. 342 of 21 November 2000).
– Tax on automotive fuel production (*see* Law Decree No. 331 of 30 August 1993, recently modified by Legislative Decree No. 48 of 29 March 2010).
– Tax on the manufacture of combustible oils (*see*, in as much as relevant, Article 21, Legislative Decree No. 504 of 26 November 1995).
– Tax on emissions of sulphur dioxide (SO_2) and nitric oxide (NO_x) (*see* Law No. 449 of 27 December 1997, Article 17, paragraphs 29–33).

Polluting products:

– Contribution for recycling virgin polyethylene; mandatory consortium for recycling virgin polyethylene (Article 1, Law No. 475 of 9 November 1988; Article 29*bis*); Law No. 427 of 29 November 1993; Article 234 of Legislative Decree No. 152 of 2006).
– Contributions to mandatory consortiums for collection, disposal and recycling (Articles 224, 233, and 236 of Legislative Decree No. 152 of 2006).

Use of environmental resources:

– Tariff for integrated water service (Article 154 of Legislative Decree No. 152 of 3 April 2006).
– Tariff for sewerage and treatment (Article 155, Legislative Decree No. 152 of 3 April 2006).

28. Subsidies, which to date have consisted of financial assistance aimed at encouraging the reduction of pollution or at financing the necessary measures in order to directly reduce pollution, can also be considered economic instruments. The following can be noted:

– Tax credits for small and medium-sized industries which, among others, have adhered to Eco-Management and Audit System (EMAS), to programme agreements for the reduction of polluting emissions, or which manufacture products bearing ecolabels – Article 4, paragraph 9, Law No. 449 of 1997.
– An income tax deduction of 55% for work upgrading energy efficiency provided by Article 1, paragraph 344 of Law No. 296 of 27 December 2006 (the 2007 Budget Law).

– Incentives for fleet renewal and the purchase of ecological vehicles provided by Article 1 of Law Decree No. 5 of 10 February 2009.
– Incentives for manufacturing reconversion and research aimed at identifying technologies and products to substitute harmful substances in order to safeguard the stratospheric ozone level.
– Article 10, Law No. 549 of 1993, modified by Law No. 179 of 31 July 2002.

29. Economic instruments also include the use of cautionary deposits, which consist of a surcharge applied on the sale of potentially polluting products: the surcharge is restored if certain conditions are respected, for example, if pollution is avoided by delivery of the used product to a collection and recycling centre. The tax on plastic bags (introduced in the early 1990s but later repealed) also deserves mention.

Markets where polluters can exchange a limited number of 'pollution rights' are being studied in Italy, but they do not yet appear to have been implemented. This system has been suggested by Organisation for Economic Co-operation and Development and is based on a model adopted in the United States of America. The limitation of the offer is reflected in a positive price for the rights, creating a disincentive to pollute (a party reducing its own pollution can sell the corresponding rights on the market), thus, creating an efficient allocation of emissions among polluters. Interventions can sustain or stabilize the prices of determined goods such as recyclable rejects. In addition, market conditions can be created to favour different forms of liability insurance for environmental damage.

30. 'Green certificates' for renewable energy production (*see* Legislative Decree No. 387 of 2003), 'white certificates' (or 'energy efficiency certificates', regulated by Ministerial Decree (*decreto ministeriale,* DM) 20 July 2004, issued in implementation of Article 9, paragraph 1, of Legislative Decree No. 79 of 16 March 1999), and the trade of emission rights are imposed by the Italian legislator in the framework of implementation of the Kyoto Protocol (aimed at creating an emission trading system related to polluting emissions from industrial plants – *see* Directive No. 2003/87/EC on emission trading, modified by Directive No. 101/2004/EC, implemented in Italy by Legislative Decree No. 216 of 2006, substituted by Legislative Decree No. 30 of 13 March 2013).

31. Sanctions for behaviour which is dangerous or harmful to environmental resources also constitute economic motivation to respect the law. They can consist of penalties for infractions, fines assessed on non-compliant polluters, and performance bonds, that is, payments made to the relevant authorities that are reimbursed once it is demonstrated that the norms or conditions imposed by such authority for performance of a particular job have been respected (e.g., performance bonds for waste transportation).

32. There are many economic instruments intended to involve private parties in environmental protection activities. The following can be mentioned:

– the possibility for companies, either individually or jointly, to participate in mixed consortiums with local entities or in mixed companies that are publicly and privately held, for the purpose of offering waste disposal services, integrated water services, or other environmental services (Articles 147 et seq. and 199 et seq., Legislative Decree No. 152 of 2006);
– voluntary consortia between producers of various packaging materials (Article 223 of Legislative Decree No. 152 of 3 April 2006): *see,* for example, the national packing consortium (Article 224 of Legislative Decree No. 152 of 3 April 2006, National Packaging Consortium 'CONAI');the national consortium for the recycling of polyethylene waste products (Article 234 of Legislative Decree No. 152 of 3 April 2006); and the national consortium for the management, collection and processing of used oils (Article 236 of Legislative Decree No. 152 of 3 April 2006);
– procedures whereby it is possible to foster broad and proper industry participation in the ecomanagement system. The following can be cited (*see also* Part 1, Chapter 1);
– the procedure to assign an 'Ecolabel' mark, regulated by EU Regulation No. 782/2013 and Regulation No. 1941/2017;
– auditors and inspectors to control the efficiency of corporate ecomanagement systems (eco-auditing), who are authorized to attribute ecological quality trademarks (ecolabels) and issue certifications that substitute those of public entities;
– implementation of environmental management systems capable of ensuring improvement of the organization and management of manufacturing activities that impact the environment (which became widespread upon adoption of a Community EMAS – currently governed by Regulation (EC) No. 1221/2009 of 25 November 2009;
– private parties (but also public entities) who can be entrusted with the uniform management of 'ecologically equipped areas, having the necessary infrastructures and systems to guarantee the protection of health, security and the environment' (companies located in such areas can utilize the services offered by the operator without the need of obtaining any form of governmental authorization, in accordance with Article 26, Legislative Decree No. 112 of 1998).

33. Italy has a limited number of large companies, whereas the number of medium and, above all, small-sized companies is quite impressive. For this reason, the use of agreements or programme contracts intended to develop common action by public and private authorities in order to achieve environmental objectives remains poorly developed.

The possibility for private parties to participate in administrative actions regarding environmental protection is currently linked to procedures that can implement general principles on environmental actions, which have also been established, within the framework of EU law, by Article 3*ter* of Legislative Decree No. 152 of 2006.

Precaution, prevention, rectification at the source as a priority and sustainable development are the foundation of the adoption of codes of conduct, environmental reports and ecobalances (currently on a voluntary basis, but which will become mandatory in the future. *See* the French example of Article 53 of *Loi Grenelle environment* of 3 August 2009).

34. Codes of Conduct do not substitute national, EU and international legislation or international treaties; they are, however, innovative instruments, negotiated as well with union counterparts, that are able to compensate environmental inefficiency, making social quality one of the instruments used to face international competitiveness (the most well-known code of conduct is *Responsible care*, adopted by the chemical industry).

35. The 'ecobalance sheet' is the accounting instrument that organically represents the interrelations between the company and the environment, by means of a quantitative and qualitative representation of the environmental impact of the productive activities and the economic effort sustained by the company. The 'ecobalance sheet' is a fundamental instrument for corporate environmental management and for corporate social responsibility, because it coherently indicates the company's 'ecological' attention level (indicating 'hidden' environmental liabilities and introducing rules of transparency in corporate decision-making and operational processes).

36. The 'environmental report' is differentiated from the ecobalance sheet and, with no requirements as to form and content, is a means of communication to all stakeholders of the results achieved, progress made and future prospects of an individual company's environmental undertaking, thus promoting accurate information in the market, as well as the participation of the company and the public in creating efficient procedures and actions aimed at environmental protection.

IV. Social and Cultural Characteristics

37. The absolute majority of the population speaks the Italian language or one of its dialects. The Constitution (Article 6) protects linguistic minorities located in border regions such as Alto Adige (approximately 300,000 inhabitants who speak a German dialect and approximately 40,000 inhabitants who use the Ladino dialect); Val d'Aosta and some valleys in Piemonte (approximately 150,000 inhabitants speak French), Friuli-Venezia Giulia (approximately 50,000 inhabitants speak Slovak). There are also some linguistic islands in other parts of the country (3,000 Serbian-Croatians in Molise; 30,000 inhabitants who speak Greek dialects in Salento and Aspromonte; 100,000 persons live in various Albanian colonies, located in Southern Italy; 15,000 Catalans live in Alghero, Sardinia).

The number of foreigners residing in Italy greatly exceeds 5 million people (according to the most recent ISTAT data there are 5,144,440 foreign residents). Most of them (more than three-fourths) are employed and prevalently live in the north of the country.

Almost all Italians are literate (98% in 1991; according to the last ISTAT population census of 21 October 2001, there were 782,342 illiterates). Education is mandatory until age 16, and only 5% of the student body terminates their studies after obtaining a simple elementary licence without any further degree (1995 ISTAT data). According to data published in 2005 based on research by the University of Castel Sant'Angelo for UNLA (National Union for the Fight Against Illiteracy) 36.52% of the population lacks any diploma: 20 million out of 53 million people who were included in the 2001 census.

The Catholic religion represents the large majority, but all of the other religious denominations present in the country in various measure are also recognized and protected (approximately 650,000 Protestants; approximately 1.6 million Orthodox; approximately 25,000 Waldenses; approximately 40,000 Jews; approximately 1.4 million Muslims; approximately 420,000 Jehovah's Witness; approximately 26,000 Mormons, approximately 180,000 Buddhists, approximately 73,000 Hindus, approximately 72,000 Sikh; etc.).

38. Public sensitivity to environmental issues is continuously increasing, but the level still remains among the lowest in Europe.

Italy's cultural and landscape heritage constitutes one of the fundamental aspects of the environment that Italy must protect and which the rest of the world must be allowed to enjoy. These rich archaeological, architectural, landscape and natural beauty resources have sizeable dimensions from both a quantitative and qualitative viewpoint. Less than 1.5 million Italians, however, appear to be members of environmental protection organizations.

The schools and universities have only recently developed themes relating to environmental information and education. Numerous university courses exist relating to the environment; for example, forestry and environmental science, environmental engineering, soil conservation and territorial planning, history and conservation of cultural resources and so on. The press and television dedicate increasing space to environmental protection themes. It is easy to predict a further increase in the near future.

The development of both social and health services lays the foundation for greater attention and sensibility towards the quality of life. Italians (and also foreigners) have access to free National Health Service for vital care and in emergency situations. Health expenditure constitutes 7%–8% of GDP (an average in line with the other European nations). Social security has seen a strong expenditure increase in recent years, in particular, with respect to the pension system. This has forced various governments to adopt measures attempting to reform the overall social security system and pensions in particular. Assistance expenditures are also paid for in part by local entities. Numerous volunteers operate within regional and local organizations (according to ISTAT 2018, 13.2% of the population above age 14 engaged in some form of volunteer activity).

39. Work habits and consumption by Italians varies noticeably between the regions in the north and those in the south. Those in the north are similar to those of other industrialized European countries, but with anomalies in many industrial districts due to the family nature of local businesses. In the south, the habits of a society undergoing a phase of development are still present. Over the past years, a strong process of urbanization has been consolidated both in the north and in the south, which initiated during the period following the end of the Second World War. Today, more than 70% of the population live in centres having more than 10,000 inhabitants, and 55% live in centres having more than 20,000 inhabitants.

Consumer protection organizations have not yet been adequately developed (they have been promoted, however, ever since Law: No. 241 of 1998). Environmental protection initiatives have been promoted both by consumer protection associations and by the numerous environmental associations active in Italy. Such associations are recognized by the Ministry of the Environment and are empowered to intervene and initiate actions before the competent judicial organs.

V. Principal Environmental Problems

40. The Italian Republic has adopted as its own objectives for the twenty-first century those set forth in Agenda 21 approved by the Rio Conference (*see* the Interministerial Committee for Economic Planning i.e., *Comitato interministeriale per la programmazione economica* – CIPE – Resolution No. 108 of 22 December 2017, which approved the National Plan for Sustainable Development). As a Member State of the EU, Italy has undertaken to implement the Sixth and the Seventh Action Programmes of the EU for sustainable development. At an international level, it has adhered to various international instruments, such as the Declaration on Sustainable Development and relative implementation plan originating from the Johannesburg Summit of 2002 and the Conference of Rio + 20 of 2012; the Conference of Paris of 2015 (COP 21), and the 2030 Agenda for Sustainable Development, approved by the General Assembly of the UN in September 2015. The first problem is that of integrating environmental policies in key sectors of sustainable growth: industry (where environmental protection legislation is already rather well-developed); energy (where the objective of a satisfactory reduction of carbon dioxide emissions remains distant); transportation (where the significant increase in the number of vehicles in circulation has resulted in insufficient progress regarding emissions and fuel quality); and tourism and agriculture (where environmental norms still need to be adequately developed).

41. Italy's waste management system is in a developmental stage, in conformity with what was provided by Directive 2008/98/EC of the European Parliament and Council, which establishes the order of priority to be followed with respect to waste prevention and management (Article 4): (a) prevention; (b) preparation for reuse; (c) recycling; (d) other kinds of recycling, such as energy recovery; (e) disposal.

According to ISPRA's Annual Report of Environmental Data for 2018, the production of urban waste reached 30.1 million tons (497 kg per year per inhabitant). The production of special wastes reached 132.4 million tons (with just over 300,000 tons of hazardous wastes). Differentiated waste collection reached the objective of 65% of urban waste in the most economically evolved regions. Landfill waste reached 19 million tons (7.8 million tons of urban waste and 11.2 million tons of special waste). Approximately 5.4 million tons of waste were sent for incineration. The other quantities of waste were subject to various types of treatment and recycling.

Some extremely critical and emergency situations involving waste management and disposal were handled by emergency and extraordinary legislative and organizational intervention (use of the power to issue urgent and occasional ordinances, law decrees and the appointment of commissioners to manage emergency situations).

42. The chemical quality testing results for surface waters (based on data transmitted by Italy to the Water Information System for Europe in 2016) were: for rivers, 75% good, 7% insufficient, and the remaining 18% unclassified; for lakes, only 48% of the water bodies were classified as good (whereas 42% were unclassified). With regard to their ecological quality status, 43% of rivers reached the quality level (38% good and 5% excellent), 41% below whereas 16% was unclassified; for lakes, only 20% reached the quality level (17% good and 3% excellent), 39% were at lower quality levels and 41% were unclassified. The chemical status of groundwater was 57.6% good, 25% poor, while 17.4% remained unclassified. (*see* data from ISPRA's Annual Report for 2018).

Marine water near the coasts also raises particularly urgent problems given its importance to the tourist industry. There has been a noticeable improvement in recent years due to activation of efficient water treatment systems in almost all of the most important public swimming areas (in 2015, out of 108 monitoring stations in coastal locations, the ecological status of bathing water was classified as 35.2% excellent, 50% good, and 14.8% sufficient – *see* data from ISPRA's Annual Report for 2018).

43. Air pollution and noise pollution from traffic is particularly high in all cities (where the major part of motor vehicles, motorcycles and scooters circulate). Restrictive circulation measures adopted in the major cities are totally inadequate. The problem will only be resolved by the creation of efficient public transportation services (favouring fast tramways and bicycle paths), incentives to improve fuel quality, and car models that have lower emission levels. Carbon dioxide emissions could also be reduced through the development of infrastructures considering the environmental impact of new works and directed towards a re-equilibrium of the relationship between road transport (approximately 80%) and train transport and sea transport. Polluting emissions from road transport have noticeably diminished over the last few years due to technological innovations (as appears from ISPRA's Annual Report for 2018, between 1990 and 2015 nitrogen oxide emissions deceased by 53.1% and those of primary particulate matter PM 2.5 decreased by 59.9%. Nevertheless, the air quality in large urban areas and in some macro areas of the country, such as the Padana Plain (also known as the Po Valley), does not yet comply with the limit values established by European legislation).

Air pollution also derives in large measure from the production of energy. The problem that Italy is facing, together with other European nations, is that of increasing energy efficiency and the production of energy from renewable sources (solar, aeolic, geothermal, hydro and biomass) on the one hand, and of rationalizing electrical consumption on the other. The reduction of greenhouse gases is also an aim of transportation and traffic energy plans that are to be prepared by the regions and by local entities. The contribution of energy processes for the production of energy to overall greenhouse gas emissions remains significant, and there are objective difficulties for Italy to achieve the reduction objectives determined by the Kyoto Protocol and consequent undertakings assumed within the EU, as well as following the Paris Agreement of 2015 (based on data collected in ISPRA's Annual Report for 2018, the total emissions of greenhouse gas diminished in the period 1990–2015 by 16.7%. Although an ongoing reduction in greenhouse gas emissions is forecast from 2015 to 2025, in the following five years, i.e., through 2030, an increase of 2.6% is expected as a countertrend).

44. Due to its climate and geographical location, Italy's natural heritage is among the most beautiful and interesting of all of Europe. Italy has implemented Directive 92/43/EEC (the Habitats Directive on the conservation of nature, flora and wild fauna, through the creation of a European ecological network of special areas of conservation – SACs – Nature 2000 Network) and Directive 2009/147/EC (for the determination of special protection areas – SPAs – for the protection of birds). In 2017, Nature Network consisted of 2,609 sites having a surface area amounting to 19.3% of the national territory. Natural areas are, however, threatened by human presence (the medium density of 200 inhabitants/km^2 reaches 500 inhabitants/km^2 in the plains and along the coasts), by a strong industrial presence (more than 5,500 installations subject to an integrated environmental authorization (*Autorizzazione integrata ambientale,* IEA) and approximately 650,000 local units of companies having more than one employee, of which one-fifth have more than ten employees) and by the expansion of building construction and infrastructures. Forests cover a lower area than the European average (approximately 30% forests, as compared to the European average of approximately 34%); and many species of fauna are threatened with extinction. The system of protected areas is, however, undergoing a phase of strong development: it presently consists of approximately 3 million hectares equal to more than 10% of the national territory (the majority of the protected areas consist of national parks (46.3%) and regional parks (49.9%)).

45. The industrialization of the 1950s, 1960s and 1970s created a significant number of gravely polluted areas (numerous areas have been declared to have a high risk of environmental crisis or have been declared critical). Programmes aimed at compiling a census of polluted areas and sites (which are much more than the number identified to date) have been initiated and the necessary cleanup programmes, recovery of abandoned industrial areas and relocation of certain industrial activities have also begun. There has been an objective increase of industrial investments, however, for environmental protection.

46. Soil conservation constitutes one of the most dramatic problems facing Italy. The land is often subject to floods, landslides and even earthquakes (particularly grave in recent years). There are also many volcanic areas in the Italian peninsula and the islands. In addition to the torrential nature of the rivers and their water basins, the causes are to be found in inadequate preventive work and the construction of buildings and infrastructures in areas that are at hydrogeological risk. Legislation addresses the problem by means of the study, monitoring and census of areas at risk (by now a complete data bank exists of events that have taken place); planning the work to be done and the restrictions to impose in individual water basins (basin plans and hydrological requirements in accordance with Law No. 183 of 1989); as well as by reorganizing the control organs and organs that have been entrusted with performing preventive and emergency work.

§2. Fundamental Principles of Environmental Law

I. Concept of the 'Environment'

47. The difficulty of rendering environmental protection laws effective derives from the same structural complexity as the object of the protection.

'Environment' is a macroscopic and indeterminate concept. The definition of 'environment' depends on factors that are particularly complex and interrelated and is connected to valuations by a plurality of subjects motivated by interests that often conflict in an incurable manner.

There are at least two opposing concepts of the environment and its relationship to man. An anthropocentric concept considers man as an active subject with respect to environmental resources and equilibrium, utilizing natural resources and guaranteeing, by means of environmental protection, his own living conditions (this is the largely prevalent theory in the law of almost all Western legal systems, in particular, in EU legislation). The ecocentric concept considers the environment and nature as values in themselves and man as a vital element who must find his place within the equilibrium of the biosphere (this theory is only found in part in law, but it influences some of the more radical proposals regarding recognition of environmental protection at the level of constitutional law). These two concepts (which are never so schematic in the legal system) conflict with the definition of diverse policies regarding environmental protection, conservation and promotion.

Environmental protection implicates the necessary activation of interdisciplinary competence for the description and definition of the values to be protected (often without the availability of solid data, even on a scientific level), both with respect to quantitative dimensions (environmental resources; factors and elements that comprise such resources; equilibrium between resources and true environmental factors) and qualitative features (objectives and manner of protection), as well as the evolution over time of the phenomena that are the object of legislative intervention.

These problematic characteristics make it extremely difficult to utilize ordinary domestic law instruments to regulate actions taken to protect the environment, as well as to define the same legal dimension of the object of protection. It is difficult to entrust courts lacking data and consolidated scientific findings with the responsibility of elaborating the principles that must be affirmed in this delicate subject matter.

48. Constitutional norms can constitute a useful reference point for the solution or formulation of these problems. Such norms are direct expressions of a specific society's social and political equilibrium in a precise historical moment. Constitutional norms can, therefore, define the principles on the basis of which the object of protection can be identified, that is, define what resources and interests society believes are relevant from a legal standpoint, with the consequent guarantees including legal guarantees; define the relationship between the needs of environmental protection and the needs of economic development (definition of the equilibrium between biosphere and technosphere); and define the criteria to be used to impose decision-making procedures and the resolution of conflicts of interest among the various parties intervening in environmental matters whether as users, operators, polluters or promoters of environmental improvement.

II. The 'Right to the Environment' and Environmental Protection Rights

49. Many constitutions explicitly recognize the right to the environment as a right of man. But the consideration of a right to the environment as a fundamental right of man has been subject to various objections both on a theoretical and on a practical level.

On a theoretical level, the difficulty of precisely identifying the object of a subjective right to the environment is noted, given the lack of preciseness of the juridical 'environmental' element. One response to this kind of objection is that other concepts that relate to the fundamental rights of man are equally vague and indefinite (one can cite the amorphous concepts of morality, public order and security: concepts that place limitations on rights). Another objection is that with respect to the environment it is not possible to predetermine the procedures to protect the relative right. It must be noted, however, that predetermining what procedure to follow to protect other rights of man that are generally recognized and consolidated in constitutional formulas is also impossible. In practice, subjective rights refer to interests that become consolidated over time, according to a static concept of the interests to be protected, whereas the environment, as the object of subjective law, has a dynamic nature (past, present and future are simultaneously considered in identifying ecological equilibrium and the environment to be protected) and has a relational structure (impeding denial to an individual holder of the right to recognition of the interests to which such relationship refers). Attempts to identify society as the owner of environmental rights (understood as a common good) highlights the diverse structure and novelty of the relationship to be protected and demonstrates that it cannot be reduced to a traditional scheme of subjective rights.

50. The same plurality and complexity of technical solutions that allow the objectives of environmental protection to be guaranteed make a static vision of law difficult with respect to a specific legally recognized value. In practice, it is difficult to identify the network of interests at play and the principle by which the predominance of one or another solution is determined to be the best in view of environmental protection. The courts are entrusted with the almost impossible task of identifying the principle of predominance, or of trying to coordinate the interests and legally recognized values involved; a task which at best can take place in an impartial and transparent manner with the active participation of the public administration, in particular, by its technical bodies.

Similarly, positive results are not achieved by present legal scholarship which, in net opposition to recognition of an environmental right as a right of man, asserts the pretext of recognition at a constitutional level of the right of nature (an opinion which is connected to an ecocentric concept: the state of nature as a value in itself and not only as a value for man).

Recognition of the right of nature corresponds to a legal-naturalistic concept that encounters technical difficulties that are almost impossible to resolve: who owns the interests of nature? What are the limits of risk of alteration of an ecological equilibrium beyond which violation of the right of nature is recognized? This position underlines how the environment must constitute a measure and quality of rights and criteria to balance constitutional values and rights that are hypothetically in conflict. The environment must, therefore, be understood not only as a right of man, but also, and above all, as an obligation which both individuals and the State must respect (including future generations), and as an objective to which not only the rights of man but also so-called economic or social rights must be directed.

Obligations relating to the environment do not only refer to obligations of conservation or abstention from behaviour that could damage it, but also to an obligation of the State as well as of its citizens to take positive action directed at guaranteeing standards of ecological *equilibrium*. The degradation of the environment also constitutes an attack on principles of substantial equality, because it is evident how environmental damage affects weaker categories of citizens in more than mere proportional terms. Protection of an environmental right is, therefore, perfectly situated within the principle of participation and substantial promotion of the human person, to which the recognition of social rights is connected.

51. The formula 'right to the environment' is, therefore, understood not in a technical sense of the existence of a subjective pretext referring to the environment, but instead as a synthetic formula used to identify a range of situations that are subjectively structured and protected in diverse manners:

> the environment as an ecological equilibrium is not a resource that can be appropriated or a resource on which individual subjective situations can be based. It is up to the legislator and public administrations to satisfy expectations of well-being and quality of life connected to environmental protection, whereas in relation to individual ecological factors or individual differentiated expectations, subjective situations can be identified that are entitled to direct protection, such as the right to a healthy environment, the right to participate in public decision-making processes, the right to be informed of the state of the environment, etc.

III. Environmental Protection in the Italian Constitution

52. When the social State is in crisis and the market is seen as the only acceptable and efficient manner of managing the economy, public action must be renovated and legitimized to mobilize interests that largely exceed the sum of individual needs. After the national question and the social question, the State can find a new source of legitimacy in ecological questions, since nature appears to be a collective good *par excellence.*

The most recent constitutions affirm principles and norms that view the environment and environmental protection as one of the values that characterizes the entire constitutional system, and which is entitled to constitutional guarantee.

The absence of explicit references in its Constitution has not impeded Italy, similar to Germany, from affirming the existence of constitutional principles regarding environmental protection by reference to the principles that protect the right to property, the right to health, or the need to protect the cultural and landscape heritage. These principles have been developed by the constitutional courts of both countries.

The principles to which reference can be made in the 1948 Italian Constitution are those set forth in Article 9 ('the Republic protects the landscape and historic and artistic heritage of the Nation'); Article 32 ('the Republic protects health as a fundamental right of man and interest of society'); Article 41 ('private economic initiative is unrestricted. It cannot be performed in contrast with social utility or in such a way as to cause damage to security, liberty, or human dignity'); and Article 44 (the part that subordinates agricultural activities to the principle of 'rational exploitation of the land').

More in general, the recognition of rights relating to environmental protection is connected to the complete and detailed regulation of social rights expressly guaranteed by the Constitution, in particular, by the principle of equality affirmed in Article 3 ('it is the responsibility of the Republic to remove social and economic obstacles which, limiting de facto the freedom and equality of citizens, impede the full development of man and his effective participation in the nation's political, economic and social organization').

Based on this written law, the Constitutional Court has been able to develop case law in which social rights have assumed the formal level of constitutional rights entitled to immediate protection, independent of an implementing norm approved by the legislator.

53. Article 9 of the Constitution protects the 'landscape' and the nation's 'historic and artistic heritage'. The norm guarantees the conservation and promotion of the objective results of man's multiple cultural activities. This affirmation of principle has allowed constitutional case law to extend such guarantee to man's 'cultural heritage', protected by the UNESCO Convention of 1968 (i.e., material heritage expressing the value of a civilization, goods or property of archaeological, historic and artistic interest, historical centres, fishing villages, castles, farm houses and typical houses, etc.) and the landscape understood not only as the entirety of natural beauty to conserve, but as the land's manner of existence, in its visual and dynamic perception and in perennial renewal.

54. The right to health is guaranteed by Article 32 of the Constitution as a 'fundamental right of man', as well as an 'interest of society'. On the basis of such affirmation, the Constitutional Court has determined it is necessary to protect the right to a healthy environment, as a condition and guarantee of the effective exercise of said right to health.

55. The protection of economic initiative (both private and public) in view of the requirement that such initiative should not conflict with security, human liberty and human dignity, has allowed environmental protection to be identified as a limit on industrial activity, thus, supplying the legal basis for maintaining the difficult balance between economic development and environmental protection, synthesized in the formula of 'sustainable development'.

With the Constitutional Revision Act No. 3 of 2001, the environment and the ecosystem' is expressly mentioned in the Constitution: it is a 'matter' attributed to the exclusive legislative power of the State. The explicit indication of such objective in the Constitution has allowed reinforcing the orientation of case law which, based on the above principles, has defined the environment as a constitutional value that everyone (citizens, local entities, the regions, the State) must pursue.

IV. The Principles of Environmental Law

56. Legal scholarship has for some time construed environmental law as law based on principles, in close correlation to the object of judicial protection.

Only principles are able to provide transversal guidelines, coordinating them in the various sectors of the legal system that are necessarily involved in defining the policies and legislation on environmental protection. Only principles can establish the correct relationship between the decisions and assessments of the legislator and the administration with the indications of technical bodies (which are essential for providing scientific data capable of defining the strategies of protection).

The principles are the indispensable parameters for balancing the different values entitled to protection by the Constitution (such as the environment, the right to health, the right to work and economic activity, etc.), and to assess the results achieved. Principles are, moreover, particularly suitable to construct guidelines for the regimes that must necessarily be adjusted to dynamic processes and a diachronistic point of view of the equilibrium of ecosystems. The need for interventions for environmental protection can be measured by observing the distance between the timing of nature and the timing of technological development. It is thus necessary to identify principles capable of directing the administration to respond with immediacy to emergency situations, as it must nevertheless govern specific situations that make the application of general and abstract rules that have been predetermined by the legislator impossible.

In the Italian legal system, the principles to be applied are those that have been developed in international declarations and those approved by European Treaties.

57. All of the principles that have been developed based on international declarations and European norms, by legal scholarship and by case law, affect in various ways the development of the administrative procedures that define environmental interests.

The reference of Article 1, paragraph 1 of Law No. 241 of 1990 to the principles of the European legal system as general principles for administrative activity therefore assumes primary importance. Such reference is certainly operative, after the further explicit reference to European principles that regard the environment made by Articles 3*bis*–3*sexies* of Legislative Decree No. 152 of 2006.

Such provisions establish that: environmental principles cannot be modified or eliminated unless by express provision of subsequent laws 'provided that compliance with European law is always guaranteed' (Article 3*bis*); as well as, in a manner that is not always clear, the principle of environmental action (Article 3*ter*), the principle of sustainable development (Article 3*quater*), the principles of subsidiarity and good faith cooperation (Article 3*quinquies*), and the right to access to environmental information and the principle of participation for purposes of cooperation (Article 3*sexies*).

There is no explicit reference to the principle of integration and the principle of balancing, which are instead essential measures in defining European policies, with particular reference to procedural rules.

Given their significance in the interpretation of all sectoral regimes that will be reviewed in the following chapters, the principles that inspire the European legal system and Italian legislation are described below, also on the basis of the case law of the Court of Justice of the EU and the Constitutional Court.

58. The principle of integration and the principle of sustainable development constitute the synthesis of all international and European principles related to environmental protection.

The principle of integration is one of the fundamental principles of the entire European legal system – *see* Article 11 of the TFEU. It is also repeated in Article 37 of the Charter of Fundamental Rights declared in Nice (which became a norm of positive law in accordance with Article 6, §1, of the TEU) – which formulates it as follows: 'a high level of environmental protection and improvement of its quality must be integrated with the policies of the Union and guaranteed in conformity with the principle of sustainable development' (*see* the Court of Justice of the EU, 29 March 1990 in case C-62/1988, 11 June 1991 in case C-300/89; 9 May 2019 in case 305/18). Through the reference to the principle of sustainable development, the need is affirmed to reconcile economic progress with environmental protection, establishing the priority of environmental needs, in the sense that their consideration does not need to prevail, but must always influence the phase when the norms are established as well as the phase when they are implemented.

The principle of sustainable development presents considerable difficulties with respect to its definition in positive law but is a fundamental criterion for orientation in determining environmental policies and the procedures that must define them (*see* Article 15 of the Rio Declaration of 1992). In the context of the classic definition contained in the World Commission on Environment and Development Report (the Brundtland Report) of 1987 ('development that meets the needs of the present without compromising the ability of future generations to meet their own needs'), sustainable development is articulated very broadly, both as a principle able to define programming objectives, as well as being a principle able to define procedural criteria for the establishment of policymaking decisions aimed at protecting environmental interests. The objectives defined on the basis of the principle of sustainable development involve at least three pillars (economic development, social development and environmental protection – as defined in the Johannesburg Declaration of 2002), and are of such magnitude and complexity that it is essential to specify that they can only come through a clear definition and application of procedural criteria (which must be considered redundant, as well as the approximate wording being susceptible to improper evaluation – and being uncritically biased towards 'sustainability' – required by Article 3*quater*, Legislative Decree No. 152 of 2006): it regards application of the principle of integration among the procedures ad decisions that involve economic development, social development and those aimed at environmental protection; but even more so it is necessary to apply the balancing principle, which is also a fundamental principle of European law, which is not referred to in Legislative Decree No. 152 of 2006.

59. The balancing principle includes the need to balance and coordinate environmental protection with other public interests, which has allowed the Constitutional Court to establish a principle of the absolute prevalence of environmental protection when acceptable limits for human health are exceeded. Only in those cases in which such limits have been respected may the legislator exercise its discretion in balancing the relationship between the needs of development, consideration of the costs of applicable technologies, and the needs of environmental protection (*see*, for example, Judgment No. 127 of 1990 on the best available technology). The Constitutional Court subsequently specified that the added value (the primacy) to be given to the environment does not imply an a priori super ordination with respect to other interests, but makes it necessary to ensure that the environmental interest is always adequately weighed in all decision-making processes (*see* Constitutional Court, Judgement No. 85 of 9 May 2013, which affirms that 'All fundamental rights protected by the Constitution are reciprocally integrated and therefore it is not possible for one of them to have an absolute prevalence over the others. Protection must always be "systematic and not divided in a series of uncoordinated norms in potential conflict among themselves" (judgment No. 264 of 2012). If this were not the case, there would be an unlimited expansion of one of the rights, which would become a "tyrant" with respect to the other recognized and protected legal situations, which constitute, as a whole, an expression of the dignity of the person'). Balancing implies the use of decision-making procedures capable of guaranteeing not only transparency and public notice, but also adequate mechanisms of democratic control. In this sense, the typical procedures of environmental law – such as EIAs, strategic environmental assessments (SEA) and IEAs – are a paradigm of environmental procedures that could be used as a reference point for all administrative procedures in this sector. In such procedures, in fact, not only is all scientific data made available and all effects measured that the decisions to be made might produce on the environment, but above all, space is given to the fundamental right to environmental information and to the right of participation, which allow determining the measures the be adopted and environmental equilibriums to be restored, maintained or promoted, that are the result of a conscious and democratically shared decision-making process.

60. The principles that define the environment (anthropocentrism; unitary concept; economic efficiency of the environment) are the premise and corollary of the principles of sustainable development, integration and balance. This category undoubtedly includes, in addition to the principle of man's centricity, the principle of the unitary nature of the environment, which allows not so much as its individual factors or components to be protected independent of each other, as much as the harmonious assemblage of strictly interrelated physical, chemical and biological conditions generating a precious equilibrium that represents the true objective of environmental protection.

This unitary concept of the environment, understood not in an objective or material sense but in view of its finality and purpose, constitutes an effective representation that allows global objectives to be pursued (which is qualitatively different than the mere sum of various sectoral interventions). It is clearly manifested in European directives regarding EIAs and integrated anti-pollution protection, to which the Constitutional Court has referred (*see* Constitutional Court, judgments No. 225 of 2009 and No. 198 of 2018; *see also* Council of State, section V, judgment No. 3000 of 6 July 2016).

The same category includes the principles that define the priority of environmental interests with respect to other interests and values that merit protection (*see* above §58), as well as the principles that attribute an economic value to environmental resources and elements, among which the fundamental principle is 'the polluter pays' (already cited in §22). This principle was regulated by part of the EU Directive No. 35/2004 and also embraced by Legislative Decree No. 152 of 2006: Article 3*ter* specifically includes it among the principles of an environmental lawsuit, and repeats it with respect to the initiation of such proceedings in Article 242 (the cost for the initiation of a lawsuit is to be borne by the polluter); Article 244 (issue of an order for the polluter to reclaim polluted sites); Article 253 (which provides a right of recourse against the responsible party to the benefit of whoever spontaneously reclaims polluted sites); and Articles 300 et seq. (which contain the regime on the indemnification of environmental damage). Both the norms on environmental taxes as well as procedures aimed at promoting, through market instruments, the actions of individuals pursuing environmental protection objectives (certification procedures, environmental management procedures, green certificates and the trading of emission quotas, environmental balance sheets) fall within implementation of the principle of the economic efficiency of the environment, but also define new perspectives in elaborating principles for administrative action in the environmental sector.

61. The *principle of prevention* and the *principle of precaution* have been affirmed because, with respect to environmental protection, prevention is always less burdensome than compensation, and it is often difficult, or even impossible, to repair the consequences of activities that place environmental resources and equilibrium at risk.

Almost all environmental decision-making is thus inspired, above all, by the principle of prevention and the assessment of scientific data that allows it to be established, in advance, whether a specific activity is capable of damaging environmental resources and their equilibrium (as correction at the source of environmental damage, which is only used if preventive measures have not had the expected effect, by reducing and eliminating pollution and the environmental alterations it causes as a priority at the source).

Although the precautionary principle is based on a review of scientific data, it anticipates the threshold of the preventive measure even in cases in which scientific uncertainty exists with respect to the consequences on the environment of specific activities (Article 15, Rio Declaration of 1992; Article 191 TFUR, expressly referred to by Article 3*ter* of Legislative Decree No. 152/2006). The lack of scientific knowledge cannot justify delaying a preventive measure that is adequate with respect to the scope of the possible risks. It is a principle having a strong potential for expansion, which implies the use of procedures aimed at implementing a structured strategy of risk analysis (including the assessment, management and communication of the risk). The Communication of the European Commission 200/1 of 2 February 2000 dealt with this issue and indicated the criteria for applying such principle. Application of the precautionary and prevention principles is frequent in the judgments of the Court of Justice of the EU (9 September 2003-C-236/01; 28 January 2010-C-77/09; 9 March 2010-C-379/08; 11 July 2013-C601/11; 4 March 2015-C-534/13; 9 June 2016-C-78/2015; 28 March 2019-C487/17), in the judgements of the Italian Constitution Court (No. 116 of 2006; No. 93 of 2013), of the Council of State (section V, judgment No. 6250 of 27 December 2013), and of the Italian Civil Court of Cassation (judgment No. 15853 of 28 July 2015 and No. 33538 of 27 December 2018).

Both the principle of prevention as well as the precautionary principle affect the manner in which some fundamental institutes of the administrative procedures are implemented, such as the administrative review and the motivation, as well as the manner in which authorization procedures are conducted, which tend to be based on the principle that environmental authorizations are not interchangeable and that such authorizations are temporary in nature, since they are structurally aimed at having their effects reviewed and monitored.

62. *Correction as a priority at the source* intervenes when the preventive protection has not had the expected outcome; such principle is applied through the reduction and elimination of sources of pollution and environmental alterations that have occurred (Court of Justice of the EU, 7 December 2016 in case C-686/15). Such principle affects the procedures that define the standards and limits of potentially polluting activities and are the basis for the urgent measures and the power to issue ordinances which must necessarily follow ad hoc procedural rules. The principles of prevention and correction at the source can also be linked to planning and programming procedures, which have a central role among environmental procedures, but which in only be indicated here in relation to the typical procedure of the SEA.

63. The right to environmental information and the right of access to environmental information are the corollary, and at the same time the premise, for all of the other principles that define the procedures for environmental protection. Environmental information also constitutes the premise of the *right of participation and co-responsibility* in the definition of environmental policies and measures. The principle of environmental information and the principle of participation are inspired (and have, at the same time, given impulse to) by the typical environmental assessment procedures (EIA, SEA, impact assessment), which constitute the strong nucleus (and, for some, the actual fundamental principles) of environmental procedures, assuming a paradigmatic character and an expansive capacity that is capable of conditioning all of the other procedures, raising problems of coordination among assessment procedures and authorization procedures (Court of Justice of the EU, 4 September 2018 in case C-57/2016).

64. The principles of subsidiarity, co-responsibility and cooperation concur in defining the role of the parties responsible for environmental protection actions, but at the same time they affect the procedures that allow the concrete implementation of such principles according to a unitary assessment of the environment understood as a unitary complex system. The co-responsibility, or shared responsibility, and cooperation are corollaries of the relational dimension (also referring to the different territorial levels of government) that characterize the environment.

Subsidiarity is a fundamental principle of the European legal system (not by chance, affirmed for the first time in the context of environmental policy – *see* Article 130, Single Act of 1986). In fact, it is necessary to have procedures able to guarantee organizational flexibility in the definition of competence, able to identify the most suitable level of government to acquire an overall and uniform vision of the protective measures to implement (*see* Article 5 of the TEU). Concurrent competence implies the need to implement procedures capable of establishing concrete forms of cooperation and coordination and the contextual assessment of environmental interests (as indicated in Article 7 of Directive 2008/01/EC on industrial emissions 'Member States shall take the necessary measures to ensure that the conditions of, and procedure for the grant of, the permit are fully coordinated where more than one competent authority or operator is involved or more than one permit is granted, in order to guarantee an effective integrated approach by all authorities competent for this procedure'): it is possible to also cite for such purpose, alongside the forms of coordinated and unified definition of the procedures (conferences of services and programme agreements, forms of simplification aimed at identifying a sole place where the procedure is carried out (*see* the 'one-stop shop' concept) and a sole procedure to assess the various authorization profiles that can be activated with reference to a specific activity (integrated environmental authorization and single environmental authorization (*Autorizzazione Unica Ambientale*, AUA).

V. Case Law of Constitutional Court

65. In Italy, constitutional case law has had to deal with many issues regarding the distribution of legislative power among the State, regions and local entities, and has attempted to resolve the complexity of the organizational scheme of the Italian public administration through the use of principles of coordination, such as affirmation of the need for effective cooperation among the various levels of territorial government by means of programme agreements, undertakings and joint services (the principles of subsidiarity and good faith cooperation are now expressly referred to in Article 3*quinquies* of Legislative Decree No. 152 of 2006).

Constitutional case law has also dealt with the distribution of legislative power between the State and the regions in view of the modifications introduced with the reform of Title V, second part of the Constitution by the Constitutional Law No. 3 of 3 October 2001, which attributed the State with exclusive legislative power for *environmental protection and protection of the ecosystem and cultural heritage* (Article 117, second paragraph, clause *s*).

66. Initially, the Constitutional Court interpreted such provision by finding environmental protection to be a transversal value entitled to constitutional protection, with respect to which there are inextricably intertwined interests within the legislative power attributed to the regions. State legislative power is attributed with direct responsibility, but this does not exclude the pursuit and enrichment of such values by the regions in carrying out their concurrent and residual legislative power (*see* judgments No. 407 and No. 536 of 2002; No. 221 and No. 307 of 2003; No. 259 of 2004; No. 62, No. 108 and No. 214 of 2005; and No. 182, No. 246 and No. 398 of 2006).

67. In the current terminology of the Constitution, the objects of environmental protection are identified using multiple terms (in Article 117, second paragraph, clause 2, 'environmental protection' is indicated next to 'protection of the ecosystem' and the 'protection of cultural heritage'; while the third paragraph of Article 117 indicates, as a matter of concurrent legislative power, the 'enhancement of environmental and cultural resources'; Article 9 of the Constitution still contains the poignant provision of 'landscape protection' and protection of the 'Nation's artistic and historic heritage' tied to the dynamic principle of the 'promotion' of 'culture' and 'scientific research' established by the first paragraph).

68. Matters that definitely interfere with environment interests are among the concurrent legislative powers of the regions (such as 'enhancement of environmental and cultural resources', the 'protection of health', 'land use control', 'civil protection', the 'production, transportation and national distribution of energy', 'ports and civil airports', the 'major transportation and navigation networks', 'technological and scientific research and support of innovation in industrial sectors'). Other matters as well, not mentioned in paragraphs 2 and 3 of Article 117, and therefore left to the residual legislative power of the regions, are definitely related to and interfere with environmental interests (agricultural and forestry can be indicated; industry, trade; crafts; manufacturing, transportation and the regional and local distribution of energy; regional and local transportation and navigation networks; hunting and fishing).

69. Subsequently the court has tried to clarify that the attribution to the State of exclusive legislative power for environmental protection corresponds to a need of uniform management in defining environmental interest. The court has, thus, held that the environment, as a collective resource, identifies a 'public function', consolidated in a clearly delineated legislative regime that only the State can guarantee in a uniform manner throughout the national territory; while the regions can only touch indirectly, in carrying out their competences, the resources entitled to environmental protection, but they cannot interfere with or modify the 'adequate and irreducible levels' of protection determined by the State (*see* judgments No. 367 and No. 378 of 2007, No. 62 of 2008; and No. 61 and No. 225 of 2009.

70. The position of the Constitutional Court on the issue of the distribution of competence between the State and the regions is summarized in judgment No. 66 of 2018, which states that the environment '... has a complex morphology, capable of including not only the protection of physical-naturalistic interests, but also cultural heritage and landscape, suitable for distinguishing in an original, specific and unrepeatable manner a certain geographical and territorial area' (Constitutional Court, judgment No. 66 of 30 March 2018, point 2.2 of the Considered in law) and that 'the environment, as repeatedly affirmed by this Court, "does not appear to be configurable as a sphere of state competence strictly circumscribed and defined, since, on the contrary, it is inextricably interrelated with other interests and competences". It "outlines a sort of "transversal" matter, with respect to which there are different competences that can be regional, while decisions that respond to needs that are worthy of a uniform regime throughout the entire national territory rest with the State" (judgment No. 407 of 2002; in the same sense, more recently, *see* judgments No. 66, No. 150 and No. 215 of 2018; No. 212 of 2017, No. 210 of 2016 and No. 171 of 2012). The national regime aimed at protecting the environment and landscape therefore "'acts as a limit on the regime that the regions and autonomous provinces dictate in other matters for which they are competent', without prejudice to the powers of the latter to approve stricter environmental protection norms while exercising their competence, provided for by the Constitution, that concur with that of the environment" (judgment No. 199 of 2014; in the same sense, *see* judgments No. 246 and No. 145 of 2013, No. 67 of 2010, No. 104 of 2008, No. 378 of 2007). It requires a broad institutional strategy, which is carried out in an extensive planning activity throughout the national territory. In such sense, the attribution to the State of exclusive competence for such "matter-objective" does not imply the absolute preclusion of regional measures, as long as they are aimed at implementing the environmental value and raising its levels of protection' (*see also* judgments No. 121, No. 126 and No. 151 of 2018).

VI. Legislative Characteristics

71. Italian legislation regarding environmental protection has also developed through sector specific interventions which have often been subject to an uncoordinated succession of laws. This is, above all, due to lack of identification of the environment as a unitary value to be protected. For example, the following interests are dealt with on an individual basis: health interests; urban interests; interests relating to water, air and soil pollution control; problems relating to wastes and waste disposal; problems relating to natural beauty, and so on. Only the most recent legislation introduces norms that directly and globally protect the environment, as in the case of regulation of the prevention of major industrial risks; laws regarding the planning of water basins in view of rational water resource management and soil conservation; those relating to environmental planning; and laws referring to EIAs.

The difficulty of identifying coherent guidelines in environmental legislation also derives from the fact that the laws were often issued during emergency situations, which is a problem common to many sources of environmental law in other legal systems (examples in the Italian legal system include the law relating to the exportation of toxic wastes; the law relating to the presence of nitrogen in drinking water; the law relating to algae in the Adriatic sea; and the law relating to major accident risks). In addition, Italian laws often are a mere implementation of EU law, with the advantage of inserting coherent principles of the 'European environmental constitution' or the disadvantage of further sectoral and partial implementation of the protection of environmental interests.

The legislative response, in addition to being 'torrential', remains episodic, giving rise to superfluous and chaotic bodies of law that lack internal coordination (there are simply too many laws, creating problems that are difficult to resolve with respect to public awareness of their contents, as well as criminal penalties that are inefficient because they are too strict in some cases and too lenient in others): the recent introduction of 'environmental crimes' in the Italian Criminal Code also leaves ample margins for the interpreter, due to the indefinite nature of the type of offence introduced. Environmental law also intervenes in a transversal manner in sectors that are the object of autonomous laws, which have analogous needs of protection (e.g., health law, labour law, energy law, urban planning and construction law, transportation law, etc.). This often leads to problems of interference among the various laws in a sector, which are often subsidiary but more often than not are in conflict with each other, with respect to both principles and competence.

The techniques and normative practices in the field of environmental protection highlight in a significant manner the 'legal crisis' involving the general and abstract laws that characterize the contemporary constitutional State (in civil law systems), and the difficulties of identifying a method of producing laws that is adequate in relation to the polyhedral nature, complexity and technicality of the matters to be regulated.

72. With reference to environmental protection, there is an inevitable subjectivity of valuation regarding definition of the interests involved, as well as difficulties arising from having to deal with emergencies caused by natural phenomena or by technological development, which necessitate intervention by means of immediate, concrete and, sometimes, temporary laws. These laws are often emergency measures geared towards solutions that are limited in time and space, and which are often the result of the negotiable nature of law, which limits itself to finding compromises between political and social subjects.

The crisis regarding the principle of certainty of the law which derives from the above is accentuated in the field of environmental protection, also due to the fact that it is necessary to work in conditions of scientific incertitude, on the basis of data that is in a constant state of flux and in the presence of social deviations that are difficult to predict or control. It is, therefore, impossible to entrust exclusive responsibility for the efficient protection of the environmental equilibrium (which will be simply favoured or damaged, not determined, by legislative intervention) to the specific laws that are promulgated. It is instead necessary to focus attention not on the mere codification of the law or the crystallization in uniform texts of the various laws that have already been promulgated, but on the identification of guidelines for legislative policies as well as for constitutional policies themselves.

On this level, constitutional law and the necessity of identifying principles and constitutional policy guidelines can suggest a diverse formulation of legal technique, which must not only rationalize existing law but, above all, identify the principles and guidelines for regulatory intervention by public authorities. The law, even if easily located in a uniform text and in organically prepared collections of laws, cannot always supply the solution to a concrete case. It is instead necessary to offer a clear reference point by identifying the basic principles to be applied by public organs and private subjects in their dealings with each other (as well as for the courts, called upon to resolve any eventual conflicts that might arise).

Many reform proposals of the Italian legislative system are aimed in this direction, but they do not go beyond a mere rationalization of certain sectors. This was the case first with some legislative decrees regarding waste and water pollution, and most recently, by Legislative Decree No. 152 of 2006 which collected the provisions relating to the principle sectors of environmental law: water, air, waste, soil conservation, reclamation and cleanup and environmental damage (also regulating the various environmental assessment procedures: SEAs (Strategic Environmental Assessment), EIAs (Environmental Impact Assessments) and IEAs (Integrated Environmental Authorizations).

VII. Environmental Protection Law and Industrial Activity

73. The multiplicity of norms regarding environmental law and the complexity of the administrative organization that exercises competence in such matters does not simplify industry's collaboration in adopting the appropriate measures to achieve environmental quality objectives that respect the limits placed on them in order to protect health and conserve natural resources.

Some characteristics of environmental law negatively impact industrial behaviour: uncertainty in identifying the applicable law; the absence or insufficiency of instruments implementing the law (the regulations, programmes and guidelines necessary to comply with laws are not always approved and issued in a timely manner); the absence of a suitable agency for the creation of the necessary technical norms, as well as the absence of suitable instruments to adequately publicize such norms; the frequency, often caused by failure to resolve pre-existing problems, of occasional and urgent ordinances adopted through the use of emergency powers which are attributed both to the Ministry of the Environment and to regional and local authorities.

A further difficulty consists of the instruments that are utilized to govern industrial activities: rigorous preventive verification of such activities (according to a 'command and control' technique); a highly differentiated system of authorizations and permits; and a repressive apparatus based on criminal sanctions (intended, in particular, to punish the lack of respect of formal rules, for example, lack of preventive authorization when required, or lack of provision of information regarding the activity being performed).

In order to have an idea of the difficulties companies face when they intend to open a manufacturing facility, it is sufficient to count the number of bureaucratic passages and the time necessary to obtain required authorizations. It must be noted, however, that the general reform of the public administration presently in course provides for reduction of the length of time and number of procedures required to obtain authorizations; unification of administrative competence; and simplified procedures in order to make industry more directly responsible in matters of environmental protection. The most recent legislation, in implementation of various EU directives, aimed at giving substance to the principle of integration, forms of integrated authorization and procedures were introduced in order to issue a single authorization to build specific kinds of installations (those having the greatest environmental impact and those of greatest economic importance, such as integrated chemical installations, the steel industry, oil refineries, power plants to produce electricity, etc.). The individual provisions are indicated in the following chapters (e.g., the IEA procedure contained in Part II of Legislative Decree No. 152 of 2006 (section III*bis* and Annexes VI through XIII of Part II).

74. The above problems are further aggravated in Italy by the difficulty of regulating environmental protection in a uniform manner throughout the entire national territory. This is due both to the significant diversities in the geophysical situations of the various regions, and to significant differences with respect to their economic structures (with major distinctions between the regions in the north and those located in the south). This is the reason why the distinction between national laws and regional laws cannot be eliminated.

An additional problem consists of the presence in the manufacturing industry of only a few large industries and a very broad and diffused web of medium and small-sized companies. It is evident that the solution to environmental law problems cannot be dealt with in the same terms for these two categories of industries. One of the problems that environmental legislation must confront in Italy is that of defining the rights and obligations of industrialists with greater precision, bearing in mind the above distinction as well as the necessity of identifying the characteristics of the passive subject of the law (the business) in relation to the needs of the environmental sector. It is necessary to establish particularly simplified forms of administrative procedures for small and medium-sized companies, as well as to institute technical assistance centres to resolve problems regarding respect of the environment through the collection and dissemination of data of environmental importance that refers to each business sector and by establishing compliance time frames with respect to emission limit values in each sector, in view of the more delicate economic *equilibrium* of the type of company involved.

§3. HISTORICAL BACKGROUND

75. Prior to the entry into effect of the Constitution of 1 January 1948, protection of Italy's natural resources and environmental patrimony was given by general laws requiring the payment of compensation for damages deriving from an illicit act (Article 2043 of the Civil Code), the law regulating relationships between neighbours (Article 844 of the Civil Code on emissions, and Article 890 on distances from unhealthy or dangerous installations), norms intended to protect health (1934 Uniform Text of Health Laws and laws of the 1930 Criminal Code) and landscape, natural beauty and Italy's archaeological, historic and artistic national heritage (special laws of 1922 and 1939, and laws promulgated even prior to the criminal laws of the 1930 Criminal Code).

The 1948 Italian Constitution does not contain laws that expressly refer to the environment as a juridical object entitled to protection, but it introduced principles that have allowed development of both legislation and case law recognizing rights connected to environmental protection.

Notwithstanding numerous petitions aimed at rationalizing legislation regarding environmental protection and creating coordinated and organic sources of law, at present no general environmental protection law has been promulgated in Italy. The relative laws all relate to different sectors faced with environmental protection problems.

Even the 1986 Law that created the Ministry of the Environment only introduced some general norms that are applicable to environmental protection (such as the payment of compensation for environmental damage and procedures for EIAs).

After the introduction of 'environmental protection' among the matters for which the State is vested with legislative power in accordance with Article 117, second paragraph, clause *s* of the Constitution, Legislative Decree No. 152 of 2006 was issued, which, as noted, attempts to contain in a single law the regulation of the most important sectors of environmental law. This law also proves, however, the extreme difficulty of adequately rationalizing and organizing Italian legislation on environmental law.

76. During the first twenty to thirty years that the 1948 Constitution was in effect, Italian legislation only indirectly protected environmental interests. Protection continued to be effectuated on the basis of prior legislation and was, from time to time, connected to the protection of health interests (1934 Uniform Text and its subsequent modifications), urban planning (Law No. 1150 of 1942 and Law No. 765 of 1967), and interests connected with Italy's historic and artistic heritage as well as its landscape heritage (Laws No. 1039 and No. 1497 of 1939).

Competence in matters of environmental protection was entrusted to the Ministry of the Interior (responsible for all police and security functions) and to the mayors, as the competent organs entrusted with protecting the hygiene of land and buildings.

The protection technique consisted of imposing restrictions and emanating prohibitions that the competent authorities were responsible to enforce (including by recourse to occasional and urgent ordinances).

77. The initiation of a legislative regime directly related to environmental interests took place in Italy prior to promulgation of a law at the level of the EC. Law No. 615 of 1966 on air pollution control and prevention constituted an important precedent with respect to protection from pollution caused by thermal and industrial plants and factories, as well as by motor vehicles. It is a law intended to directly protect the quality of the air, but it also contains norms whose primary purpose is to impede the alteration of atmospheric conditions rather than merely control individual sources of emissions.

In addition, Italy already had laws generally intended to protect health and environmental interests at the same time: examples are the law regarding solid urban waste disposal (Law No. 366 of 1941) and laws regarding protection of the population from ionized radiation (Law No. 1860 of 1962).

78. During the 1970s, Italy, similar to other European nations, manifested a new sensitivity towards environmental protection at the same time that positions were being taken at an international and regional level (UNESCO declarations on cultural heritage in 1968; Club of Rome 1970; UN Conference in Stockholm 1972; First Action Programme of the EC 1973).

The legislative system of environmental protection remains sectoral and specific, however, in terms already foreshadowed by Law No. 615 of 1966 on air pollution control (authorizations issued based on tables of polluting substances and acceptable limits; implementation of technical controls and surveillance organs, etc.). Environmental protection always refers to individual resources and is connected to the need to protect health: its purpose is the repression of activities that pollute natural resources. Law No. 319 of 1976 on water pollution control is an example (although it provides for sectoral planning instruments such as regional water cleanup plans which, however, remained unimplemented for a long period of time).

During the 1970s, environmental protection became identified as an autonomous sector of law, but it was always connected with the protection of the interests related to it. There is, therefore, environmental protection connected with the National Health Service (Law No. 833 of 1978); environmental protection connected with land use planning and zoning law (with competence attributed to the regions by means of DPR No. 616 of 1977); and landscape protection (Law No. 431 of 1985).

Contemporaneously with the evolution of European directives issued during the 1970s and the beginning of the 1980s, sectoral law specifically referring to environmental interests began to develop (as in the case of modifications to the water pollution control law introduced by Law No. 650 of 1979 or the first organic waste disposal law: DPR No. 915 of 1982).

79. During this phase, competence in environmental law was expanded to include the regions and provinces, and protection techniques also began to be linked to planning forecasts.

Throughout the 1980s, increased attention to environmental protection developed at the same time that EC initiatives were intensified (the EC's Second, Third and Fourth Action Programmes) and the seriousness of environmental emergencies was verified (calamitous events such as Chernobyl). This led to the attribution of environmental protection interests at a central level, by means of the creation of the Ministry of the Environment (Law No. 349 of 1986).

Law No. 349 of 1986 constitutes an essential passage in determining that the environment should be the object of an autonomous regime. The 1986 Law did not specify, however, whether the ministry and the competent organs in matters of environmental protection simply coordinate competence connected with environmental interests (health, urban planning, agriculture and forests, hunting and fishing, local police, etc.), or whether they are able to act in an autonomous manner in a determined sector, with their own uniform characteristics.

80. The tendency towards a non-sectoral but autonomous regime in environmental protection manifested itself during the second-half of the 1980s and during the 1990s on an international level (Brundtland Report of 1987, UN Rio Conference of 1992 and UN Kyoto Conference of 1997), on a Community level (the Third and Fourth Action Programmes of 1982, 1986, 1992, and even more so the Fifth Action Programme of 1993–1999, aimed at dealing with environmental problems on the basis of the principle of sustainable development, the integrated management of protection instruments, and the principle of collaboration between public and private authorities, and in the Sixth Action Programme *Environment 2010: our future, our choice*, 2002–2012, which concentrates on four priority areas of intervention: climactic change, biodiversity, environment and health and sustainable waste and resource management), as well as on a national level, with legislation modelled on a uniform view of the problem. The following laws can be cited in this regard: the laws on the prevention of major industrial risks (DPR No. 175 of 1988), soil conservation and the planning of water basins (Law No. 183 of 1989), environmental planning and, more in general, the protection of special areas (Law No. 341 of 1985 on landscape protection and Framework Law No. 394 of 1991 on protected areas).

Subsequently, there was a move in the direction of protection aimed at prevention and the rational management of resources by means of sectoral laws implementing community directives adopted at the end of the 1980s and during the 1990s. They include implementation of directives on air pollution control (DPR No. 203 of 1988), laws on water resources and the disposal of wastewater (Law No. 36 of 1994 and DPR No. 152 of 1999), as well as the law on the management and disposal of urban and industrial wastes (DPR No. 22 of 1997).

81. The tendency to no longer protect only individual environmental factors but instead ecological equilibrium, that is, the environment understood in its entirety, has not yet found mature legal expression. Protection techniques have, however, been refined and exceed a merely restrictive and sanction-imposing conception, as quality objectives and principles of co-responsibility in the protection of environmental resources have been introduced (in particular, this perspective is present in Decree No. 152 of 1999 on water pollution control).

An important move in this direction can be seen from the initiatives taken by the Ministry of the Environment as well as by various studies that have been made, including at the time of formulation of the laws, by the National Environmental Protection Agency and by the ARPA: the first was created by means of Law No. 61 of

1994, and the latter by numerous regional laws during subsequent years (the national agency has now become part of ISPRA, *see infra*).

82. On an administrative level, reform of the public administration as well as of administrative procedures favours greater direct access of citizens and industry to environmental information and allows the use of collaboration mechanisms between private industry and the public administration, in accordance with the orientations of the community's Fifth and Sixth Action Programmes, which have only been partially implemented in some Italian laws (programmatic agreements between private parties and public authorities on waste disposal, Legislative Decree No. 152 of 2006; there are forms of collaboration evidenced by voluntary agreements or programme contracts on air pollution caused by motor vehicles); Community regulations on ecolabels and ecoaudits were implemented (*see* Legislative Decree No. 216 of 1993, DM No. 413 of 1995, as well as the introduction above).

83. Other important laws were also promulgated during the 1990s: laws on energy savings (Laws Nos 9 and 10 of 1991), hunting (Framework Law No. 157 of 1992 on fauna protection); numerous laws intended to implement international conventions such as the law to safeguard stratospheric ozone (Law No. 549 of 1993); the Convention on climate change (Law No. 65 of 1994); the Convention on EIAs in a transborder context (Law No. 640 of 1994); the UN Convention of the Rights of the Sea of Montego Bay (Law No. 89 of 1994); the Geneva Convention limiting the use of certain conventional weapons harmful to the environment (Law No. 715 of 1994); the Paris Convention prohibiting the development, production, storage and use of chemical weapons (Law No. 496 of 1995); the Treaty of New York regarding a total nuclear test ban (Law No. 484 of 1998); and the Convention of cooperation and common fight against hydrocarbon pollution (Law No. 464 of 1998).

84. The attempt to reorganize, coordinate and rationalize environmental law was implemented by Delegating Law No. 308 of 15 December 2004 and subsequently by Legislative Decree No. 152 of 3 April 2006 ('environmental regulations'), which deals with some of the most significant issues of the environmental regime, including them in a sole context; it lacks, however, any reference to a sufficiently organic framework of principles (*see* Part I of Legislative Decree No. 152/2006). It regulates: the procedures for SEAs and for EIAs (Part II); the rules on soil conservation, the fight against desertification, water pollution control and water resource management (Part III); waste management and the reclamation of polluted sites (Part IV); air pollution protection and the reduction of atmospheric emissions (Part V), as well as claims for compensation for environmental damage (Part VI). Equally important and fundamental sectors are not included, such as those related to land use control, with particular reference to protected areas, and those related to the energy regime, which is one of the most delicate and complex sectors of environmental law. The complex issue of implementation of the Kyoto Protocol also remains autonomous, just as other important issues need to be organized (such as biodiversity and Genetically Modified Organisms).

85. In recent years Italian legislation has implemented the changes made in the various sectors by European regulations and directives. The following are noted: Directive 2014/52 EU, which led to modifications of the provisions of Legislative Decree No. 152 of 206 on the EIA (*see* Legislative Decree No. 104 of 16 June 2017); Directives 2010/75/EU and 2015/2193/EU which led to the reorganization of norms on atmospheric emissions set forth in Legislative Decree No. 46 of 4 March 2014, as well as Legislative Decree No. 183 of 15 November 2017 and Legislative Decree No. 167 of 20 November 2017; the directive on environmental crimes, implemented by Law No. 68 of 22 May 2015, which included in the Italian legal system the sanctions regime for administrative and criminal offences in matters of environmental protection.

Italy, together with the EU, joined and participated in the international conventions and conferences that have taken place in recent years in the context of the UN. Reference is made to Law No. 204 of 4 November 2016, with which Italy implemented the Paris Agreement of 2015 (COP 21) and started changing legislation in the context of the circular economy and the green economy, consistently with the Sixth and Seventh Action Programme approved by the EU, also as implementation of the guidelines established by the XXI Rio Agenda (*see* Law No. 221 of 28 December 2015 and CIPE Resolution No. 108 of 22 December 2017, which approved the National Strategy for Sustainable Development; *see also* Law 166 of 19 August 2016 on the limitation of food waste; Law No. 221 of 28 December 2015 on promoting the green economy; as well as Article 34 of Legislative Decree No. 152/2006. The Directives of the European Parliament and the Council that reformed the rules of the EU on wastes are still being implemented: No. 849 – and No. 852 of 30 May 2018, which are aimed at promoting the principles of the circular economy and the careful, efficient and rational use of natural resources.

§4. The Role of Governmental Bodies in the Formulation and Administration of Environmental Policies

I. Government Bodies and Their Competencies

86. Environmental policies are, above all, the competence of the national Parliament. Both the Chamber of Deputies and the Senate of the Republic have instituted permanent parliamentary commissions for environmental matters. The parliamentary commission examines all draft laws dealing with environmental protection and issues its own opinion on all other projects that could involve, even indirectly, the matters for which it is competent. The Parliament has approved all of the major environmental protection laws that are cited above. In particular, the Parliament annually (in principle) approves a 'European Delegation Law' which indicates the directives of the EU regarding environmental protection that Italy must implement. This law indicates, in fact, the manner in which EC laws are to be implemented: parliamentary laws; delegation of powers to the government; regional laws; or general governmental regulations or administrative acts. The implementation of community laws can also be entrusted directly to the regions. The Parliament also approves an annual 'European Law', through which measures are adopted to adapt Italian legislation to European law that has been implemented.

In addition, the national Parliament is competent to authorize ratification of international conventions to which Italy is a party that involves environmental protection, as well as approve the relative implementing laws.

87. The Ministry of the Environment was created by Law No. 349 of 1986 as an autonomous structure responsible for directing and coordinating the sector. Previously, competence relating to environmental interests was entrusted to individual sectors of the central and local administration. Starting from 1973, some of Italy's national governments created ministries 'without portfolio', that is, lacking a traditional ministerial structure and unable to incur expenses, responsible for coordinating legislative initiatives and administrative activity in this sector. After Legislative Decree No. 300/1999 (the 'Bassanini Reform'), the ministry changed its name to the Ministry for the Environment and Land, and in 2006, by means of Legislative Decree No. 181 of 18 May 2006, converted into Law No. 233 of 17 July 2006, its name was again changed upon the transfer of competence for the sea.

Most recently, the Ministry for the Environment, Land and Sea was reorganized by DPR No. 142 of 10 July 2014. The ministry is articulated in seven general directorates, corresponding to the fundamental functions that they perform regarding: (a) waste and pollution; (b) the protection of land and water; (c) the protection of nature and the sea; (d) the climate and energy; (e) environmental assessments and authorizations; (f) sustainable development and environmental damage and the relationship with the European Union and international bodies; (g) general affairs and staff.

The ministry is responsible for coordinating the national public administration and its various consultative bodies, as well as overseeing the central administration's relationships with the regions. The ministry also has programming and planning responsibilities with respect to the identification and study of environmental crisis areas. Until 1998, it was also responsible for programming actions favourable to the environment, but these programming responsibilities were transferred to the regions by means of DPR No. 112 of 1998.

The ministry is competent to assess the environmental impact of the projects set forth in Annex I of EC Directive No. 337 of 1985 (and its subsequent modifications). It is competent to authorize the major industrial installations and has the power to issue occasional and urgent ordinances for the protection of environmental resources.

The ministry can also exercise substitute powers when the regions or local entities fail to adopt the necessary measures for environmental protection, with particular reference to EU or international obligations.

The ministry can utilize an operative nucleus of the military police to effectuate controls ('Operational Ecology Unit of the Carabinieri'). The minister also plays an important role with respect to environmental information and education. Further, the Environmental Minister presents a report to Parliament regarding the state of the environment (the statistical data can be found on ISPRA's website).

88. The creation of a ministerial entity capable of performing a role of coordination function has not produced the desired results to date, given that Italian legislation has maintained its segmentation and has continued its characteristic partial interventions, without receiving the resources required to consolidate a system of technical organisms capable of providing support that is indispensable to the ministry's activity. In particular, in addition to the ministerial structure, the characteristics of autonomy and independence of the central administration's technical bodies should also be reinforced, in order to provide – on the basis of a useful dialogue even with other technical and scientific operators (both of apparatus and from the universities and industry) – information and the preparation of technical standards that are at the heart of an effective environmental protection policy.

The same competencies entrusted to the Ministry of the Environment are superimposed, without substituting them, in matters relating to environmental protection that have remained the responsibility of other ministries: the Ministry of Agricultural, Food and Forestry Policies, which oversees environmental development in the context of agricultural activity, forestry, food products and fishing, coordinating its activities with the Ministry of the Environment with respect to soil conservation and the management of parks and natural reserves; the Ministry of the Economy and Finance, competent for programming expenses, including those regarding the environment; the Ministry of Cultural and Environmental Heritage, responsible for protecting the landscape and Italy's historic, artistic and cultural heritage; the Ministry of Health, competent to issue laws regarding water, air and soil pollution, as well as regarding protection of interior environments, protection of workers' health and protection of residential interiors; the Ministry of Economic Development, which has broad competence regarding the environmental impact of industrial activities and in matters relating energy and mining resources; the Ministry of Infrastructures and Transportation, which is competent with respect to the effects on the environment of activities relating to rail, land and sea transport, matters relating to infrastructures, in particular, those of viability, as well as with respect to water works and soil conservation; the Ministry of Education, University and Research, which coordinates environmental education; the Ministry of Foreign Affairs, which coordinates Italy's participation in the formulation of international treaties and participation in the relative international organizations that are competent in environmental matters; and the Ministry of the Interior, which supervises environmental emergencies, major accident risks and the use of harmful toxic substances when exercising its general competence in matters of public security.

89. The Italian central administration also has technical organisms:

ISPRA, *Istituto Superiore per la Protezione e la Ricerca Ambientale* (Institute for Environmental Research and Protection), which took over the functions that had been belonged to A.N.P.A., subsequently A.P.A., and later A.P.A.T., and which is regulated by Law Decree No. 132 of 28 June 2016, converted, with modifications, into Law No. 133 of 6 August 2008. ISPRA has recently been assigned functions that had previously been attributed to other consultative bodies of the Ministry of the Environment (DM 1° March 2018); ISPRA performs technical and scientific functions to support the Ministry of the Environment;

ENEA, *Agenzia nazionale per le Nuove Tecnologie, l'Energia e lo sviluppo economico sostenibile* (National Agency for New Technologies, Energy and Sustainable Economic Development), originally created by Law No. 282 of 1991 to promote the pacific use of nuclear energy, which was later reorganized by Legislative Decree No. 257of 2003 and Law No. 99 of 2009, currently governed by Article 4 of Law No. 221 of 28 December 2015, which places the entity under the supervision of the Ministry for Economic Development;

IRSA, *Istituto di Ricerca sulle Acque del Consiglio Nazionale delle Ricerche* (National Water Research Institute of the National Research Council), conducts technical-scientific consulting for the Ministry of the Environment, and is considered in various laws to be the institute of reference, among which most recently Legislative Decree No. 30 of 16 March 2009 and MATTM Decree No. 56 of 14 April 2009;

ISPESL, *Istituto Superiore per la Prevenzione e la Sicurezza del Lavoro* (Institute for the Prevention of Workplace Accidents and Workplace Security), is involved with research, clinical trials, controls, assistance, high level training, information and documentation of the prevention of workplace accidents and illness, the safety of workplace environments as well as the promotion and protection of health in workplace and non-workplace environments; it was dismantled by means of Law No. 122 of 30 July 2010 and its functions were attributed to INAIL, *Istituto Nazionale Assistenza Infortuni sul Lavoro* (National Institute for Occupational Accidents);

Istituto Superiore della Sanità (Health Institute) is a technical-scientific organ of the National Health Service, is a public entity and performs technical-scientific functions and responsibilities and technical coordination in matters for which the Ministry of Health is competent.

90. The regions have legislative power in many areas relating to environmental law (land use control, health, infrastructures, transportation, tourism, energy production and transmission, enhancement of cultural resources and so on).

The regional councils have issued numerous laws in matters for which they are competent, often anticipating solutions of the national legislator and in some cases directly implementing EC directives. Regional legislation normally moves within the framework of the fundamental principles established by national legislation, including with respect to environmental protection. The result is that the regional laws often do not create noticeable differences between regions but aspire to relatively homogeneous models of administration and protection. Not all of the regions are, however, similarly timely in implementing the principles established in national legislation. The regional competence has been used in different manners both in the context of defining standards and limit values, and with respect to preparing plans relating to air pollution control, water pollution control, waste disposal, industries that present a risk to the environment, and the protection of nature by means of the creation of national and regional park systems.

The State only transferred its own administrative functions to the regions starting from 1977 by means of Decree No. 616 of 1977. Among others, this decree transferred environmental protection functions connected with urban planning (Article 80); functions with respect to nature protection, and natural reserves and parks (Article 83); those relating to hunting and fishing (Articles 99 and 100); those relating to soil hygiene and the hygiene of residential areas, water works and water and air and noise pollution control (Article 101). The State has also delegated other functions for which it is competent in environmental matters to regional organs, for example, the protection of natural beauty, in as much as it relates to its identification, protection and relative sanctions for damage caused to it (Article 82, Decree 616/1977). The regions also act in matters involving environmental protection, in as much as they are responsible for sanitary and hygiene issues relating to urban environments; as well as exercise functions with respect to agriculture and forests, the hydrogeological system and soil conservation.

Constitutional case law, in particular during the 1980s, recognizes the competence of the regions with respect to the environment. But the lack of a specific definition both in the Constitution and in applicable law of 'environment' has allowed the national legislator to subtract legislative and administrative power from the regions in various matters regarding the environment, defining environmental interests as uniform and undivided interests which can only be regulated by the nation's central administration.

By means of Decree No. 112 of 1998, in the framework of a broader reform of regional and local administrations, the State provided for the transfer to the regions of almost all administrative and programming functions relating to environmental protection, reserving for itself the exclusive role of directing and protecting uniform national interests.

This tendency was definitively consolidated by the reform of Title V of the Constitution (the cited Constitutional Law No. 3 of 2001), which attributed the State with legislative power to determine objectives and limits of protection of the environment and the ecosystem. By means of Legislative Decree No. 152 of 3 April 2006, the primary administrative functions in this regard were again concentrated at the State level (even though in many sectors these functions remain delegated to the regions).

91. The competence of the provinces regarding environmental protection was redefined by means of the general law on local autonomies: Law No. 142 of 1990 (which merged with the uniform text on local entities, Legislative Decree No. 267 of 18 August 2000). The province has control and programming functions in the territorial context in which it is competent (which constitutes an intermediary territorial level between the municipal level and the broader regional level), collaborating and sustaining the actions of the municipalities and minor local entities as well. The various laws in the sector attribute competence to the provinces in matters regarding the protection of environmental interests (soil conservation and hydrogeographic regulations, ordinances on air and water pollution control, discharges and waste treatment plants, as well as with respect to toxic and hazardous wastes).

The municipalities and their relative associations are competent in matters of health protection. The municipalities are also competent in important matters relating to waste disposal and water pollution control. The regulatory powers of the municipalities relating to sewage systems, unhealthy and dangerous works and noise pollution control are also important.

The competence of the municipalities and provinces is also undergoing a phase of significant reorganization following the reform initiated by Law No. 59 of 1997 and Decree No. 112 of 1998, and the subsequent constitutional reform of 2001. The distribution of competence between municipal and provincial organs is defined by the regional laws that are approved by the regions in the process of the reform under way. The general trend, however, is coherent with the regulatory system that has been in effect through the present.

The recent Law No. 56 of 2014 initiated reconsideration of the role of the provinces, allowing some of their functions to be attributed directly to the regions (with the reform they remained partially unimplemented, and the provinces maintain a coordinating role in environmental matters, with reference to the areas of their competence).

92. In addition, the local health agencies, operative units of the municipalities which are part of the larger network of the National Health Service, continue to perform functions that sometimes regard environmental protection when related to health protection. These functions are presently distinguished between those attributed to the ARPA (Regional Environmental Protection Agencies), which have substituted the local health agencies with respect to technical functions, and controls regarding environmental protection.

II. The Present Role of Governmental Institutions

93. Parliament and the government perform a fundamental role in the formation and implementation of the normative regime in the environmental protection sector. But the coordination and stimulation deriving from the decisions of the organs responsible for performing the functions of the central government are conditioned by at least three factors.

First of all, the major policy orientations in environmental matters are formulated and decided in international law conventions and norms and, above all, in the context of the policies adopted by the EC and EU. The role played by the Italian Government and Parliament remains central, however, both with respect to participation in the formulation of EC laws and, in particular, with respect to definition of the manner in which international norms and EC directives and regulations are implemented in Italy's domestic legal system.

Second, preparation of the norms and action programmes in environmental matters reflects, in a more significant manner than in other sectors, the difficulties faced by the Italian institutional system in coordinating public action and adopting normative techniques inspired by criteria of clarity and coherence. The Ministry of the Environment has been performing an active role for the past few years, but the fragmentation of competence among many other ministries and the absence of a strong relationship with national technical organs and regional organs have rendered attempts to rationalize the production of laws in this field episodic and scarcely efficient to date.

Third, the implementation of European law escapes in large part the government's and the Ministry of the Environment's capacity of control. This is due not only to the absence of an efficient and technically prepared centralized bureaucratic apparatus, but also because the concrete definition of environmental protection now depends in large part on the administrative and legislative acts of the regions and local entities.

94. In practice, all levels of government are involved in environmental protection (international, supranational, national, regional, local) simultaneously in such a way as to render the adoption of the principle of separation in the distribution of competence difficult, if not impossible. Instead, flexible principles of coordination and the absence of rigid hierarchical schemes are necessary in this subject area.

Undoubtedly, emergencies that involve the biosphere at a worldwide level condition the exercise of local powers. Problems in regional areas necessitate coordinated solutions, with respect to which the Member States of supranational organizations must adopt their own decisions. At the same time, there are problems faced by individual and specific territories which raise the need for protection involving uniform and multiregional interests, which cannot be delegated to the local communities.

It is, therefore, necessary to apply the principle of co-responsibility and cooperation affirmed in point 7 of the Rio Declaration of 1992 to the territorial dimension of environmental interests, and the principle of concerted action by all interested parties in accordance with the concept of subsidiarity affirmed in the Fifth Community Policy and Action Programme on behalf of the environment, which corresponds to a fundamental principle established by the Treaty of the EC (Article 5). Principles were further developed in the Sixth and Seventh European Action Programmes as well as, most recently, in the adhesion to the 2030 Agenda for Sustainable Development of the UN, at the same time as the Paris Agreement of 2015.

The principle of subsidiarity is also applicable today with respect to the domestic relationships between the central State and the regions on the basis of Article 118 of the Constitution (as modified by Law No. 3 of 2001 that revised the Italian Constitution). This principle implies a presumption of general competence in favour of the level of government that is the closest to a nation's population (in Italy the municipal and provincial administrations); definition of the competence of the broadest level of government on the basis of explicitly stated attributes (those attributed to the central State or the regions); and a margin of flexibility in the application of such principles, allowing the broadest level of government to intervene in relation to the dimensions, interests, problems and objectives that necessitate a uniform or in any event unitary action. It is particularly easy to recognize the necessity of a strong role to be played by the central government in the field of environmental protection. This is due first of all to the reasons that have traditionally justified a centralized policy (international responsibilities, responsibilities deriving from membership in the EU, the need to protect raw materials and resources of particular importance, the timeliness of State intervention in emergency situations, etc.); and second and above all, to the need to guarantee a determined qualitative dimension for the environment, which only a broader level of intervention and a stronger and more efficient decisional level are capable of doing.

95. The role of the regions must instead be strengthened in view of the optimal territorial context of environmental interests. The regions must be entrusted with responsibility for administering and managing the services that are indispensable in order to guarantee, on a concrete and efficient level, the quality standards established at a central level. The environment must receive strong protection from the central government, but, in as much as it is also essential to the local community, it must also be managed at a regional governmental level.

Currently, the greatest responsibility for the environment rests with the central government, in particular, with the Ministry of Protection of the Environment, Land and Sea.

The regions have important responsibilities, because they maintain the functions that were transferred to them by delegation of powers during the 1990s, and they are able in practice to coordinate the planning and programming of the most complex sector (such as water resources and soil conservation, wastes and the relative waste management and disposal systems, water pollution control, etc.).

96. The provinces are characterized by their coordination and programming responsibilities for the areas for which they are competent (with specific reference to waste disposal plans and permits for discharges, and monitoring air pollution).

The municipalities are responsible for the issuance of authorizations in sectors that they can more easily control and monitor (their functions are a more direct control of the territory and local policing).

The instruments of coordination and collaboration assume a determinant role among the various levels of government (municipal, provincial, regional and State).

§5. Sources of Environmental Law

97. There are no sources of law in the Italian legal system that were expressly created for or that are governed as a function of environmental protection. In order to achieve the objectives of protection, the legislator and various governmental administrations utilize the multiple sources of law provided by the Constitution and by the Italian legal system.

98. In the absence of explicit constitutional norms, the right to the environment is defined above all by the 'primary laws' of the national Parliament and the regional councils (based on the exclusive legislative competence that Article 117, II paragraph, clause *s*, attributes to the State on matters regarding 'the protection of the environment and the ecosystem'); as well as by regional laws (on matters related to environmental protection, such as health, land use planning and landscape protection). Legislation has rarely identified general and abstract principles and norms, in accordance with the nature of this source of law. The laws of primary legislation often specify precise concepts and regulate concrete cases in which environmental emergencies are verified. This occurs due to both the inevitable concrete nature of public action in environmental matters, and the fact that Parliament has exclusive competence in the Italian constitutional regime to impose limits and controls on the initiatives of private parties (*see*, in particular, Article 41 of the Constitution). Uniform texts and norms containing principles regarding environmental protection are in the course of preparation; but as of today, principles in this area must instead be sought in the case law of the Constitutional Court, which develops them on the basis of the norms contained in the 1948 Constitution and the EU's legal system. In this framework, the judgments of the Italian Constitutional Court (whose judgments have *erga omnes* effect) constitute an important source of environmental law.

99. The length of time required by parliamentary procedures to approve laws (due both to the bicameral structure of Parliament and to the excessive number of laws that are approved each year) has led to the frequent use by the government, including in environmental matters, of its own power to issue urgent acts (law decrees) having the force of law, which enter into effect the same day that they are approved and published and which must be converted into law by the Parliament within the following sixty days. The use of this power is fully understandable in cases of natural disasters and environmental emergencies. The government has utilized this power too often and in an excessively far-reaching manner, so that entire sectors of the legal system dealing with environmental protection have been subject to repeat emergency decrees issued by the government (such as waste management and major risk protection).

A judgment of the Constitutional Court declared the practice of reiterated law decrees illegitimate in the absence of new reasons for urgent measures (judgment No. 360 of 1996). During the most recent legislative period, the Parliament broadly utilized its power of legislative delegation, thus reducing the need for the government to intervene relying on its emergency powers. The most recent organic reforms regarding the environment (waste regulation, Decree No. 22 of 1997; water pollution control, Decree No. 152 of 1999; and most recently Decree No. 152 of 2006 reorganizing environmental legislation) were adopted in the form of delegated decrees (acts having force of law that the government adopts on the basis of a precise delegation from Parliament that establishes the object, time frame and directional principles to which the decree must conform).

The legislative delegation of power through its annual European Delegation law constitutes one of the manners in which Parliament ensures that EC directives are implemented. It must be emphasized that almost all of the standards and principles of Italian environmental legislation are in implementation of European laws (both principles of Treaties and those resulting from regulations and directives, which deal with all significant sectors of environmental protection): the European norms of reference will be noted in describing the regime's individual sectors.

100. The regulation of important sectors and definition of fundamental environmental legal principles are also entrusted in many cases to secondary laws. Regulatory laws in Italy are within the competence of the central government

(government regulations that are approved by the individual ministries) as well as the local administrative organs (regional regulations, provincial and municipal regulations).

Regulations are in principle subordinate to primary law. In accordance with a precise hierarchical scale, governmental regulations prevail over those issued by the ministries, which in turn prevail over those issued by the regions, which prevail over those issued by local entities. There are many cases, however, in which the primary law allows the regulations to derogate from the norms of the same law, thus attributing to organs having regulatory power the responsibility of governing and modernizing entire sectors of protection.

101. Technical norms have decisive importance in the regulation of environmental protection. Technical norms, precisely due to the specific nature that characterizes their content (in particular, scientific knowledge that is often controversial and precarious due to the rapid obsolescence of the data on which it is based) emphasize the inadequacy of both the ordinary institutional organs entrusted with promulgating laws and the relative procedural regimes (joint action by various ministries, opinions of the Council of Ministers, controls of legitimacy or financial coverage, etc.). The normal procedures for the promulgation of laws, in fact, do not facilitate on the one hand an accurate and knowledgeable evaluation of the contents and enforcement consequences of technical provisions, and on the other hand timely revaluation of the same. The promulgation of these laws, thus, very often ends up taking place by means of a formal vote of confidence of the legislator in favour of whoever prepared the text of the technical rules. In addition, often the experts to whom the preparation of these texts is entrusted are designated subjects, or in any event represent the same recipient subjects of the laws or only some of the recipient subjects, with all of the evident consequences from the standpoint of political concepts of democracy, diffusion of knowledge of the law, transparency and responsibility that should characterize the lawmaking process.

102. Urgent and occasional ordinances (acts issued by administrative authorities based on necessity and urgency) often assume importance in the Italian legal system in matters and with respect to the objectives indicated in a generic manner by the law. These ordinances are differentiated from other administrative orders due to the absence of pre-established and typical contents. Such ordinances raise delicate problems of legitimacy due to the obligations deriving from them on citizens and industries that are unsupported by a direct parliamentary law. Entire sectors of environmental protection are governed by such ordinances in the absence of an organic law. This is verified both in relation to the exercise of occasional and urgent powers by the Ministry of the Environment, and with reference to ordinances issued in accordance with the competence of the ministry responsible for functions of civil protection. Emergency powers can also be exercised by other administrative organs competent in matters relating to the environment: the presidents of the regional councils; the presidents of the provinces; and the mayors.

In view of this situation, a more decisive attempt to rationalize the existing law is desirable in order to create a clear and uniform legal system for the entire subject area, eliminating the inconsistencies and gaps resulting from the complex stratification of the laws that has been registered up through the present.

103. The attempt at reorganization made by Legislative Decree No. 152 of 2006 constitutes an important starting point (for the first time the most important sectors of the regime were included in a sole legislative act). But the Italian legal system still needs an organic reference framework (which could consist of a law setting forth principles, capable of providing direction both for detailed legislation and for the work of the administrations and courts). The principles specified, in summary and synthetic terms, in Title I of Legislative Decree No. 152 of 2006 (which were only introduced by Legislative Decree No. 4 of 2008 which modified it), do not correspond to such need and require additional, ample clarifications. The positive aspect consists of the explicit reference that Legislative Decree No. 152 of 2006 makes to the principles of EU Treaties (which, as already noted, is the indispensable reference point for interpreting the outstanding legislative regime in Italy).

Part I. Pollution Control

Chapter 1. General Law

by *Stefano Grassi*

§1. Introduction

104. Protection from various forms of pollution constitutes the principal object of environmental protection legislation in Italy, as in other countries. Notwithstanding the large quantity of laws in existence, a general law regarding environmental protection has not yet been approved, in contrast with other legal systems. Some existing norms and laws do establish, however, common principles for the definition of acceptable limits and environmental protection procedures.

105. These norms and laws do not consist solely of the principles deriving from the norms set forth in the Italian Constitution and EU law directly applicable in the Italian legal system, but also include norms of the Italian Civil and Criminal Codes, which define institutes and cases applicable to multiple kinds of pollution, as well as norms of general application in administrative law regarding procedures and controls that involve private activities referring to or impacting environmental values. Legislative Decree No. 152 of 2006 contains a general regime. Title I refers to some general principles of EU environmental law and indicates some interpretative guidelines of the sources of environmental law. Both in this law and in other sector laws, uniform procedures for the issuance of authorizations and the location of industrial activities have also recently been introduced. The regime regarding the right to information and, in particular, access to environmental information can also be cited (but this issue also regards forms of protection for citizens with respect to acts and activities that impact the environment), as well as laws aimed at guaranteeing the participation of citizens in proceedings defining environmental interests.

§2. Principles of Civil Law

106. In Italy, as in other legal systems, the norms protecting property rights constituted one of the first forms of protection of environmental resources. In the context of the Italian Civil Code, reference can be made to the norms allowing home owners to protect their property from access and interference by third parties

(Article 841 of the Civil Code, on the right to close one's property at any time; Article 844 of the Civil Code, which protects against emissions of smoke or heat, noise, vibrations, etc. emanating from neighbouring property that exceed normal acceptable levels).

In practice, the protection deriving from norms that define traditional property rights is totally insufficient with respect to the requirements of effective protection of environmental resources and values. The same norms of the Civil Code are intended to balance the interests of property owners to enjoy and fully utilize the resources that are the object of their property rights with the interests of neighbours and the community at large (e.g., Article 842 of the Civil Code on the norms that allow access to privately owned property by authorized hunters and fishermen; Article 843 of the Civil Code on the right of neighbours who need access to common property to build or repair a wall or perform other work to property that they own individually).

The necessity to balance the interests of private property owners and the interests of neighbours and society was confirmed, with an innovative formula, by Article 42 of the Italian Constitution. The constitutional norm places the private property regime among 'economic relationships' and not among the fundamental rights of man, giving the ordinary legislator responsibility for defining the equilibrium among ownership interests and public interests, guaranteeing the acquisition and enjoyment of property but establishing limits in order to assure a societal function. This has led to the possibility of the public authority to adapt property rights to the protection of group interests, among which environmental interests assume an important role.

The legislator can, for example, allow access to privately owned property, not only to protect traditional hunting interests, but also to protect societal interests in exploiting environmental resources. An example is legislation allowing access to areas of natural beauty and landscapes (Legislative Decree No. 42 of 22 January 2004).

The norms that regulate access to private property in relation to a 'right of access to nature', for example, can also be cited, as well as norms allowing access by mushroom hunters or collectors of medicinal plants and norms that permit public access to land included in natural parks (recognition of such right is normally conditioned, however, on precise conditions established by the administrative authority).

107. Article 844 of the Civil Code, which prohibits emissions exceeding acceptable limits, has been utilized by the courts as an environmental protection instrument. Protection from pollution deriving from emissions of smoke, heat, noise, etc. is currently entirely regulated by the norms dealing with air, water and soil pollution control. The norms of the Civil Code indirectly protect the environment from pollution, in that they aim to protect the rights of property ownership. Case law has distinguished emissions which fall within acceptable limits (which are considered legal), from those exceeding normal limits that cannot be eliminated because they are indispensable to the manufacturing industry (if reasonable, they are allowed with eventual forms of indemnification); and those exceeding acceptable limits to such a degree that they are considered illegal, and are, thus, subject to enjoinment and the payment of compensatory damages.

The principle of acceptable emission limits does not coincide in case law with the limit values established by pollution control norms. In fact, reference must be made to the concrete condition of the places involved and generally recognized socio-economic values existing at the time the emission is made: the valuation is, therefore, made on a case-by-case basis by the court. The most frequent controversies are those between a private landowner and a neighbour who performs a manufacturing activity. Emissions deriving from manufacturing activity are normally held to be legal unless they impede the significant productive use of the property that is subject to the emission, and unless there are reasonably priced available alternative technologies (normally the courts impose adoption of the technical measures required to contain emissions within limits on the party performing the manufacturing activity).

108. The laws regarding reclamation and hydrogeological restrictions are related to the principles set forth in the Civil Code. Articles 857–865 of the Civil Code establish a series of principles regarding land reclamation, which still guide the special regimes adopted at both a national and regional levels. The function of reclamation works is neither limited to hygiene protection (e.g., the reclamation of swampland to combat negative consequences on health), nor are hydraulic works and ground exploitation limited to agricultural purposes (as implementation of agricultural development plans that have characterized the Italian economy starting from the 1930s). The most recent body of law attributes reclamation works with responsibility for environmental preservation and enhancement, by means of a system of norms aimed in its entirety at regulating powers that also pertain to 'the landscape and urban structure of the territory, soil conservation and environmental protection, nature conservation, and the regulation and use of (Italy's) water patrimony'. In addition to these obligations for which the landowner is responsible can be added, always from an environmental protection viewpoint, the norms that regulate building construction, imposing certain distances between buildings (Articles 890 et seq. Civil Code), and those requiring the repair of river beds and embankments (Articles 915 et seq. Civil Code).

109. Mention should also be made of antique institutions such as 'civic uses' (based on customs and traditions as effective as real rights that guaranteed everyone belonging to a particular community the right to utilize, for his own subsistence and well-being, specific parts of the territory and its resources for fishing, hunting, grazing, wood gathering, etc.). The protection of territorial and ecological equilibrium in favour of the local community constitutes the new objective of civic uses. The Constitutional Court has recognized 'a specific uniform interest of the national community to conserve civic uses' because they guarantee a rational use of territorial resources and determine its form, thus, promoting conservation (Constitutional Court, judgment No. 46 of 1995 and Law No. 396 of 1991, Article 1). Laws regarding the reorganization of civic uses date back to the 1920s (Law No. 1766 of 16 June 1927), but recent norms have also recognized and given new life to this institute (Article 10, Law No. 491 of 1993 on the reorganization of regional and State competence regarding agriculture and forests; Article 12, Law No. 97 of 31 January 1994 and now, Law No. 168 of 20 November 2017 – *see* Constitutional Court, judgement, No. 113 of 2018).

110. The principles of the Civil Code are also at the base of the complex regime of liability for environmental damage. Such regime has assumed a specific dimension in environmental protection as implementation of the EU principle 'the polluter pays' (*see*, Articles 298 et seq., Legislative Decree No. 152 of 2006, Part IV).

§3. Criminal Law

111. There are laws providing for criminal sanctions in each sector relating to pollution control. The Criminal Code provides for some crimes which in a general manner consist of behaviour considered as criminal (criminal offences or transgressions). The environment is indirectly protected by laws that establish the crimes of causing a fire (Articles 423 et seq. Criminal Code); provoking flooding, landslides or avalanches (Articles 426 et seq.); poisoning water or food products (Articles 439 et seq.); the intentional spread of plant or animal diseases (Article 500); unauthorized water deviations and modification of the state of places (Article 632); damage (whoever destroys, loses or causes deterioration to the real or personal property of a third party or renders it wholly or partly unusable: Article 635 Criminal Code); disfiguring and defacing a third party's property (Article 639); interference with lawful occupation and rest (through noise, Articles 658 and 659); and the reckless throwing of objects (Article 674).

The prohibition against damage to the archaeological, historic and artistic national heritage (Article 733) and the destruction or defacement of natural beauty (Article 734) more specifically refer to environmental crimes. The latter crime is quite liberally defined as it punishes whoever, by means of construction, demolition or otherwise, destroys or alters the natural beauty of places subject to special protection. It, therefore, does not only contemplate damage to specific environmental elements but also the destruction or deterioration of natural beauty. Problems in applying this law involve not only the case of landscape damage deriving from television antennas fixed to the roofs of buildings located in historic centres, but also the destruction of vegetation or activities that gravely and permanently alter or pollute the natural components of a landscape.

112. Directive No. 2008/99/EEC of 19 November 2008 of the European Parliament and Council obligates Member States of the EU to introduce criminal sanctions for grave violations of Community environmental protection law (the types of crime are listed in Article 3 of the Directive). Law No. 96 of 4 June 2009 delegated the Italian government with promulgating a decree to implement the directive. The law of delegation included among its guidelines the introduction of the liability of public entities for environmental crimes (Legislative Decree No. 231 of 2001 regulated some cases of criminal liability for public entities, but even though it had a specific delegation of power, the 2001 legislator omitted extending the liability of public entities to environmental crimes).The delegation of power remained unimplemented until 2015, when Law No. 68 of 22 May 2015 was approved, which inserted a chapter in the Criminal Code expressly dedicated to environmental crimes (such as crimes of environmental pollution, environmental disaster, illicit trafficking of waste, etc.). This law also provides for a reduction of the applicable penalty in the case of remediation/environmental cleanup at the offender's expense and includes environmental crimes among the list of offences that constitute grounds for the administrative liability of legal entities (*see*, *infra*, Part IV).

113. There is a tendency to dilate the use of the criminal law in legislation (in part to comply with international law and EU law obligations), but there is also a tendency to sustain that criminal law must be utilized as an *extrema ratio* (according to the formulation of 'minimalist' criminal law). An indication in the first regard can be seen by the exclusion of some of the most important environmental cases in point from the decriminalization process initiated during the past few years in Italian criminal legislation. Thus, the application of substitute penalties in the case of environmental crimes has been excluded. There are recent laws, however (in particular, with respect to water pollution control), in which broad forms of decriminalization have been implemented, justified by recognition of the low efficiency of the criminal penalties with respect to behaviour damaging environmental interests and resources.

114. The need for environmental protection and the difficulty in defining the juridical 'value' that is the object of protection force the criminal legislator and legal scholars to reconsider some of the principles that had inspired the norms of criminal law. The breadth and complexity of the concept of environment (and thus of the juridical value being protected) implicates the difficulty in identifying what behaviour prejudicing the environmental value should be the object of the criminal norm. It is also difficult to respect the principle of legality of the sanction: the definition of behaviour and of the value to be respected must, in fact, be deferred in large part to secondary norms and, in particular, to technical norms (the only ones capable of timely and adequately defining the notions destined to integrate the environmental protection regime).

There are problems adapting the traditional concept of causation (there are phenomena involving systematic and non-linear causation) and, with reference to the subjective element, there is a tendency to accentuate forms of objective liability (violation of rules intended to prevent environmental damage is sufficient to constitute the crime as much as the subjective element of guilt). Criminal law has become instrumental with respect to the function of sanctions, imposing penalties requiring that environmental damage be remediated when possible.

§4. PRINCIPLES OF ADMINISTRATIVE LAW

115. In defining administrative powers and proceedings in the context of environmental protection some steady orientations appear, on the basis of which some general principles of environmental administrative law can be identified.

One tendency is to subject the activity of private parties that impacts on the environment and which is potentially polluting (such as projects and installations, manufacturing activity, etc.) to authorization by the competent administrative power. This regime would allow a private party to exercise a specific right only after a public authority has evaluated the compatibility of the activity with public interests. The requirement of prior authorization is related to the European principle of prevention. By means of the authorization, the public authority can require the private party to respect certain limitations and can regulate the manner in which the activity is performed: private activity will, thus, be coherent with public interests, and environmental public interests will prevail over private interests.

116. In the context of environmental protection, the general norms regulating administrative procedures normally exclude the possibility of authorizing activity of a private party based on the administration's lack of response with respect to a permit request. The evaluation of conformity of a private party's activity impacting on the environment and, thus, on public environmental interests must be the object of a precise and express valuation of the administration's organs ('silence amounting to assent' is not allowed).

The general principle of silence amounting to assent does not apply to acts and procedures regarding cultural and landscape heritage, the environment, protection from hydrogeological risks (as well as in in the sectors of national defence, public security, immigration, asylum, citizenship, or health and public safety).

Environmental authorizations must establish a certain structure and balance in the regime on the operating procedures that must be applied to perform activities capable of impacting environmental interests, and it is therefore necessary that the conditions to carry out both the preliminary reviews as well as subsequent audits and controls that the authorized activity presupposes and requires be expressly indicated and specified (*see* Constitutional Court, judgments No. 307 of 1992, No. 302 of 1988, No. 437 of 1992, No. 194 of 1993, No. 26 of 1996 and No. 62 of 2008. In the same sense, *see*, EU Court, 28 February 1991, in case 360/87. *See also* the judgments of the EU Court on 19 September 2000 in case C-287/98 and 14 June 2001 in case C-230/00).

There are some cases comparable to silence amounting to assent when the possibility of the tacit renewal of the authorization exists, if the renewal is requested with the prescribed period but the administration has not acted before the expiration date (*see* Article 124, paragraph 8, Legislative Decree No. 152/2006). For example, it is possible to temporarily continue operating a discharge, in compliance with the requirements contained in the expired authorization, until the adoption of a new measure, but if the discharge contains hazardous substances the renewal must in any case be granted expressly within and no later than six months from the expiration date. The same principles apply to authorizations for atmospheric emissions – *see* Article 269, paragraph 7, Legislative Decree No. 152 of 2006).

117. The discretion in applying principles of prevention and precaution regards, in particular, the assessment of risks deriving from acts capable of impacting environmental interests: the procedure allows the point of equilibrium to be identified with respect to the acceptability and management of such risks. The method is that indicated by the TEU for the preparation of environmental policy (considering available scientific and technical data, environmental conditions, the potential benefits and costs of action or lack of action, and the situation of economic and social development – *see* Article 191, §3, of the TFEU).

This results in the absorbing nature of the preparatory stage and reasons for the environmental protection measures adopted. The scope of the preparatory stage and the need to justify the assessments that are made on competing interests require that the justification, or in any case an explanation, of the logical process followed be indicated, not only in measures referring to individual situations but also in measures having overall effectiveness such as planning and programming measures.

118. The absolute requirement of the valuations that are the competence of administrative organs responsible for environmental protection was also affirmed by the norms that have attempted to simplify administrative proceedings. When the opinion of a technical organ is indispensable for the issuance of an authorization or adoption of an ordinance, the competent administrative organ can ordinarily acquire the data necessary for its decision-making process from other offices or entities when the necessary technical opinion is not timely provided. However, this is not possible when the technical organ is competent in matters of environmental protection. The inertia of the competent technical organ in matters pertaining to safeguarding environmental interests can only be surpassed, in some cases, by a decision of the political body (*see*, for example, with respect to EIAs, the possibility to rely on the decision of the Council of Ministers when the technical organisms delay providing their assessments – *see* Article 25 of Legislative Decree No. 152 of 2006).

The necessity of a valuation by the competent environmental protection authority does not exclude that a private party can, and in some cases must, present and certify technical data necessary for the decision-making process. In such manner, not only are the proceedings simplified, but the control that the public administration will be able to perform on the basis of the data supplied will be more efficient. It also forces the private party to assume greater responsibility in defining premises and limits for the safeguarding of environmental interests. The law on administrative proceedings excludes, however, the possibility to use simplified procedures when environmental interests are involved (the technical assessments of the competent bodies cannot be substituted by other forms of certification or the technical assessment of different organs: *see* Article 16, paragraph 3 and Article 17, paragraph 2 of Law No. 241 of 1990).

Cases of simplification are allowed for specific categories of operators with reference to activities that do not pose significant risks to the environment and health.

With respect to waste, it is possible to cite disposal and recovery activities carried out through a simplified procedure, i.e., after reporting the commencement of activity (*see* Articles 214–216 of Legislative Decree No. 152 of 2006). Registration with the National Register of Environmental Operators can also be cited, which is only subject to notice and self-certification (Article 212 of Legislative Decree No. 152/2006).

With respect to air pollution, the ordinary authorization procedure is flanked by a 'derogation' procedure provided for the plants set forth in Article 272 of Legislative Decree No. 152 of 2006 (those with reduced or insignificant air pollution. These are cases in which the emissions are considered to be of scarce significance, and therefore they are not subject to the application of Legislative Decree No. 152 of 2006 (*see* the list of such activities referred to in Article 272, paragraph 1 – Part I of Annex IV of Part V of the Decree; as well as paragraphs 4*bis* and 5 of Article 272). Article 272, paragraph 2, cit., also attributes the competent authority with the power to issue, for specific categories of plants, identified in relation to the type and manner of production, special authorizations of a general nature relating to each individual category of plant in which emission limit values are established, the requirements, adjustment times, sampling and testing methods and frequency of controls: the operators of the plants or activities can only begin operating after they have communicated that the plants or activities are included in the mentioned list, with a prior indication of the date the plant will start operating or when the activity will initiate.

119. The dynamic nature of the factors making up the environmental balances defined in the individual authorizations necessitates ongoing monitoring of the results achieved: environmental authorizations are therefore issued with limited temporal effectiveness.

For example, the authorization for discharges is valid for four years (*see* Article 124, Legislative Decree No. 152 of 2006); the authorizations for waste management plants have a duration of ten years, which is reduced to two years in the case of experimental plants (*see* Article 211, Legislative Decree No. 152 of 2006); and the simplified procedures provide that the communication must be renewed every five years (Article 215, paragraph 5, and Article 216, paragraph 5, Legislative Decree No. 152 cit.). The authorizations for atmospheric emissions have a limit of fifteen years (but such term is allowed only to the extent that during the period of validity of the qualification, the power of the competent authority can be applied to modify the authorization's requirements or to adjust them to technological progress – *see* Constitutional Court, judgment No. 250 of 2009). The IEA normally has a five-year duration (with an extension of this term if the plants have environmental certification – *see* Article 29*octies*, Legislative Decree No. 152 of 2006).

The temporary nature of the authorization regards submission to continual and periodic audits, with the obligation of the authorized company to update, over time, the management procedures of the authorized facility.

Upon the expiration of the period of validity, the competent administration must review the prerequisites and terms of the authorization, establishing criteria that conform to the activity that is the object of the enabling measure, also considering the continual updating of the emission limits and standards established by the legislator. In fact, there is an obligation that the renewal of the authorization or concession be requested far in advance – *see* the one-year term provided for authorizations of discharges and for emission authorizations – because it is necessary to guarantee continuity with respect to the prerequisites, terms and limits imposed in the authorizing measure.

Landscape authorizations and EIAs also have a validity of five years, and must be renewed upon their expiration (Article 146, paragraph 4, Legislative Decree No. 42 of 2004).

120. With respect to environmental protection, the public administration's control powers assume a very important role. The authorizations themselves constitute an *a priori* control of the authorized activity. The necessity of conforming the performed activities to environmental conditions, as well as to the evolution of the best available technologies, requires that in many cases the authorizations be granted for a limited period of time, that they be subject to periodic control of their legitimacy, and that they be further subject to an intense web of monitoring and verification of the authorized activities. From this standpoint, the responsibilities entrusted to the technical organs that support administrative action (e.g., the ARPA) and the mechanisms of sharing the technical data available and identification of the best available technologies with the professional and business categories involved are of major importance.

Controls are conducted first of all by requiring monitoring activity (technical measurements and periodic observation or ongoing monitoring of compliance with the terms of the authorizations): the controls are implemented by the authorized party, based on operating procedures that require the initiation of internal processes within the productive cycles, with an obligation of collaboration by communicating the data and inspections and monitoring activity entrusted to the administration's technical bodies.

The monitoring procedures are explicitly provided for in environmental legislation (*see* the various forms of control indicated in Legislative Decree No. 152 of 2006: Articles 28 and 29 with respect to EIAs; Articles 128 through 132 on control of discharges; *see* the principle set forth in Article 178, paragraph 1 regarding waste management; Article 248 regarding the remediation of contaminated sites; and Articles 268, 269, 274, 276, 288, and 296 regarding atmospheric emissions).

The multiple techniques and procedures to conduct the controls results in operating difficulties, which, in the European context, have led to the issue of a recommendation (of the European Parliament and the Council, No. 2001/331/EC of 4 April 2001), which provides the minimum criteria for environmental inspections in the Member States, laying the foundation for the identification of uniform criteria to ensure that control procedures are more efficient.

Negative monitoring results can create the conditions for the suspension and – in the most serious cases – the revocation of the environmental authorization. Monitoring also serves the function of identifying the conditions for the review of authorizations and to indicate adjustment to the best technologies.

The B.A.T. ('best available technologies') tend to impose the ongoing improvement of plant performance from an environmental protection standpoint. The obligation to incorporate new technologies over time is, however, conditioned on the ability to bear the costs that the adjustment of the facilities requires (the B.A.T-.N.E.E.C.: 'best available technology not entailing excessive cost' are imposed).

The rules aimed at identifying the methods to be used to adjust to the best available technologies and the guidelines for the continual updating of the environmental performance of the plants is therefore particularly important. (Articles 29*bis*,

Legislative Decree No. 152 of 2006, refers to the information published by the European Commission or by international organizations: the 'B.R.E.F.', 'B.A.T.', 'CBAT reference documents', prepared by the European IBC Bureau, in accordance with a procedure in which the public and interested parties can also participate – are determined according to the 'Seville process' (*see* Articles 13 and 75 of Directive 2010/75/EU). *See* EU Court, judgment 22 January 2009 in case 473/07 on the importance of the 'BREF' documents, as well as EU Court, judgment 15 January 2004 in case C-235/02.

With respect to another sector in which the adoption of the best available technologies and the definition of the criteria for the selection and performance of environmental work, reference can be made to Annex 3 of Part IV of section V of Legislative Decree No. 152, which refers to Article 242, paragraph 8, of the same decree, regarding remediation, environmental cleanup, and the operational or permanent safety of polluted sites.

The following articles of Legislative Decree No. 152 of 2006 can also be cited: 98 (water savings); 100, paragraph 2 (designing sewerage networks); 101, paragraph 2 (determination of the emission values of water discharges by the regions); 108, paragraph 3 (discharges of hazardous substances, with reference to plants subject to A.I.A.); 182, paragraph 3, on waste disposal; 208, paragraph 12 (on the review of the authorization for waste disposal and recovery facilities); 270, on conveying atmospheric emissions; 271, paragraph 3, on identifying emission limits in the atmosphere by the regions; 275, paragraph 7, on the emission of volatile organic compounds (VOC).

§5. Procedures to Implement Environmental Protection (Emission Limits and Standards: Urgent Measures)

121. The manner in which emission limits, standards and quality objectives are determined, as well as the instruments to implement environmental protection strategies are defined in complex terms and articulated by the EU legislator, by the national legislator and by the regional legislators.

It is useful to draw attention to the procedures that are intended to result in the direct regulation of emission sources (standards and emission limits); the planning and programming procedures designed to coordinate actions in specific territorial areas or areas of intervention; and the ordinance powers to be used to fill the gaps in ordinary procedures and to deal with emergencies.

122. The State, regions and local entities have power to determine the emission limits in the various areas of environmental law and to identify the technologies or specific technical solutions that must be used in the individual activities that can affect resources and environmental equilibrium.

It is possible to cite, as an example, the manner in which the State establishes emission limits, indicating a maximum and a minimum value for protection from atmospheric pollution, in the Annexes to Part V of Legislative Decree No. 152 of 2006, with the possibility of procedures for modifications integrations (*see* Articles 271 and 281 of Legislative Decree No. 152 of 2006).

The emission standards and limits must be defined in flexible terms (with the possibility of reducing them or making them more stringent in relation to particular situations of a health risk or for areas that require specific environmental protection (procedures are envisaged at a regional or a provincial level, by means of planning or programming instruments aimed at the remediation of compromised areas).

With respect to reclamation, emission limits are defined by an ad hoc procedure carried out based on a risk assessment (Article 242 et seq., Legislative Decree No. 152 of 2006).

123. The planning and programming tools adopted in the various areas of environmental protection play a central role and contribute to defining a comprehensive vision of the objectives of environmental protection.

They consist of a significant number of programmes that cannot be easily reconstructed (in which the criteria for the distribution of financial resources for environmental protection measures are also determined) and planning tools that define the objectives and rules that apply to both public as well as private parties in carrying out their activities (as in the case of urban planning and the planning of activities that more directly impact the environment).

It is possible to cite the following: in the waste sector, the plans for recovery and disposal plants of major national interest, approved by a decree of the President of the Council of Ministers, having heard the Unified Conference and been included in the economic and financial programming document; the region waste plan, which is linked to the regional reclamation plan (*see*, in Legislative Decree No. 152 of 2006: Article 195, paragraph 1, clauses *f* and *g*, for national plans; Article 199 for the regional plan; Articles 250 and 251 for the reclamation plans of individual sites); in the area of air pollution, the national programme for emissions reduction (provided by Legislative Decree No. 171 of 21 May 2004) and the regional remediation plans (provided by Legislative Decree No. 351 of 4 August 1999, on the protection of air quality, and by Legislative Decree No. 183 of 21 May 2004, related to ozone in the air), as well as the programme on the quality of air in urban areas (set forth in Article 3, paragraph 5, of Legislative Decree No. 152 of 3 August 2007); in the area of land management, the basin plans (set forth in Article 65, Legislative Decree No. 152 of 2006), the water management and protection plans (Articles 117 and 121, Legislative Decree No. 152 of 2006), abstracts from the hydrogeological structure plans (Articles 67 and 68, Legislative Decree No. 152 of 2006); in the field of landscape protection plans, the landscape plan (Article 143, Legislative Decree No. 42 of 22 January 2004, with respect to which the regions can choose whether to subject the territory to specific rules on use through such plan, or whether to integrate the consideration of landscape values in the urban planning-territorial plans), and plans related to national and regional parks (Article 12, Law No. 394 of 6 December 1991).

The need to harmonize and simplify the legislative framework was attempted in Article 57 of Legislative Decree No 112 of 1998, which introduced the territorial coordination plan entrusted to the provinces, which is able to assume the value and effects of a protection plan in the areas of nature protection, environmental protection, land management and the protection of natural beauty, provided that the definition of the relative provisions takes place in the form of an agreement between the province and the competent administrations, including the national administration.

124. The principle of correction at the source justifies the introduction of ordinance powers, and in any case, measures aimed at obtaining emergency interventions. It is possible to cite both the sanctioning-restoration ordinances that ordinarily govern the individual areas of environmental protection as well as contingent and urgent ordinances, adopted to cope with emergency situations aside from ordinary procedures.

Contingent and urgent ordinances have caused delicate problems in terms of legality, because such ordinances result in obligations for citizens and corporations, without the law having previously identified the criteria and prerequisites for their adoption.

Contingent and urgent ordinances can be issued to cope with unexpected and unforeseeable situations of grave and imminent danger for society that cannot be resolved using ordinary instruments (*see* Constitutional Court, judgment No. 196 of 2009).

Legislation and case law allow contingent and urgent ordinances when: it can be demonstrated that it is impossible to act using any other typical measure (residual nature of ordinances); the temporary nature and time limits for the adopted measure have been established; a minimum of procedures have been provided aimed at allowing adequate justification, based on technical reviews that allow the proportionality between the emergency situation to be dealt with and the scope of the urgent power that is exercised to be assessed.

It is also necessary for this type of ordinance that an administrative review with a debate be conducted as a prerequisite for the legitimacy of their enactment.

It has been established that this type of review cannot be repeated for a period exceeding eighteen months for each special form of waste management; the term can only be extended when there is a demonstrated need.

Article 5, Law No. 225/1992 allows the President of the Council to adopt ordinances that attribute special powers to a commissioner entrusted with managing the emergencies that derive from national disasters or from dangers to public health or safety. This type of ordinance has also been broadly used to deal with emergency situations regarding waste management and other areas of environmental protection.

The procedures related to management by commissioners are approved from time to time in derogation of outstanding law and regulations. The Constitutional Court recognized the legitimacy of such ordinances on the condition 'that they are "derogations limited in time, that do not repeal or modify outstanding law" (ex multis, judgments No. 127 of 1995; No. 418 of 199; No. 127 of 1995) (judgment No. 237 of 2007). In any case, such ordinances 'must be justified with reference to the law that is derogated from and with a precise indication of the reasons for the derogation' (Council of State, VI, judgment No. 701 of 10 February 2015).

Article 135, paragraph 1, clause *e* of Legislative Decree No. 104 of 2010 attributes a functional role to the T.A.R. Lazio, granting it exclusive jurisdiction for controversies related to the emergency ordinances set forth in Law No. 225 of 1992 (as well as those relating to the 'overall management of the waste cycle').

125. The case of the ILVA (Società siderurgica italiana) plant in Taranto – the second most important industrial steel production plant in Europe which has been active since 1905 – is an emblematic example of the use of emergency decrees in cases of necessity and urgency – law decrees – to allow the continuation of industrial activity in large plants, including when there is a serious environmental and health crisis, in order to avoid negative consequences on the national production system as well as maintenance of employment levels.

The management of the environmental – employment crisis of the ILVA plant was dealt with through the adoption of numerous emergency legislative acts (Law Decree No. 207 of 3 December 2012; Law Decree No. 61 of 4 June 2013; Law Decree N. 101 of 31 August 2013; Law Decree No. 136 of 10 December 2013; Law Decree No. 91 of 24 June 2014; Law Decree No. 1 of 5 January 2015; Law Decree No. 92/15 of 4 July 2015; Law Decree No. 191 of 4 December 2015; Law Decree No. 98 of 9 June 2016; Law Decree No. 243 of 29 December 2016; Law Decree No. 244 of 30 December 2016).

By means of this sequence of law decrees, the government progressively introduced an ad hoc regulatory system to manage environmental crisis situations regarding industrial facilities of primary importance, providing for: (a) the direct obligation to review the IEA as a necessary and sufficient condition for allowing continuation of the industrial activity, overcoming and at the same time conditioning the precautionary powers of the criminal court; (b) the use of the outcome of the health damage assessment – *valutazione del danno sanitario* (VDS) as the basis for the request to review the AIA (but is unable to result in an immediate modification); (c) the use of extraordinary administration as a tool to counteract the repeated failure of the private operator to comply with the requirements and conditions provided in the IEA.

The various measures adopted to deal with the environmental crisis deriving from the prior operation of the ILVA plant resulted in both criminal and civil proceedings, which also raised issues regarding the constitutionality of the various law decrees (Constitutional Court, judgments No. 85/2013 and No. 58/2018), as well as at the EU level (an infraction procedure was initiated by the European Commission in 2014, still in course). Two petitions were also filed with the Court of Human Rights against the Italian Republic (Cordella and others, petitions No. 54414/13 and No. 54264/15), for violation of the public's right to health caused by the Italian government's failure to take sufficient and timely action with respect to the environmental pollution caused by the ILVA plant.

In 2018, the multinational Arcelor Mittal purchased the ILVA plant after receiving the favourable opinion of the European Antitrust Authority. The new ownership must implement the environmental remediation plan approved by the MATTM.

§6. Integrated Environmental Protection

126. The complexity of the organization of environmental interests necessarily involves all levels of government. The prevailing tendency is the concentration of the exercise of administrative functions, after the revision of Title V of the Constitution (which attributes 'environmental protection and protection of the ecosystem' exclusively to State legislation – Article 117, second paragraph, clause *s*) of the Constitution), and in relation to the frequent need to ensure the uniform exercise of protective functions (based on principles of subsidiarity, differentiation and adequacy – Article 118, first paragraph, Constitution), on which the entire approach of Legislative Decree No. 152 of 2006 (and subsequent corrective measures) is based.

At a central level, the Ministry of the Environment has not been able to effectively implement its role as a centre of coordination for environmental policies with respect to the other numerous departments involved in defining the objectives of environmental protection. At a local level, it is unclear what responsibilities have been entrusted to the competence of the territorial entities, and above all the regions. It is therefore necessary to implement procedures capable not only of simplifying, but above all, of enhancing the coordinated exercise of the functions in the field of environmental protection.

127. One of the first possibilities of procedural simplification was identified in the environmental sector, consisting of the *Conference of Services* (*conferenza di servizi*: a procedure aimed at allowing the various administrations, in a meeting where they are represented, to evaluate all of the interests involved in the activity to be authorized).

The use of this simplification and coordination model was introduced for the first time in 1987 in the field of waste management, and subsequently it was also applied to environmental protection (the Conference of Services is currently governed in general by Articles 14 through 14*quinquies* introduced in Law No. 241 of 1990).

Participation in the Conferences of Services of the administrations entrusted with environmental protection is aimed at guaranteeing the completeness of the administrative review and the possibility to indicate the terms and modifications that may be required to obtain approval for the final project.

The dissent of one of the administrations involved in the authorization procedure does not preclude the possibility for the administration to issue the authorization (justifying the contrast with the dissenting opinion). If the dissent among ministries cannot be overcome, the final decision rests with the Council of Ministries.

128. The programme agreements provide for the assumption of obligations by the competent administrations to implement procedures for the realization of particularly complex works (urban renewal projects; infrastructures to be created at the same time as other public and private works). The programme agreements are provided for the coordinated performance of the administrative action and are stipulated for the purpose of adopting, according to a predetermined time schedule, planning and programming acts and authorization measures. The agreements are normally stipulated to resolve industrial crisis situations in high-risk areas (the agreement can finance industrial reconversion programmes together with repair and restoration work that enables the improvement of the state of the environment).

The programme agreement signed by all of the competent entities can define the procedural arrangements, including in derogation from outstanding law, but must nevertheless comply with the acceptable limits of contamination for sites or rules for the management of emissions, the same as the rules on waste management, etc. (*see* the Council of State, judgment No. 11 of 3 January 2002).

129. The paradigm of the procedures used to implement the need for a contextual examination of environmental interests with respect to other public interests (implementing principles of integration, sustainable development and balance) consists of the IEA procedure introduced by Directive 96/61/EC of the Council of 24 September 1996 Integrated Pollution Prevention and Control (IPPC), subsequently modified and currently codified in the Directive of the European Parliament and Council 2008/1/EC of 15 January 2008. In 2010, the European Parliament and the council modified the rules on the integrated prevention and control of pollution arising from industrial activities and integrated previous directives in one legislative corpus (*see* Directive 2010/75/EU).

The directive's objective is to unify the authorization procedures in order to allow an integrated approach to pollution control by industrial installations (Annex 1 lists the industrial activities subject to the regime), preventing, when possible, emissions in the air, water or soil, considering waste management, or, at the least, minimizing them in order to achieve a high level of environmental protection overall.

The *AIA* is issued by the competent authority on the basis of the use by the installation's operator of the best available technologies (whose development must be followed by the authorities), adopting a programme for the gradual reduction of emissions, including by means of a periodic review and update of the conditions of the authorization.

The IEA serves to provide uniform and integrated management of the conditions of use of installations that have a significant impact on individual environmental factors, applying in a sole procedural process the entirety of principles of prevention and precaution, rectification at the source, information and participation and summary sustainable development, that characterizes the overall environmental legal system (Constitutional Court, judgment No. 85 of 2013).

Legislative Decree No. 372 of 4 August 1999 initially implemented the directives, while Legislative Decree No. 59 of 18 February 2005 provided a more organic implementation. At present, Decree No. 128 of 2010 included the IEA regime set forth in Part II of Legislative Decree No. 152 of 2006 (introducing the new Title III*bis* and Annexes VI through XIII of Part II).

The operator of the plant must notify the competent authority of the state of implementation of the requirements set forth in the authorization and report significant information related to the performance of the activity. The administration, through its control bodies, subjects the plant to inspections and periodic controls (Articles 29*decies*, Legislative Decree No. 152 of 2006, which governs, in particular, two types of controls: ordinary controls – *see* paragraph 3 – and extraordinary inspections – *see* paragraph 4).

Any breach of the authorization's requirements or the performance of activity in the lack of a valid title results in a sanction procedure. In minor cases, the operator receives a simple warning that can be accompanied by an order to suspend the activity in the case of repeat non-compliance. If the repetition of the offending conduct can result in damage – or even the mere danger of damage – to the environment, the revocation of the authorization and closure of the plant can be ordered. In cases of severe violations, a 'warning and contemporaneous suspension of the activity (…)' can be ordered (Article 29*quattuordecies*, Legislative Decree No. 152 of 2006).

Some recent Italian laws have already created procedures characterized by the simultaneous review of all of the environmental and other public interests involved.

One example is the procedure for the approval of projects and authorization of the creation of waste disposal and waste treatment plants. Whoever intends to realize the project must present, together with the request, all of the technical documentation for the construction of the plant required by the laws and regulations on urban planning, environmental protection, workplace health and security, and public hygiene. Approval of the project, which can also be given by joint authorities, therefore implicates the evaluation of all environmental interests involved.

The approval procedure for the installation does not, however, substitute an EIA when such is required due to its size or location. Any authorization only substitutes the need to obtain all the other ordinances or opinions that the competent authorities must issue in relation to the creation and authorization of the installation (Article 208, Legislative Decree No. 152 of 2006).

Other examples are contained in the procedures relating to the authorization of installations for energy production (*see* Article 1, paragraph 2, Law Decree No. 7 of 2002, on power plants producing more than 330 MW of thermal power; Article 12 of Legislative Decree No. 387 of 2003 on power plants producing energy from renewable sources; and Article 25 of Law No. 99 of 2009, and subsequent Legislative Decree No. 31 of 2010 on nuclear power plants).

With respect to some industrial activities (referable to small and mid-sized companies) – for which the IPPC is not mandatory, an AUA is provided (*see* Article 23, Law No. 35 of 2012). By means of the AUA, the procedures required for the issue of individual authorizations to which the industrial activity is subject are included in a sole procedure.

Municipal authorizations to proceed with environmental cleanup and recovery projects of polluted sites substitute all of the other measures and opinions that are provided for by the relevant legislation (*see* Article 242 of Legislative Decree No. 152/2006).

Finally, Article 23 of Legislative Decree No. 112 of 1998 has attributed the municipalities with administrative functions concerning the realization, enlargement, cessation, reactivation, location and relocation of manufacturing facilities, including the issuance of building permits and authorizations. The subsequent Articles 24 and 25 of Decree No. 112 of 1998 establish that the competent municipality must organize a sole office responsible for the proceedings (a sole counter or 'one-stop shop' – *sportello unico*, Article 24) and evaluate in a sole proceeding urban planning interests, health interests and environmental protection and security interests (Article 25). In this case as well, the final authorization substitutes all of the other authorizations, opinions, agreements, approvals and so on required by law. The authorization is issued in a context of joint services only after the valuations of the various competent organs have been obtained. The municipalities must establish procedural rules that guarantee the transparency of the procedures and must open the proceedings to the observations of parties representing group interests.

§7. Procedures for EIAs

130. Projects, acts and activities that have a potentially significant impact on the environment are subject to EIA procedures. In this way, the legislator has created a general regime intended to prevent environmental pollution and damage.

The procedural model was implemented, as known, for the first time in the United States (*see* the National Environmental Policy Act approved by Congress on 31 December 1969). In the EU legal system, it was subsequently introduced by Council Directive 85/337/EEC of 27 June 1985 (subsequently modified by Directive No. 97/11/EEC of 3 March 1997, by Directive No. 2003/35/EC of 26 May 2003, by Directive 2011/92/EU, and more recently modified and integrated by Directive 2014/52/EU), according to an approach that is less extensive on an operative level (in that it only applies to the projects listed in specific annexes).

The European norms require that determined projects are subject to an EIA procedure prior to issuance of the relative authorization. The EIA identifies, describes and evaluates, in a suitable manner for each particular case and according to a predetermined procedure, the direct and indirect effects of the project on environmental factors: man, fauna, flora, soil, water, air, climate, landscape, material goods and cultural heritage, as well as interaction between all of the above factors.

A first Annex to the EU directive indicates the projects for which an EIA is mandatory. They are projects that have definite and important direct or indirect effects on environmental resources, for example, raw oil refineries; thermal power plants having more than 300 MW of power; installations for the final storage of radioactive wastes; steel and iron mills; chemical plants; ports; dams destined to hold more than 10 million m^3 of water; and installations for the elimination of toxic and hazardous wastes. A second Annex to the EU directive lists the projects for which each of the Member States must determine (either on a case-by-case basis or in accordance with predetermined criteria) whether a particular kind of project is subject to an EIA. Both with respect to the projects set forth in the first annex, and for those of the second annex, it is necessary to submit any variations that result in modifications that might have a significant negative impact on environmental matrices to a new EIA.

131. The principles on which EIA procedures are based are essentially the following: the party proposing the project must supply all of the information necessary for evaluating the direct and indirect effects that the project could have on the environment, by means of filing an environmental impact study. The public administration can request the proposing party to present additional information in order to better identify the project's purposes and objectives. The actual valuation is made after completion of an inquiry: it states the environmental impact information and issues a final determination that can be either positive or negative. The final determination may also be positive but issued requiring that certain restrictions and conditions be respected.

Italian legislation requires a *valutazione di impatto ambientale – VIA*, hereinafter EIA, for the projects indicated in the EU directive's first Annex. More specifically, it requires the presentation of a special study by the private or public subject proposing the project; an inquiry is performed by a technical commission working on behalf of the Ministry of the Environment; and an opinion as to environmental compatibility must be given by the Ministry of the Environment itself (which incorporates the opinion expressed by the technical commission). The decision as to whether or not to issue the authorization for the project rests, however, with the competent administrative organ. When the Ministry of the Environment's opinion as to the project's environmental compatibility is negative, authorization to continue with the project can only be granted by a resolution of the Council of Ministers. This latter provision has obviously been criticized because it allows the government to permit the project to proceed notwithstanding its negative impact on the environment.

132. The party proposing the project must make the environmental impact study public, both by filing the project so that the public has free access to review it, and by informing the public in a comprehensible manner through the press.

133. The EU directives were implemented with considerable delay in the Italian legal system. An initial partial implementation of the principles of the directive was contained in the temporary regime set forth in Article 6 of Law No. 849 of 1986 (which created the Ministry of the Environment), which remained in effect until 2006. On the basis of a DPR dated 12 April 1996, EIA procedures were introduced for works of regional competence, and all of the regions have promulgated specific regimes. Special types of EIAs were introduced for certain types of work of public interest (*see* Article 1, Law No. 433 of 2001, and Article 165 of Legislative Decree No. 163 of 2006).

134. The EU Court of Justice has condemned both the delay in implementing directives and the incomplete nature of the implementing regime (Court of Justice, judgment of 8 November 2007 in case C-40/07).

135. Legislative Decree No. 152 of 2006 (corrected by subsequent Legislative Decrees No. 4 of 2008 and No. 128 of 2010) sets forth an organic procedure for EIA, and also includes SEA. In the most recent modification introduced by Legislative Decree No. 128 of 2010, the IPPC was included and coordinated with the EIA and SEA. Another modification was introduced by Legislative Decree No. 104 of 2017, which adjusted the Italian regime to Directive 2014/5/EU. By means of such decree the government simplified, harmonized and rationalized the EIA procedures, also in relation to coordination and integration with other procedures aimed at the issue of environmental opinions and authorizations, thus reinforcing the quality of the EIA process, aligning it with the principles of smart regulation (*see* Constitutional Court, judgment No. 198 of 2018).

The EIA applies both to projects subject to national authorization as well as to projects authorized by the regions. The national regulations establish fundamental principles and are an exercise of the State's exclusive competence in this area. The regional laws must be adjusted, for works within the scope of regional and local competence, to the procedural principles established by Legislative Decree No. 152 of 2006. The Constitutional Court has excluded the admissibility of regulatory acts by the regions that conflict with the procedural rules imposed by the State – *see* judgments No. 225 and No. 234 of 2009 as well as No. 215 of 2015, No. 232 of 2017 and No. 198 of 2018). The regions can only define the organizational procedures for the exercise of the relative functions, in compliance with national and European legislation (Articles 7*bis*, paragraph 8 of Legislative Decree No. 152/2006).

Case law has emphasized the nature of a sub-procedure of the EIA with respect to the main procedure aimed at the approval of the project.

The positive or negative judgment on environmental impact therefore has significant consequences on the conclusion reached by the project approval procedure and can be appealed autonomously (Council of State, section VI, judgment No. 5092 of 14 October 2014).

Nevertheless, it is clear that the EIA, when necessary, cannot be omitted or the measure that approved the project can be repealed.

136. The projects for which it is necessary to activate the EIA are indicated in the annexes to the directives, but all projects that might have significant repercussions on the environment, both due to their nature and to their size and location, must be subjected to the EIA procedure (in this sense *see*, Court of Justice, judgment of 16 March 2006, in case C-332/04). In Legislative Decree No. 152 of 2006, the annexes to Part II list the projects that are the competence of the State – annexes I and II – and those that are the competence of the regions – annexes III and IV (the lists were updated by Legislative Decree No. 104/2017, expanding the projects entrusted to the competence of the State. For projects that have potentially significant negative effects on the environment, it is, therefore, necessary to initiate a procedure aimed at verifying whether submitting to an impact assessment is required (screening or 'verification of exclusion' – *see* Article 20 of Legislative Decree No. 152/2006 and Annex V of Part I of the Decree, which defines the criteria for such verification). The verification must also be made for modifications or extensions of projects that have already been authorized or which are in the course of being realized, which could have significant negative repercussions on the environment. The verification procedure is conducted by the Environmental Impact Technical Commission.

Case law must often deal with the problem of whether modifications of the installations and projects that had previously been subject to the EIA procedure require a new EIA: it is noted that a new assessment is necessary only in the case of 'modifications or extensions of the projects set forth in Annex I or Annex II' of the European Directives 'already authorized, realized or which are being realized, which can have significant negative repercussions on the environment' (*see* Council of State, IV, judgment No. 5525 of 11 November 2014).

The Court of Justice specified that the assessment of the environmental impact of a project, when the authorization procedure is articulated in various stages, must in principle be carried out as soon as it is possible to identify and evaluate all of the effects that the project might have on the environment (EU Court, 7 January 2004 in case C-201/02; EU Court, 28 February 2008 in case C-2/07).

The EIA must be conducted during the final planning stage (in some cases the assessment is made on a preliminary project, but it is necessary that the project be at an equivalent level of the feasibility project, and nevertheless allows the complete assessment of the environmental impact that it might produce). The EIA cannot be circumvented by dividing the planning phases (the objective of the procedure is to assess the overall impact of the project on the environment and the entirety of its effects, not only of the projected work but also of the use and exploitation of the installations resulting from such work).

The application of the interested party must include an environmental impact study containing all of the data necessary for the assessment, with an analytical indication of the project and the measures to be taken to reduce the impact and identify the possible alternatives considered as well as the reasons why a specific solution was chosen. The project and the relative study must also contain a non-technical summary to allow the activation of the participating public institutes involved (*see* Articles 22 and 23, Legislative Decree No. 152 of 2006). The costs of the study, as well as the subsequent costs related to carrying out the EIA procedure, shall be borne by the proponent (*see* Article 33, Legislative Decree No. 152 of 2006).

In the context of the preparatory stage, it is also possible to implement a stage seeking an indication by the administration of the information and data that it is necessary to integrate and further specify (the scoping procedure – Articles 19–21 of Legislative Decree No. 152/2006). In such procedure, the competent authority gathers all information that is useful for clarifying the project, also hearing the opinion of experts, and it deliberates – after the convocation of the interested parties, to find consent on a proposal for work – on the content and priorities that the proponent must develop in the EIA study.

At a State level, the preliminary phase, with the subsequent technical opinion on the EIA, is done by the Technical Commission for the verification of the environmental impact – EIA and SEA. In each region, a technical body is created that is capable of carrying out the administrative review and expressing a technical opinion on the EIA.

This preliminary phase also takes place in front of the environmental impact technical commission and requires adequate public notice (in some cases there is an obligation for a public hearing). All of the authorities that might be interested in the project must be informed, so that they are able to express their opinion on the information provided by the project proponent, as implementation of the principle of the broadest participation possible in the EIA project by interested parties (*see* Constitutional Court, judgments No. 227 of 2011; No. 93 and 178 of 2013; and No. 178 of 2018). The recent Legislative Decree No. 104 of 2017 provides for the publication of the EIA application and the relative documentation on the website of the competent authority (Article 24, Legislative Decree No. 152/2006), and also governs the manner in which the public inquiry is conducted (Articles 24*bis* of Legislative Decree No. 152/2006).

Once the opinions and observations of the administrative authorities as well as of any other interested party have been obtained, the final measure of the procedure – for projects that are the competence of the State – is approved by the Minister of the Environment, and if necessary, because cultural heritage is involved, jointly with the Minister of Cultural Heritage. If there is conflict among the competent ministries, or after the period for the issue of the measure has expired without action, the proponent or the individual ministries can request that the Council of Ministers issue such measure (Article 25 of Legislative Decree No. 152/2006).

The EIA measure is always integrated in every type of authorization required for the realization of the project, and in particular in the IEA, when it is necessary (Article 26 of Legislative Decree No. 152/2006).

It is also possible for the EIA to be issued in the context of a sole measure that is inclusive of every other type of environmental authorization required by outstanding law to realize and operate the project (Article 27, sole measure in environmental matters – *provvedimento unico in materia ambientale* in procedures that are the competence of the State; Article 27*bis*, sole regional authorization – *provvedimento autorizzatorio unico regionale* in procedures that are the competence of the regions).

Legislative Decree No. 104/2017 established that the periods within which the procedural phase and within which the final EIA measure must be issued are mandatory. Once the deadline established by the law has expired, the procedure must be archived.

The final EIA is communicated to the authority entrusted with the procedure for the approval of the project. The decision on the EIA is published in the official journal or in the official bulletin of the regions, as well as in a national daily newspaper and on the website of the Ministry of the Environment. The period within which to file a judicial appeal starts to run from such date (*see* Article 27, Legislative Decree No. 152/2006).

In the decision containing the EIA, the deliberating authority must indicate the conditions on which a positive assessment is made, as well as the reason of the choices made and an indication of the manner in which the outcome of an activity deemed to be compatible will be assessed (*see* Articles 26 and 28 of Legislative Decree No. 152 of 2006). The reason for the final measure on the EIA is required, given its discretionary nature (*see* in this regard, among many, Council of State, VI, judgment No. 129 of 18 January 2006; Council of State, VI, judgment No. 2851 of 17 May 2006; T.A.R. Veneto, judgment No. 1225 of 2 November 2016). The justification is even more significant after the choice made by the legislator to absorb in the final judgment on the EIA all of the authorizations and opinions on the environment that are necessary for the approval of the project, unifying in a single procedure the assessment of the environmental impact of the project.

The resolution on the EIA remains valid for five years; in fact, the projects subject to it must be realized within five years from the publication of EIA measure (*see* Article 26, paragraph 6, Legislative Decree No. 152 of 2006). The EIA measure can, however, take into consideration the characteristics of the project, establish a longer period and extensions can also be granted upon the request of the proponent. Upon the expiration of the period of effectiveness, however, the EIA procedure must be repeated.

The EIA normally includes among the conditions required for a favourable decision the activation of *post operam* monitoring and the creation of environmental observatories aimed at verifying both compliance with the requirements of the EIA as well as the development of the environmental impact during the execution and management stages of the authorized work.

The monitoring is aimed at verifying compliance with the environmental requirements defined in the final EIA measure, but also at acknowledging new situations and factors that were not considered in the final EIA measure.

Supervisory activity is carried out with respect to the execution of the works subject to EIA. In the case of failure to comply with the requirements and terms indicated in the EIA, it is possible to warn the owner of the project that the necessary corrective measures must be implemented. In more serious cases, the suspension or even the repeal of the final EIA measure can be ordered.

The EIA must be performed prior to the realization of the individual projects. If the project is realized in the lack of the required EIA, the relative authorizations can be repealed.

The most recent reform (Legislative Decree No. 104/2017), consistently with the case law of the Court of Justice of the EU (judgment 28 February 2018, C-117/17), introduced the possibility of submitting projects and activities realized in the lack of an EIA measure to a 'posthumous' EIA procedure. The regularization is not limited to examining the future impact of the work that was realized, but also the environmental impact starting from its realization (*see* Constitutional Court, judgment No. 120 of 2010).

137. The SEA (*valutazione ambientale strategica*) was introduced as implementation of EC Directive No. 2001/42/EC of 27 June 2001 of the EC Council. It is an environmental assessment of plans and programmes, in such a way as to anticipate the consideration of environmental interests during the phase in which the development guidelines for territorial and landscape planning are determined as well as the programming of economic activities.

Different from the EIA, which is required when projects can produce *negative* effects on the environment, the SEA must be used when the plans and programmes might have *significant* impacts on the environment and cultural heritage.

The SEA is mandatory for plans to assess and manage the quality of ambient air in the following sectors: agriculture, forestry, fishing, energy, industry, transportation, waste and water management, telecommunications, tourism, territorial planning or land use, as well as for plans that determine the reference framework for the approval, authorization, and area where the projects set forth in the annexes to the directive will be located or built (these projects are currently listed in Legislative Decree No. 152 of 2006, which implemented the directive in Italy – Articles 6 et seq. of Legislative Decree No. 152 of 2006).

138. The SEA procedure is regulated by Legislative Decree No. 152 of 2006 in terms that are totally analogous to the EIA procedure (evaluation of whether the procedure is required – Article 12; preparation of an environmental report – Article 13;

consultations – Article 14; assessment of the environmental report upon the conclusion of the consultations – Article 15; decision – Article 16; information regarding the decision – Article 17; monitoring subsequent to approval of the plan – Article 18).

The judgment on environmental compatibility is made through a summary statement that must be annexed to the measure approving the plan or programme. The SEA consists, in fact, of integrating environmental interests in planning procedures. In this way, the plans and programmes include all of the information and assessments, which can subsequently be used in the EIA procedure for projects that implement planning tools. In fact, the legislative regime expressly provides that the data collected in the SEA procedure must be considered in the subsequent EIA procedure (Article 10, paragraph 5, of Legislative Decree No. 152 of 2006).

139. A particular form of preventive environmental assessment consists of an impact assessment on the protected areas (*valutazione di incidenza*) identified by Directive No. 92/43/EEC of 21 May 1992 regarding the conservation of natural and semi-natural habitats and wild fauna and flora (Sites of Community Importance – SCI – and SAC), also as implementation of the directive on the conservation of wild birds (Directive No. 79/409/EEC of 2 April 1979), with reference to SPA.

The Habitat Directive was implemented by DPR No. 357 of 8 September 1997 (subsequently modified by DPR No. 120 of 12 March 2003), and consequently SCI were identified which, together with the SPA (set forth in the Birds Directive No. 79/409/EEC), are part of the 'Nature 2000 Network', i.e., the European ecological network of SAC.

European legislation provides for both planning and programming activity for the protection of biodiversity and bird species, with the implementation of specific management plans or management plans that are integrated with other development plans. In line with European principles and the hermeneutic criteria developed by the commission, it was found that an obligation exists to perform an impact assessment even with reference to general urban planning instruments (and variants), and not only those implementing individual works', even if they are 'outside of a site included in the Natura 2000 Network'. In other words, 'the assessment must be performed each time there is the probability of a significant impact and can only be omitted when there is certainty of a lack of impact', but 'national administrations must nevertheless justify the lack of impact' (Council of Administrative Justice for the Region of Sicily – C. GARS, judgment No. 4 of 15 January 2014).

The procedure regarding the impact assessment takes place in the same manner as the EIA, through the presentation, by the proponents of the works, of a study aimed at identifying and assessing the main effects on sites of Community Importance (SCI) or on SAC. The study is subject to the assessment of a competent authority, which considers the guidelines and monitoring criteria specified by decrees of the Ministry of the Environment on 3 September 2002 and 17 October 2007.

The procedure is also implemented with reference to SCI that have been proposed for inclusion in the list of the 'Habitat' Directive.

140. Until a few years ago there was neither any specific obligation in the Italian legal system to assess the health effects of certain polluting activities, nor was the relative application methodology defined. In relation to the worsening of complex situations of pollution (as in the case of large industrial poles inserted in heavily urbanized contexts, such as ILVA in Taranto), the need to guarantee the protection of the well-being of the environment with legal instruments able to fulfil both the function of obtaining the appropriate scientific knowledge, as well as of transposing the results of the reviews conducted to binding legal effects on the parties involved, became inevitable. The VDS originated in the above context upon the initiative of the regional legislator (specifically, the Region of Puglia, *see* Regional Law No. 21 of 24 July 2012), which conceived it as a means to determine the existence of critical factors from a health standpoint due to the activity of some specific categories of installations (subject to the EIA and the IPPC regime). The VDS consists of the preparation of a specific report aimed at determining whether there are critical health issues.

The national legislator (*see* Article 1*bis* of Law Decree No. 207/2012) delegated the regime on the methodological criteria useful for the preparation of the VDS report to an inter-ministerial decree adopted jointly by the Ministry of Health and the Ministry of the Environment (*see* DM 24 April 2013).

The health impact assessment (*valutazione di impatto sanitaria – VIS*) was the object of a specific regulatory regime by the national legislator (which followed the individual initiatives taken by the regions), with the modification of Article 26 of Legislative Decree No. 152 of 3 April 2006 (*see* Article 9, paragraph 1, Law No. 221 of 28 December 2015). Specifically, paragraph 5*bis* has been added, which requires the proponent to prepare a VIS in relation to the projects set forth in clause 1 of Annex II to Part II and the projects regarding thermal power stations and other combustion plants with thermal output in excess of 300 MW. The document must be prepared in conformity with the guidelines that the Higher Institute of Health (*Istituto superiore di sanità*) published in February 2016 titled 'Guidelines for the integrated assessment of environmental and health impact (VIIAS) in environmental authorization procedures (SEA – Strategic Environmental Assessment, EIA – environmental impact assessment, IEA – integrated environmental authorization)'.

§8. The Procedures to Implement Voluntary Environmental Protection Tools

141. Starting from the V Community Action Programme (1993–2000), alongside the traditional command and control policy, the search for tools and practices aimed at fostering the participation of companies in the strategy of sustainable development and environmental protection was added.

The Green Paper published by the European Commission on 18 July 2001 introduced the principle of corporate social responsibility (referring to the 'voluntary integration of social and ecological concerns in business operations and their relations with stakeholders').

With reference to environmental protection, corporate social responsibility implies a path towards 'eco-awareness' and 'eco-compatibility', that can be implemented through a self-regulation process, implicit in the concept of social responsibility, that should initiate from the environmental control and monitoring of the company's activities; continue with the implementation of compatible solutions on an environmental level; and end, in a self-sustaining manner, with the enhancement of the ecological goals achieved in the market, and more generally, with respect to the public.

The tools and procedures by means of which it is possible to promote the broad and correct participation of companies in the ecomanagement process have been articulated, in particular, in the procedure for the award of the 'Ecolabel'; in the 'ecoaudit' environmental audit system; in certification systems or tradable permits (including in relation to the emissions market); and in codes of conduct and environmental reports and balance sheets.

142. There are many forms of product certification (aimed at providing information, on a voluntary basis, regarding compliance with standards and technical rules in order to render products eco-compatible 'from cradle to grave', ensuring their EIA. In European law, the procedure to award the 'Ecolabel' should be cited, which is governed by Regulation (EC) No. 66/2010 of the European Parliament and the Council of 25 November 2009, modified by Regulation EU No. 782/2013 of 14 August 2013.

The Ecolabel regards 'any goods or services which are supplied for distribution, consumption or use on the Community market whether in return for payment or free of charge' (Article 1, first paragraph Regulation EC 66/2010), excluding medicinal products for human or for veterinary use, or any type of medical device (Article 1, second paragraph).

The specific criteria for the award of the EU Ecolabel are established for groups of products.

The evaluation of the prerequisites is entrusted to a EU Ecolabeling Board, consisting of the competent bodies of all Member States and by representatives of other stakeholders (Article 5, Regulation EC 66/2010).

'The most significant environmental impacts' are taken into consideration, 'in particular the impact on climate change, the impact on nature and biodiversity, energy and resource consumption, generation of waste, emissions to all environmental media, pollution through physical effects and use and release of hazardous substances' (Article 6, third paragraph, clause *a*), Regulation EC 66/2010); 'the substitution of hazardous substances by safer substances, as such or via the use of alternative materials or designs, wherever it is technically feasible' (clause *b*), the 'potential to reduce environmental impacts due to durability and reusability of products' (clause *c*), the 'net environmental balance between the environmental benefits and burdens, including health and safety aspects, at the various life stages of the products' (clause *d*), the 'social and ethical aspects' (clause *e*), the 'criteria established for other environmental labels' (clause *f*), the 'principle of reducing animal testing' (clause *g*).

The award of the label and related terms of use are determined by the competent bodies designated by each Member State of the EU. In Italy, competence rests with the Commission for the EU Ecological Quality Label for products and for the European Union ecomanagement and audit system, created by DM No. 413 of 1995, as modified by DM No. 263 of 1998, care of the Ministry of the Environment.

The administrative review is conducted by ISPRA, with an audit by accredited laboratories of the technical Inspectorate care of the Ministry of Productive Activities.

There are also environmental product statements and forms of voluntary certification entirely governed by technical rules and managed by private associations (which public entities also participate in): *see*, for example, the ISO 14020 series – which refers to environmental labels and statements; the ISO 14040 series – related to the life cycle assessment; and the UNI (Ente nazionale italiano di unificazione) and CEI (Comitato elettrotecnico italiano) training and accreditation activities.

143. The use of environmental management systems able to ensure improvement of the organization and management of companies with an environmental impact, the adoption of the European Union Eco-Management and Audit System (EMAS) has spread.

The EMAS system is currently regulated by Regulation (EC) No. 1221/2009 of 25 November 2009.

The parties adhering to it can be private companies and organizations, but also public entities. The parties who request registration for the first time must perform an environmental analysis in compliance with the requirements established by the EC Regulation, develop and apply an environmental management system considering the best practices of environmental management for the sector involved, conduct an internal audit and prepare an environmental statement in conformity with Annex IV of such regulation.

The eco-management system must be accredited by an independent auditor.

The parties registered with the 'EMAS' system can enjoy benefits both on the level of participation in public procedures (such as those for the allocation of financing or the award of contracts), as well as with respect to simplification of the authorization procedures.

144. The procedures aimed at implementing the green certificate system and 'white certificates' are particularly significant, also in the context of implementation of the Protocol of Kyoto.

The procedure related to green certificates involves a determination by the administration of the amount of energy originating from renewable sources must be included in the system. Producers and importers of electrical energy from conventional sources must demonstrate that they have a quantity of energy produced or acquired that originates from renewable sources (green obligation).

The operator of electrical services issues green certificates based on a procedure that qualifies the production activities from renewable sources, attributing the producer with an owner's account in which such certificates are deposited.

Parties who are obligated to produce a certain quantity of energy from renewable sources can directly produce the quantities of energy imposed on them through autonomous investments; or they can buy the equivalent quota and relative rights from renewable energy producers, thus acquiring the green certificates.

It is a procedure that allows the activation of a market in which the parties who carry out activities, through energy production, having a strong environmental impact are given an incentive for the eco-compatible management of their activities and to engage in transactions and investments that are functional to such result. The administration is responsible for preparing a platform for the purchase-sale of the certificates.

Similarly, but with reference to the distribution of energy, are cases of 'white certificates' or 'titles of energy efficiency'. In this case as well, the administrative authority organizes a market for the trading of certificates related to the implementation of projects for the efficient use of energy by final users (e.g., the substitution of boilers, insulation, cogeneration).

The procedures implementing the Protocol of Kyoto resulted in a trading system of pollution rights in relation to the emissions of industrial plants and airline operators in order to ensure environmental protection through the reduction of greenhouse gases (*see*, most recently, Directive 2009/29/EC). In this case as well, the administration (at a European level, the Commission), establishes the overall quantity of consumable resources.

Since 2013 a decision of the Commission establishes an overall cap on allowable emissions, using calculation criteria that refer to the total quotas issued by the Member States for the period considered.

Legislative Decree No. 30 of 13 March 2013 established the Italian regime.

In practice, the trading system of quotas is based on the requirement of prior authorization to emit greenhouse gases and the allocation of quotas authorizing the operator who owns a plant to issue a specific quantity of such gas, with the obligation to return a number of emission quotas each year equal to the total emissions of its plant during the course of the prior calendar year.

The individual plant owners can exchange the emission quotas in relation to the needs of each company. There can therefore be operators who, in the case of emissions that exceed what is allowed, can acquire quotas from other operators, or operators who, having succeeded in positively modifying the functioning of their plants, can sell their excess quotas or capitalize them, setting them aside for future use.

145. Precaution, prevention, correction as a priority at the source and sustainable development are at the basis of the adoption of codes of conduct, and environmental reports and balance sheets (at present voluntary, but in the future mandatory – *see* the French example of the 'Loi Grenelle environment', No. 967 of 3 August 2009, Article 53).

The codes of conduct do not substitute national, EU and international legislation, or international conventions; they are, however, innovative tools – which are also negotiated with the union counterpart – capable of offsetting environmental inefficiency, placing societal quality as one of the tools to deal with international competitiveness (the most well-known code of conduct is *Responsible care*, adopted by the chemical industry).

The *environmental balance sheet* – or 'ecobalance' – is the accounting tool capable of representing, in an organic manner, the interrelations between company and environment, through a quantitative and qualitative representation of the environmental impact of productive activities and the economic effort sustained by the company.

The 'ecobalance' is a fundamental tool for corporate environmental management and for the company's social responsibility, because it organically highlights the company's level of 'ecological' attention (indicating 'hidden' environmental liabilities, introducing rules on transparency in decision-making processes and in the company's operations).

The 'Environmental Report' is distinguished from the environmental balance sheet and has the role, with freedom of form and content, of communicating to all stakeholders the results achieved, progress made and future prospects of the environmental undertaking of the individual company, thus enhancing, through correct information, the participation in the market of both the company and the public in creating policies and efficient actions for environmental protection.

§9. The Right to Environmental Information and Participation

146. Principles aimed at guaranteeing the right to environmental information (access to information and to data, guarantee of an adequate flux of information, etc.) and at permitting all interested parties to participate in environmental proceedings constitute general principles of the environmental protection regime.

It is obvious that the guarantee of environmental information and the right of adequate participation in decision-making processes constitute an indispensable premise for the proper definition of environmental interests. In this context, citizen participation becomes a structural element of the regime itself, and, thus, not a simple means to the end, but an end in itself. The environment (or better, the regulation of environmental protection) is the result of a series of choices and compromises reached in balancing the values with which the need for protection comes in conflict. This leads to the inclusive nature of the procedural rules aimed at verifying the relative principles to be applied and the manner in which such valuation should be made.

Given the strict connection between substantive and procedural rules in this field, the general principles regarding the right to information and participation are discussed in greater detail in Part V *infra*.

Chapter 2. Water Pollution

by *Antonio Borzì*

§1. Principal Sources of National Law

147. Italian law on water has two fundamental features:

- qualitative protection, which essentially consists of protecting existing water resources from pollution;
- quantitative protection, aimed at ensuring a balance between available water and sustainable water consumption, that is, the proper use of all water resources by guaranteeing society's use of water in accordance with a rational scale of priorities, which is the principal objective of *water resource management.*

148. The Italian legal system, even though it has made significant progress integrating these two features, has currently still not achieved uniform regulation of qualitative and quantitative water pollution control. Specifically, the regulation of water use is still contained in the *Uniform text on water and electrical systems*, adopted by Royal Decree No. 1775 of 11 December 1933 (modified in 1999 and in 2006).

149. Until June 1999, Italian law dealing with water pollution control primarily consisted of Law No. 319 of 10 May 1976, *Water Pollution Control Law* (as modified and integrated by Law No. 690 of 8 October 1976, Law No. 650 of 24 December 1979, and Law No. 172 of 17 May 1995), in addition to a lengthy series of legislative decrees implementing Community law.

150. In June 1999, Legislative Decree No. 152 of 11 May 1999 entered into effect. It entirely reorganized this sector and abrogated Law No. 319/1976 and Legislative Decrees Nos 515/1982, 130/1992, 131/1992, 132/1992 and 133/1992.

151. In 2004, the Parliament approved a delegating law for the government to coordinate and integrate outstanding environmental legislation and prepare uniform laws, inclusive of the sectors of water pollution control and water resource management (Article 1, paragraph 1(b), Law No. 308 of 15 December 2004). This delegation of power was implemented by Legislative Decree No. 152 of 3 April 2006, which contains all of the standards on soil conservation (previously contained in Law No. 183 of 18 May 1989), water resource management (Law No. 36 of 5 January 1994) and water pollution control (Legislative Decree No. 152/1999).

152. By means of Legislative Decree No. 152 of 2006 (the 'Decree'), the Italian legislator also implemented Directive 2000/60/EC (which *establishes a framework for Community action in the field of water policy*), intended to achieve the following objectives (*see* the Commission Communication to the European Parliament and Council *Towards sustainable water management in the European Union* of 22 March 2007, COM 128):

- to expand protection to all waters: inland and coastal surface waters and groundwater;
- to achieve a 'good status' for all waters by 2015;
- to base water management on river basins;
- to combine emission limit values with Environmental Quality Standards (EQS);
- to ensure that water prices provide adequate incentives for water users to utilize water resources more efficiently;
- to involve citizens more closely.

153. This chapter will review the specific regime on water pollution control, in accordance with Part III, section II of the 2006 Decree, whereas water resource management and soil conservation will be reviewed in another chapter.

154. It is noted, however, that the following laws also regard the protection of water quality: (a) the laws regulating bathing water, and (b) the legal regime on drinking water.

(a) Legislative Decree No. 116 of 30 May 2008 entitled *Implementation of Directive 2006/7/EC concerning the management of bathing water quality and repealing Directive 76/160/EEC,* is aimed at protecting human health from the risks deriving from poor quality bathing water, defined as *surface water or any part of it which the competent authority expects will be used for bathing.* The decree contains rules for the monitoring, classification and management of the quality of bathing water, including information to be made available to the public. More specifically, it provides that subsequent to monitoring and evaluating data, water identified as bathing water be classified according to a quality scale that ranges from 'poor' to 'excellent'.

    The regions, in addition to increasing the number of areas where bathing water is classified as 'excellent' or 'good' quality, should have ensured by means of a plan containing adequate management measures that by the end of the 2015 bathing season, that all bathing water would at least be 'sufficient'.

    Further, the municipalities must intervene with timely and adequate management measures whenever they become aware of unexpected situations that have, or which are likely to have, a negative impact on the quality of bathing water or the health of bathers (informing the public and, if necessary, temporarily prohibiting bathing).

    The rules set forth in Legislative Decree No. 116 of 2008 integrate those of Part III of the Decree and, in effect, follow the same approach, aimed at the dynamic protection of water resources in view of the progressive improvement of water quality.

(b) In order to protect human health from the negative effects deriving from water contamination, guaranteeing that it is wholesome and clean, Legislative Decree

No. 31 of 2 February 2001 contains provisions on the *quality of water intended for human consumption*, as implementation of Directive 98/83/EC (the Drinking Water Directive). 'Water to be used for human consumption' means not only water used for drinking, to prepare foods and beverages, or other domestic uses, but also water used by the food industry to manufacture, process, conserve or distribute products used for human consumption, whereas it excludes natural mineral water and recognized medicinal water because they are subject to other specific laws.

Water to be used for human consumption must conform to the biological and chemical parameters established in Annex I to the decree. Derogations are allowed, limited to cases in which the supply of compliant water cannot be guaranteed using suitable means, as long as always within limits in which there is no potential danger to public health. In the event it is verified that the limits have been exceeded, the water service manager must take corrective action to restore water quality and the mayor, in addition to the obligation to inform consumers, can take precautionary measures to protect health, based on the extent of the variance from the limit values imposed.

The decree provides for a series of internal controls to be performed by the integrated water service manager, as well as external controls performed by the Provincial Health Agencies, which use testing laboratories of the Regional Environmental Protection Agency (ARPA). The system of sanctions set forth in Legislative Decree No. 31 of 2001 only contemplates administrative penalties for anyone providing water destined for human consumption that does not conform to the legal limits (more rigorous sanctions are applied to food businesses and the managers of buildings in which water is provided to the public), as well as for anyone who violates the measures approved by the authorities to restore the quality of the water resource (including limits on use). It should be noted, however, that the Italian Criminal Code punishes the intentional or negligent poisoning of water intended for consumption (Articles 439 and 452 of the Italian Criminal Code).

In 2016 the regime on radioactive substances in water to be used for human consumption was substituted by the regime set forth in Legislative Decree No. 28 of 15 February 2016.

§2. Objective Scope of Application

155. The primary objective of Italian law on water pollution control is the pursuit of *sustainable and long-lasting* uses of water resources, with priority for drinking water, aiming at the improvement of the state of water and adequate protection of water destined for special uses, by means of the prevention and reduction of pollution as well as the purification of polluted water bodies (Article 73).

The legal regime used to achieve these ambitious results is very articulated and can only be described in a general manner.

156. The basic choice made in 1999 (and therefore in advance with respect to the decisions taken at a Community level by means of the Framework Directive of

2000), was to not limit protection to individual points of wastewater discharges, but rather to consider the qualitative protection of the receiving water body as a logical priority, along the lines of the model law introduced with respect to air pollution, which, together with the regulation of emission sources aims at guaranteeing that air quality reaches specific objective values over time. Legislative Decree No. 152 of 1999, thus, constituted a radical change of approach to the problem of water pollution with respect to Law No. 319/1976. Legislative Decree No. 152 of 2006, currently in effect, confirms the model of protection introduced in 1999 and, on the basis of Directive 2000/60/EC, it enriches it from at least two viewpoints: a closer relationship between the quantitative and qualitative protection of water resources (e.g., by application of the principle 'the polluter pays'), and greater attention to some territorial areas that require special protection.

157. In brief, the rules on water pollution control contained in the decree (Part III, section II, Articles 73 et seq.) are intended to protect the quality of water resources by (a) regulating water discharges; (b) providing quality objectives for receiving bodies of water and measures to ensure that they are achieved; and (c) introducing special protection for specific territorial areas worthy of protection.

I. Regime on Discharges

158. Discharge is defined as any release made exclusively by use of a stable system that seamlessly links the production cycle of wastewater with the receiving body of surface water, soil, subsoil or a sewage system, independent of its polluting nature, and even if subjected to preventive treatment, with the specification that the permits provided by Article 114 are excluded in the case of dams (Article 74, paragraph 1, clause ff).

Said definition plays a central role in the regulation of water pollution control, above all, because it constitutes the legal reference point to determine the limits of the scope of application of provisions on wastes, since Article 185 of the decree excludes *wastewater, except for liquid wastes* from the scope of application of the provisions of Part IV of the decree.

The central element for the definition of a discharge (eliminated in 2006 but reintroduced by Legislative Decree No. 4 of 2008) is that of linkage: starting from Legislative Decree No. 152 of 1999, case law has clarified that 'discharge' means a *direct* discharge in receiving bodies, because interruption of the functional linkage between the source of production of wastewater and the receiving body results in the wastewater being regulated by the regime on wastes, as in the case of wastewater collected in tanks and removed using tankers (Criminal Court of Cassation, section III, judgment No. 42529 of 9 October 2008). Moreover, the decree's use of the expression *stable connection system*, with respect to that of an *exhaust* (in 1999), makes it clear that a discharge does not require the delivery point to be reached by means of a classic 'plumbing' system, but any objective and long-term drainage system is sufficient if it channels wastewater (Court of Cassation, Criminal Chamber section III, judgment No. 35888 of 3 October 2006; Idem, judgment No. 16162 of 27 January 2016).

The decree provides that all discharges must be authorized and comply with specific emission limit values determined in accordance with law; whenever controls confirm that the discharge exceeds legal limits, lacks authorization or does not comply with the terms of the authorization, criminal or administrative penalties are applied, both monetary fines and other sanctions (such as the suspension or revocation of the authorization).

The regime on discharges varies, above all, depending on the type of waste. With reference to wastewater, Article 74 distinguishes among:

- *domestic wastewater*: wastewater originating from residential homes and services, prevalently deriving from human metabolism and domestic activities (paragraph 1, clause g);
- *industrial wastewater*: any type of wastewater discharged from buildings or installations in which commercial or manufacturing activity is performed, other than domestic wastewater and storm water runoff (clause h);
- *urban wastewater*: the mix of domestic wastewater, industrial wastewater, and/or storm water runoff channelled into sewage systems, even if separately, originating from settlements (clause i).

There is also wastewater *assimilated to domestic wastewater*, that is, wastewater which, due to legislative definition, constitutes industrial wastewater, but which is subject to the regime on domestic wastewater discharges based on the level of pollution that it causes; the list, contained in Article 101, paragraph 7, can be 'expanded' by the regions, as long as it regards *water having qualitative characteristics that are equivalent to domestic wastewater.* Law No. 221 of 28 December 2015 inserted paragraphs 7*bis*, which governs the assimilation of wastewater originating from oil mills.

The distinction based on the type of wastewater is significant, above all, with reference to the regime on authorizations and the regime of emission limit values: discharges of domestic wastewater (and assimilated wastewater), when discharged into public sewers, do not require authorization; in the case of discharges of industrial wastewater, the request for authorization must be supplemented with the information required by Article 125. With respect to the limit values of the discharge, while the emission concentrations set forth in Tables 1 and 2 of Annex 5 to Part III apply to discharges of urban wastewater, industrial wastewater is subject to the limit values set forth in tables 3 and 3/A of the same Annex.

159. Discharges in soil, subsoil and groundwater is normally prohibited. Discharges *in soil* are only allowed in specific mandatory cases (Article 103), among which discharges of domestic wastewater of isolated settlements, buildings or installations, as well as discharges of urban or industrial wastewater that have been verified to be technically impossible or excessively costly with respect to the environmental benefits that could be obtained by discharging such wastewater in surface water. In any event, discharges in soil must conform to the limits set forth in Table 4 of Annex 5 and cannot contain specific substances (indicated in point 2.1 of said Annex). This also applies to discharges in *groundwater and in subsoil*, which is only allowed in the cases contemplated by Article 104 of the decree.

One of the instruments indicated by the decree used to improve water bodies consists of the *adjustment of the sewage system, connection and treatment of water discharges in the context of the integrated water service* (Article 73, paragraph 2, clause d). Article 100 requires that urban centres, starting from a specific size (in excess of the equivalent of 2,000 inhabitants, where 'equivalent inhabitant' means a biochemical oxygen demand at five days equivalent to 60 g of oxygen per day), have sewage systems for the discharge of urban wastewater. These infrastructures must be planned, realized and maintained using the criteria of the best available technologies at sustainable costs. In the case of isolated settlements, installations and buildings, the regions must identify other kinds of waste treatment that achieve the same level of environmental protection.

160. Discharges *in a public sewer* impact both the need for authorization, with the exception of domestic wastewater, as well as the entity that is competent to issue the authorization which, except in the case of a different regional regime for such kind of discharge, is the Optimal Territorial Area – *Area Territoriale Ottimale* (ATO) Authority (i.e., the authority that regulates the Integrated Water Service, for which reference is made to the chapter on water resource management and soil conservation) whose functions are indicated in section 9).

161. With respect to a discharge in *surface water*, the decree requires that discharges of urban wastewater be subjected to diversified treatment depending on the size of the user being serviced (measured in equivalent residents) and the characteristics of the receiving body (e.g., fresh water or salt-coastal water): the important factor is that discharges of both urban and industrial wastewater in surface water conform to the limits set forth in Annex 5 or those established by the regions (Article 105).

II. Water Quality

162. Italian law on water pollution control places attention not only on control of the individual emission points, but also on the overall quality of the receiving water body. The number of discharges into the same water body varies, and, thus, the determination of a *standard* emission limit, equal for all situations, risks being an insufficient form of protection for the bodies of water that are the most greatly impacted, either because they are subject to an elevated number of discharges or are small water bodies. The result that Italian law intends to achieve is that of adhering to a specific system of emission limits for each water body that guarantees the quality of the resource. Article 101, paragraph 1 provides that *all discharges are regulated on the basis of compliance with quality objectives for water bodies;* this is the reason why the regions can intervene in regulating emission limits (Article 101, paragraph 2). The different levels of government involved in determining emission limits for discharges are reviewed below. It is important to note, however, that in order to be effectively implemented, the Italian legislator's plan requires an enormous effort just to discover what water resources exist, and subsequently to programme interventions.

Article 120 of the decree requires the regions to prepare and implement programmes aimed at awareness and verification of the qualitative and quantitative status of the surface and groundwater within each water basin. This results in a need for monitoring and the subsequent classification of the most important water bodies located within the territory (identified according to the procedures indicated in Annexes 1 and 3 to Part III of the decree, the object of numerous amendments, the most recent made by DM 6 July 2016 and DM 15 July 2016). These activities allow the presence of specific chemical pollutants to be studied, as well as the ecological status of water bodies to be specifically surveyed ('ecological status' means *the quality of the structure and functioning of aquatic ecosystems associated with surface water*, Article 73, paragraph 2, clause *t*). The combination of data on the chemical status with data on the ecological status results in the overall expression of the state of a surface water body, which can range from 'poor' to 'excellent'. In relation to such classification, the regions must determine and adopt the necessary measures to reach or maintain the environmental quality objectives imposed by the decree (including measure making emission limits for discharges more rigorous with respect to the limits set forth in the decree). Similarly on this issue, with respect to the quality of groundwater Legislative Decree No. 152 of 2006 was integrated (and in part modified) by the rules of Legislative Decree No. 30 of 16 March 2009 entitled *Implementation of Directive 2006/118/EC on the protection of groundwater against pollution and deterioration.*

III. Areas Subject to Special Protection

163. In implementing the provisions of Directive 2000/60/EC, Legislative Decree No. 152 of 2006 reinforced the protection of water bodies located in areas entitled to special protection.

The decree requires a register of protected areas (Article 117), as well as the obligation that the Water Basin Management Plan include a cartographic representation of protected areas and monitoring results, an indication of the environmental objectives established for protected areas, and the measures required to achieve them (Annex 4-A). The decree also provides specific rules for monitoring (Annex 1, paragraphs A.3.1.1. and A.3.7), and the specification and delineation of boundaries for water bodies located in protected areas (Annex 3, paragraphs B.3.4; B.3.4.2.).

The register is required for the following types of protected areas:

(i) designated areas for the abstraction of drinking water;
(ii) designated areas for the protection of aquatic species that are important from an economic standpoint;
(iii) bodies of water to be used for recreational purposes, inclusive of designated bathing areas;
(iv) nutrient-sensitive areas, including those designated as vulnerable zones and sensitive areas;
(v) designated areas for the protection of habitats and species, in which the maintenance or improvement of the state of water is important for their protection, including pertinent sites of the Nature 2000 network created pursuant to

Directives 79/409/EEC and 92/43/EEC, respectively implemented by Law No. 157 of 11 February 1992 and Presidential Decree No. 357 of 8 September 1997 – ZPS and SCI.

The register is maintained by the Basin Authority, after consultation with the ATO Authority, based on data provided by the regions and must be kept updated for each hydrographic district.

On the basis of the list set forth in Annex IX, it appears that not all protected areas are regulated by Legislative Decree No. 152 of 2006 (or by Directive 2000/60/EC): certain kinds of areas are created on the basis of other laws of this sector. Article 77, paragraph 4 specifies that *water located in protected areas must conform to the quality objectives and standards set forth in Annex 1 to Part III of the Decree, within the deadlines set forth therein, unless in the case of a different provision of the relevant law that established the individual area.*

Among protected areas, the decree provides specific regulations for sensitive areas, areas vulnerable to nitrates of agricultural origin, areas vulnerable to pesticides, areas vulnerable to desertification and protected areas of surface water and groundwater to be used for human consumption: these consist of water bodies and portions of land that have a common need for *specific pollution control and purification measures* (Articles 91 et seq.).

In the tradition of the Italian legal system, therefore, the term 'protected area' refers to territories that have naturalistic or environmental significance according to Law No. 394 of 6 December 1991 (the Framework Law on Protected Areas), which created parks (national and regional) and natural wildlife reserves (national and regional). The expression 'natural areas', according to the above legal meaning, also appears in the decree, for example, when the criteria for the creation of protected areas appear among the objectives of basin planning (Article 56, paragraph 1, clause *m*), as well as Article 65, paragraph 3, or when a specific regime is established for the collection and discharge of water in these particular areas (Article 164).

Nothing appears to prohibit the Basin Authorities from also including the parks and reserves set forth in Law No. 394 of 1991 (and regional implementing legislation) in the register of 'protected areas' required by Article 117 and Annex IX; the directive expressly refers not only to Community law, but also to national and local legislation as legal sources creating protected areas to be included in the register (Directive 2000/60/EC, Annex IV).

Protected areas are subject to particular attention from a punitive profile as well, with more rigorous administrative sanctions for whoever makes discharges that exceed the legal limits in such areas (Article 133, paragraph 1).

§3. Planning and Programming Instruments

164. Truly effective water pollution control, capable of ensuring qualitative and quantitative conditions for the resource compatibly with the need for sustainable development, requires a preventive monitoring phase of the state of the water bodies and subsequent strategic planning of interventions.

165. Section II of Part III of the decree, dedicated to water pollution control, contemplates two distinct planning instruments: the Water Management Plan and the Water Pollution Control Plan; these are in addition to the Basin Plan provided by section I of Part III, which contains provisions on soil conservation and the fight against desertification.

166. In order to prepare the Management Plan, the Basin Authority must guarantee the participation of all of the institutional entities having competence with respect to water pollution control.

With respect to the content of the Plan, Article 117, paragraph 2, of the decree refers to the provisions of Annex 4, section A of Part III, which reproduces the provisions of Directive 2000/60/EC. The index, contained in an annex, consists of:

(a) a general description of the district's characteristics, including any protected areas, as well as an indication of the monitoring networks of the qualitative state of water (pages 1–4);
(b) the list of environmental objectives established for surface water, groundwater and protected areas (including cases of extension or derogation, page 5);
(c) a summary of the economic analysis of water use made according to the forecasts of Annex 10;
(d) a summary of the measures required to achieve quality objectives for the water bodies, including controls of discharges (page 7);
(e) a summary of the measures taken with respect to public information and consultation, with the relative results and any consequent modifications to the plan (page 9), as well as an indication of the competent authorities within each district (page 10).

In order to combine flood risk management with the protection of river ecosystems, the Basin Authorities, together with the other competent entities, are responsible for preparing a management programme for river basin sediments in the context of the Management Plan, as a cognitive, management and planning tool for activity related to the morphological structure of river corridors (paragraph 2*quater*, inserted by Law No. 221 of 2015

The Management Plan must also contain an index of any more detailed programmes or management plans approved for the district basin or related to specific sub-basins, sectors, thematic or types of water, together with a summary of the content.

167. The Management Plans for the hydrographic districts must be updated every six years (paragraph 2*bis*, inserted by Law No. 97 of 2013). With respect to sector plans, particular importance is given to the Regional Water Pollution Control Plan, set forth in Article 121 of the decree.

In addition to interventions aimed at guaranteeing achievement or maintenance of the quality objectives, the Protection Plan contains measures required for the qualitative and quantitative protection of the water system.

168. Specifically, the Water Pollution Control Plan contains (Article 121, paragraph 3, as well as Annex 4, section B, to Part III of the decree):

(a) the results of cognitive activity;
(b) specification of environmental quality objectives and specific use;
(c) a list of water bodies having a specific use and of the areas requiring special measures of pollution prevention and purification;
(d) integrated and coordinated qualitative and quantitative protective measures for the water basin;
(e) an indication of the timeframe for the work and relative priorities;
(f) the testing programme of the effectiveness of the projected work;
(g) reclamation of water bodies;
(h) the data possessed by the competent authorities and agencies with respect to monitoring groundwater and water to be used for human consumption in the areas involved, surveyed and periodically updated by the existing monitoring network, to be published in such a way that it is available to the public;
(i) the economic analysis set forth in Annex 10 of Legislative Decree No. 152 of 2006 and the measures to implement the provisions set forth in Article 119 on cost recovery for water services; and
(j) the financial resources provided by outstanding law.

The Water Pollution Control Plan is approved after a very articulated procedure which requires the participation of the provinces, Ministry of the Environment, and above all, the Basin Authority, which is also entrusted with determining the objectives on a district scale to which the regional plans must conform and with specifying the priorities of the work regarding water pollution control.

More specifically, the regions approve the Water Pollution Control Plan after consultation with the provinces, and transmit it to the Ministry of the Environment as well as to the competent Basin Authority, which verifies the conformity of the Water Pollution Control Plan with the Basin Plan and District Plan, as well as with the objectives previously specified by said authority, expressing a binding opinion. The Water Pollution Control Plan is definitively approved by the region, which must update it every six years.

During the bureaucratic process creating the Plan, particular attention is paid to public information and consultation (Article 122).

The law specifies that *upon a justified request, the regions shall authorize access to the documents of reference and the information on the basis of which the draft Water Pollution Control Plan was prepared.* The fact that the request must be 'justified' is a deviation with respect to general principles on environmental information, which exclude subordinating access to the allegation of a specific interest. Further, Article 14 of Directive 2000/60/EC does not specify that a justification be cited as a prerequisite for a request.

It is difficult to reconstruct the relationships among the Basin Plan, Water Management Plan, and Water Pollution Control Plan, and even the Constitutional Court has intervened on this issue.

169. The district Basin Plan is defined in Article 65 of the decree as a territorial plan for the sector and as a cognitive, regulatory and technical-operative instrument, by means of which actions and rules on use are planned and programmed that are aimed at soil conservation, defence and enhancement and the proper use of water, based on the physical and environmental characteristics of the territory involved.

170. The Water Management Plan regards the entire basin district and is an internal articulation of the Basin Plan. Consequently: (a) the Water Management Plan must be adopted and approved using the same procedures established for the Basin Plan (adoption by the Basin Authority, subject to SEA, approved by a decree of the President of the Council of Ministers, *see* Article 66); (b) similar to the Basin Plan, the provisions of the approved Water Management Plan are immediately binding on public administrations and entities, as well as on private parties, when expressly specified in the Plan (Article 65, paragraph 4).

The Water Management Plan is, therefore, placed on the same legal level as the Basin Plan, regards the same territorial area, but differs from the Basin Plan because its exclusive object is water pollution control (it does not include soil conservation).

171. The Water Pollution Control Plan is defined by Article 121 as a specific sector plan and, different from the Water Management Plan, it regards an individual water basin; it must conform to the Water Management Plan (and the Basin Plan), as well as the orientation and objectives defined by the Basin Authority on a district level (in this regard, *see* Constitutional Court, judgment No. 254 of 2009).

The decree provides that the regions can prepare a programme of measures that integrates the Water Pollution Control Plan to guarantee that quality objectives are achieved, whose contents are determined by Annex 11 of the decree (Article 116; on this point *see* Constitutional Court, judgment No. 251 of 2009).

To ensure the effectiveness of the measures, any new measures or modifications approved in the context of an updated plan must be implemented within three years from their approval (Article 116, paragraph 1*bis*, added by Law No. 97 of 2013).

§4. Authorization Procedures

172. All discharges require prior authorization. Such obligation, required since 1999, expresses one of the fundamental principles of the Italian legal system in terms of water pollution control.

Exceptions are made for domestic wastewater discharges in sewage systems, which are always allowed as long as the regulations established by the integrated water service manager, approved by the competent ATO Authority, are complied with.

Authorization must be requested:

(a) in the case of new discharges;
(b) in the case of the transfer of an activity to another location; and

(c) in the case of establishments or settlements that are subject to a change of use, are enlarged or restored, or from which a discharge originates having characteristics that are qualitatively and/or quantitatively different with respect to the pre-existing discharge.

If the discharge does not have different qualitative or quantitative characteristics, notice must be given to the competent authority, which, after verifying the compatibility of the discharge with the receiving body, adopts any measures that might be necessary.

The authorization is issued to the owner of the activity from which the discharge originates (but the decree also regulates the establishment of a consortium for the discharge, Article 124), who is responsible for the costs of the procedure, inclusive of controls and inspections by the competent authority.

If the authorization regards the discharge of industrial wastewater, the application must contain (Article 125):

- an indication of the quantitative and qualitative characteristics of the discharge and the annual volume of water to be discharged, with a description of the overall discharge system, inclusive of the operations that are functionally related to it as well as the eventual system to measure the flow of the discharges, if required;
- an indication of the equipment used in the manufacturing process and in the discharge systems, as well as the water treatment systems used to comply with emission limit values;
- specification of the point where control sampling should be conducted;
- a description of the type of receiving body.

Further information, such as the installation's production capacity and the hourly need for water, are necessary in the case of discharges of specific substances (those set forth in Table 3/A of Annex 5 to Part III of the Decree, deriving from the productive cycles indicated in said table).

Except in the case of a different regional regime, the province or the ATO Authority is the competent authority if the discharge is in a public sewer.

There is a ninety-day term for compliance from receipt of the application, as long as the installation is not subject to an IEA; in such case the terms set forth in Article 29*quater* of Legislative Decree No. 152 of 2006 are applied.

The same applies to the duration of the authorization, with the exception of what is provided by Article 29*ocites* for the AIA (normally a five-year duration). The authorization is valid for four years from the date it is issued.

Renewal must be requested one year prior to the expiration. A timely request for renewal allows the discharge to be temporarily maintained in accordance with the requirements specified in the previous authorization, until a new measure is adopted. Renewal of an expired measure is subject to a time limit in the case of authorizations of discharges containing hazardous substances: the activity must immediately cease if six months have passed from the authorization's expiration without the issuance of an express renewal.

173. The decree contains two important specifications with respect to authorization requirements:

(1) *in general*, in relation to the technical characteristics of the discharge, its location and the local environmental conditions, the authorization contains additional technical requirements aimed at guaranteeing that the discharge, inclusive of the operations that are functionally related to it, is made in conformity with the provisions of the Decree and without causing any damage to the receiving body, public health and the environment;
(2) *in the specific case* of the discharge of a course of water in which no natural flow is verified for more than 120 days per year, or of an insignificant water body, the authorization must also consider the no-flow period and the dilution capacity of the water body in other periods and must establish requirements and limits in order to guarantee the self-purification of the receiving body and the protection of groundwater.

§5. Specific Instruments of 'Direct Regulation'

174. The classic instrument to contain water pollution consists of determining an emission limit value for discharges, defined as the *limit of acceptability of a polluting substance contained in a discharge, measured in concentration, or in mass per unit of product or raw material that is processed, or in mass per time unit*, by Article 74, paragraph 1, clause *oo* of the decree.

Said provision also establishes some general rules with respect to emission limits for discharges:

- values can also be determined for specific groups, families or categories of substances;
- emission limits for substances are normally applied at the point where the emissions leave the installation (*see* section 6 *infra* with respect to where samples must be taken);
- the effect of a wastewater treatment plant must be taken into account in determining the installation's emission limit values, on the condition that an equivalent level of environmental protection is guaranteed overall and that increased polluting loads are not brought into the environment;
- emission limits are applied without considering eventual dilution.

This latter point merits clarification because the prohibition of dilution is very significant in practice.

The decree provides in Article 101, paragraph 5 that *emission limit values cannot be achieved by dilution using water removed exclusively for this purpose.* Case law has held that the prohibition is general and is not limited to regulation of the discharge of hazardous substances. With respect to specific hazardous substances, however (those set forth in Article 101, paragraph 4), the law: (a) repeats that they cannot be diluted using cooling water, wash water or water removed exclusively for the purpose of partial discharges prior to its treatment in order to adjust them to the limits established by the decree; and (b) requires the competent authority, at the time of authorization, to separate the discharge point of said substances from those of cooling water, wastewater or water used for the production of energy.

175. The parties who must collaborate in determining emission limit values are:

(a) The State: the limit values are set forth in Annex 5 to Part III of the decree and are diversified according to the type of discharge and delivery; the annexes can also be modified by regulations or decrees of the Minister of the Environment in order to adjust them to technological or scientific progress or to implement supervening Community law (Article 75, paragraphs 3 and 4).

(b) The region: the regional administration, in compliance with the quality objectives, can determine limits that are *different* from national limits, considering the maximum admissible loads and best available technology. Said limits, however, cannot be *less restrictive* than those provided: (a) in Table 1, relative to the discharge of urban wastewater in surface water bodies; (b) in Table 2, relative to the discharge of urban wastewater in surface water bodies located in sensitive areas; (c) in Table 3/A, for the productive cycles set forth therein; or (d) in Tables 3 and 4, for those substances indicated in Table 5. The most suitable instrument to introduce different limits is the Water Pollution Control Plan, in which all of the indications on the quantitative and qualitative state of the receiving water body are indicated.

(c) The Optimal Territorial Ambit Authority (*autorità d'ambito territoriale ottimale*): the ATO Authority is competent to adopt, in compliance with national and regional regulations, the technical standards, regulatory requirements and limit values for the discharge of industrial wastewater in sewage networks and approves the regulation for the discharge of domestic wastewater in sewage systems (Article 107, with respect to the abolishment of the A.A.T.O.).

(d) The Authority Competent to issue the authorization. It is necessary to distinguish two different cases:
   (i) if the discharge relates to an installation that is subject to an IEA (Title III-*bis*, Part II of Legislative Decree No. 152 of 2006), the rule is that limits on the discharge are determined on the basis of the best available technologies (and the limits provided by national, regional and sector regulations can be derogated from *in melius*, but not *in peius*);
   (ii) if the discharge does not relate to an installation subject to AIA, the authority that issues the authorization, in relation to the technical characteristics of the discharge, its location and the local environmental conditions, can determine additional technical requirements with respect to those indicated in the decree in order to guarantee that the discharge occurs in conformity with outstanding law and without damage to the receiving body, public health or the environment (Article 124, paragraph 10). With respect to the limit values for hazardous substances, the authorizing subject has the power to establish more rigorous limits than those established by State or regional law, when such limits impede or prejudice the quality objectives provided by the Water Pollution Control Plan, including due to other discharges of hazardous substances (Article 108, paragraph 2).

176. The other fundamental instrument of direct regulation with respect to water pollution control consists of determining quality objectives for the water bodies in which the discharges flow. It is not superfluous to repeat that the functional connection between quality objective and emission limit for the discharge, in which the emission limit must be suitable to guarantee compliance with quality objectives, constitutes an important change of approach to the issue of water pollution that has matured in Italian legislation starting from Legislative Decree No. 152 of 1999.

Outstanding law contemplates two different objectives:

(i) environmental quality objectives, which apply to all significant surface water and groundwater and which are defined on the basis of the capacity of the receiving body to maintain natural self-purification processes and to support broad and diversified community wildlife and plants (Article 76, paragraph 2);

(ii) quality objectives for specific use, which determine the state of suitable water bodies in order to guarantee particular uses of the resource: (1) surface freshwater for the production of water suitable for human consumption; (2) water used for bathing; (3) water suitable for the life of fish; (4) water used by molluscs (Article 76, paragraph 3 and Article 79).

Establishing EQS representing the concentration of a specific pollutant or group of pollutants in water, sediments or biota that cannot be exceeded in order to protect human health and the environment is particularly important (*see*, specifically, Articles 78 through 78*decies* of the Decree, inserted by Legislative Decree No. 172 of 13 October 2015).

§6. Control System

177. With respect to controls, the decree continues the regime introduced in 1999, when it was established for the first time that the competent authority must adopt a suitable prevention programme in order to ensure a periodic, widespread, effective and impartial prevention system and subsequent controls.

178. In the case of discharges in public sewers, said controls are added to those organized by the integrated water service manager in the manner provided by the servicing agreement (Article 128).

The competent authority is authorized to perform the necessary inspections, controls and sampling in order to verify compliance with emission limit values, the requirements set forth in authorizations or regulations, and the conditions that led to the creation of the discharges. The owner of the discharge must provide the information requested and allow access to the places where the discharge originates (Article 101, paragraph 4, and 129).

All discharges, with the exception of domestic discharges and those assimilated to domestic discharges by regional legislation, must be made accessible for sampling by the authority responsible for controls at the point used as a reference for the sampling, which is normally done immediately upstream of the release into the delivery point in all natural watersheds, surface water and groundwater, inland and marine, sewers, soil and subsoil (Article 101, paragraph 3. The special rule provided by Article 108, paragraph 5 applies to industrial wastewater containing hazardous substances; on this point *see also* the definition of emission limit value in Article 74, paragraph 1, clause *oo*).

179. In the case of discharges containing hazardous substances, there is the possibility that the owner will be required, at the time of authorization, to outfit installations with automatic control instruments and to conserve the relative results so that they are available to the control authority for at least three years (Article 131).

180. In addition to controls that are the competence of administrative bodies, the decree provides that it is possible to require forms of 'self-control', both for wastewater treatment plants and for the owners of discharges of hazardous substances (Annex 5, paragraphs 1.1. and 2.). In terms of self-control, it should again be noted that whenever an installation is subject to an IEA, the relevant provisions of section III*bis*, Part II of Legislative Decree No. 152 of 2006 are applied.

181. Upon verifying that the requirements of the authorization have not been complied with, in addition to the eventual application of administrative and criminal penalties, the competent authority responsible for performing the control must:

- issue a warning, establishing a deadline within which the irregularity must be eliminated;
- issue a warning, and at the same time suspend the authorization for a specific period of time if there is any danger to public health or the environment;
- revoke the authorization if the requirements set forth in the warning are not complied with, as well as in the case of repeat violations or situations of danger to public health or the environment.

There is a substitute mechanism if the controls are not performed, on the basis of which the Minister of the Environment initially requires the region to comply within six months, or within a shorter term if necessary for environmental protection. In the case of persistent inertia, the Minister of the Environment can exercise substitute power (with the costs borne by the non-compliant entity), upon a resolution of the Council of Ministers, and a commissioner *ad acta* is appointed.

§7. Administrative and Criminal Sanctions

182. The decree establishes three major categories of behaviour subject to sanctions: when emission limits are exceeded; discharges lacking authorization, or which are made with a suspended or revoked authorization; and breach of the requirements contained in the authorization or the specific requirements that may be imposed in individual cases by the competent authorities.

183. An administrative fine ranging from EUR 3,000 to EUR 30,000 is assessed when emission limits are exceeded (Article 133, paragraph 1). The emission limits to which the penalty refers are those established by the State, the regions, the ATO Authority or at the time of authorization. Criminal sanctions, with the cumulative penalty of detention and a fine, are instead applied only when the limits for certain hazardous substances are exceeded in discharges of industrial wastewater, as well as when the same limits are exceeded by the manager of the treatment plant. The amount of the sanction varies according to the substances whose parameters have been exceeded (Article 137, paragraphs 5 and 6).

An administrative fine ranging from EUR 6,000 to EUR 60,000 is applied in the case of discharges of domestic wastewater, sewage systems that lack proper authorization, or discharges made during the suspension or revocation of an authorization; the fine is reduced for discharges originating from isolated buildings used for residential use (Article 133, paragraph 2). Criminal sanctions, with an alternative penalty of detention or a fine, are instead applied in the case of discharges of industrial wastewater, with aggravation of the penalty (detention from three months to three years) if such discharges contain any hazardous substances (Article 137, paragraphs 1 and 2).

Failure to comply with the requirements set forth in the authorization or other specific requirements is subject to an administrative fine ranging from EUR 1,500 to EUR 15,000 (Article 133, paragraph 3). In the cases of discharges of industrial wastewater containing certain hazardous substances, however, a criminal sanction of detention of up to two years is applied (Article 137, paragraph 3).

The sectoral sanctions apply in addition to the cases already provided for by Article 29*quattuordecies* of the decree with respect to IEA.

184. In addition to these three fundamental categories of unlawful behaviour, the new regime provides for a series of additional situations subject to sanctions:

- violation of the regulations on the use of manure for livestock cultivations, which, depending on the behaviour involved, is punished by an administrative fine ranging from EUR 600 to EUR 6,000 (Article 133, paragraph 5) or a criminal penalty (Article 137, paragraph 14);
- violation of prohibitions against discharges in soil and subsoil, punished by a criminal penalty of detention of up to three years (Article 137, paragraph 11);
- violation of the prohibition against the disposal of sludge in freshwater or brackish water, punished by an administrative penalty (Article 133, paragraph 6);
- violation of regional regulations on fresh rainwater or wash water, subject to criminal penalty (Article 137, paragraph 9);
- violation of the obligation to allow access to settlements by the entity entrusted with monitoring, punished by detention for up to two years (Article 137, paragraph 8);
- violation of the requirements for the installation and management of automatic monitoring, punished by detention for up to two years (Article 137, paragraph 4).

185. Additional cases subject to penalties regard behaviour related to territorial areas or water entitled to specific measures of protection:

- violation of the provisions on prohibited activities and intended use in areas subject to protection of surface water and groundwater to be used for human consumption, set forth in Article 94, is punished by an administrative fine ranging from EUR 600 to EUR 6,000 (Article 134);
- discharges that exceed legal limits in a protected area or in water bodies located in protected areas are punished by an administrative fine of not less than EUR 20,000 (Article 133, paragraph 1, second clause);
- violation of urgent measures on discharges, or the use of resources that relate to water capable of supporting the life of fish, are punished by a criminal penalty (a fine ranging from EUR 1,500 to EUR 15,000, Article 137, paragraph 10); whoever violates suitable measures taken to restore the quality of water capable of supporting the life of fish is subject to the same penalty;
- similar violations referring to water capable of supporting mollusc life are subject to criminal penalties (Article 137, paragraph 12).

186. The decree's system of penalties is completed by provisions that specify that the region is the competent entity to issue administrative fines (except for the competence of the municipalities in two marginal cases, Article 135, paragraph 1); exclude the possibility of a reduction of said sanctions (Article 135, paragraph 4); and require that the proceeds be used to purify water bodies (Article 136). Two other important provisions introduce forms of incentives for the restoration and repair of the damages provoked by unlawful behaviour. It is possible, for example, to subordinate the benefit of the conditional suspension of the penalty to the payment of damages and performance of necessary security, reclamation and cleanup work, as well as reduce the amount of administrative and criminal penalties by one-half to two-thirds of the amount of the fine for whoever has entirely remediated the damage (Articles 139 and 140).

Finally, it is necessary to note that the Italian Criminal Code punishes whoever damages public water and the intentional or negligent poisoning of water or food (Articles 439 and 452), as well as the crimes against the environment punished by section VI*bis*.

§8. Economic Instruments

187. The principal economic instrument with respect to water resources consists of the tariffs of the Integrated Water Service, that is, the consideration that water users must pay to use public services for the collection, adduction and distribution of water for non-industrial use, sewage systems and wastewater treatment.

Reference is made to the chapter on water resource management and soil conservation with respect to the description of the tariff system connected to the Integrated Water Service; it is important to note, however, that the decree also links cost recovery for water services to the achievement of quality objectives for water bodies.

On the basis of Article 119, the competent authorities, in order to achieve quality objectives, consider the principle of recovery of costs for water services, inclusive of environmental costs and those related to the resource, according to the principle 'the polluter pays'.

In this way, the price of water becomes an instrument that provides adequate incentives to water users to utilize water resources efficiently and to contribute to the achievement and maintenance of environmental quality objectives (Article 119, paragraph 2).

188. The reference to 'environmental costs', interpreted together with the connection to quality objectives, would require the price of water to include not only the cost of individual services, but also those sustained by the public administration to purify contaminated water bodies. However, as is clearly stated in Directive 2000/60/EC, cost recovery does not hinder financing specific preventive or reclamation measures aimed at achieving quality objectives.

189. The principle 'the polluter pays' requires that consideration for the use of the resource be differentiated depending on the use of the water (at least for the residential, industrial and agricultural sectors). Specifically:

(a) concession fees for derivations of public water must consider environmental costs and the costs of the resource in relation to the use of water;
(b) tariffs for water services to be borne by the various sectors that use water, such as civilian, industrial and agricultural sectors, must contribute sufficiently to cost recovery.

Rigorous application of the principle 'the polluter pays' in determining water service tariffs almost always translates into an increase of tariffs, with an increase of negative effects on the economic and social fabric of some territories. For these reasons, Article 119 requires the social, environmental and economic repercussions of cost recovery to be considered, as well as the geographic and climatic conditions of the region or regions involved. Directive 2000/60/EC, on its part, also leaves a margin of manoeuvre to Member States in implementing the provisions on cost recovery for water services (Article 9, paragraph 4).

§9. Institutional Framework

190. The distribution of competence among different levels of government with respect to water pollution control reflects the general tendency in Italian environmental legislation: the State is responsible for determining standards, above all, technical standards; the regions prevalently carry out planning functions; whereas local entities, even when acting in the form of an association (A.A.T.O.), are responsible for operative administrative functions.

191. It should be noted, however, that Legislative Decree No. 152 of 2006 grants broad space for rule-making to the regions in contexts that have strong practical significance, such as the regulation of rainwater or the use of livestock manure in agriculture, with respect to the Constitution, which attributes the State with exclusive competence for rule-making (promulgating laws and regulations) in the environmental sector (inclusive of the quantitative protection of water resources and water use planning, *see* Constitutional Court, judgment No. 251 of 2009). The Italian legal system does not waive support from the regions, which are entrusted with integrating the general regime imposed by national laws with regional regulations.

192. Having made these general comments, the primary powers of the different levels of government are set forth below:

State:

(i) The State exercises its competence prevalently by means of the MATTM. Among its principal secondary *standardization* functions are the following:
  - Modification of the annexes to adjust them to technical progress or to implement supervening Community technical standards (Article 75, paragraphs 2 and 3).
  - Determination of technical rules for the reuse of wastewater, after consulting with the Ministry of Agriculture and Forestry, the Ministry of Health, and the Ministry of Productive Activities (Article 99, paragraph 1).
  - Determination of technical procedures related to the movement of seabeds consequent to laying submarine cables and pipelines, together with the Ministry of Productive Activities, Ministry of Infrastructures and Transportation and the Ministry of Agriculture and Forestry (Article 109, paragraph 5).
  - Specification of the criteria related to containment of the environmental impact of aquaculture and fish farming, together with the Ministry of Agriculture and Forestry and the Ministry of Infrastructures and Transportation, and upon agreement with the permanent Conference for Relations among the State, regions and the autonomous provinces of Trento and Bolzano (Article 111).
  - Regulation of water discharges directly in the sea for oil and gas exploration, research and cultivation in the seas (Article 104, paragraph 5).
  - In some cases, the State intervenes by means of other ministries, such as specification of general technical rules on the use of livestock manure and mill water for cultivations, which is left to the competence of the Ministry of Agriculture and Forestry (in accordance with the procedure set forth in Article 112, paragraph 2), and determination of the criteria for the preparation of management projects for catchment areas, established by means of a Decree of the Minister of Infrastructures and Transportation (as provided by Article 114, paragraph 4).

(ii) The State has limited functions of *active administration*, such as in the following cases:

- identification or reidentification of sensitive areas every four years, having heard the State – Regional Conference (Article 91, paragraphs 2 and 6);
- authorization of discharges of water resulting from the extraction of hydrocarbons in deep-sea geological deposits, together with the Minister for Economic Development (Article 104, paragraph 3).

(iii) The President of the Council of Ministers has substitute power with respect to the regions and local entities when their demonstrable inactivity could result in the breach of obligations deriving from membership in the EU, create grave danger to health or the environment, or result in non-compliance with obligations to provide public information (Article 75, paragraph 2).

(iv) Further, it should be noted that the State level of government has final approval of the Water Management Plan, by means of a Decree of the President of the Council of Ministers, since it is excerpted from the Basin Plan (adopted previously by the Basin Authority).

Basin Authority:

The Basin Authority is responsible for:

- Adopting the Water Management Plan, which is excerpted from the Basin Plan (Article 117, paragraph 1).
- Establishing the register of protected areas (Article 117, paragraph 3).
- Establishing objectives at a district level, which the Water Pollution Control Plans must comply with, as well as the priority of the actions to be taken (Article 121, paragraph 2).

Regions:

(i) The power that qualifies the region's role in the context of the water pollution control regime is undoubtedly the approval of the Water Pollution Control Plan. An entire series of functions provided by various provisions of the decree are included in the scope of such power, either because they are required for the preparation of the plan, or because they are carried out by means of the planning instrument.

The following activities are preliminary with respect to the plan:

- The implementation of specific data collection programmes useful for describing the characteristics of the water basin (Article 118, paragraph 2).
- The drafting and implementation of programmes to determine and verify the qualitative and quantitative state of surface water and groundwater within each water basin (Article 120, paragraph 2).

The following fall within the scope of the Region's planning activity (*see* Article 121, paragraph 4):

- The determination of more rigorous environmental quality objectives or specification of further uses for water bodies and the relative quality objectives (Article 76, paragraph 7). Similarly, the regions can provide less rigorous objectives or extend the deadlines within which quality objectives must be achieved in the cases and according to the procedures established by the decree (Article 77, paragraphs 6 et seq.). Derogations are also provided for quality objectives regarding water destined for a specific use (Articles 81, 86 and 89).

- The determination of the quality class for each significant water body (Article 77, paragraphs 1 and 2) and adoption of the measures to be taken in order to achieve the environmental quality objectives within the deadlines established by the decree (Article 77, paragraphs 1 and 2).
- The specification and classification of waters intended for a specific use (Articles 80, 82, 84, 85, 87 and 88).
- Programmes to maintain or adjust the quality of waters intended for a specific use to the relative quality objectives (Article 79, paragraph 3).
- The specification, having heard the Basin Authority, of additional sensitive areas with respect to those designated by the decree (Article 91, paragraph 4); the same is provided with respect to areas that are vulnerable to nitrates of agricultural origin (Article 92, paragraph 4). The regions also designate the areas vulnerable to pesticides and the areas vulnerable to desertification (Article 93). Further, upon the proposal of the ATO Authority, the regions determine protected areas of surface water and groundwater intended for human consumption (Article 94).
- Approval of specific rules on agricultural water savings, based on planned use, proper identification of needs in the sector and controls on water purification (Article 98, paragraph 2).
- The adoption of rules and measures aimed at enhancing water recycling and the reuse of treated wastewater (Article 99, paragraph 2).
- The determination of emission limits that differ from State limits (Article 101, paragraph 2).

(ii) The following are among the rule-making functions of the regions:

- The specification of suitable treatment systems for isolated settlements, installations or buildings that cannot be reached by the public sewage system (Article 100, paragraph 3).
- The specific regulation of discharges for sewage systems originating from agglomerates subject to a strong seasonal fluctuation of inhabitants (Article 105, paragraph 5).
- The introduction of supplemental rules to control discharges of civilian and manufacturing settlements connected to public sewers, related to the functioning of waste pretreatment plants, and compliance with the limits and requirements of the relative authorizations (Article 107, paragraph 4).
- The regulations on use for cultivations (Article 112, paragraph 2).
- The regulation of rainwater and wash water (Article 113, paragraph 3).
- Adoption of a special regime on the restitution of waters used for hydroelectric production, for irrigation and in water treatment plants, as well as water deriving from boring or drilling, unless related to the research and extraction of hydrocarbons (Article 114, paragraph 1).
- The regime on transformations and soil and topsoil management within a range of at least 10 m from the banks of rivers, lakes, ponds and lagoons (Article 115, paragraph 1).

- The regime on the phases of temporary authorizations for discharges of wastewater treatment plants for the time required for their start-up (Article 124, paragraph 6), as well as regulation of the procedures for approval of projects for urban wastewater treatment plants (Article 126).

(iii) In some cases, the regions also have authorization functions:
- Handling seabed movements deriving from the laying of submarine cables and pipelines (Article 109, paragraph 5).
- Approval of the basin management project, in view of regulating the digging, removal of gravel and removal of sludge of dams (Article 114, paragraph 2).

(iv) The regions are also responsible for:
- Ensuring the broadest possible dissemination of information on the status of water quality (Article 75, paragraph 5; Article 101, paragraph 8 and Article 123), as well as the biennial publication in the Regional Official Bulletins of a report on urban wastewater disposal in the areas for which they are competent (Article 101, paragraph 9).
- Adopting measures to ensure that the concentrations of priority pollutants do not significantly increase in sediments or the biota (Article 78, paragraphs 8 and 12).
- Issuing administrative sanctions (Article 135, paragraph 1).
- Preparing programmes of measures, as integration of the Water Pollution Control Plans, intended to achieve the quality objectives set forth in Article 116 of the decree.

ATO Authority:

The ATO Authority's competence regards issues that are more directly involved in the organization of wastewater sewage and treatment services:

- Determination of the technical rules, regulatory requirements and limit values for discharges in public sewage systems (Article 107, paragraphs 1 and 2).
- Authorization of the disposal of liquid wastes at wastewater treatment plants (Article 110, paragraph 2).
- Authorization of discharges in public sewers (Article 124, paragraph 7) and the relative controls (Article 128).

Provinces and Municipalities

In addition to the role that local entities perform as members of the ATO Authority, the provinces and municipalities have operative administration functions (authorization and control). In fact, the decree only attributes the province with the function of authorizing discharges outside of public sewage systems (Article 124, paragraph 7) and ordering the relative controls (Articles 128 et seq.). Some regions, however, have also created a role for municipal entities, attributing them with competence to authorize (and control) domestic wastewater discharges outside of public sewage systems.

Law No. 56 of 7 April 2014 – which adopted a series of provisions on metropolitan cities, provinces and the union and merger of municipalities to update the systems with respect to principles of subsidiarity, differentiation and adequacy – redefined the organization and powers of the provinces, nevertheless recognizing their functions in safeguarding and enhancing the environment (Article 1, paragraph 85, clause *a*).

§10. Summary Considerations

193. Starting from the 1999 reform, the Italian legal system on water pollution control has overcome some defects that had originally characterized it, conditioning the level of efficiency and hindering achievement of satisfying results in terms of the maintenance and improvement of water resource quality.

The current law has some important strengths:

- it is more organic and less fragmentary since it is contained almost entirely in a sole legislative act: Legislative Decree No. 152 of 2006;
- it creates a sufficiently clear framework for the distribution of competence among the various levels of government;
- it designs a protection strategy based on planning long-term policies linking quality objectives for water bodies with the regulation of individual discharges (in advance with respect to Community legislation).

In addition to these strengths, some critical factors should be noted which risk compromising the effectiveness of the legislative choices:

- a control system that is structurally inadequate to perform its functions due to the lack of human, technical and economic resources;
- a system of sanctions that is incapable of being an effective deterrent for unlawful behaviour.

As regards the first issue, the role of the Environmental Protection Agency was strengthened by approval of Law No. 132 of 28 June 2016 on 'the Creation of a National Environmental Protection Network and the regulation of ISPRA'. With respect to whether the system of sanctions is an effective deterrent, a step forward consists of the inclusion in the Italian Criminal Code of a specific section dedicated to environmental crimes (section IV, Chapter 2).

Chapter 3. Air Pollution

by *Antonio Borzì*

§1. The Principal Sources of Italian Law

I. The Main Stages of the Evolution of Legislation on Air Pollution

194. Prior to the formulation of a specific regime intended to contain air pollution, various laws aimed at protecting other legal interests, such as health and public safety or property, were shaped to fit environmental needs.

In particular, these laws are the following:

- Article 674 of the Criminal Code *dangerous throwing of objects*, which provides that it is a crime, in those cases not permitted by law, to provoke emissions of gas, vapours or smoke capable of offending or molesting persons.
- Articles 216 and 217 of RD No. 1265 of 27 July 1934, *Uniform Text of Health Laws, which regulates unhealthy work, i.e. those activities that produce vapours, gas or other unhealthy exhalations or which are in another manner dangerous to the health of inhabitants*. The mayor has the power to issue specific precautionary ordinances in relation to these activities.
- Article 844 of the Civil Code, 'emissions', on the basis of which protection is provided to property owners against emissions originating from neighbouring property which exceed normal levels of tolerability.

Such laws continue to be used even recently to provide general coverage of the gaps left by 'environmental' laws (*see* the chapter on radiation – electromagnetic pollution).

195. By means of Law No. 615 of 13 July 1966, *Air Pollution Control Law* (the so-called anti-smog law), the first provisions directly aimed at containing air pollution were introduced in the Italian legal system, therein defined as *emissions of smoke, dust, gas and odours of any kind in the atmosphere that can alter the normal conditions of healthy air and therefore directly or indirectly harm human health and damage public or private property* (Article 1).

The reference to the definition of air pollution is sufficient to demonstrate that protection from air pollution was originally strictly linked to the protection of public health and the defence of public and private property; the law did not contemplate damaging effects on the environment in its entirety, considered as ecological equilibrium, a concept that only became part of the legal system with DPR No. 203 of 1988 (*see* Article 2(1)).

196. The Air Pollution Control Law was the result of a traditional approach, based on controlling emissions from the most significant sources: residential heating systems and the relative fuels (Articles 8–19), industrial plants (Articles 20 and

21) and motor vehicles (Articles 22–24), and it remained in effect, limited to the part regarding residential heating systems, until Legislative Decree No. 152 of 2006 was enacted.

197. Prior to formulating a more modern and efficient approach, it was necessary to wait for the issuance of Department of the Presidency of the Council of Ministers (DPCM) of 28 March 1983, which implemented the law reforming the healthcare system and introduced for the first time the regulation of air quality based on the identification of maximum limits for concentrations of diverse pollutants in the air and exposure limits for living beings. If said limits were exceeded, the decree required the regions to prepare special recovery plans for the progressive improvement of air quality (Article 3).

The 1983 Decree's regulation of air quality, together with the 1966 Law, with respect to the part controlling emissions from industrial plants, were modified and supplemented by DPR No. 203 of 24 May 1988 *Implementation of EEC Directives 80/779, 82/884, 84/360 and 85/203 on air quality, specific pollutants, and pollution produced by industrial plants, in accordance with Article 15 of Law No. 183 of 16 April 1987.*

198. In general, DPR No. 203 of 1988 regulated: (a) the authorization regime for emissions from industrial plants, distinguishing among new plants, existing plants, substantial modifications to plants, power stations and oil refineries; (b) limit values for polluting emissions and the relative methods for sampling, testing and assessment, attributing the State with the power to determine the minimum and maximum values (Article 3, paragraph 2, clause *a*), and the regions with the power to establish emission limits for plants, bearing in mind State guidelines (Article 4, clause *d*); (c) the limit values and guidelines for outdoor air pollution and the relative sampling, testing and assessment methods; (d) the system for the protection of air quality, differentiated in a national plan and in regional plans for air quality cleanup and protection; and (e) the product standards for fuels and their use.

199. Among the numerous legislative initiatives that implemented DPR No. 203 of 1988, DM 12 July 1990 was of particular significance, *Guidelines for containing polluting emissions from industrial plants and establishing emission limit values*, even though most of the rules contained in it were aimed solely at controlling emissions from existing plants. The decree specified: (a) the guidelines for containing emissions from existing industrial plants; (b) minimum and maximum emission values for existing plants; (c) general sampling, testing and assessment methods for emissions; (d) the criteria for the use of available technologies to control emissions; and (e) time frames for the progressive adjustment of existing plants.

DPR No. 203 of 1988s rules on air quality were implemented by two DMs issued the same day (20 May 1991): the first *Criteria for the preparation of regional plans for the redevelopment and protection of air quality,* and the second *Criteria for data gathering relating to air quality.*

Said regulation, together with cited DPCM of 28 March 1983, was significantly innovated by Legislative Decree No. 351 of 4 August 1999, issued as implementation of Directive 96/62/EC on the assessment and management of the quality of *ambient air*, a term used to define *outdoor air in the troposphere, excluding work places* (Article 2, paragraph 1, clause *a*), recently substituted by Legislative Decree No. 155 of 13 August 2010.

During the 1990s, the 1966 Air Pollution Protection Law was also substituted with respect to its regulation of motor vehicles, whose principal source remains Legislative Decree No. 285 of 1992 (*New Code of the Road*) and the relative implementing decree (DPR No. 495 of 16 February 1992).

II. An Overview of Legislative Sources Currently in Effect

200. The general law containing the regime on atmospheric emissions is set forth in Part V of Legislative Decree No. 152 of 3 April 2006, which repealed DPR No. 203 of 1988 and Law No. 615 of 1966 (and their relative implementing decrees).

Part V was significantly modified by Legislative Decree No. 128 of 29 June 2010 (hereinafter the 2010 'Corrective'), which primarily regards the following:

- the determination of the applicative scope of the laws, both with respect to other regimes, such as that on incinerators and co-incinerators of waste, and the relationship between sections I and II of Part V;
- the need for an authorization related to the entire plant and no longer for each individual installation;
- the introduction of rules on the control of emissions aimed at standardizing sampling, analysis and control methods of the conformity of the measured value with the legislative limit;
- the distribution of competence between the State and regional level, above all, with respect to residential heating systems (subsequent to the Constitutional Court's judgment No. 250 of 2009).

Legislative Decree No. 46 of 3 March 2014 implemented Directive 2010/75/EU on industrial emissions (IPPC) through further modifications and integrations of Legislative Decree No. 152 of 2006. Among the most significant modifications are the inclusion in the 2006 Legislative Decree of provisions on the incineration and co-incineration of waste (section III*bis* to Part IV), previously contained in Legislative Decree No. 133 of 2005.

Legislative Decree No. 183 of 15 November 2017, again through modification of Legislative Decree No. 152 of 2006, implemented EU Directive 2015/2193 of the European Parliament and of the Council of 25 November 2015 on the limitation of atmospheric emissions of certain pollutants originating from medium combustion plants, as well as the reorganization of the legal framework on plants that produce atmospheric emissions, in accordance with Article 17 of Law No. 170 of 12 August 2016.

Article 268 defines air pollution as *any modification of atmospheric air due to the introduction of one or more substances in quantities and with characteristics that could harm or endanger human health or air quality or that could harm material goods or compromise legitimate uses of the environment* (paragraph 1, clause *a*).

With respect to the wording previously in effect (*any modification of the normal composition or physical state of atmospheric air due to the presence of one or more substances in quantities and with characteristics that could alter normal environmental conditions and air health; constitute a danger or cause direct or indirect prejudice to human health; compromise recreational activities and other legitimate uses of the environment; alter the biological health of human beings; compromise recreational activities and other legitimate uses of the environment; alter biological resources and ecosystems and public and private tangible property*, Article 2, paragraph 1, DPR No. 203 of 24 May 1988), the reference to the 'normal composition' of the atmosphere has disappeared, a fact that is difficult to understand both from a technical standpoint and from a legal standpoint, and greater emphasis has been placed on whether the emission is capable of being harmful, both in terms of damage and danger, eliminating the reference to the broader concept of 'alteration' of the environmental resource.

Section I is dedicated to the prevention and limitation of atmospheric emissions originating from activities and industrial plants, including residential heating systems that do not fall within the scope of section II (Articles 267, 269, paragraphs 14 and 282). The following are subject to specific regulation: the authorization regime, inclusive of plants and activities in derogation of the law, that is, those that cause reduced air pollution and insignificant levels of pollution (Articles 269, 270, 272 and Annex IV), excluding incinerators, co-incinerators and the thermal treatment of waste and plants subject to integrated environmental permits (Article 267, paragraphs 2 and 3, as well as section III*bis*, Part II, Legislative Decree No. 152 of 2006); emission limit values (Article 271, Annexes I, V and VI); large thermal plants (Articles 273, 274 and Annex II); medium-sized combustion plants (Article 273*bis*); emissions of VOC, including with specific reference to plants for the warehousing, transportation and distribution of fuels (Articles 275–277 and Annexes III, VII and VIII); powers to apply sanctions and to issue orders (Articles 278 and 279); as well as repeals and the transitory regime (Articles 280 and 281).

Section II regards residential heating systems (except those that are subject to the regulation of section (i), specifically: technical requirements for systems, including emission limit values (Articles 285, 286 and Annex IX); qualification procedures for the operation and notice of the installation of heating systems (Articles 284 and 287); regulation of controls and sanctions (Article 288); as well as determining which provisions have been expressly repealed (Article 289) and regulating the transition phase (Article 290).

Section III is dedicated to fuels, and specifically regards: product standards for the fuel that can be used in the plants and heating systems referred to in sections I and II (Articles 291–293 and Annex X), provisions to enhance their combustion efficiency (Article 294); and fuel for maritime use (Article 295). With further regard to fuels, there are specific provisions on controls and sanctions (Article 296), repeals (Article 297), and the transitory regime (Article 298), as well as a specific defining framework for each sector involved (Articles 268, 283 and 292).

201. A summary overview of the contents of Legislative Decree No. 152 of 2006 makes it clear that the decree does not exhaust the sources currently in effect that regard air pollution. References to provisions not contained in the decree are, therefore, inevitable, to the clear disadvantage of providing certainty as to the applicable regime.

More specifically, the following do not fall within the scope of Legislative Decree No. 152 of 2006:

(a) the regulation of air quality (Legislative Decree No. 155 of 13 August 2010, modified by Legislative Decree No. 250 of 24 December 2012) and regulation of limits on vehicular traffic (Article 7 of the Code of the Road);
(b) the regulation of the constructive characteristics of motor vehicles (Code of the Road and implementing decrees), and regime of the fuels to be used by them (Legislative Decree No. 66 of 21 March 2005, modified by Legislative Decree No. 55 of 31 March 2011);
(c) the legal regime for the protection of stratospheric ozone (Law No. 549 of 28 December 1993 and implementing decrees, as well as DPR No. 147 of 15 February 2006);
(d) national emission limits for specific air pollutants (Legislative Decree No. 81 of 30 May 2018);
(e) the regulation of VOC emissions for some products (Legislative Decree No. 161 of 27 March 2006).

It should also be noted that the integrated environmental permit procedure set forth in section III*bis*, Part II of Legislative Decree No. 152 of 2006 substitutes the procedure regulated by the legislation in this sector. The integrated environmental permit, which is based on the application of the 'best available technologies', can provide for stricter emission limit values than those established by the regulatory framework (Article 271, paragraph 16 as well as Article 29*sexies*, paragraph 3 of Legislative Decree No. 152 of 2006).

With respect to small and medium-sized plants not subject to the AIA, the goals of procedural integration and simplification are pursued through the Single Environmental Permit (AUA) (Article 23, Law Decree 9 February 2012, converted into Law No. 35 of 4 April 2012, as well as Presidential Decree No. 59 of 13 March 2013).

202. In view of completeness, the sources related to the exchange of emission quotas of greenhouse gas, in accordance with the mechanism of the Protocol of Kyoto, should also be mentioned:

Law No. 120 of 1 June 2002 'Ratification and implementation of the Protocol of Kyoto to the framework Convention of the United Nations of climactic changes, signed in Kyoto on 11 December 1997';
Legislative Decree No. 30 of 13 March 2013, 'Implementation of Directive 2009/29/EC, amending Directive 2003/87/EC so as to improve and extend the greenhouse gas emission allowances trading scheme of the Community'; as well as Legislative Decree No. 79 of 3 May 2016, which ratified and implemented the Doha Amendment to the Protocol of Kyoto, signed in Doha on 8 December 2012.

§2. The Objective Legislative Scope of Application

203. There are three primary objective areas of intervention in which the environmental legislator has traditionally acted to contain air pollution.

The first is represented by regulations aimed at controlling primary sources of emissions, that is, industrial plants and activities, heating systems and motor vehicles, by means of specifying emission limit values for pollutants, introducing constructive and operating requirements, and subjecting activities to an authorization regime or to other sources of control by the authorities (e.g., the validation of motor vehicles). It is possible to include in this context even the most recent instrument of intervention, represented by the establishment of a maximum quantity of emissions for specific pollutants that it is possible to emit overall in the atmosphere.

The second regulatory area of intervention consists of legislation on air quality. Individual sources of emission are not regulated, but rather the quality of ambient air, which is affected by human activity, bearing in mind the reciprocal interaction of the different substances that are harmful to health and the environment. Legislation limiting traffic in urban areas is related to the general regulation of air quality.

The third area of intervention refers to fuel, both fuel used by industrial plants and residential heating systems, and fuel used by motor vehicles.

I. Sources of Emissions

A. Domestic Emission Undertakings to Reduce Limits for Some Pollutants

204. Legislative Decree No. 171 of 21 May 2004 (*Implementation of Directive 2001/81/EC on domestic emission limits for some air pollutants*) established annual domestic emission limits for SO_2, nitrogen oxide, and VOC to be reached within 2010 and maintained in the following years.

The decree was repealed by Legislative Decree No. 81 of 2018, 'Implementation of Directive (EU) 2016/2284 of the European Parliament and of the Council of 14 December 2016, on the reduction of national emissions of certain atmospheric pollutants, amending Directive 2003/35/EC and repealing Directive 2001/81/EC'. The national limits are applied through 31 December 2019.

The new decree is aimed at improving air quality, safeguarding human health and the environment, and ensuring a more effective participation of citizens in decision-making processes through:

- national commitments to reduce anthropogenic emissions of SO_2, nitrogen oxides, non-methane VOC, ammonia and fine particulate matter (starting from 2020);
- the preparation, approval and implementation of national air pollution control programmes;
- emission monitoring obligations (with the preparation of inventories and forecasts by ISPRA);
- monitoring obligations of the impacts of air pollution on ecosystems;

- obligations to communicate documents and information to the European Commission and to the European Environmental Agency;
- more effective information aimed at citizens, using all the information systems available, especially through the institutional site of MATTM.

B. Industrial Plants and Activities

205. Part V, section I of Legislative Decree No. 152 of 2006 regulates industrial plants and residential heating systems not regulated by section II and the activities that produce atmospheric emissions, and it establishes the emission values, requirements, sampling and testing methods for emissions and the criteria to assess conformity of the measured values to the limit values (Article 267, paragraph 1). The reference to 'industrial plants' has, therefore, lost a meaning that is strictly normative, and has survived in a descriptive sense (*see*, for example, the reference contained in Article 214, paragraph 8).

206. With respect to incinerators and co-incinerators of waste, as well as other thermal waste treatment plants, it provides that:

- for all categories of industrial plants mentioned, the emission limit values and other restrictions are determined by the sole authorization or AIA (it is not necessary that these plants obtain separate emission authorizations);
- for incinerator and co-incinerators of waste, the limit values and restrictions are determined on the basis of section III*bis* of Part Four of Legislative Decree No. 152 of 2006 and the regional air quality plans;
- for other thermal waste treatment plants (a category identified based on the difference with the definitions contained in cited section III*bis*), the emission limits and restrictions are determined in accordance with Articles 270 and 271;
- Legislative Decree No. 152 of 2006 continues to be applied to atmospheric emissions for the other plants and activities located in the same facility in which there is an operating incinerator, co-incinerator or thermal waste treatment, as well as for waste treatment subject to a simplified authorization process (Article 214, paragraph 8, exempts them from application of the rules on air quality and air pollution).

Plant means: *the machinery or system or entirety of machinery or fixed systems destined to carry out a specific activity in an autonomous manner, including in a broader constructive cycle* (Article 268, paragraph 1, clause l).

The plant can consist of a single machine as well as of a system of machinery, and is characterized by its fixed structure and functional autonomy.

207. Even after the 2010 Corrective, the definition of 'plant' maintains its central role from various standpoints:

- with reference to the regime on modifications to the facility, defined as the installation of a new plant or start-up of a new activity, or modification of an existing plant or activity (Article 268, clause *m*; Article 269, paragraph 8);
- with respect to the conveyance of emissions, with the general rule that requires a sole emission point for each plant (Article 270, paragraph 5);
- with respect to emission limit values, which continue to be decisive for industrial plants and activities (Article 271).

Large thermal plants are subject to special regulation, that is, thermal plants *having a nominal thermal power in excess of 50MW* (Article 268, paragraph 1, clause *gg*), to be used for the production of energy, with the exclusion of those that directly use the products of combustion in the manufacturing cycle (in accordance with Article 273, clause 15); the decree also regards VOC (Articles 275–277).

In the framework of the regulation of industrial emissions, Legislative Decree No. 216 of 4 April 2006: Implementation of Directives 2003/87 and 2004/101/EC on the exchange of emission quotas of greenhouse gas in the Community, with reference to the project mechanisms of the Kyoto Protocol, must also be noted.

The manager of an industrial plant included among the kinds of plant specified in Annex A must obtain authorization to emit greenhouse gas. The authorization is issued by the competent national authority, specified as being the National Committee for the Management and Implementation of Directive 2003/87/EC, created at the Ministry of the Environment.

C. *Residential Heating Systems*

208. Section II of Legislative Decree No. 152 of 2006 provides that to prevent and limit air pollution, residential heating systems must have a nominal thermal power that is less than 3 MW, whereas residential heating systems having nominal thermal power equal to or in excess of 3 MW, are subject to the provisions of section I (Article 282).

The scope of application of the majority of the provisions of section II (Articles 284–286) are limited to (a) residential heating systems; (b) whose nominal thermal power falls within the interval between the minimum threshold value of 0.035MW and 3MW. Residential heating system means 'a heating system whose heat production is exclusively destined, even in non-residential buildings, to providing heat or air-conditioning for rooms or heating water for hygienic and sanitary use' (Article 282, clause *d*, which distinguishes among centralized and individual systems), while the system's 'nominal thermal power' is the total of the thermal power of the system's individual heating systems (Article 282, clause *e*).

209. The fundamental elements of the regulation of residential heating systems pursuant to section II of Legislative Decree No. 152 of 2006 can be summarized as follows:

(a) the obligation for the manufacturer of residential heating systems to certify, for each model produced, conformity with the technical characteristics set forth in

Article 285 and suitability to comply with emission limit values set forth in Article 286. The suitability must result from specific tests carried out in accordance with the relevant EN standards by accredited laboratories in accordance with standard UNI CEI EN ISO/IEC 17025 for the test methods relating to the parameters for which the measurement is carried out. The reports must be kept at the manufacturer's disposal. Each residential heating system put on the market must be accompanied by the certification and installation instructions (Article 282, paragraph 2*bis*);

(b) the installer's obligation to also declare that the installation has a certificate of conformity (in the context of the declaration of conformity provided by DM No. 37 of 22 January 2008). The installer must also provide the party responsible for operating and maintaining the heating system (or the principal who commissioned the installation work, if the party responsible for the heating system has not yet been identified) with the list of ordinary and extraordinary maintenance and must ensure compliance with emission limit values, so that such list can be included in the booklet for the central heating installation in accordance with DPR No. 412 of 26 August 1993;

(c) special provisions for medium-sized residential heating systems, i.e., residential heating systems of 1 MW or more (such as a registration obligation with a register of authorizations);

(d) the determination of emission limits and constructive requirements for heating systems established by Annex IX, as well as by the air quality plans and programmes that might establish additional technical characteristics and more restrictive values when necessary to obtain compliance with air quality objectives and values (Articles 285 and 286);

(d) the annual control of emissions (the lack of which is automatically subject to sanction pursuant to Article 288, paragraph 4), with the results annotated in a special booklet (in accordance with DPR No. 412 of 1993);

(f) a licence for personnel operating heating systems whose power exceeds 0.232 MW (Article 287);

(g) a system of sanctions for the manufacturer, the installer and the heating system manager (Article 288).

The norms on air pollution contained in Legislative Decree No. 152 of 2006 are supplemented by legislation on energy savings for buildings (DPR No. 412 of 1993, DPR No. 551 of 1999, and Legislative Decree No. 102 of 4 July 2014)), energy efficient buildings (Legislative Decree No. 192 of 2005 and subsequent modifications, DPRs No. 74 and No. 75 of 16 April 2013) and plant safety (DM No. 37 of 2008 and Law No. 46 of 1990, of which only Articles 8, 14 and 16 remain in effect).

D. Motor Vehicles

210. Another classic source of emission regards motor vehicles, whose primary legislative source is found in Legislative Decree No. 285 of 30 April 1992, *New Code of the Road* (and its implementing regulations). Article 75 provides that only validated motor vehicles are allowed to circulate, that is, a type of motor vehicle whose prototype has been tested to ensure compliance with the technical requirements and constructive and functional characteristics set forth in special ministerial decrees (Article 71). Further, in order to guarantee the effective compliance with these requirements by all motor vehicles placed in circulation, control of conformity of the individual vehicle to the validated model must be performed at the manufacturing plant (Article 77). Finally, there is an obligation to maintain circulating vehicles in a condition of maximum efficiency in order to guarantee safety and contain pollution (Article 79).

The provisions related to the constructive characteristics of vehicles, including with respect to emissions and anti-pollution devices, normally derive from Community law and are issued by means of a DM in accordance with Article 229 of the Code of the Road. The same source is used to regulate the constructive characteristics of agricultural machinery (Articles 104 et seq.) and operative machinery (Article 114).

II. Air Quality

211. Efficient action to contain air pollution cannot be based solely on the control of individual emission points; a similar approach ignores the overall phenomenon and fails to offer an effective remedy to the consequences of the presence of pollutants on human health and environmental matrixes. The regulation of air quality considers air pollution starting from its effects, that is, from the concentration of harmful substances in the atmosphere, using that as the starting point to establish diversified measures to reduce, contain and maintain the values that were found.

212. The current regulatory framework is set forth in Legislative Decree No. 155 of 13 August 2010 which, in implementing Directive 2008/50/EC (which substituted 96/62/EC) simplified, at least from a quantitative profile, the panorama of outstanding sources on air quality by abrogating Legislative Decree No. 351 of 1999 and the secondary implementing regulations, as well as the special provisions of Legislative Decree No. 183 of 21 May 2004 (relating to ozone) and Legislative Decree No. 152 of 3 August 2007 *Implementation of Directive 2004/107//EC on arsenic, cadmium, mercury, nickel and polycyclic aromatic hydrocarbons in the air* (*see* Article 21). The result is a lengthy regulatory text that is difficult to read, even when compared to the directive from which it was transposed, consisting of twenty-two articles and twenty-seven annexes and appendixes.

With respect to the pre-existing regulation, there are, nevertheless, important new elements:

- the provision of a series of instruments to guarantee a homogeneous air quality measurement, assessment and management system throughout the national territory;
- the introduction of measures to rationalize the air quality measurement system which guarantee its efficiency, effectiveness and cost-effectiveness;
- strengthening the role of the recovery and action plans, above all, with the possibility to modify the emission limits of industrial plants;

- the introduction of regulations to ensure coordination among the different planning instruments provided by outstanding law;
- providing for the State's subsidiary intervention by the adoption of national measures if it appears from a special administrative procedure that none of the possible measures that have been identified by the regions in the air quality plans resolve the issue, because the limits are exceeded primarily due to emission sources for which the regions lack administrative and legislative competence;
- particular attention for the regulation of information to be provided to the public on the state of air quality.

The provisions of Legislative Decree No. 155 of 2010 are intended to ensure the quality of 'ambient air', that is, the quality of external air in the troposphere, thus, with the exclusion of the air that is inhaled at the workplace, whose cleanliness is protected by the provisions of Legislative Decree No. 81 of 2008.

213. Public intervention to protect air quality is articulated in three fundamental phases:

(1) determination of the levels of concentration of pollutants that might cause harmful short and long-term effects;
(2) zoning and classification of the territory, followed by the measurement and assessment of air quality using an efficient monitoring network;
(3) preparation of measures to restore air quality or maintain it if the limit values have not been exceeded.

Sub (a). Legislative Decree No. 155 of 2010 provides:

(a) limit values for concentrations in ambient air of SO_2, nitrogen dioxide, benzene, carbon monoxide, lead and PM10;
(b) the critical levels for concentrations in ambient air of SO_2 and nitric oxide;
(c) alert thresholds for concentrations in ambient air of SO_2 and nitrogen dioxide;
(d) the limit value, objective value, obligation of concentration of exposure and national objective for the reduction of exposure to concentrations in ambient air of PM2.5;
(e) the objective values for concentrations in ambient air of arsenic, cadmium, nickel and benzopyrene;
(f) target values, long-term objectives, alert thresholds and information thresholds for ozone.

In accordance with the definitions set forth in Article 2 of the decree, 'limit value' means the level established on the basis of scientific knowledge, including with respect to the best available technologies, in order to avoid, prevent or reduce the damaging effects on human health or for the overall environment; such level must be reached within a specific deadline and cannot subsequently be exceeded. The concept of 'target value', that is, 'the level established to avoid, prevent or reduce the harmful effects on human health or for the overall environment', is partially different and refers to some specific pollutants. Said limit must be reached within a specific deadline, if possible, not to be confused with that of a 'long-term objective', which means the 'level to be reached long-term by the use of proportional measures, in order to ensure the effective protection of human health and the environment'. In order to protect human health from risks deriving from exposure, even if of brief duration, 'alert thresholds' have been specified which require immediate intervention; they exclusively refer to the 'critical level' for natural matrixes, that is, the level 'established on the basis of current scientific knowledge, beyond which direct negative effects can exist on receptors such as trees, other plants or natural ecosystems, with the exclusion of human beings'.

Sub (b). Territorial zoning constitutes the basis on which the assessment of ambient air quality is organized (Article 1, paragraph 4, clause *c*). The overall territory is subdivided into zones and urban centres. The distinction is important because the same decree requires the prior identification of urban centres and subsequent identification of other areas. An urban centre consists of an urban area or an entirety of urban areas that have, in relation to their urban structure, resident population and residential density, specific characteristics established by the decree (Article 2, paragraph 1, clause *f*, as well as Appendix 1). The other areas have been primarily identified on the basis of aspects such as the territory's load emission, orographic characteristics, weather-climatic characteristics and degree of urbanization, in order to identify the areas in which one or more of such aspects are predominant in determining the level of pollutants and group such areas in zones distinguished by the homogeneity of the predominant characteristics. The zones can also consist of areas that are not contiguous among themselves, as long as they are homogeneous from the standpoint of their predominant characteristics. It is possible, for example, to distinguish with a territory its mountain areas, valleys, coastal areas, areas with a high density of urbanization and areas characterized by a high load emission in reference to one or more specific sectors (e.g., traffic and/or industrial activity). In specifying the areas, as long as this is compatible with the criteria set forth above, reference must be made to the administrative confines of local entities (Appendix I, pages 7 and 8).

Territorial zoning is followed by the classification of the zones and urban centres. Each zone and urban centre is classified in order to determine the manner in which air quality is assessed. The classification is made using assessment thresholds: a higher assessment threshold and a lower assessment threshold. The first represents the level below which assessments in fixed sites can be combined with indicative measurements or modelling techniques, the second the level below which the use of modelling techniques or an objective estimate is provided, even on an exclusive basis (Article 2, paragraph 4, clauses *z* and *aa*), as well as Article 5. Lastly, the classification serves to establish the techniques to be used to measure and assess air quality.

The zoning and classification activities are the competence of the regions (and autonomous provinces), but they are subject to the consent of the Ministry of the Environment, which, relies on the ISPRA for the assessment of zoning and classification projects approved by the regions (Article 3, paragraph 3, and Article 4, paragraph 3).

This is only one of the mechanisms introduced by Legislative Decree No. 155 of 2010 to guarantee that the air quality assessment and management system complies everywhere with 'elevated and homogenous qualitative standards in order to ensure that the same situations of pollution are assessed and managed in a similar manner' (Article 1, paragraph 4, clause *a*; on this point *see* paragraph 10).

Air quality assessment is based on a measurement network and an assessment programme. The measurement network includes the system of measurement stations for air pollutants that are used to assess air quality according to the provisions of the decree that establishes the minimum number and location (*see* Article 7, as well as Annexes III, IV and V). The assessment programme not only indicates the measurement network, but also the other techniques, among which modelling, that are different than measurement in fixed sites, by means of which an assessment is made of air quality. The programme is adopted by the regions and, in this case as well, there is an assessment of conformity by the Ministry of the Environment, made with ISPRA's assistance.

Legislative Decree No. 155 of 2010 introduced a series of important rules on the measurement of air quality, with the intent to overcome some critical factors that emerged from the application of the pre-existing regulation:

- the measurement stations that are not included in the measurement network and the assessment programme cannot be used to assess air quality;
- the stations included in the network and inserted in the programme must conform to the technical rules of the decree and must comply with the quality objectives provided by Annex I to the decree (*see* Article 17);
- the number of measurement stations provided by the programme must be chosen in compliance with standards of efficiency, effectiveness and cost-effectiveness: it is necessary to avoid a useless excess of measurement stations;
- the measurement network is subject to public management and control: the stations must be managed by the regions (and autonomous provinces), or, upon express delegation, by the ARPA or by other public or private parties (in the latter case under the control of the regions or ARPA);
- the State and regional EIAs, State and regional integrated environmental permits, and the authorizations provided by Legislative Decree No. 152 of 3 April 2006 for industrial plants that produce atmospheric emissions can provide for the installation or adjustment of one or more measurement stations of ambient air quality by the proponent only if the region or autonomous province or, upon delegation, the ARPA, deems such stations necessary for the measurement network or for the assessment programme.

Sub (c). Once the areas have been identified and classified, it is necessary to plan short-term actions to avoid the risk that limit values and alert thresholds are exceeded; measures to restore air quality over a lengthier period of time; as well as the measures to be implemented to preserve air quality when there is no risk that limit values will be exceeded.

214. Legislative Decree No. 155 of 2010 provides for different types of plans:

(1) Plans to achieve limit values. This is to be used if, in one or more areas inside of zones or urban centres, the levels of SO_2, nitrogen dioxide, carbon monoxide, benzene, lead, PM10 and PM2.5 exceed the respective limit values (Annex XI). The plan must provide the necessary measures to impact the primary sources of emission that have an influence on such areas where the limit values are exceeded, and to reach the limit values within the prescribed terms or in the shortest amount of time possible if the term has already expired (this is the case of all pollutants, with the exception of PM2.5, whose initial expiration was set for January 2015).
(2) Plans to pursue target values. This is to be used if, in one or more areas within the zones or urban centres, the target value has been exceeded for PM2.5 (Annex XIV), as well as arsenic, cadmium, nickel and benzopyrene (Annex III). The plan contains the measures that do not result in disproportionate costs required to impact the principle emission sources that have an influence on such areas where the limit values have been exceeded, and to pursue the target values within the deadlines established by the annexes (set for 31 December 2012 for the last four substances indicated). Article 9, paragraph 2 of the decree specifies that the achievement of the target value does not result, for industrial plants subject to integrated environmental permits, in more rigorous conditions than those related to the application of the best available technologies. It is an exceptional rule with respect to what is established by Article 29*septies* of Legislative Decree No. 152 of 2006 which allows more rigorous supplemental measures in AIA if necessary 'to ensure compliance with EQS'. Article 13 contains a special regulation for the plan to pursue a target value for ozone.
(3) Plans to achieve critical levels. These are to be used if, in one or more areas within zones or urban centres, the values of SO_2 and nitric oxide exceed the critical levels set forth in Annex XI. The plan provides the necessary measures to impact the primary sources of emission that influence the areas where the values are exceeded and to reach critical levels within the prescribed terms.

The decree also provides for action in the areas in which limit values and target values are achieved, by the adoption of measures required to preserve the best ambient air quality compatible with sustainable development (Article 9, paragraph 3 and Article 13, paragraph 3).

It is important to note that the plans related to an area within a zone or an urban centre where the levels have been exceeded must take action with respect to all of the primary emission sources, whether specific or spread out, that influence such area even if they are located in other areas or in other zones and urban centres of the region or autonomous province.

The plans are approved by the region (or autonomous province) by means of a procedure that ensures consultation with the interested local authorities.

On the basis of an approach based on the principle of subsidiarity (Article 118, paragraph II, Constitution and Article 3*quinquies* of Legislative Decree No. 152 of 2006), coordinated interregional actions are possible, as well as the definition of measures of a national nature if it is determined that the regional air quality plans are unable to ensure that limit values will be achieved in areas where they are exceeded that are heavily influenced by emission sources over which the regions do not have administrative and legislative competence.

(4) Action plans for the risk that alert thresholds are exceeded. The regions (or autonomous provinces) must adopt this plan to identify the short-term measures to be taken in the case of the risk that the alert thresholds established by Annex XII for SO_2 and nitrogen dioxide are exceeded.

(5) Action plans for the risk that limit values and target values are exceeded. These are short-term plans in the case of the risk of exceeding limit values and target values provided by Annexes VII and XI for ozone and SO_2, nitrogen dioxide, carbon monoxide, benzene, lead, PM10 and PM2.5. Such plans are adopted if specific contingent circumstances can be identified which do not have a structural or recurrent nature, which can result in values being exceeded or which can prejudice the process of achieving limit values or the pursuit of target values and which, due to such nature, are predictable and can be countered by the remediation plans set forth in Articles 9 and 13.

The action plans provide short-term measures, aimed at reducing the risk or limited the duration of the period when the values are exceeded, including, if necessary, interventions to limit or suspend activities that contribute to the onset of the risk of exceeding the limit values, the target values and alert thresholds.

(6) Plans to achieve the long-term objective for ozone. This is to be adopted if, in one or more areas within the zones or urban centres, the levels of ozone exceed the long-terms objectives and are lower or equal to the target values set forth in Annex VII. They contain measures that do not result in disproportionate costs necessary to impact the principal emission sources that influence such areas and to pursue the long-term objectives within the prescribed deadlines.

The range of plans provided by Legislative Decree No. 155 of 2010 is, therefore, very articulated: the measures to be implemented are identified and modulated based on the objectives and purposes of each planning instrument. From this standpoint, the provisions of Article 11 which refer to Legislative Decree No. 152 of 2006 merit special attention, which provide that the air quality plans can intervene on emission limits, the criteria for localization, the requirements for operating industrial plants, as well as the characteristics and use of fuel. Further, the plans can provide for: (a) criteria to limit vehicular circulation; (b) emission limit values, operating requirements and criteria for the localization of waste treatment plants that produce atmospheric emissions; (c) emission limit values, operating requirements and criteria for the localization of industrial plants subject to integrated environmental permits which produce atmospheric emissions; (d) requirements to prevent or limit emissions in the atmosphere that are produced during the course of the activities carried out at any work site; (e) requirements to prevent or limit atmospheric emissions produced from moored boats; (f) specific measures to protect the juvenile population or to limit atmospheric emissions that are produced during agricultural activities and practices; and (h) requirements to limit outdoor combustion, in particular, in an agricultural, forestry and work site context.

215. Legislative Decree No. 155 of 2010 also regulates the transmission of information. The following are obligated to provide information: public administrations are responsible for providing updated, clear, comprehensible and accessible information to the public (Article 18); the regions must inform the Ministry of the Environment and ISPRA; and the Ministry of the Environment must inform the European Commission (Article 19).

216. Strictly related to the regulation of air quality is the regime limiting vehicular traffic to contain air pollution.

Power rests with the Mayor (or different authority specified by the regions). If the Mayor fails to act, the regions (or the different authority specified by the regions) intervene in substitution. The instrument used is that of an order, provided by Article 7 of the Code of the Road (Legislative Decree No. 285 of 1992), which is used in the cases and with the criteria specified by the air quality plans. The method and duration of the limitations must be functional to the purposes of the various plans regulated by Legislative Decree No. 155 of 2010. In the lack of plans, or if the plans do not specify the cases and criteria of limitation of vehicular circulation, the Mayor retains the power to impose such limitations for reasons related to air pollution by means of the orders provided by the Uniform Text of the laws regulating local entities (Legislative Decree No. 267 of 18 August 2000).

III. Fuels

217. Fuel to be used in plants is regulated, above all, by sections I and II of Legislative Decree No. 152 of 2006, as set forth in section III of said decree.

In said plants, including residential heating systems having a thermal power that is less than the limit value, only the fuels specified in Annex X of Part V of Legislative Decree No. 152 of 2006 can be used, on the conditions set forth therein. One of these conditions, introduced by the 2010 Corrective, is that the materials and substances listed in Annex X must not be waste in accordance with Part IV of Legislative Decree No. 152 of 2006.

The 2010 Corrective also established that the combustion of materials and substances that do conform to Annex X, or which are otherwise waste in accordance with Part IV of Legislative Decree No. 152 of 2006, are subject to outstanding laws on waste. From the literal tenor of the law it appears that the qualification of waste directly depends on the objective fact of the non-conformity of the fuel used when compared to the standards specified in Annex X, rather than by the conditions provided by the concept of waste (*see* the chapter on waste, unless there is an indirect obligation to dispose of non-conforming materials deriving from the obligation to exclusively use the fuels provided by the Annex).

218. Another novelty of the 2010 Corrective is the possibility for the regions, autonomous provinces or other authorities to introduce additional limits or prohibitions regarding fuels, as long as 'in the cases and manner provided by Part V' of Legislative Decree No. 152 of 2006, for example, by means of an authorization (Article 271, paragraph 5), even if general (Article 272, paragraph 2), or by means of a law or general measure for the industrial plants set forth in Article 272, paragraph 1 (Article 271, paragraph 3).

Such legislation also requires industrial plants to have equipment capable of contributing to enhancing combustion efficiency, such as temperature sensors and continuous analysers of free oxygen and carbon monoxide.

The managers of certain plants must also annually notify ISPRA and the Ministry of the Environment of the quantity and sulphur content of the fuels used. On the basis of these communications, ISPRA provides a report to the Ministry of the Environment, which in turn prepares a document that must be sent to the European Commission.

219. Legislative Decree No. 66 of 21 March 2005 contains the technical specifications for gasoline and combustible diesel.

Distributing gasoline or diesel having characteristics different than those provided by the decree is prohibited, except for specific quantities and by means of a distribution network approved by a special decree (DM 29 March 2006), above all, for particular uses, for example, fuelling antique cars.

Article 5 provides that distributing fuels destined to all or some categories of vehicles can be subject to more severe characteristics than those provided by the decree in order to protect public health in specific urban centres, or the environment in specific critical areas from an ecological standpoint, if air pollution or polluted groundwater constitutes or could presumably constitute a serious and recurrent risk to human health or the environment.

Gasoline and diesel are also subject to reporting requirements to Customs Offices, tax deposits that import fuels and to manufacturers, as well as to APAT (ISPRA), which prepares an annual report for the Ministry of the Environment, which, in turn, must communicate the data to the European Commission. ISPRA publishes an annual report on the quality of gasoline and diesel fuel sold the previous year.

Legislative Decree No. 66 of 2005 (modified over the past few years by Legislative Decree No. 55 of 2011 and by Legislative Decree No. 51 of 2017) requires the reduction of greenhouse gas as well as sustainability criteria for biofuels.

The Customs Office and the Finance Police are responsible for applying sanctions for violations of Legislative Decree No. 66 of 2005.

220. Legislative Decree No. 128 of 30 May 2005 should also be mentioned, which is aimed at promoting the use of biofuels or other renewable fuels in substitution of diesel fuel or gasoline for transportation. The stated objective is to contribute to the attainment of national objectives in terms of the reduction of emissions of greenhouse gas and safety in the supply of environmentally sound energy, as well as the promotion of sources of renewable energy.

§3. Planning and Programming Instruments

221. Different types of sources concur in producing air pollution, and, thus, prevention and containment measures must necessarily involve differentiated objective areas of intervention. This requires the adoption of planning and programming instruments to rationalize and coordinate action measures.

The most recent legislation signals the return of state level planning, which had disappeared in 1998 due to the effect of Article 82 of Legislative Decree No. 112 of 1998, which had repealed the National Plan for the Protection of Air Quality.

222. Legislative Decree No. 171 of 2004 (implementation of Directive 2001/81/EC) introduced the National Programme to Reduce Emissions, functional to reaching the national objectives for emissions of SO_2, nitrogen oxide, VOC and ammonia.

The programme was confirmed by Legislative Decree No. 81 of 2018. It is prepared with the support of ISPRA and ENEA (*Ente Nazionale Energia Atomica*) and approved by a Decree of the President of the Council of Ministers, upon an opinion of the Unified Conference.

The national programme consists of the following:

(a) evaluation of the contribution of national emission sources in terms of the impact on air quality in the national territory and neighbouring Member States;
(b) the recognition of the existing national strategic framework for air quality and pollution control, with an indication of the relative policy priorities and the relationship between these priorities and those relating to emission-related sectors affected by reduction commitments. The programme also shows the relevant functions assigned to the national, regional and local authorities by the outstanding regulations;
(c) evaluation of the progress achieved through existing policies and measures, including those provided by the air quality plans set forth in Legislative Decree No. 155 of 2010 of the relative degree of conformity to national and European obligations and the expected development if such policies and measures are not modified;
(d) identification, on the basis of the assessment set forth in clause *a* and the information set forth in clauses *b* and *c*, of a framework of possible additional policies and measures with respect to those provided by clause *c*, which can be chosen for the purposes set forth in paragraph 1;
(e) identification, based on the framework set forth in clause *d*, of specific sets of policies and measures;
(f) analysis of the sets provided by clause *e* in terms of the expected impact on the reduction of emissions and, where possible, on air quality and the environment and in terms of costs, with an indication of the method of analysis and, if possible, the relative uncertainties;
(g) selection of the measures and policies to be implemented and determination of the timeframe for their approval and implementation, as well as the relative review;
(h) identification, based on the division of functions provided by the outstanding regulations, of the competent parties responsible for implementing the selected measures and policies;
(i) assessment of the consistency between the selected policies and measures and the sector tools. The programme indicates the manner in which the selection considered the sector tools and identifies the cases in which the sector tools must be adapted to the programme.

Implementation of the programme is incumbent on all administrations, whether State, regional or local, and for such purpose a coordination board has been established at the Presidency of the Council.

223. In the Italian legal system, environmental planning and programming is prevalently entrusted to the level of the regional government. The air quality plans provided by Legislative Decree No. 155 of 2010 assume particular importance.

It should be noted that, in view of the integration of the environment in other sector policies (e.g., with respect to energy, transportation, zoning), Legislative Decree No. 155 of 2010 increased the coordination mechanisms between air quality plans and other planning instruments provided by the Italian legal system. The regions, in adopting the air quality plans, must ensure the coordination of such plans and the objectives established by them with other sector planning instruments and with the planning instruments of local entities (Article 9, paragraph 7). Further, in preparing the plans, coherency with the requirements contained in the domestic programme set forth in Legislative Decree No. 81 of 2018 must be ensured, as well as in the noise action plans (previously Legislative Decree No. 194 of 19 August 2005), regional measures to promote renewable energy (Article 2, paragraph 167 of Law No. 244 of 24 December 2007), and in all the other regional and local planning and programming instruments, such as energy plans, transportation plans and development plans. At the same time, the competent authorities for the preparation and updating of such plans, programmes and measures must ensure their consistency with the requirements contained in the air quality plans (Article 9, paragraph 11; coordination norms for planning related to ozone are set forth in Article 13).

The necessity of integration also inspires the provisions of Article 22 of Legislative Decree No. 155 of 2010, which requires the regions to ensure consistency among the scenes of emissions, prepared in conformity with what is dictated by such decree, and planning and programming instruments provided in other sectors such as energy, transportation and agriculture.

Subregional level planning mostly regards motor vehicle circulation and mobility (urban traffic plan, traffic plan for extra-urban roadways, multi-year programmes to rationalize circulation by the creation of integrated bicycle paths, etc.).

§4. Direct Regulation: Specific Instruments

224. With respect to sources of emission, the primary instrument to contain air pollution consists of establishing an emission limit value, defined as an *emission factor, the concentration, percentage or mass flow of pollutants in emissions that cannot be exceeded* (Legislative Decree No. 152 of 2006, Article 268, paragraph 1, clause *q*.

Section I of Part V of Legislative Decree No. 152 of 2006 provides for differentiated limits depending on the age of the industrial plants, their type and the activity performed, with a series of special provisions, contained in the annexes and not in the text, that render an exhaustive treatment of the regulation of limit values extremely difficult and of scarce use.

225. It is instead more useful to specify the sources and procedures that determine limit values.

In brief, the interested subjects are as follows:

(i) The State: the emission limit values and restrictions to be applied to emissions conveyed and spread by industrial plants and emissions or activities are identified in Annexes I and V, which can be modified and supplemented in accordance with Article 281, paragraph 5 (Article 271, paragraph 2). The annexes primarily contain the emission limit values for plants built prior to 1988; integration, therefore, essentially involves establishing the limit values and restrictions for new plants and those built prior to 2006.

(ii) The Region: Regional intervention, by means of a specific measure on emission limit values and restrictions for plants and activity must consider, if available, air quality plans and programmes (Article 271, paragraph 3). By means of such plans and programmes, the region can also establish more restrictive limit values and requirements than those specified by the State when necessary to achieve and comply with air quality values and objectives (Article 271, paragraph 4, *see* paragraph 2.2). Article 271, paragraph 3, saves regional laws issued while DPR No. 203 of 1988 was in effect.

(iii) The Competent Authority: the authorizations establish emission limit values and restrictions by means of an administrative procedure based on the best available technologies and the provisions of State and regional laws, and evaluate the overall emissions of the plants and activities of a facility. The State limit values (as well as those contained in authorizations about to expire, in the case of renewal) are parameters that cannot be derogated *in peius*, except for the possibility of the competent authority to establish emission limit values in the authorization that are more restrictive than (even) those established by the air quality plans and programmes (Article 271, paragraph 7, a power generally introduced with the 2010 Corrective). For substances for which emission values are not established by State and regional legislation, the authorization provides for special limit values with reference to those provided for similar substances from a chemical viewpoint, which have analogous effects on health and the environment.

226. Legislative Decree No. 152 of 2006 also establishes important rules on the identification of plants and conveyance of emissions:

- emissions that are spread out must be conveyed to an emission point, when technically possible on the basis of the best available technology (Article 270, paragraph 1); – except in the case of a different provision, the emission limit values apply to each emission point (Article 271, paragraph 5);
- in general, each plant must have a sole emission point (Article 271, paragraph 5); Article 271, paragraph 6 provides specific rules for the application of limit values when assurance of a sole emission point per plant is not technically possible, including for safety reasons;
- the emissions (homogeneous from a chemical-physical standpoint) of various plants, having similar technical and building characteristics and located in the

same establishment, can be conveyed to a single point; similar plants must, in any case, be considered as a single industrial plant in order to determine limit values (Article 271, paragraph 4).

The above summarizes the general regulation of emission limit values. Specific norms regulate large thermal plants and VOC emissions, while the limit values for incinerators and the co-incineration of wastes are provided by section III*bis* of Part IV of Legislative Decree No. 152 of 2005. It should be noted that in all cases in which the kind of installation is subject to an IEA, the procedure established by the section III*bis*, Part II of Legislative Decree No. 152 must be followed.

227. With respect to residential heating systems, set forth in section II, the emission limit values are specified in Article 286 and Annex IX of Part V of Legislative Decree No. 152 of 2006, as well as by the air quality plans and programmes (which can establish more restrictive limits than State limits when necessary to achieve and comply with air quality values and objectives). The conformity of the heating systems to the established values must be controlled at least annually by the person responsible for their use and maintenance.

On the basis of Legislative Decree No. 285 of 1992, the emission limit values for motor vehicles are determined by decrees issued by the Minister of Transportation, together with the Environmental Minister and Health Minister, when establishing the constructive and functional characteristics of such vehicles.

Turning from the regulation of sources of emission to the protection of air quality, the specific instruments of protection consist of limit values, alert thresholds, target values and the critical levels provided by Legislative Decree No. 155 of 2010.

With reference to the specific instruments of protection adopted in the sector of fuels, as is clearly seen from what is set forth above, the primary instrument used in this sector to protect ambient air is the establishment of maximum limit values for concentrations of specific pollutants (sulphur, lead, benzene, aromatic hydrocarbons, etc.) in this kind of product.

§5. Authorization Procedures

228. The classic form of authorization, understood as the public administration's consent to perform an activity subsequent to the preventive control of compliance with all legal pre-requisites, is an indispensable instrument for environmental protection. It should also be noted that on a general level, instruments aimed at simplification, such as silence-assent and the 'certified notice of the initiation of activity', are generally excluded from this regime (Articles 19 and 20 of Law No. 241 of 1990 and subsequent modifications).

229. Legislative Decree No. 30 of 2013 requires authorization to emit greenhouse gas for the plants specified in its annex.

The authorization is issued by a national committee created at the Ministry of the Environment composed of six members, three of whom are appointed by the Environmental Minister and the other three by the Minister of Productive Activities.

230. Subsequent to the modifications made by the 2010 Corrective, the authorizations provided by Part V, section I of Legislative Decree No. 152 of 2006 are no longer issued for each system, but by plant, defined as *a sole and stable complex, configured as an overall productive cycle, subject to the decision-making power of a sole manager, where one or more systems are present or one or more activities are carried out that produce emissions by means, for example, of mobile devices, manual processes, deposits and movements. A plant is also considered to be the place used on a regular basis to carry out one or more activities (Article 268, paragraph 1, clause h).*

On the basis of the timeframe of the laws substituted by Legislative Decree No. 152 of 2006, section I of the decree distinguishes among plants prior to 1988, those prior to 2006, and new plants.

The division is important with respect to the emission limits for heating systems, both with respect to the application of the transitional regime, and the timeframe and manner in which pre-existing plants are adjusted to the new legal regime (Article 281 as well as Article 3, paragraphs 28 and 29 of the 2010 Corrective).

231. The authorization regime for industrial plants, outlined in Legislative Decree No. 152 of 2006, contemplates: (a) an ordinary authorization regime; (b) cases of exclusion from the obligation to obtain authorization; (c) cases of heating systems and activities in derogation of the regime (i.e., subject to simplified authorization procedures):

(a) the ordinary procedure, set forth in Article 269, can be outlined as follows:

- The request for authorization, together with the documentation provided by paragraph 2 (among which the project with a description of all of existing heating systems and activities), is necessary in the case of the installation of a new plant, the transfer of a plant from one place to another, or the substantial modification of a plant, meaning a modification 'resulting in an increase or qualitative variation of emissions, or which alters the conditions of their technical conveyance' (Article 269, paragraphs 2 and 8, as well as Article 268, paragraph 1, clause *mbis*).
- The competent authority is the region or another authority specified by a regional law (Article 268, paragraph 1, clause *o*), unless in the case of exceptions.
- In order to issue an authorization to instal new plants, the competent authority calls a conference of services in which the interests involved in other proceedings (in particular, those for which the Municipality is competent for town planning and the protection of public health) are reviewed contemporaneously; at the time of renewal, the competent authority initiates an autonomous procedure informing the interested Municipality, which can provide an opinion (Article 269, paragraph 3). The administrative procedure is based on the best available technologies, as well as on the requirements of State and regional law and by the air quality plans and programmes. An important provision introduced by the 2010 Corrective

requires that the authorization process must evaluate a plant's total emissions, including those originating from other sources, as well as the state of the interested area's air quality (Article 271, paragraph 5).

- The procedural duration is 120 days, or 150 days (in the case of a request for supplemental documentation).
- If the procedure does not conclude within the above terms, the plant manager can apply to the Ministry of the Environment within the following sixty days to seek substitute authorization (and must also notify the competent authority).
- If the ministry does not respond (it is necessary for the interested Municipality to be heard) within the established deadlines (90 or 150 days), it is possible to contest the lack of a response by means of recourse to an administrative court.
- The issuance of the relative authorization by the competent authority precludes the substitution power of the Ministry of the Environment (Article 281, paragraph 8, introduced by the 2010 Corrective).
- The content of the authorization, specified in Article 269, paragraphs 4–6, includes an indication of the emission limit values and other constructive and operating requirements for the plant, including an indication of the fuels utilized. The 2010 Corrective introduced the possibility to require limit values for each pollutant (expressed in annual mass flows) referring to a plant's overall heating systems and activities.
- The authorization remains effective for fifteen years (DPR No. 203 of 1988 did not provide for an expiration); the competent authority can, however, require that the authorization be renewed prior to its expiration if a modification of the requirements is necessary to comply with air quality limit values (Article 269, paragraph 7, as modified by Corrective 2010).
- Paragraph 8 regulates the regime of modifications to the plant. 'Modification of the plant' (Article 268, paragraph 1, clause *m*) means *the installation of a heating system or initiation of an activity in a plant or modification of a heating system or activity in a plant, which results in a variation with respect to what was indicated in the project. (…) or in the authorization set forth in Article 269, par. 3.; modifications relating to the manner of use or fuels used fall within the definition*. The plant manager must notify the competent authority in the case of (any) modifications, which will order the plant manager to file a request for authorization if he feels that the modification is 'substantial' (in the meaning set forth above). The substantive modification of a heating system can result in an update or renewal of the authorization depending on whether the administrative procedure is limited to the heating systems and activities affected by the modification or the entire plant (when such need arises due to the evolution of the environmental situation or best available technologies). Renewal, differently than an update, results in the initiation of a new fifteen-year period.

(b) Article 269 exonerates plants for the deposit of mineral oils, including liquefied gas (paragraph 10), as well as those excluded from the scope of application of section I (Article 267, paragraphs 2 and 3, for example, waste incinerators, as well as Article 272, paragraph 5, for example, plants for national defence).

(c) The ordinary authorization procedure is flanked by the regime 'in derogation', provided for the plants set forth in Article 272 which, according to the terminology borrowed from pre-existing legislation, are considered to provoke reduced or insignificant air pollution.

Article 272, paragraph 1 refers to plants in which only the systems and activities specified in Part I of Annex IV are present, whose emissions are of scarce significance (subsequent to the 2010 Corrective, the systems already provided by Article 269, paragraph 14 are now included in the Annex). Such plants are not subject to authorization, however, the competent authority (to issue the authorization following an ordinary procedure) can provide, by means of its own general measure, that the plant managers must notify it of the date the plant will begin to function or when the activities will initiate. The region can establish, including by laws or a general measure, special emission limit values and requirements based on the best available technologies for all of the systems and activities provided by Article 272, paragraph 1, including construction and operating requirements and the fuel used. Limit values and requirements can also be established by the air quality plans and programmes (*see* Article 271, paragraphs 3 and 4).

If the plants set forth in Article 271, paragraph 1 are subject to emission limit values, the regional legislation specifies the sampling and analysis methods for emissions to be used in controls and can impose monitoring obligations on the operator. If the combustion plants set forth in paragraph 1 are subject to emission limit values, the authority responsible for the control can decide not to conduct, or to limit, the controls on emissions if the operator has a declaration of conformity for the plant issued by the builder that attests the conformity of the emissions to the limit values and if, based on documentary checks, the specific technical instructions on use and maintenanace indicated in the declaration are duly applied.

Article 272, paragraph 2 also attributes the competent authority with the power to issue special authorizations of a general nature for specific categories of industrial plants, determined in relation to the type and mode of production and related to each individual category, establishing emission limit values, requirements – including those relating to the conditions of use and fuels utilized, terms for compliance, sampling and analysis methods and frequency of controls. The emission limit values and requirements are established in conformity with Article 271. The general authorizations are adopted on a priority basis for plants having the types of installations and activities listed in Part II of Annex IV to Part V.

The manager of industrial plants subject to general authorization must apply for a general authorization with the competent authority at least forty-five days prior to installation. The competent authority can cancel the authorization by means of its own measure in the event the prerequisites provided by the general authorization, the requirements of State or regional law, or air quality plans and programmes are breached, as well as when there are particular situations of a risk to health, or areas that require special environmental protection. The manager can always opt for the ordinary procedure set forth in Article 269, while the use of the ordinary procedure is mandatory for the plants having heating systems or activities not referred to in the general authorization.

The general authorizations scheme does not apply in cases where substances or mixtures are used in the system or activity having an indications of danger H350, H340, H350i, H360D, H360F, H360FD, H360Df and H360Fd in accordance with current European legislation on the classification, labelling and packaging of substances and mixtures; in these cases the operator must request an ordinary authorization (in accordance with Article 269).

Legislative Decree No. 152 of 2006 expanded the use of a simplified regime for general authorizations with respect to pre-existing legislation, which can now be broadly used and is not limited to just a few activities.

§6. Control System

232. As is the case for other sectors of environmental protection, with respect to air pollution controls it is necessary to distinguish between control functions, which are of an administrative nature, and control activities, which are of a technical nature and which are normally performed by the ARPA (*see* the Constitutional Court, judgment No. 120 of 2010, with respect to such distinction).

233. In relation to 'industrial' plants and activities, Legislative Decree No. 152 of 2006 distinguishes between the authority competent to issue the authorization, that is, the region or the entity delegated by it, and the authority competent to perform the control, which is 'the authority regional law entrusts with controlling compliance on a regular basis with the authorizations and provisions', as set forth in section I (Article 268, paragraph 1, clause *p*).

The emissions authorization also requires, among its other obligations, an indication of the frequency of the controls that the plant manager must carry out, whose results he must refer to the competent authority (Article 269, paragraph 4, clause *b*). The authorization also contains an indication of the monitoring methods and systems that must be used by the manager during self-monitoring; in the case of the use of different monitoring methods or systems, or monitoring which does not conform to the authorization, the manager is subject to the criminal sanction provided by Article 279, paragraph 2 (Article 271, paragraph 18, introduced by Corrective 2010).

If the manager verifies during the monitoring that he must implement that there is a difference between the required emission values and the values that are measured, he must notify the competent control authority within twenty-four hours.

Naturally the administrative authority is also responsible for controls. The initial control of compliance with the authorization must be performed by the responsible authority within six months from the date one or more heating systems become operational or one or more activities are initiated in the authorized plant (Article 269, paragraph 6). The authority responsible for the control is authorized to make all of the on-site inspections that it deems necessary to verify compliance with the authorization (Article 269, paragraph 9).

234. The 2010 Corrective introduced technical standards of reference with respect to sampling methods and the analysis of emissions, measurement principles and the procedures aimed at guaranteeing the quality of the emission monitoring systems (Article 271, paragraph 17, which refers to a specific supplemental ministerial decree in Annex VI). These standards are the only ones that can be used during the authorization or control process, and the use of different methods is ineffective (Article 271, paragraph 18). With respect to sanctions as well, the limit values are considered to have been exceeded only if the difference between the limit values and measured values is verified by the competent authority or judicial police by controls carried out according to the standardized sampling and analysis methods (Article 271, paragraph 20). Further, it provides that if the controls of the administrative authority (or judicial police) and those of the manager that are carried out contemporaneously provide different results, it is necessary to repeat the control on the basis of the reference methods and adjust the monitoring requirements contained in the authorization whenever, including during the phase in which the analysis are repeated, the difference remains (Article 271, paragraph 19 as well as paragraph 20 if the difference regards the exceeding of emission limit values). If necessary, the adjustment of the authorization can also regard the emission limits, demonstrating the importance of the choice of the method for measuring emissions with respect to the results of the testing in terms of the values that are determined.

235. With respect to residential heating systems, the authority responsible for the control is specified in Article 283, paragraph 1, clause *i* as the authority that conducts the necessary controls, assessments and inspections with respect to the energy efficiency of buildings (provided by Article 9 and by Annex L of Legislative Decree No. 192 of 19 August 2005 and by Presidential Decree No. 412 of 26 August 1993), or by the different authority indicated by regional law. The competent authority can utilize external organisms with specific technical expertise, in accordance with what is provided by Legislative Decree No. 192 of 2005.

236. With reference to fuels, spot checks are required of the characteristics of heavy fuel oil, diesel and marine diesel, produced or imported and destined to be marketed, which are carried out by the Customs Office's chemical laboratories as well as by any other subjects indicated by Article 295. Controls are also performed at industrial plants in order to verify that the use of a fuel conforms to the characteristics required by section III, Part V of Legislative Decree No. 152 of 2006. Jurisdiction rests with the authority competent to control industrial plants (Article 296, paragraph 2).

Legislative Decree No. 66 of 2005 requires spot checks of the conformity of gasoline and combustible diesel with legislative parameters. The Customs Office has been entrusted with these controls in accordance with Law No. 689 of 1981, including by use of the control powers provided by Legislative Decree No. 504 of 1995 (Uniform Law on Production and Consumption Tax), and by the Finance Police.

237. With respect to motor vehicles, once approval of the prototype has been issued, the Ministry of Infrastructures and Transportation can verify the conformity of the vehicles manufactured to the model that has been approved, and the costs related to such verification are borne by the recipient of the approval (Article 77 of

Legislative Decree No. 285 of 1992). Another type of control, also within the competence of the Ministry of Transportation, is made at the time of the periodic mandatory check-up of circulating vehicles. The municipalities are instead attributed with control functions for exhaust gas emissions from circulating vehicles.

238. The most important requirement with respect to the protection of air quality is the guarantee of a continuous and reliable control system. That presumes the creation of a complex air monitoring network system that is capable of supplying reliable, homogenous and comparable data, which allows a cognitive picture to be formed that is as precise as possible of the state of air quality and its evolving dynamics.

§7. Administrative Sanctions

239. Among the cases of air pollution subject to sanctions, an important place is occupied by the kind of air pollution set forth in Article 278 of Legislative Decree No. 152 of 2006 regarding industrial plants that fall within the scope of section I, Part V of Decree.

240. The competent authority, either the region or the province, in the case of breach of the requirements contained in the authorization, according to the seriousness of the infraction, must proceed as follows:

- issuance of a written warning, assigning a deadline within which the irregularities must be eliminated;
- issuance of a written warning, with the simultaneous suspension of the authorization of installations and activities that are non-compliant with the requirements of the authorization, in the case of situations presenting a danger to health or the environment;
- revocation of the authorization with reference to the installations and activities that are non-compliant with the requirements of the authorization, in the case of lack of adjustment to the requirements ordered by the warning and in the case of repeat violations of the requirements set forth in the authorization that create situations of danger and damage to health or the environment.

Notwithstanding the explicit reference to the seriousness of the infraction as a parameter to be utilized for the choice of the sanction, the sanctions are not progressive. In fact, the written warning and the warning with simultaneous suspension of the relative activity are alternatives, depending on whether or not there is any danger to health or the environment. Revocation of the authorization and the closure of the plant necessarily presupposes the preventive exercise of the power to issue a warning. The above is without prejudice to the possibility that a court might order precautionary measures, and the court's injunctive power is in addition to the criminal sanctions provided by subsequent Article 279.

If, during the controls carried out by the competent authority for the control or by the judicial police, the non-conformity of the measured values to the prescribed limit values, the competent authority shall, by an order, require the operator to restore conformity in the shortest possible time.

The cessation of operations of the system must always be ordered if the non-conformity could result in danger to human health or a significant deterioration of air quality at a local level (Article 271, paragraph 20*bis* and 278, paragraph 1*bis*).

241. An administrative sanction of EUR 1,000 is applied to anyone who makes a modification to a plant that is non-substantive without providing notice to the competent authority as provided by Article 269, paragraph 8 (Article 279, paragraph 1, prior to the 2010 Corrective such behaviour was criminally sanctioned by means of a fine of up to EUR 1,000).

242. Except for those cases in which the behaviour constitutes a crime (*see infra*), the violation of the requirements set forth in Articles 276 and 277 regarding VOC emissions from fuel distribution and storage plants is punished by an administrative sanction ranging from EUR 15,493 to EUR 154,937 (Article 279, paragraph 7, which provides for suspension of the authorization in the case of repeat violations).

243. With respect to residential heating systems, Article 288 provides for a series of cases subject to administrative sanction that are aimed at the manufacturer, the installer and the party responsible for operating the system.

In the case of operation of a residential heating system that does not comply with the technical characteristics set forth in Article 285, the following are subject to an administrative penalty ranging from EUR 516 to EUR 2,582:

(a) the manufacturer, or if the certification provided by Article 282 is missing, the producer and the installer in the cases subject to Article 284, paragraph 1;
(b) the party responsible for the operation and maintenance of the system, in cases subject to Article 284, paragraph 2.

In the case of a residential heating system that does not comply with the emission limit values set forth in Article 286, paragraph 1, the following are subject to an administrative penalty ranging EUR 516 to EUR 2,582:

(a) the manufacturer and the installer if the certification or instructions provided by Article 282 are missing;
(b) the manufacturer if the certification and instructions provided by Article 282 exist and it appears from the booklet for the system that the required controls and maintenance have been carried out, as long as the duration stablished for the life cycle of the system is not exceeded;
(c) the party responsible for the operation and maintenance if the certification and instructions provided by Article 282 exist and it appears from the booklet for the system that the required controls and maintenance have not been carried out or the duration established for the life cycle of the system has been exceeded.

The party responsible for operating the heating system is punished if the required annual control is not performed or if a heating system having power greater than 0.232 MW is operated without the necessary licence.

244. In addition to a monetary fine, the law also provides for injunctive relief, by ordering that the heating system be adjusted: failure to comply constitutes the crime set forth in Article 650 of the Italian Criminal Code (*Breach of the Authority's measures*).

The competent authority, as specified in Article 283 of Legislative Decree No. 152 of 2006, is responsible for assessing sanctions in accordance with the procedure set forth in Law No. 689 of 1981.

The obligations required by Legislative Decree No. 30 of 2013 on the emission of greenhouse gas are also subject to administrative sanction in the case of non-compliance (*see* Article 36). The committee is the competent authority, and the provisions of Law No. 689 of 1981 are applicable.

245. With further reference to the regime of polluting sources, administrative sanctions are provided with respect to motor vehicles: whoever issues a declaration of conformity for types of vehicles other than those that have been approved; whoever manufactures or places in commerce vehicles that do not conform to the approved prototype; whoever circulates with a vehicle that presents alterations of the manufacturing characteristics; or whoever circulates with a motor vehicle which did not undergo a mandatory periodic check-up (Articles 76–80, Legislative Decree No. 285 of 1992).

246. With respect to fuel, an administrative fine is assessed in the following cases: (a) with reference to residential heating systems, whoever burns materials or substances that do not conform to what is required by law; or (b) whoever does not use the enhanced combustion technologies provided by Article 294 of Legislative Decree No. 152 of 2006 in such heating systems.

If waste is burned, the provisions set forth in Part IV of Legislative Decree No. 152 of 2006 and Legislative Decree No. 133 of 2005 are applicable.

The same behaviour is a crime if it regards industrial plants.

247. Legislative Decree No. 66 of 2005 punishes by means of an administrative fine, unless the fact constitutes a crime, whoever places in commerce gasoline or diesel that does not conform to legislative requirements. The sanctions are applied to managers of tax deposits, distribution systems and commercial storage. The prefect is the competent authority.

248. Legislative Decree No. 161 of 2006 provides that whoever places paints, varnishes and other body shop products containing VOC in commerce in which the label is missing, incomplete or has evidently been altered or falsified shall be punished by an administrative fine, unless the same constitutes a crime. The region with territorial jurisdiction or the different authority indicated in the regional law is responsible for assessing such fine.

Legislative Decree No. 81 of 2018 refers to outstanding law (Article 9) in cases of the infringement of the implementation measures of the National Emission Reduction Programme.

§8. Criminal Sanctions

249. In providing an overview of the sources of protection of air quality, it has already been noted that in order to contain air pollution, the crime set forth in Article 674 of the Italian Criminal Code regarding the hazardous throwing of objects is still applicable.

In addition to said general provision, the Italian legal system contemplates a multitude of crimes introduced in the Italian Criminal Code by Law No. 68 of 28 May 2015 (*see* Part IV 'Environmental Crimes' *infra*).

The Italian legal system envisages a multitude of crimes typified by the sources in this sector.

250. Legislative Decree No. 152 of 2006 punishes violations of obligations related to heating systems that fall within the scope of section I, Part V as fineable offences. Such offences regard: (a) emissions without authorization or with an expired, suspended or revoked authorization; (b) emissions that violate the requirements set forth in the authorization; (c) exceeding the limit values set forth in the tables; and (d) the failure to communicate data on emissions (Article 279).

251. The 2010 Corrective introduced some important specifications with respect to verifying the crime of exceeding emission limit values. For purposes of determining whether a crime has been committed, the limits are considered to have been exceeded only if the competent control authority or judicial police verify a difference between the measured values and the required values based on the sampling methods and analysis listed in the Annexes to the Decree (Article 271, paragraph 20).

For the most part, the crimes provided by Legislative Decree No. 152 of 2006 are formal crimes that punish behaviour that does not directly result in damage or danger to the environment. In this case, the legal interest that is directly protected is the environmental regulation carried out by the public authorities as well as, only indirectly, ecological equilibrium. This is the case notwithstanding the fact that legal scholarship is debating the conformity of these provisions with the principle of 'offensiveness' in criminal matters.

The decree normally provides alternative penalties of detention and a fine, resulting in the possibility of a voluntary payment pursuant to Article 162*bis* of the Italian Criminal Code (i.e., the payment of an amount of money to extinguish the crime). The choice of a finable offence also results in a reduced statute of limitations. The sanction of arrest up to one year (Article 279, paragraph 5) is always applied only when exceeding the limit values also results in exceeding the air quality limit values (a condition that is difficult to verify from the standpoint of a causal connection).

252. With respect to fuels, an alternative sanction of detention or a fine is applied: (a) with reference to the industrial plants set forth in section I, Part V of Legislative Decree No. 152 of 2006, to whoever burns materials or substances that do not conform to legislative requirements; and (b) to whoever does not use the enhanced combustion technologies provided by Article 294 of the decree in said plants.

Legislative Decree No. 161 of 2006 punishes with an alternative sanction of detention or a fine whoever places in the market paints, varnishes and products of body shops having a VOC content greater than that established by law, as well as whoever alters or falsifies the relative labels (DPCM of 25 March 2011 extended through 31 December 2011 the initial term of the prohibition of products having a VOC content greater than the values set forth in Annex II of Legislative Decree No. 161 of 2006 in non-EU countries).

§9. Economic Instruments

253. One of the principal economic instruments in the environmental sector consists of environmental taxation.

Until 2007, the two principal sources of environmental taxation were Law No. 449 of 27 December 1997 (Article 17, clauses 29–33), and Law No. 448 of 23 December 1998 (Article 8).

The first imposed a tax on emissions of SO_2 and NO_x produced by large combustion plants having a nominal thermal power equal to or greater than 50 MW.

The second introduced the carbon tax, in particular, providing for the recalculation of the excise tax on mineral oils (fully operative starting from 1 January 2005), and the introduction as of 1 January 1999 of a tax on consumption in the amount of EUR 1,000 per tonne for carbon, petroleum coke and natural bitumen emulsified with 30% water ('Orimulsion'), used in combustion plants. Legislative Decree No. 26 of 2 February 2007 ('Implementation of Directive 2003/96/EC reorganizing the Community framework on the taxation of energy products and electricity') repealed cited Article 8 and modified Legislative Decree No. 504 of 1995 ('Uniform Law on Production and Consumption Tax').

254. In addition to environmental taxes, among the economic instruments providing incentives aimed at improving air quality, the fund for financing investments for the realization of bicycle paths or walkways created by Law No. 208 of 28 June 1991 by the Treasury Ministry should be noted.

A source of financing works promoting bicycle mobility was created, by means of Law No. 366 of 19 October 1998, by the Ministry of Transportation. Such fund, financed with resources of the Ministry of Public Works and the Department of Urban Areas, is divided on an annual basis among the regions in accordance with regional allotment plans prepared in consideration of the projects for bicycle mobility presented by the municipalities and provinces.

Legislative Decree No. 128 of 30 May 2005, aimed at promoting the use of biofuels, provides economic interventions in the form of tax benefits on biofuels and incentives to initiate biomass cultivations.

Incentive campaigns to 'scrap' non-ecological motor vehicles are instead less known. Over the years the forms of intervention have varied, from a straightforward cash contribution on the purchase or scrap price of the abandoned automobile, through an exemption from payment of ownership tax for some tax periods.

In general, Legislative Decree No. 81 of 2018 provides that the measures providing incentives, benefits and facilitations in the fields of climate, transportation, industry, agriculture, energy and residential heating must be consistent with the implementation of the policies and measures of the national programme.

§10. Institutional Framework: The Division of Responsibilities among Diverse Territorial Levels of Government

255. The division of administrative functions among diverse levels of government appears not only from national law in the sector, but also from Legislative Decree No. 112 of 1998 and regional laws that completed the *Bassanini* reform on administrative decentralization in that, as has already been noted, national law refers to regional legislation on more than one occasion.

256. The fuel sector does not have particular problems with respect to the distribution of competence given that, for obvious needs of uniformity throughout the national territory, the regulation of product standards and the relative sampling methods must be exclusively reserved to State organs. The State (Customs Agency) is responsible for controls of gasoline and diesel fuel, while the entity responsible for controlling the plants has competence for the fuels set forth in Part V of Legislative Decree No. 156 of 2006.

257. The structure of competence in the context of the regulation of polluting sources is instead more differentiated.

258. With respect to motor vehicles, the functions are divided between the State and municipalities. The State is responsible for the following:

- establishing technical requirements for polluting emissions of motor vehicles;
- ascertaining the constructive and functional characteristics of motor vehicles at the time of approval of the relative prototype;
- regulating the periodic check-ups with reference to polluting emissions produced.

259. The municipalities are instead attributed with control functions regarding polluting emissions originating from circulating vehicles.

260. With reference to residential heating systems, competence is divided as follows:

- Municipalities exercise control functions on the heating systems and also have the power to issue sanctions (due to the effect of the reference to the provisions of Legislative Decree No. 192 of 2005).
- The region can modify which authority is competent to issue administrative sanctions by means of a regional law.
- The region is responsible for functions concerning the licensing of specialized personnel used to operate thermal plants (inclusive of the regulation of licensing courses, after Constitutional Court judgment No. 250 of 2009 and subsequent modifications made by the 2010 Corrective).
- The State establishes the prerequisites for the organisms that the competent authority can use to perform controls (Article 288, paragraph 8).

261. With respect to functions relating to the regime of industrial plants in accordance with section I, Part II of Legislative Decree No. 152 of 2006, the division of functions primarily regards the State and regional levels.

262. The State is responsible for the following:

- establishing emission limit values and requirements for the operation of industrial plants;
- determining methods of sampling, analysis and valuation of pollutants, including reference standards;
- identifying criteria for the utilization of the best available technologies and criteria for compliance by existing industrial plants;
- exercising substitute power, issuing the general authorizations set forth in Article 272, paragraph 2.

263. The regions are attributed with the following functions:

- establishing emission limit values within the national range;
- establishing emission limit values, considering air quality plans and programmes, with the possibility to establish more restrictive values than national limit values, if necessary to achieve and comply with limits and quality objectives (Article 271, paragraphs 3 and 4);
- establishing, by means of a law or general provisions, specific limit values and requirements for constructing and operating the heating systems set forth in Article 271, paragraph 1.

The region, or the authority chosen by it, has authorization functions, with the exception of offshore platforms and offshore regasification plants for liquefied natural gas, which must be authorized by the Ministry of the Environment (Article 268, paragraph 1, clause *o*).

The competent control authority is specified by regional law (if the regional law is silent, the competent control authority is the authority that issues the authorization, Article 268, paragraph 1, clause *p*). The authority responsible for the control is attributed by Legislative Decree No. 183 of 2017 with the power to order the restoration of the conformity of a plant exceeding the prescribed emission limit values or the cessation of activity if the non-conformity can result in danger to human health or a significant detriment to air quality at a local level.

264. The State is competent to issue the authorization to emit greenhouse gas and approve the plan for assigning emission quotas (Legislative Decree No. 30 of 2013).

265. With respect to EIAs, competence is distributed between the State and region depending on the kind of installation involved.

The State, and, in particular, the President of the Council of Ministers, approves the programme to reduce emissions provided by Legislative Decree No. 81 of 2018.

266. The maximum level of complexity in the distribution of competence to diverse levels of government is reached in the context of the regime aimed at directly protecting air quality.

Legislative Decree No. 155 of 2010 introduced some procedural and institutional measures to guarantee the homogeneity of the assessment and management of air quality throughout the national territory. In addition to consent by the Ministry of the Environment of regional zoning programmes classifying and assessing air quality and the regional project adjusting the existing measurement network (Articles 3–5), the creation of a Coordination Committee is noted, which consists of representatives of central and regional administrations, responsible for the preparation of orientations and guidelines in relation to aspects of common interest, permitting the joint review of issues related to the application of Legislative Decree No. 155 of 2010, including for the purpose of guaranteeing a coordinated and homogeneous implementation of the new rules and to prevent situations of non-compliance (Article 20; the Committee's specific competence is established by the individual provisions of the Decree).

With respect to the division of functions among different levels of government, the following functions are reserved to the State:

- preparing the national programme to reduce emissions and implement measures;
- establishing limit values and alert thresholds;
- establishing objective values and long-term objectives for ozone;
- establishing procedures for the information to be provided to the public concerning the registered levels of air pollution and in the event alert thresholds are exceeded;
- determining criteria for data gathering regarding environmental air quality and the criteria and techniques of measurement, with particular reference to the location and minimum number of data gathering stations and reference methods for measurement, sampling and analysis;
- determining criteria for the preparation of regional air quality plans as well as issuing guidelines to determine the measures to be introduced in the plans related to sectors not regulated by State laws;
- establishing procedures to guarantee quality provided to verify compliance of the ambient air quality measures as well as procedures to approve sampling instruments and instruments to measure air quality;

- ordering limits on the circulation of motor vehicles outside of inhabited centres (competence of the Prefects);
- maintaining and annually distributing a fund to be used for works that promote the use of bicycles.

The regions are attributed with the following functions:

- preparing air quality plans;
- assessing air quality in view of planning;
- orientation and coordination of air pollution monitoring systems;
- responsibility for ensuring the quality of the data gathered at a provincial or local level;
- approval of plans to allocate financing for bicycling mobility.

The provinces are entrusted with the following functions:

- preparing traffic plans for extra-urban road networks;
- preparing projects for bicycle mobility with reference to provincial road networks and connections between the centres of diverse municipalities.

Reference is made to the reform of provincial entities set forth in Law No. 56 of 7 April 2014.

The municipalities are attributed with the following functions:

- preparing urban traffic plans;
- issuing measures limiting circulation for all or some categories of vehicles in inhabited centres;
- adopting adequate measures aimed at achieving sustainable mobility, among which: programme agreements for the implementation of home-work travel plans for personnel of public entities and businesses; incentives and measures for public services and forms of multi-property ownership of motor vehicles;
- preparing projects for bicycle mobility, limited to municipal road networks.

§11. Conclusions

267. The entry into effect of Legislative Decree No. 152 of 2006, improperly called the 'Environmental Code' or the 'Uniform Environmental Law', has without doubt led to a significant quantitative decrease of the sources on air pollution control. Regardless, the primary limitation of environmental legislation in the Italian legal system remains the excessive proliferation of general laws and administrative acts of various kinds and levels, from laws and acts having the effect of a law to ministerial decrees, with and without regulatory power.

In fact, a significant part of outstanding law, above all, with respect to air quality, remains independent of the decree, with the aggravating factor that the coordination mechanisms among the different regimes are frequently insufficient.

268. Only with the enactment of Legislative Decree No. 155 of 2010, has a partial inversion of the tendency occurred: a decrease of sources on a quantitative level which, however, even due to the obligations assumed in the EU context, has not been accompanied by a corresponding simplification of the rules.

Another critical aspect of the Italian legal system with respect to air pollution consists of the excessive complexity of the transitory regime.

This is not surprising, considering the fact that the rules regulating the passage from the pre-existing to the new regime express the basic tension that exists between the need to pursue, in the briefest time possible, the highest level of protection allowed by modern technologies, and the need to apply environmental law gradually, in order to avoid the increase of costs that implementation of the new standards places on companies in difficulty.

It should be noted in this regard that the Italian legislator again does not leave much space to the Community perspective, which tends to promote the application of best available technologies (Legislative Decree No. 155 of 2010 does signal a slight improvement in this case as well).

With respect to a few years ago, however, the battle to contain air pollution is producing results that are increasingly satisfying, above all, due to the full effectiveness of air quality measurement and monitoring systems.

The regime's major merits can largely be seen in the sectors where the Community legislator has been active: constructive and functional characteristics for motor vehicles, product standards for certain fuels, and air quality standards for major pollutants are areas in which Italy recently forced itself to fully and properly implement the objectives established at a Community level.

Chapter 4. Waste Management

by *Antonio Borzì*

§1. Principal Sources of National Law

269. The first Italian law that dealt organically with the issue that, in current terminology, is defined as waste 'management' is Law No. 366 of 20 March 1941. The *collection, transportation and disposal of solid municipal wastes* are qualified as public interest activities not only due to legal aspects relating to protecting public hygiene and decorum, but also due to the impact the use of wastes has on the national economy (not by chance considered to be one of the methods for 'disposing' of wastes, together with dispersion and destruction).

The law does not define what is intended by the term 'waste' but is limited to distinguishing between waste located in public areas or areas destined to public use (external waste), and waste produced by installations (internal wastes), which is subject to a specific tax (for the collection and transportation of internal solid municipal wastes).

The solid municipal waste collection, transportation and disposal service has been removed from the market and entrusted to the municipalities, which can create special waste management companies.

The law promotes the industrial and agricultural use of wastes. In 1941, however, the reuse of wastes was not appreciated in terms of decreased pressure on the ecosystem, but essentially for its positive impact on the national economy. On the contrary, even in the context of the EC with respect to the regime on wastes, the most authentically 'environmental' objectives were only flanked with those of protection of the sole market starting from 1986 (by means of the Single European Act).

Italy's participation in the EEC influenced subsequent Italian legislation, which moved in a new institutional context and new context of values sustained by the Republican Constitution, which entered into effect on 1 January 1948. The new Constitution expressly provides for landscape protection and protection of Italy's historical-artistic heritage (Article 9), as well as the protection of health as a fundamental right of man and an interest of society (Article 32). These roles are entrusted to the Republic, and, thus, to all public entities having territorial autonomy, starting from the regions, which the 1948 Constitution granted with legislative power, but which only began to function starting from 1970.

270. In the evolution of Italian legislation, the second important phase is represented by DPR No. 915 of 10 September 1982, in which Italy implemented Directive 75/442/EEC on wastes for the first time, together with Directives 76/403/EEC on the disposal of polychlorinated biphenyls and polychlorinated terphenyls and 78/319/EEC on toxic and hazardous wastes.

A legislative definition of 'waste' appeared in the Italian legal system for the first time. It defines waste as any substance or object deriving from human activity or from a natural cycle that is *abandoned or destined to be abandoned.* The meaning of the term 'abandoned' is narrower than the expression 'to dispose of' used by the

Community legislator, but it should be noted that as originally drafted, Directive 75/442/EC referred to *outstanding national laws*.

DPR No. 915 of 1982 confirms the role of the municipality as the subject responsible for providing on an exclusive basis for the collection, transportation and disposal of municipal wastes; the State is responsible for the waste treatment regime, above all, by providing technical rules (the characteristics of toxic and hazardous wastes were specified and general technical rules introduced on the construction and location of treatment centres in an inter-ministerial Committee Resolution dated 27 July 1984). With respect to other territorial entities, the region is entrusted with planning and authorizing facilities, whereas the province has control power with respect to waste disposal (as well as authorization power, which the regions often delegate to the provinces).

It is clear that the 1982 rules are focused on the waste and waste disposal regimes and, above all, on the confinement in landfills of waste produced by human activity. The decree provides a very marginal role for waste recycling, reuse and energy recovery, which is almost limited to a simple statement of principle inserted to comply with Community obligations.

271. Law No. 475 of 9 November 1988 was approved shortly thereafter. By introducing the category of 'secondary raw materials', it initiated a principle of Italian law that has become consolidated: the tendency to remove manufacturing by-products that can be reused economically from the legal regime on wastes. In the wake of this tradition, in which diverse national legislation was approved that varies due to the type of act and its legal effect (ranging from Law Decrees to Ministerial Circulars), a law was approved in 2002 that 'authentically interprets' the definition of waste (Article 14 of Law Decree No. 138/02, converted into Law No. 178/2002), which, however, the European Court of Justice (ECJ) has held on more than one occasion conflicts with Community law (judgment 11 November 2004, in case C-457/02, *Niselli* and judgment 18 December 2007, in case C-263/05, *Commission of the European Communities v. Italian Republic*).

272. Legislative Decree 22 February 1997 (the so-called Ronchi Decree, based on the name of the Environmental Minister who proposed it), is the third stage, undoubtedly the most important one, in the evolution of the Italian legal framework on waste management. The Decree, which adjusted Italian law to the innovations regarding waste provided by Community legislation (*see* Directive 91/156/EEC), introduced principles, objectives and definitions that remain the cornerstones of the current regime. The approach of the 1982 legislation has been substantially confirmed with respect to the role of public subjects.

273. The norms set forth in Part IV of Legislative Decree No. 152 of 2006, (TUA) contain the current, general Italian waste management regime, and constitute the 'backbone' of Italian law on waste. Legislative Decree No. 205 of 3 December 2010, the general regime on waste management, was amended in order to implement the Waste Framework Directive 2008/98/EC.

The provisions of Part IV of Legislative Decree No. 152 of 2006 do not exhaust the panorama of Italian legal sources that deal with waste, either to regulate the management of specific categories of waste or to regulate specific waste treatment methods (*see* Articles 177 and 227 of Legislative Decree No. 152 of 2006). The most important sector laws will be discussed below.

It should be noted that the Directives of the European Parliament and the Council which reformed the rules of the EU on waste are still being implemented – No. 849 – and No. 852 of 30 May 2018 – which are aimed at improving the quality of the environment, protecting human health, ensuring the careful, efficient and rational use of natural resources, promoting the principles of the circular economy, increasing energy efficiency and reducing the EU's dependence on imported resources, all of which are goals already pursued by the Italian regime in force.

274. Within the Italian legal system, the regime on radioactive wastes is treated as a separate regime. It is principally regulated by Legislative Decree No. 230 of 17 March 1995 (*Implementation of Directives 89/618/Euratom, 90/641/Euratom, 96/29/Euratom and 2006/117/Euratom on ionizing radiation*), recently modified by Legislative Decree No. 23 of 20 February 2009 entitled *Implementation of Directive 2006/117/Euratom on the supervision and control of shipments of radioactive wastes and spent nuclear fuel*; recently amended by Legislative Decree No. 45 of 4 March 2014. Such legislative decree contains provisions on the classification of radioactive wastes, the national regulatory authority on nuclear safety and radiation protection (a department of ISPRA), and the national programme for the management of spent fuel and radioactive waste. The provisions of Law No. 99 of 23 July 2009, implemented by Legislative Decree No. 31 of 15 February 2010, are also noted.

§2. The Law's Objective Scope of Application

I. The Scope of Application of the Law on Waste

275. The scope of application of the law on waste regards the provisions of Article 185 and the meanings of important concepts such as 'waste' and 'by-product' (Articles 183 and 184*bis*) and 'secondary raw materials' (Article 184*ter*).

Article 185 of Legislative Decree No. 152 of 2006 regulates cases of exclusion from the scope of application of Part IV of the Environmental Code; they are mandatory exclusions often characterized by their functional aspect, which cannot be integrated by national legislator (EC Court of Justice, 18 December 2007, case C-194/05, C-195/05, Commission v. Italy, respectively 54 and 53).

Part IV of the Environmental Code does not apply to land (in situ), including contaminated unexcavated soil and structures permanently connected to land, without prejudice to what is provided by Articles 239 et seq. with respect to the reclamation of contaminated sites (Article 185, paragraph 1, clause *b*) and uncontaminated soil and other naturally occurring material excavated in the course of construction, or if it is certain that it will be reused for building purposes in its natural state and in the same site in which it was excavated (Article 185, paragraph 1, clause *c*). The last paragraph of Article 185 specifies that uncontaminated excavated soil and other naturally occurring material used in sites other than where they were excavated, must be assessed in accordance with Article 183, paragraph 1, clause *a* (definition of waste), 184*bis* (by-product) and 184*ter* (*end of waste*).[1]

The topic is linked to the management of 'excavated soil and rock', which has great practical relevance ranging from construction to the realization of large infrastructures, and which is subject to a specific regime set forth in Article 8 of Law Decree No. 133 of 2014 ('Unblock Italy') and in the implementing regulation DPR No. 120 of 13 June 2017.

Article 185 does not apply, among others, to gaseous effluents emitted into the atmosphere (subject to Part V of the Environmental Code, Article 185, paragraph 1, clause *a*), radioactive wastes (subject to a specific regime, Article 185, paragraph 1, clause *d*), some materials – among which waste from grass clippings and pruning – that are non-hazardous and which are subject to normal agricultural and animal husbandry practices or used in agriculture, in forestry or the production of energy from such biomass (Article 185, paragraph 1, clause *f*).

Drain water is also excluded since it is subject to other EU regimes and national implementing regulations.

The provisions of Article 185 determine the reciprocal limits of the law on waste management and other sector environmental regimes (such as the regime on water pollution, in order to distinguish 'drainage' from 'liquid waste' (*see* the chapter on water pollution).

276. 'Waste' means: *any substance or object that its holder discards or has decided or is obliged to discard* (Article 183, paragraph 1, clause *a*). As clarified by the EU Court of Justice, the scope of application of the concept of waste depends on the significance of the term 'discard' (ECJ, judgment 18 December 1997, in case C-129/96, *Inter – Environnement Wallonie*, p. 26; interpretative guidelines were prepared in June 2012 by the Commission's Directorate-General for environmental policy on the principal definitions of Framework Directive 2008/98/EC).

Wastes, defined as above, are classified according to two criteria: origin and characteristics of hazardousness. Wastes are differentiated on the basis of origin as either 'municipal' or 'special' wastes. Municipal wastes are domestic wastes and wastes included in the categories set forth in Article 184, paragraph 2 (such as wastes deriving from breaking up roads or green areas). 'Special' wastes are wastes deriving from the productive activities (commercial, artisan and industrial activities) indicated in Article 184, paragraph 3. There is also the category of special wastes assimilated to municipal wastes. Assimilation only regards non-hazardous wastes and is decided by the municipalities (which apply special criteria determined by the Ministry of the Environment). The distinction between municipal wastes (including assimilated wastes) and special wastes primarily regards organization of waste management services and opening the relative activities to competitors.

Wastes are further classified as hazardous and non-hazardous wastes. Hazardous wastes are identified by an asterisk in the list of wastes contained in Annex D to Part IV of the decree. The law establishes an absolute presumption that domestic wastes are non-hazardous. Hazardous wastes require particular waste management

1. The topic is linked to the management of 'excavated soil and rock', see most recently Art. 8 of Law Decree No. 133 of 2014 (the so-called 'Unblock Italy' law) and implementing regulation.

precautions (Article 178, paragraph 1). Mixing hazardous and non-hazardous wastes or different categories of hazardous wastes is prohibited, for example (Article 187), and disposal facilities must meet specific building characteristics depending on the classification of the wastes delivered to them (*see* Legislative Decree No. 36 of 2003 on landfills).

The Court of Justice of the EU plays a fundamental role in interpreting the law on wastes (the Italian Constitutional Court refers to *fixed points of interpretation* in judgment No. 28 of 2010). The Community court, starting from the objectives of the Waste Directives and the principles of prevention and precaution, has extensively interpreted the concept of waste to include objects that can be economically reutilized (*see* judgment 28 March 1990, in the joined cases C-206 and 207/88, *Vessoso e Zanetti*, 12; judgment 15 June 2000, in the joined cases C-418 and 419/97, *Arco*, 2000, 39, and judgment 22 December 2008 in case C-238/07, *Commission of the European Communities v. the Republic of Italy*, 46).

277. The 'by-product' category has been consolidated by this case law. 'By-product' means the production residue (i.e., what is accidentally produced during the manufacture of a material or an object, which is not the objective of the manufacturing process). In specific situations, by-products are not considered to be wastes because the manufacturer did not intend to dispose of them, but rather exploit them on economically advantageous conditions (starting from judgment 18 April 2002, in case C-9/00, *Palin Granit*, 32).

This concept was codified in the European context by Framework Directive 2008/98/EC, implemented in the Italian legal system by Legislative Decree No. 2015 of 2010 (even if the Italian legislator had already introduced its own concept of by-product).

Pursuant to the Environmental Code, a by-product is any substance or object that satisfies the conditions set forth in Article 184*bis*, paragraph 1, or which complies with the criteria established based on Article 184*bis*, paragraph 2 (Article 184, paragraph 1, clause *qq*, of the Environmental Code).

The concept of 'by-product' is 'self-applicative' when the prerequisites provided by paragraph 1 of Article 184*bis* have been satisfied. Therefore, any substance or object that satisfies all of the following conditions is a by-product and not waste:

(a) the substance or object originates from a manufacturing process, is an integral part of it, and the primary aim of such process is not the production of such substance or object;
(b) the use of such substance or object is certain, during the production process or a subsequent production process of use, by the manufacturer or third parties;
(c) the substance or object can be used directly without any additional processing other than standard industry practice;
(d) the further use is legal, i.e., the substance or object satisfies, for the specific use, all prerequisites for products and the protection of health and the environment, and will not result in an overall negative impact on the environment or human health.

Nevertheless, by means of a ministerial regulation, based on the above conditions, measures can be adopted to establish qualitative or quantitative criteria to determine whether specific types of substances or objects are considered by-products and not waste.

DM No. 264 of 13 October 2016 specified identifying criteria to facilitate demonstrating the existence of the prerequisites for qualifying production residue as a by-product rather than as waste (two interpretative circulars have been issued regarding the Decree of the Ministry of the Environment: Protocol No. 3084 of 3 March 2017 and Protocol No. 77619 of 30 May 2017).

With respect to the concept developed by the EU courts, the current concept is characterized by the lack of reference to the economic value of the by-product and the use of the indeterminate concept of 'normal industrial practice' to determine when the object was subject to preliminary transformation prior to reuse.

The regime on the end of waste should also be noted.

In accordance with Article 184*ter* of the Environmental Code:

> waste ceases being waste when it is subject to recovery, including recycling operations and preparation for reuse, and when it satisfies specific criteria, to be applied in compliance with the following conditions:
>
> a) the substance or object is commonly sued for specific purposes;
> b) there is a market or demand for such substance or object;
> c) the substance or object complies with technical requirements for the specific objectives and complies with outstanding regulations and standards applicable to the products;
> d) the use of the substance or object will not result in overall negative impacts on the environment or human health.

The recovery operation can simply consist of controlling the waste to verify whether it satisfies the criteria established in conformity with the above conditions. The criteria set forth in paragraph 1 have been adopted in conformity with what is established by the EU regime, or, in the lack of EU criteria, on a case-by-case basis of specific types of waste by means of one or more decrees of the Ministry of the Environment, in accordance with Article 17, paragraph 3 of Law No. 400 of 23 August 1988. If necessary, the criteria include limit values for polluting substances and consider all possible negative effects on the environment of the substance or object (Article 184*ter* of the Environmental Code). An example of application of this standard is represented by DM No. 22 of 14 February 2013 on secondary solid fuels.

II. The Principles and Qualifying Features of Italian Law on Waste Management

A. The Objectives of the Legal Framework on Waste Management

278. Waste management is expressly considered to be a public interest activity, that is, a worthy objective to be pursued by public authorities, each while exercising its competence. Its principal objective is to guarantee that waste is recycled or disposed of without endangering human health or prejudicing the environment to the extent possible, specifically: (a) without creating risks for water, air, the soil, fauna and flora; (b) without causing inconvenience due to noises or odours; and (c) without damaging the landscape and sites of particular interest (Article 178, paragraph 2).

B. Fundamental Principles

279. Article 178, paragraph 1 of Legislative Decree No. 152 of 2006 provides that 'waste management shall comply with the principles of precaution, prevention, sustainability, proportionality, accountability and cooperation of all subjects involved in the production, distribution, use and consumption of goods from which wastes originate, as well as the principle of the polluter pays. For such purpose waste management is done according to criteria of effectiveness, efficiency, affordability, transparency, technical and economic feasibility, as well as in compliance with outstanding law on participation and access to environmental information'. The sector specific provision repeats what has already been established in general by Articles 3*bis* through 3*sexies* of the Environmental Code on environmental standards:

(a) The principles of proximity and self-sufficiency are particularly significant for purposes of the organization of the waste management service.

    Waste disposal and the recovery of mixed municipal waste is done using an integrated and adequate network of facilities, considering the best available technologies and the overall cost-benefit ratio in order to:

    (i) obtain self-sufficiency in the disposal of non-hazardous municipal wastes and waste from their processing in the best territorial contexts;
    (ii) allow waste disposal and the recovery of mixed municipal wastes in suitable facilities closest to the places of production or collection to reduce the movement of such waste, considering the geographic context or need for specialized facilities for specific types of waste;
    (iii) use the most suitable methods and technologies to guarantee a high level of environmental protection and protection of public health.

        Article 182, paragraph 3, prohibits the disposal of non-hazardous municipal waste in regions different than the regions where the waste is produced, unless there are any regional or international agreements, if the territorial characteristics and economic technical opportunity to achieve optimal levels of serviced users requires it.

For fractions of municipal waste subject to differentiated collection aimed at recycling and recovery, unrestricted circulation throughout Italy is always allowed between entities or companies registered in the specific categories of the National Register of Environmental Managers in accordance with Article 212, paragraph 5, in view of enhancing their recovery as much as possible, favouring the principle of proximity to recovery facilities (Article 181, paragraph 5).

Article 35, paragraph 6, of Law Decree No. 33 of 19 September 2014 (the so-called Unblock Italy law) clarified that 'in accordance with Legislative Decree No. 152 of 3 April 2006, as there are no basin restrictions on processing municipal waste in energy recovery facilities, the above facilities must nevertheless ensure priority of access to municipal waste produced in the regional territory until the relative need is satisfied, and to process municipal waste produced in other regions only for authorized residual availability. In a complimentary manner, special hazardous waste with only an infective risk is also allowed in compliance with the principle of proximity established by Article 182bis, paragraph 1, clause *b*, of the cited Legislative Decree No. 152 of 2006 and general laws that govern this matter, on the condition that the facility has a dedicated loading system cut to size that also excludes any contact between the personnel and the waste'.

(b) Article 179 of the Environmental Code presents the hierarchy of waste, i.e., 'an order of priority of what constitutes the best environmental option'. In line with the hierarchy, measures must be adopted aimed at encouraging options that guarantee, in compliance with Article 177, paragraphs 1 and 4, and 178 of the Environmental Code, the best overall result, 'considering health, social and economic impacts, inclusive of technical feasibility and economic viability' (paragraph 2). The forecast – through references to technical feasibility and economic viability found in the definition of best available technologies[2] – expresses the need to make waste management choices while balancing interests. With reference to individual flows of waste, the waste hierarchy can be derogated from on an exceptional basis 'if justified, in compliance with the principle of precaution and sustainability, based on a specific analysis of the overall impacts of the production and management of such waste, both from an environmental and health profile, in terms of life cycle, as well as from a social and economic profile, inclusive of technical feasibility and the protection of resources' (paragraph 3).

The hierarchical order of priority in waste management is: (a) prevention; (b) preparation for reuse; (c) recycling; (d) another type of recovery, for example energy recovery; and (e) disposal.

In exercising their respective spheres of competence, the public administrations must take initiatives aimed at enhancing compliance with the waste management

2. Article 5, para. 1, clause l*ter*).

hierarchy, in particular those listed in the fifth paragraph of Article 179 (among others: the promotion of clean technologies; the provision of 'green' contracts; and the 'energetic' use of waste).

In the waste hierarchy the first place is occupied by prevention, understood as the 'measures used before a substance, material or product becomes waste that reduce: (1) the quantity of waste, including through the reuse of products or the extension of their life cycle; (2) the negative impacts of waste produced on the environment and human health; (3) the content of hazardous substances in materials and products' (Article 183, paragraph 1, clause *m*) of the Environmental Code).

Initiatives aimed at promoting waste prevention are exemplified in Article 180 of the Environmental Code. These include economic instruments, an analysis of the life cycle of products, the use of quality systems, the use of the best available technologies, the enhancement of environmental information; the provision of clauses in calls for tenders that enhance the prevention capability of the tenderer; the implementation of agreements, programme contracts, memorandums of understanding aimed at prevention.

The Environmental Code provides an articulated programme on two levels with respect to prevention: national, by MATTM, which indicates the objectives, establishes the prevention measures and the indicators to verify and assess progress in the implementation of the measures (Article 180 and Annex L of Part IV) as well as regional, of an implementational nature, integrated in the Protection Plans (*see* Article 199 of the Environmental Code).

Recovery is defined as 'any operation whose principal result is to allow waste to play a useful role, substituting other materials that would otherwise be used to fulfil a particular function or prepare them to fulfil such function, in the facility or market in general'. Annex C of Part IV of the Environmental Code contains a non-exhaustive list of recovery operations (Article 183, paragraph 1, clause *t*).

In the context of recovery, the Environmental Code provides for an internal hierarchy, so that 'the measures aimed at waste recovery through preparation for reuse, recycling or any other recovery operation of material are applied on a priority basis with respect to the use of waste as a source of energy' (Article 179, paragraph 6 of the Environmental Code).

The preparation for reuse consists of 'control, cleaning, disassembly and repair activities through which products or parts of products that have become waste are prepared in such a way that they can be reused without any other pretreatment' (Article 183, paragraph 1, clause *d*).

Initiatives aimed at enhancing preparation for reuse are indicated in Article 180*bis*, which contemplates the use of economic instruments; the creation and support of repair/reuse centres; the introduction of quantitative objectives; the provisions of educational measures and the use of programme agreements; the implementation of measures for extended producer responsibility; and the possibility to provide spaces in collection centres for the exchange of used goods ready to be reused.

Recycling includes 'any recovery operation through which wastes are processed to obtain products, materials or substances to be used for their original function or for other purposes' (Article 183, paragraph 1, clause *u*). Recycling assumes that the waste is collected in a differentiated manner. Differentiated collection means 'the collection in which a flow of waste is kept separate based on the type and nature of the waste to facilitate specific processing' (Article 184, paragraph 1, clause *p*).

Article 181 of the Environmental Code implements the same objectives as Directive 2008/98/EC:

- within 2015, separate collection, at least for paper, metals, plastic and glass, and if possible, for wood, as well as adoption of the necessary measures to achieve the following objectives;
- within 2020, the preparation for the reuse and recycling of waste such as, at minimum, paper, metals, plastic and glass originating from households and possibly from another origin, to the extent that such waste flows are similar to domestic waste in a percentage of at least 50% in terms of weight;
- within 2020 the preparation for reuse, recycling and other types of recovery of material, including landfill operations that use waste in substitution of other materials, waste from construction and non-hazardous demolition, excluding naturally occurring material defined in item 17 05 04 of the list of wastes, will be increased at least to 70% in terms of weight.

Article 205 provides that in each territorial context, i.e., in every Municipality where there is no A.T.O., the differentiated collection of municipal waste must be ensured for the following minimum percentages of waste produced: at least 35% within 31 December 2006; at least 45% within 31 December 2008; at least 65% within 31 December 2012. The third paragraph of such Article governs a bonus and penalty measure applied to the tax for landfill waste borne by the A.T.O. or the Municipality.

The use of waste as fuel, or as a means to produce energy, is the last option in the context of the internal waste recovery hierarchy. With respect to incinerators for municipal wastes, the distinction between recovery and disposal is established based on the energy efficiency of the facility, through application of the R1 formula, a further novelty introduced with the implementation of the framework directive (which formula has recently been modified by DM 7 August 2013, with the inclusion of a climate correction factor).

Disposal occupies the last place in the waste hierarchy and is the residual processing operation of a waste; disposal includes 'any operation different than recovery, even when the operation has the recovery of substances or energy as a secondary consequence'. Annex B to Part IV of the Environmental Code contains a non-exhaustive list of disposal operations (Article 183, paragraph 1, clause *z*). Disposal in landfills is governed by Legislative Decree No. 36 of 13 January 2003, while it is necessary to refer to the provisions of section III*bis* of Part IV of the Environmental Code for incineration. Waste disposal must be done in safe conditions after verification, by the competent authority, of the technical and economic impossibility to conduct recovery operations. As already noted, disposal outside of the region of non-hazardous waste is prohibited (Article 180, paragraphs 3 and 3bis, of the Environmental Code).

§3. Planning and Programming Instruments

280. In the context of the regime on waste, the Italian legal system attributes particular importance to planning management activity (an activity that EU law considers to be mandatory (EC Court of Justice, case C-82/06, *Commission of the European Communities v. the Italian Republic* of 14 June 2007). The plan is where strategic decisions are made regarding waste management; the above objectives and principles are achieved and implemented in the plan, specifically with respect to the waste hierarchy and principles of self-sufficiency and proximity.

By means of Legislative Decree No. 205 of 2010, the content of planning instruments includes objectives and prevention measures on waste production, with the goal of separating economic growth from the environmental impact related to the production of waste.

The Environmental Code attributes a primary role to the regions with respect to waste management planning; the State's planning powers are limited to recycling and disposal facilities of pre-eminent national interest, as well as establishing national objectives for waste prevention.

The regional plan provides for strategic decisions on wastes, such as those regarding the location of disposal facilities, which have undoubted political and social significance (Article 199; in case law, *see* T.A.R. Umbria, judgment No. 542 of 2 July 2007, and more recently T.A.R. Lazio, Rome, judgment No. 121 of 9 January 2013); decisions which must be taken to ensure adequate public notice and the maximum public participation (paragraph 1).

The regional waste management plans include an analysis of existing waste management in the geographic area involved, the measures to be adopted to improve the environmental efficiency of the different waste management operations, as well as an assessment of the manner in which the plans contribute to implementing the objectives and provisions of Part IV of the Environmental Code. The regional plans are coordinated with other regional planning instruments provided by outstanding law (e.g., those on territorial governance).

The content of the regional waste management plans is indicated in Article 199 of the Environmental Code. The plan must contain, among others, a quantitative and qualitative description of waste flows and an assessment of the trend of such flows; an assessment of the need for additional treatment facilities; and the criteria to determine areas that are not suitable for the location of the facilities.

Part of the plan is dedicated to initiatives aimed at limiting waste production and favouring reutilization, recycling and recovery (including for energy).

An integral part of the regional plan consists of the plan to reclaim contaminated areas, which in addition to specifying and describing the sites to be reclaimed must also establish the order of priorities of the work to be performed, indicate the manner in which the reclamation must be implemented, specify the manner in which materials that are removed will be disposed of, and quantify the necessary financial costs.

The plans must be adjusted to the new regime within 2013 and must be updated every six years.

§4. AUTHORIZATIONS PROCEEDINGS

281. Waste management is subject to control by the public administration by means of a system of preventive authorizations, as well as the obligation to register with a special waste register that contains the details of waste managers.

I. Authorizations

282. Legislative Decree No. 152 of 2006 contemplates two kinds of authorization: (1) authorization following an ordinary procedure: in this case, waste disposal or recovery can only be performed with the express consent of the public administration, which has verified that the petitioner has the prerequisites established by law; or (2) authorization following a simplified procedure: in this case, the activity can be initiated once a specified period of time has passed from a notice sent to the competent Authority.

Regardless of the type of procedure involved, wastes must be recovered or disposed of without danger to human health and without the use of procedures or methods that could damage the environment (Article 178, paragraph 2, and Article 214, paragraph 1).

A. *Ordinary Authorization Proceedings*

283. The prototype of the first kind of authorization (ordinary authorization) is represented by a *sole authorization for new waste disposal and recovery facilities* (Article 208 of Legislative Decree No. 152 of 2006). The name originates from the fact that said instrument not only authorizes the construction of the facility, but also authorizes its owner to carry out the activity. It is qualified as a 'sole' authorization because while Legislative Decree No. 22 of 1997 was in effect, these two factors were connected to two distinct authorizations (one approving the project for the facility and the other authorizing performance of the activity).

The authorization's principal characteristics can be summarized as follows:

(i) *Object*: an authorization is required to build and manage new waste recovery or disposal facilities, that is, the operations set forth in Annexes C and B to Part IV of Legislative Decree No. 152 of 2006, as well as for any substantial variations (variations during construction or operations that result in modifications subsequent to which the facilities no longer conform to the original authorization). Instead, a 'temporary deposit' does not require authorization; a temporary deposit is the grouping of wastes prior to collection in the place of production in accordance with the conditions established by Article 183, paragraph 1, clause *m*) of Legislative Decree No. 152 of 2006 (conditions which respect the composition of wastes, quantity and time of deposit).

(ii) *Contents*: the authorization must take at least the following factors into consideration:
- the types and quantities of wastes to be disposed of or recovered;

- the technical prerequisites, with particular reference to the compatibility of the site, the equipment used, the types of maximum quantities of waste and procedures for the monitoring, control and audit of the conformity of the facility to the approved project;
- the precautionary and safety measures to be taken;
- the location of the authorized facility;
- the method to be used for each type of operation;
- the provisions related to closure of the facility and the necessary work done afterwards;
- the financial guarantees required;
- the expiration date of the authorization;
- atmospheric emission limits for thermal waste treatment, even if accompanied by energy recovery.

Proceedings:

- Whoever intends to build and manage new waste recovery or disposal facilities or make substantial variations to existing facilities must file a special application with the competent administrative authority, usually the region.
- The application must be accompanied by the final project for the facility and the necessary technical documentation required by outstanding urban planning regulations, environmental protection law, and laws on workplace health and safety and public hygiene. If the facility is subject to an EIA, the application must also be accompanied by the notice of the project sent to the competent authority for the above purposes, and the procedure is suspended until a decision is made on the work's environmental compatibility.
- Within thirty days from receipt of the application, someone is appointed to be in charge of the proceeding and a special Conference of Services is convened, at which representatives from the competent regional offices, the ATO Authority and relevant local entities, as well as the petitioner participate (the Conference of Services is an institute of administrative simplification pursuant to the general law on administrative proceedings, Law No. 241 of 1990, which is referred to when it is necessary to evaluate various public interests in a sole proceeding, or when the consent of more than one public administration is required for the same activity).
- Within ninety days from being convened, the Conference of Services, using technical consultants such as the ARPA, examines the application (it evaluates the project, acquires and evaluates all elements relating to the project's compatibility with environmental and territorial needs, obtains an EIA when required by outstanding law, etc.) and, after completing its review, the Conference of Services transmits its conclusions to the regions along with the relative acts.
- On the basis of the conclusions of the Conference of Services in the case of a positive evaluation, the regional administration approves the project and authorizes the construction and management of the facility or, in the case of a negative evaluation, it rejects the petition with a reasoned opinion.

- The proceedings must be completed within 150 days from the date the application is filed, a term which can only be interrupted once upon the request for additional documentation by the subject in charge of the proceedings. In the event said term is not complied with, the Ministry of the Environment can intervene as a substitute power.

Duration: The authorization remains effective for ten years and is renewable; however, the requirements of the authorization can be modified prior to its expiration after at least five years have passed from its date of issue in the case of critical environmental conditions, in view of the development of the best available technologies.

Effect: The approval substitutes to all effects visas, opinions, authorizations and concessions from regional, provincial and municipal bodies; if necessary, it constitutes a variant to municipal instruments. In the latter case, the modification of the zoning plan deriving by law from the request for an authorization does not require a SEA (Legislative Decree No. 152 of 2006, Article 6, paragraph 12). The authorization also results in a declaration of public utility, urgency and work that cannot be postponed.

It is important to specify that some kinds of waste recovery or disposal facilities (such as those having a capacity of more than 10 tonnes per day) are subject to the rules on IPPC set forth in section III*bis,* Part II of Legislative Decree No. 152 of 2006, which requires an IEA (Article 213).

It is also necessary to consider the sector regime dedicated to some kinds of disposal or recovery activities that integrate the provisions of Legislative Decree No. 152 of 2006, such as those on landfills (Legislative Decree No. 36 of 2003) or waste incineration (Articles 237*bis* et seq. of the Environmental Code, included by means of Legislative Decree No. 46 of 2014).

In addition to the sole authorization, Legislative Decree No. 152 of 2006 contemplates other authorization procedures:

- renewal of the authorization to companies that have environmental certification (Article 209). At the time of renewal of the authorization for management of the facility, subjects that have EMAS or ISO 14001 certification or which operate in the context of the Ecolabel system can substitute the authorization with a self-certification given to the competent authority;
- authorization for research and experimentation facilities (Article 211). This applies to experimental disposal or recovery facilities realized on a non-profit basis, which generally have a capacity of less than 5 tons per day. The timeframe for the authorization procedure has been halved with respect to that established by Article 208, and the authorization remains effective for two years, which can be extended for a maximum term of four years.

B. Simplified Authorization Proceedings

284. Simplified authorization proceedings have particular practical significance. For specific waste disposal or recovery activities, it is sufficient to notify the province of the initiation of the activity.

It is only possible to use this procedure for activities involving non-hazardous waste disposal in the place where the wastes are generated (self-disposal), as well as for hazardous and non-hazardous waste recovery operations specified by the Ministry of the Environment in decrees establishing the type of wastes, the originating cycle, permissible treatment activities, emission values for the facilities and, in general, conditions to ensure that wastes are treated without danger to human health and without using procedures or methods that could damage the environment. At present, the ministry has only issued technical rules for the recovery of hazardous wastes (DM No. 269 of 17 November 2005, and DM No. 161 of 12 June 2002) and non-hazardous waste (DM 5 February 1998); therefore, notwithstanding the provisions of Legislative Decree No. 152 of 2006, the simplified procedure cannot be used for self-disposal operations.

Waste recovery activities using this simplified procedure can be initiated ninety days after a notice sent to the province, which must record the company in a special register.

The province is responsible for automatically verifying whether or not the petitioner has the prerequisites indicated in State technical norms. In the lack of these prerequisites, the province issues an ordinance setting forth the reasons for its decision that prohibits the initiation or continuation of the activity until the petitioner renders it compliant with outstanding law, within the deadline and in accordance with any requirements established by the public administration.

The notice must be renewed every five years or whenever there is a substantial modification of the treatment operations.

The construction of facilities that recover wastes in a manner that allows the simplified procedure to be used is, nevertheless, subject to national and Community law on air quality and atmospheric pollution from industrial facilities.

By means of Law No. 221 of 28 December 2015, a specific simplified procedure was introduced for aerobic composting facilities of biodegradable waste deriving from agricultural and nursery activities or from kitchens, cafeterias, markets, gardens or parks.

If the facility has a treatment capacity of less than 80 tons per year and is to be used exclusively to treat waste collected in the municipality where the above wastes are produced (as well as in neighbouring municipalities), it can be built and placed in operation by means of notice of the start of activity in accordance with the Consolidated Text of the laws and regulations on building, set forth in Presidential Decree No. 380 of 6 June 2001, after obtaining the opinion of the ARPA (*see* Article 214, paragraph 7*bis* of the Environmental Code for the details).

II. Registration in the National Register of Environmental Waste Managers

285. The Italian legal system requires anyone engaged in waste management to be registered in a special national Register (National Register of Environmental Waste Managers – *Albo nazionale gestori ambientali*). The register is maintained by the Ministry of the Environment and is divided into a national committee, whose office is located at the ministry, as well as regional sections established at the Chambers of Commerce of the regional capitals (the Register can be consulted via internet at the address <www.albogestoririfiuti.it>).

The following subjects must be registered in the register:

- companies engaged in non-hazardous waste collection and transportation;
- companies that collect and transport hazardous wastes;
- companies that remediate contaminated sites;
- companies that remediate asbestos contaminated goods;
- companies engaged in the commerce and trading of wastes without detaining said wastes.

Registration is required, according to simplified and more economic procedures, for the initial producers of non-hazardous wastes who engage in the collection and transportation of their own wastes as well as the initial producers of hazardous wastes who engage in collection and transportation activities of up to thirty kilos or thirty litres per day of their own hazardous wastes. The producer of the wastes is required to register when the collection and transportation activities are an integral and an accessory part of the company's activity from which the wastes are generated (such as companies engaged in demolitions). These cases of registration were introduced after Italy was condemned for violating Community law on wastes, which requires Member States to provide for the mandatory registration of subjects engaged in waste collection and transportation *on a professional basis* (ECJ, judgment 9 June 2005, in case C-270/03, *Commission of the European Communities v. Italian Republic*).

Simplified registration also regards companies that collect and transport wastes of electric and electronic equipment in accordance with Decree No. 65 of 8 March 2010 of the Minister of the Environment, together with the Ministers of Economic Development and Health, as well as special public companies, consortium of municipalities and management companies of public services pursuant to Legislative Decree No. 267 of 18 August 2000, for municipal waste management services for waste produced in such municipalities.

§5. Specific Instruments of 'Direct Regulation'

286. One of the objectives of waste legislation is to ensure an ongoing control of wastes, from the time they are generated through disposal or recovery. Legislative Decree No. 152 of 2006, in addition to the obligation to obtain authorization or to register with the register of waste managers, also requires subjects involved in waste management to annotate the loading and unloading of wastes in a waste register, and transportation of wastes must be accompanied by an identification form.

Specifically, the following subjects are required to maintain a loading and unloading register:

- anyone who performs waste collection and transportation on a professional basis;
- merchants and intermediaries (without detention) of wastes;
- companies and entities engaged in waste disposal and recovery;
- consortia created for the recovery and recycling of particular categories of wastes;
- initial producers of hazardous wastes;
- initial producers of non-hazardous wastes deriving from industrial and artisan activities, as well as from waste disposal or recovery or from water treatment.

Legislative Decree No. 152 of 2006 also contemplates the possibility of exoneration, for example farmers who have a sales volume of less than EUR 8,000 per year or entities or companies that produce non-hazardous wastes that do not have more than ten employees (Article 189, paragraph 3, and 190, paragraph 1).

It is necessary to record information on the qualitative and quantitative characteristics of wastes in the registers; the companies engaging in disposal and recovery activities must also record: (a) the origin and destination of wastes; (b) the loading and unloading dates and the means of transportation used; and (c) the treatment method utilized.

287. Annotations must be made in accordance with specific deadlines.

The same subjects must compile the loading and unloading register and must notify the Chamber of Commerce annually of the quantity and qualitative characteristics of the wastes generated by their activities by filling out a form known as a Single Environmental Statement Form – *Modello unico di dichiarazione ambientale.* The data which is processed in the waste registry, whose central office within ISPRA and outlying offices within ARPA (*Agenzie regionali di protezione dell'ambiente*), and is fundamental for the proper planning of waste management activities.

The identification forms that must accompany waste transportation are an integral part of the loading and unloading register (Article 193). The following must appear from the documentation: (a) the name and address of the producer and holder of the waste; (b) the origin, type and quantity of waste; (c) the receiving facility; (d) the date and route that the waste will travel; and (e) the name and address of the consignee.

The form is neither required for the transportation of municipal wastes, which is carried out by the public service manager, nor for occasional and sporadic transportation by producers of non-hazardous wastes that do not exceed the quantity of 30 kg or 30 l.

The forms, numbered and stamped by the Chamber of Commerce or by the Tax Authority, must be prepared in four copies that are signed by the producer (or holder) and countersigned by the shipper. One copy remains with the producer (or holder) and the other three are countersigned by the consignee: of these three copies, one remains with the consignee and two with the shipper, who must forward one copy, including by certified email, to the producer (or holder) of the waste (who will, therefore, have two copies of the document: one held at the time the waste is delivered to the shipper, and the other countersigned by the consignee of the waste).

The receipt of the fourth copy of the form, countersigned and dated when received by the consignee, releases the producer (or holder) from liability for episodes of unlawful waste management subsequent to the date the waste is delivered. If the copy of the form does not arrive within three months from the date the waste was delivered to the shipper, the holder must notify the province that it has not received the document (Article 188, paragraph 3, clause *b*). Obviously, the exoneration from liability does not include the case in which the holder participates in the crime of unlawful waste management committed by the shipper and consignee, and the holder is obliged to verify whether the final consignee of the waste has a suitable authorization for waste disposal or recovery.

By means of Legislative Decree No. 205 of 2010, the Italian legislature introduced a computerized waste tracking system System for Checking the Traceability of Waste (SISTRI) to manage hazardous special waste; the system was supposed to have substituted the documentary requirements described above. Such system was based on the use of two electronic devices: a black box (i.e., a transponder), to be mounted on the means used to transport waste to trace its movements, and a USB device equipped with electronic signature software, to be used to communicate data on waste.

SISTRI's goal was to prevent the illegal management of hazardous special wastes (the management of the information processes and flows contained in SISTRI was entrusted to the Environmental Protection Unit of the Carabinieri).

Problems arose, however, with the implementation and functioning of such system (over time its use was limited and later suspended).

SISTRI was abolished by Article 6 of Law Decree No. 135 of 14 December 2018.

A national Electronic Register for the traceability of wastes, which is managed directly by MATTM, was created to substitute SISTRI. Entities and companies that engage in waste treatment, producers of hazardous wastes and the entities and companies that collect or transport hazardous wastes on a professional basis or who operate as merchants and intermediaries of hazardous wastes, consortia established for the recovery and recycling of particular kinds of waste, as well as municipalities with reference to non-hazardous wastes, are all required to enrol with this register.

The organization and functioning of the national Electronic Register, the registration procedure for the subjects required to register as well as anyone else who wishes to voluntarily enrol, as well as the obligations incumbent on them, according to criteria of graduality in view of the progressive participation of all operators, are established by the Minister of the Environment together with the Minister for Economic Affairs and Finance, having heard the Minister for Economic Development, the Minister for Public Administration and the Minister of Infrastructures and Transportation, as well as the Minister of the Defence for the aspects within its competence. The regulations should also include sanctions for failure to enrol.

The traceability of wastes is guaranteed through all of the obligations described above until the register is fully operative.

§6. Control System

288. The Italian legal system provides for periodic controls at facilities and companies that dispose of or recover wastes, even if they were authorized by a simplified procedure. The controls also regard waste collection and transportation, especially of hazardous wastes, in order to verify their origin and destination.

The provinces are primarily responsible for controlling all waste management, trading and commerce of wastes and for verifying any violation of the laws on wastes. The provinces have created their own local administrative police organs to carry out their functions, and they use specialized public organisms such as the ARPA for technical activities (such as sampling and laboratory testing). ARPA's role is especially intense with respect to facilities that are subject to an IEA (Article 29*decies* of Legislative Decree No. 152 of 2006).

Anyone entrusted with supervisory functions is authorized to perform inspections, control and sampling in facilities or companies that generate wastes or that engage in waste management. Industrial secret cannot be invoked to prevent controls, and the persons entrusted with the control are, in turn, obliged to respect confidentiality.

The provinces do not have exclusive competence for controls aimed at verifying administrative and criminal violations regarding wastes, which are also performed by other administrative and judicial police organs, some of which are institutionally aimed at combating environmental crimes, such as the branch of the military police entrusted with environmental protection (*Comando carabinieri tutela ambientale*) or the State Forestry Corps (*see* Article 195, paragraph 5).

With respect to waste disposal and recovery facilities, especially large facilities, the manager is responsible for performing self-controls, subject to the provisions of section III*bis*, Part II of Legislative Decree No. 152 of 2006. In the case of landfills, the manager must also annex a surveillance and monitoring plan to the application for authorization, which must indicate all of the measures required to prevent accident risks caused by the functioning of the landfill and to limit their consequences.

Further, the manager must file with the authority that authorized the facility a report at least once each year on the types and quantities of wastes disposed of, the results of the surveillance programme and the controls performed (Articles 8 and 10 of Legislative Decree No. 36 of 2003).

§7. Administrative and Criminal Sanctions

289. Article 208, paragraph 13, of Legislative Decree No. 152 of 2006 is significant with respect to providing a regime of sanctions in the sector of waste management. In the case of non-compliance with the requirements specified in the authorization, the granting authority can provide as follows, depending on the gravity of the offence:

- issue a warning, assigning a deadline within which the breach must be cured;
- issue a warning, with the contemporaneous suspension of the authorized activity for a specific period of time in situations of danger to health or the environment;

– revoke the authorization and close of the facility, in the case of continued non-compliance with the requirements imposed by the warning or repeat violations that result in danger or damage to health or the environment.

290. In accordance with Article 192, the mayor's ordinance has the nature of a sanction for violation of the prohibition against abandonment, uncontrolled deposits or the dumping of wastes in surface and underground water.

In these cases, in addition to administrative and criminal sanctions, the polluter is required to remove the wastes, properly dispose of or recover them, and restore the status of the affected sites. The mayor can issue an ordinance indicating the operations that are necessary for such purpose and the deadline for compliance, after which enforcement proceedings are initiated against the responsible subjects, including recovery of any amounts that had to be advanced.

An ordinance can also be issued against the owner of the area (or owner of another real property right), but only in cases of malicious intent or negligence. Determining the grave negligence of the owner of an area in which third parties abandon wastes is not a simple operation. According to case law, the property owner's duty of diligence does not extend to the point of requiring constant vigilance, exercised night and day, to impede third parties from invading the area (Council of State, section V, judgment No. 935 of 8 March 2005), whereas prolonged inertia or the failure to adopt simple measures to impede access to the area are considered to be significant factors (T.A.R. Campania, Naples, judgment No. 9795 of 2008; T.A.R. Puglia, Lecce judgment No. 587 of 2008).

In any case, Article 192 requires the mayor to initiate an adversarial process against the recipient of an order of forced removal, by providing notice of the proceedings.

It should be noted that mayors, especially in cases of serious situations of waste abandonment that can endanger public hygiene or safety, due to either the amount of waste or the hazardous nature of the abandoned material (such as asbestos), often use their contingent and urgent power to issue orders provided by other laws (such as Articles 50 and 54 of Legislative Decree No. 267 of 2000 entitled *Uniform text of the legal structure of local entities* and Article 32 of Law No. 833 of 1978, entitled *Creation of the National Health Service*).

Whoever abandons or deposits wastes in an uncontrolled manner or who dumps wastes in surface or underground water must also pay an administrative fine ranging from EUR 105 to EUR 620 (from EUR 25 to EUR 150 for abandoning non-hazardous and non-cumbersome wastes on the ground). If the same behaviour refers to a legal entity, the owner of the company or manager of the entity is subject to criminal sanctions (Article 256, paragraph 2), and whoever is non-compliant with a mayor's ordinance of removal is subject to detention for up to one year (the conditional suspension of the penalty can be subordinate on compliance with the obligation).

291. The following behaviour is also punished by administrative sanction:

– non-compliance with notice requirements, maintaining the loading and unloading register, and filling out forms (Article 258);

- the temporary deposit at the production site of a modest amount of medical wastes (200 L or an equivalent quantity), in violation of the provisions of DPR No. 254 of 2003 (from EUR 2,600 to EUR 15,500);
- the demolition of motor vehicles without delivering the licence plates, registration certificate and ownership certificate to the Public Motor Vehicle Registry and annotating such delivery in its vehicle entry and exit log (from EUR 260 to EUR 1,550);
- the holder's failure to deliver used oils or polyethylene waste products to the respective Consortia (from EUR 260 to EUR 1,550);
- the failure of anyone obliged to do so to participate in the Consortia set forth in Articles 233–236 (from EUR 8,000 to EUR 45,000);
- violation of the provisions on the management of packaging, according to what is set forth in Article 261.

292. Law No. 221 of 2015 introduced specific sanctions for whoever abandons small-sized waste or waste of products produced by smoking (Article 255, paragraph 1*bis*).

293. The missing or late filing of the MUD, the missing or incomplete maintenance of the loading and unloading register, the transportation of waste without a waste identification form or with an incomplete or inaccurate waste identification form is punished by an administrative fine (Article 258); a criminal sanction is applied if the transportation without a waste identification form (or with an incomplete or inaccurate waste identification form) regards hazardous waste, as well as in cases of certificates of waste analysis containing false indications of the nature, composition and chemical-physical characteristics of the waste or transportation with a false certificate. The penalties are decreased if the waste flow can nevertheless be reconstructed using the documentation held by the waste holder or manager.

Once the National Electronic Register becomes fully operative, the administrative fines established by a regulation of MATTM will be applied.

294. The panorama of crimes relating to wastes is quite articulated and it is often difficult to determine the reciprocal boundaries between different types of crime.

Legislative Decree No. 152 of 2006 punishes whoever engages in the collection, transportation, recovery, disposal, trade and brokerage of wastes without the mandatory authorization, registration or notice, by differentiated penalties according to whether the behaviour respects hazardous or non-hazardous wastes (Article 256, paragraph 1). The classification of the waste not only effects the amount of the sanction, but also the possibility, in the case of non-hazardous wastes, of being able to resort to a cash settlement, that is, to extinguish the offence by the payment of an amount of money equal to one-half of the maximum fine (Article 162*bis* of the Italian Criminal Code).

The same treatment is provided for owners of companies and managers of entities that abandon or deposit wastes in an uncontrolled manner or who place them in surface or underground waters (there is an administrative sanction when an individual is involved), and for anyone engaging in the unauthorized mixing of wastes (Article 256, paragraphs 2 and 5).

Article 256, paragraph 3 establishes more serious penalties for the unauthorized creation of a landfill (in this case as well with a more severe sanction when the offence involves hazardous wastes); case law has identified some factors used to distinguish such behaviour from the simple abandonment or uncontrolled deposit of wastes. More specifically, a landfill is considered to be abusive when: (a) a minimum period of time has passed from the deposit of the materials (according to the definition of landfill set forth in Legislative Decree No. 36 of 2003); (b) an area is used as a receptacle for wastes, with the construction of works and the use of equipment; (c) the sites are degraded; and (d) the abandonment of materials is definitive.

295. Again with respect to landfills, Article 16 of Legislative Decree No. 36 of 2003 punishes non-compliance with the procedures for admitting wastes to landfills, mixing wastes, and dumping wastes for which the landfill is inappropriate (e.g., hazardous wastes placed in landfills for inert wastes). Special crimes regarding incineration are also provided by Article 261*bis* of the Environmental Code.

Article 261*bis* of the Environmental Code provides and punishes crimes related to the illegal combustion of waste.

Another case of a crime (and, therefore, more serious than an offence punished by a fine) is organized activity for the illicit trafficking of wastes (previously set forth in Article 260 of Legislative Decree No. 152 of 2006 and currently in Article 452*quaterdecies* of the Italian Criminal Code). Whoever, in order to obtain unjust profit using various operations and continuous, organized activities and means, transfers, receives, transports, exports, imports or in any event abusively manages significant quantities of waste is punished by detention ranging from one to six years, increased to three to eight years in the case of radioactive wastes. This crime is almost always committed together with the crime of criminal conspiracy, including allegations of mafia-related activity (Articles 416 and 416*bis* of the Italian Criminal Code); by means of Law No. 136 of 13 August 2010 ('Extraordinary Anti-Mafia Plan, as well as delegation of powers to the Government for anti-mafia laws'), competence for investigations relating to such crime was attributed to the Anti-Mafia District Management (a department within the public prosecutor's office specialized in pursuing mafia-related crimes).

§8. Economic Instruments

296. The principal economic instrument regarding wastes regards the management of municipal (and assimilated) wastes.

With reference to such service, there was an overlap over time of different taxes and tariffs due to spotty application throughout Italy. Legislative Decree No. 507 of 1993 established an 'Annual Tax on Solid Municipal Waste' (TARSU); Legislative Decree No. 22 of 1997 introduced the 'Environmental Hygiene Tariff' (Article 49, TIA1), whose nature as a tax was confirmed on various occasions, (Constitutional Court, judgment No. 238 of 2009; among many, *see* Court of Cassation, judgment

No. 3756 of 9 March 2012; Court of Cassation, section I, judgment No. 2320 of 17 February 2012). Article 238 of Legislative Decree No. 152 of 2006 regulates the tariff for municipal waste management (later referred to as the 'Integrated Environmental Tariff', TIA2), whose non-tax nature has been confirmed (Article 14, paragraph 33 of Law Decree No. 78 of 31 May 2010, converted by Law No. 122 of 30 July 2012, which is an interpretative law). Starting from 1 January 2013, the tariff was replaced by TARES, i.e., the municipal tax on waste and services, introduced by Article 14 of Law Decree No. 201 of 6 December 2011, converted with modifications in Law No. 214 of 22 December 2011 (the so-called Save Italy law).

TARI, the 'waste tax', is currently applied, together with TASI, which is the component related to services of the IUC (single municipal tax; the other component is IMU, which is a property tax). TARI is governed by Article 1, paragraphs 641 through 668, 704 and 705 of Law No. 147 of 27 December 2013. The prerequisite for TARI is the possession or holding for any reason of premises or open areas, regardless of how they are used, that are capable of producing municipal waste. In accordance with paragraph 650, TARI is paid based on a tariff that is proportional to the calendar year coinciding with an autonomous tax obligation. In calculating the tariff on the basis of the tax, the Municipality can alternatively (*a*) consider the criteria determined by regulation set forth in *D.P.R. No. 158 of 27 April 1999 (the method normalized by TIA1, see paragraph 651);* (b) calculate the tariff in proportion to the average ordinary quantity and quality of waste produced per unit of surface area, in relation to the uses and types of activity performed as well as the cost of the waste service, in accordance to what is provided by paragraph 652.[3] In any case, paragraph 654 provides that the investment costs and costs to operate the service must be completely covered, including the costs set forth in Article 15 of Legislative Decree No. 36 of 13 January 2003 (i.e., the costs to dispose of waste in landfills), except for the costs related to the disposal of special waste, which the relative producers must provide for directly at their expense, demonstrating that such waste was treated in conformity with outstanding law. Starting from 2016, the Municipality must also consider standard requirements in calculating the costs.

Law No. 147 of 2013 provides that 'the municipalities that have created precise measurement systems for the quantity of waste delivered to the public service can, by means of a regulation pursuant to Article 52 of Legislative Decree No. 446 of 1997, apply a tariff having the nature of a fee, in lieu of TARI' (Article 1, paragraph 668).

297. The principal features of the integrated waste management service are briefly described below:

- similar to what occurs with respect to water service, (for which reference is made to the chapter on water resource management), municipal waste management is organized based on territorial areas or basins called ATO;
- a government service authority is created as a legal entity for each ATO and local entities are required to participate in it;

3. Criteria provided for TIA2, by Art. 238, para. 2 of the Environmental Code.

- the government service authority organizes the service and determines the form of management; entrusting management and the related control, and approval of the ATO plan (Article 3*bis* of Law Decree No. 138 of 13 August 2011);
- the integrated waste management service includes: (a) the establishment, management and implementation of the entire service, inclusive of managing and constructing the facilities; and (b) the collection, differentiated collection, trading and complete disposal of all municipal and assimilated wastes produced within the ATO. The service must be organized in a way that guarantees the self-sufficiency of waste disposal for each ATO and the presence of a complex technological facility, inclusive of a landfill.

An important novelty is represented by attributing a national regulatory authority with functions for the regulation and control of the waste cycle, including differentiated, municipal and assimilated waste.

The legislative choice (Law No. 205 of 2017 – Budget Law 2018) fell on the Authority for electricity, gas and the water system, an independent administrative authority established by Law No. 481 of 1995 for the electricity and gas sectors, which has been given the new name of the Regulatory Authority for Energy Networks and the Environment (ARERA).

In accordance with law, ARERA is responsible for ensuring accessibility, usability and widespread homogenity throughout the national territory as well as adequate quality levels in conditions of efficiency and cost-effectiveness of management, harmonizing economic and financial objectives with general social and environmental objectives and the appropriate use of resources, as well as for ensuring that the infrastructure is adjusted to the goals imposed by European legislation, thus overcoming the infringement proceedings that have already been initiated, with consequent economic benefits for the local authorities affected by such procedures (*see* section 9 *infra* on the details of the attributed functions).

Another important tax on wastes is the special tax for leaving solid wastes in a landfill, regulated by Law No. 549 of 28 December 1995 (and by integrating regional laws). This tax, created in order to favour the decrease of waste production and the recovery of raw materials and energy from wastes, is applied to the manager of the landfill, who has an obligation of recourse against anyone delivering wastes.

Further, whoever operates, even if not on an exclusive basis, an abusive landfill activity and anyone who abandons, unloads or engages in the uncontrolled deposit of wastes is also subject to this tax (in addition to the sanctions set forth in section 7 and an additional administrative sanction equivalent to three times the tax).

The Framework Directive introduces in a general manner the policy tool of extended producer responsibility.

Premise No. 27 of Directive 2008/98/EC establishes that 'the introduction of extended producer responsibility (…) is one of the means to support the design and production of goods which take into full account and facilitate the efficient use of resources during their whole life cycle, including their repair, reuse, disassembly and recycling without compromising the free circulation of goods on the internal market'.

Article 8 of the Directive deals with extended producer responsibility, that prefigures measures that 'may include an acceptance of returned products and of the waste that remains after those products have been used, as well as the subsequent management of the waste and financial responsibility for such activities. These measures may include the obligation to provide publicly available information as to the extent to which the product is reusable and recyclable'.

The sectoral legislation is based on extended producer responsibility with respect to waste, which regards, for example, waste from electrical and electronic equipment (RAEE, Directive 2012/19/EU), waste from accumulators (2006/66/EC) and end-of-life vehicles (2000/53/EC).

Article 183 of the Environmental Code defines, in clause *g*), the producer of the product as 'any individual or legal entity that professionally develops, manufactures, transforms, processes, sells or imports products', while extended producer responsibility is set forth in a general manner in Article 178-*bis*.

Specifically, it is established that:

> in order to reinforce prevention and facilitate the efficient use of resources during the entire life cycle, including the phases of reuse, recycling and recovery of waste, avoiding compromising the free circulation of goods in the market, can be adopted, upon consultation of the interested parties, by one or more decrees of the Minister of the Environment having a regulatory nature, having heard the unified Conference set forth in Article 8 of Legislative Decree No. 281 of 28 August 1997, the manner and criteria for introducing extended producer responsibility understood as any individual or legal entity that professionally develops, manufactures, transforms, processes, sells or imports products, in the organization of the waste management system and acceptance of returned products and waste that remains after their use. For the same purposes, one or more decrees of the Minister of the Environment, together with the Ministry of Economic Development, can establish the manner and criteria for:
>
> a) waste management and the related financial responsibility of producers of the product. The decrees set forth in this clause shall be approved together with the Ministry for the Economy and Finance;
> b) the publication of information related to the extent that the product is reusable and recyclable;
> c) the design of products aimed at reducing their environmental impact;
> d) the design of products aimed at reducing or eliminating waste during production and the subsequent use of the products, ensuring that the recovery and disposal of products that have become waste is done in compliance with the criteria set forth in Articles 177 and 179;
> e) is aimed at enhancing and encouraging development, production and the marketing of products suitable for multiple use, that are technically long-lasting and which, after they become waste, are suitable for adequate and secure recovery and disposal compatible with the environment.

In accordance with the third paragraph 'the decrees set forth in paragraph 1 can also provide that waste management costs are partially or entirely sustained by the producer of the product that is the cause of the waste. If the producer of the product participates in part, the product's distributer shall be responsible for the difference until such costs have been entirely covered'.

Paragraph 2 specifies that 'The extended producer responsibility of the product is applicable subject to responsibility for waste management in accordance with Article 188, paragraph 1, and without prejudice to outstanding legislation on flows of waste and specific products'.

There are other provisions of Legislative Decree No. 152 of 2006 that regard extended producer responsibility:

- Article 180, paragraph 2, on the reuse of products.
- Article 206*ter*, paragraph 1, on 'Agreements and program contracts to provide incentives for the purchase of products deriving from post-consumer materials or from recovering scrap and materials originating from the disassembly of complex products'.
- Article 216*ter* on the content of the three-year report of MATTM to the European Commission on implementation of the framework directive on waste.

The principle of shared responsibility has guided the regime for packing material consortium (CONAI and production chain consortium, Articles 223 and 224 of the Environmental Code) and that of the consortium related to specific categories of waste (Articles 233 and 237 of the Environmental Code). The same holds true for collective management systems for specific categories of waste, regulated by sectoral legislation. The reference is to systems regulated by Article 10 of Legislative Decree No. 49 of 14 March 2014 on RAEE: these consortia, whose by-laws were approved by MATTM and which 'have autonomous legal personality of private law, are non-profit and operate under the supervision of the Ministry of the Environment and the Ministry of Economic Development, which shall approve standard bylaws within 6 months from the entry into force of this Legislative Decree'. Collective systems are also provided in the sector of batteries, accumulators and the relative waste.

§9. Summary Framework of Competence

298. Different from what occurs with respect to air pollution and water pollution control, Part IV of Legislative Decree No. 152 of 2006 contains some provisions that specify the principal responsibilities of the different levels of government (Articles 195 through 198).

I. The State

299. Article 195 of cited Legislative Decree No. 152 provides a long list of the duties attributed to the State that refer to an essential function of orientation and coordination for the sector. Such function is carried out, among others, in accordance with paragraph 1 of Article 195 (i) by:

- defining the general criteria and methodology for integrated waste management, the preparation of sector plans and the organization and implementation of differentiated collection of municipal waste;
- determining the guidelines on the minimum content of authorizations and for energy recovery activities;
- adopting a national communication and environmental awareness plan;
- identifying, in compliance with the constitutional attributes of the regions, recovery and disposal facilities of primary national interest to be built to modernize and develop the country;
- determining the quality objectives of waste management services;
- determining the general criteria, differentiated for municipal wastes and for special wastes, in order to prepare regional plans, with specific reference to determining guidelines, together with the unified conference, for identifying ATO, to be created in accordance with Article 200, and to coordinate such plans.

Paragraph 2 of Article 195 grants the State further powers, including:

- indicating the criteria and manner of adoption, in accordance with principles of unity, completeness and coordination, of technical rules for waste management, hazardous waste and specific types of waste;
- determining the qualitative and quantitative criteria for the assimilation of special wastes and municipal waste, for purposes of collection and disposal;
- determining the requirements and technical resources and financial expertise needed for waste management activities, including the general criteria for determining financial guarantees on behalf of the regions.

Article 206*bis* of Legislative Decree No. 152 of 2006 – as modified most recently by Law No. 221 of 28 December 2015, which approved 'Environmental provisions to promote green economy measures and to contain the excessive use of natural resources' (the so-called 'Related Environmental Law') – also attributes the Ministry of the Environment, which exercises them through ISPRA, with supervisory and monitoring functions on waste management. More specifically, the ministry is responsible for:

- supervising the management of waste, packaging materials and packaging waste;
- providing for the permanent preparation and updating of criteria and specific action objectives, as well as for the definition and permanent updating of a reference framework on waste prevention and waste management, including through the preparation of guidelines on waste management methods to improve their effectiveness, efficiency and quality, to promote the spread of good practices and the best available technologies for prevention and differentiated waste collection;
- verifying the quality levels of the services provided;

- preparing the parameters to identify standard costs and define a fair and transparent tariff system based on the principle of the EU's legal system that 'the polluter pays' and the full coverage of investment and running costs;
- preparing one or more standard draft service contracts as set forth in Article 203;
- verifying whether the objectives established by the EU on waste have been achieved and determining compliance with extended producer responsibility by producers and importers of goods.

By means of Article 35 of Law Decree No. 133 of 12 September 2014, as converted into Law No. 164 of 11 November 2014, the State has been attributed, in particular the President of the Council of Ministers, with new functions aimed at identifying infrastructures and strategic facilities of major national interest.

As noted, Law No. 205 of 2017 attributed ARERA with regulatory and control functions for the waste cycle, including differentiated, municipal and assimilated waste, specifically with respect to:

(a) issuing guidelines on the separation of accounting and administrative management, the assessment of the costs of the individual services, including for purposes of the proper breakdown by functions, geographic area and categories of users, and the determination of measurement indexes of the efficiency and cost-effectiveness of management in view of the services provided;
(b) determining the quality levels for the services, after hearing the regions, operators and consumer associations, as well as supervising the manner in which services are provided;
(c) spreading knowledge and transparency of the conditions in which services are performed for the users' benefit;
(d) protecting users' rights, including through the assessment of claims, requests and reports made by users and consumers, whether individually or jointly;
(e) determining standard schemes of service contracts set forth in Article 203 of Legislative Decree No. 152 of 3 April 2006;
(f) preparing and updating the tariff method to determine the fees for the integrated waste service and the individual services which constitute the management activity in order to cover operating and investment costs, including the remuneration of capital, based on the evaluation of efficient costs and the principle the polluter pays;
(g) establishing criteria to determine the tarriffs for access to waste treatment plants;
(h) approving the determined tariffs, in accordance with outstanding law, by the optimal territorial governance body for the integrated service and by the operators of the treatment plants;
(i) controlling the proper preparation of the area plan, making observations and findings;
(l) formulating proposals related to the activities included in the integrated waste management system to be subject to a concession or authorization regime in relation to market competition conditions;
(m) formulating proposals for a review of the existing regime, as well as reporting cases of grave non-compliance and improper implementation;
(n) preparing an annual report to Parliament on the activity performed.

II. The Regions

300. The duties attributed to the regions are expressly provided for and listed in Article 196 of Legislative Decree No. 152 of 2006. They are orientation and coordination functions with respect to local entities, programming functions and administrative activity functions.

The orientation and coordination functions include (i) the regulation of waste management activities, including differentiated collection of municipal waste, even if hazardous, (ii) incentives to reduce waste production and to recover waste and (iii) the promotion of integrated waste management.

The programming functions include the preparation, adoption and updating of regional waste management plans, and determining the boundaries of the ATO for the management of municipal and assimilated waste.

Further, administrative functions include authorization for waste disposal and recovery operations, even for hazardous waste, and the approval of projects for new waste management facilities, including hazardous waste, as well as the authorization to modify existing facilities.

Article 196 expressly provides that the regions can also use ARPA to carry out such functions.

III. The Provinces

301. In accordance with Article 197 of Legislative Decree No. 152 of 2006, the provinces are responsible in general for administrative functions regarding the planning and organization of waste disposal and recovery at a provincial level.

Specifically, the duties of the provinces include the control and verification of reclamation and management activities, intermediation and the trading of waste as well as determining the areas that are suitable for the location of waste disposal facilities as well as areas that are not suitable for the location of waste recovery and disposal facilities.

The provinces can also use public organisms with specific technical skills, including ARPA, to exercise their functions.

Article 1, paragraphs 51 through 100, of Law No. 56 of 7 April 2014 – which contains a series of provisions on metropolitan cities, provinces and on the unions and mergers of municipalities in order to adjust their legal systems while waiting for the reform of Title V of Part II of the Constitution to principles of subsidiarity, differentiation and adequacy – redefined the organization and duties of the provinces, recognizing environmental protection and enhancement functions to such entities (paragraph 85).

IV. The Municipalities

302. The municipalities concur in the management of municipal and assimilated wastes in the context of the activities performed at the level of the ATO.

Further, the municipalities must adopt specific regulations in order to:

- ensure hygienic-sanitary protection during all phases of municipal waste management;
- specify procedures for the municipal waste collection and transportation service;
- specify procedures for the delivery, differentiated collection and transportation of municipal and assimilated wastes in order to guarantee the separate management of different kinds of wastes and promote their recovery;
- guarantee the separate and adequate management of hazardous municipal wastes and wastes originating from exhumation and disinterment;
- enhance forms of delivery, collection and transportation of primary packaging wastes in collaboration with other commercial sectors, establishing minimum standards that must be complied with;
- determine the procedures for weighing municipal wastes prior to sending them to recovery and disposal;
- assimilate, by quality and quantity, special non-hazardous wastes to municipal wastes, in accordance with the criteria prepared by the State.

V. The ATO Authority

303. The ATO Authority is the governmental body for integrated waste management in which all of the local authorities located within the ATO must participate (*see* section 8 *supra* for a review of its functions).

VI. The ISPRA and the ARPA

304. ISPRA and the ARPA are the principal technical-scientific consulting bodies, respectively of the State and regions and the other local entities, even with regard to wastes. They establish the national environmental protection system, regulated by Law No. 132 of 28 June 2016 (to which reference is made for greater details).

§10. Conclusions

305. At the beginning of this chapter it was noted that Italian law is characterized by periodic attempts to 'escape waste' by the approval of various kinds and levels of legislation, that have excluded some kinds of reusable by-products from the group of laws regulating wastes. The ECJ has found Italy non-compliant due to this and other behaviour found to conflict with Community law (*see*, for example, with respect to the ratification and implementation of regulations on landfills, ECJ, judgment 26 April 2007 in case C-135/05, and judgment 10 April 2008 in case C-442/06).

The history of the definition of 'waste', tied to the legislative codification of the category of 'by-product', demonstrates how necessary it is in this sector to find a point of equilibrium between private economic initiative and a rigorous environmental protection policy; this point of equilibrium must be adjusted to different needs and the current times, which explains the rigid attitude adopted by Italian law when it was still necessary to create an 'environmental conscience' among producers.

Another factor that favours evasion of the rules is the high level of complexity that the panorama of legal sources on wastes has reached: there is much legislation, at diverse levels and different in nature, distributed among general laws (Legislative Decree No. 152/06, Part IV) and sector regulations (e.g., regulations on landfills, medical wastes, mining wastes, RAEE, used oils, batteries, vehicles no longer in use and wastes from ports). This is not just an Italian phenomenon, but reproduces the EU's legal framework, which, for the first time since 1975, the new Framework Directive (implemented by Legislative Decree No. 205 of 2010 in the Italian legal system) has attempted to simplify.

Passing from the norms to their actual implementation, there is significant divergence in Italy among the various areas of the country (in particular, between northern and southern Italy), with respect to planning, organizing and managing the municipal waste collection, transportation, disposal and recovery service.

There is a higher percentage of differentiated collection in northern Italy, and over time the quantity of wastes sent to landfills has diminished, to the advantage of other kinds of waste treatment.

The scene is different moving downwards towards southern Italy. There are environmental emergencies in more than one region (e.g., Lazio, Puglia, Campania and Calabria), that have compelled the State government to take extraordinary measures (using recourse to Law No. 225 of 1992 on civil protection), appointing a government Commissioner with special powers in each region (even in derogation of outstanding law, but without prejudice to constitutional principles and Community law), who exercises many of the powers ordinarily attributed to the regions and local entities.

Waste management, in particular municipal waste, is still undergoing organizational difficulties, the lack of competition and infrastructures that are inadequate with respect to the objectives imposed by outstanding law, to the extent that there have been calls to attribute regulatory functions for the sector to an independent administrative authority (as is already the case for water services).

Chapter 5. Reclamation of Polluted Sites

by *Antonio Borzì*

§1. Principal Sources of National Law

306. Until the mid-1980s, the term 'reclamation' in legal language was associated almost exclusively with the reclamation of wetlands or land with a poor capacity to retain water, in order to render them suitable for human settlements, whether residential areas or manufacturing facilities, with the exception of the legal regime on clearing landmines and explosives (Legislative Decree Luogotenenziale No. 320 of 12 April 1946, which is still in effect). With the law on environmental damage (Article 18 of Law No. 349 of 1986, the Italian legislator's preference emerged for restoration of the status of contaminated sites with respect to the payment of an equivalent monetary amount, but Article 5 of Law No. 441 of 29 October 1987 (*Reconversion into law, with modifications, of Law-Decree No. 361 of 31 August 1987, containing urgent measures for waste disposal*) is the first that associates 'reclamation' with the removal of wastes and polluting substances from the soil, subsoil and underground waters.

307. Another decade passed before there was an organic reclamation regime for contaminated sites when Legislative Decree No. 22 of 5 February 1997 was promulgated, since Article 5, *supra* of the 1987 law was limited to attributing the regions with the power to approve reclamation plans for contaminated resources, with the provision that the consequent costs would be borne by the State (through the creation of a special environmental protection fund). DM 16 May 1989 was issued to implement Law No. 441 of 1987, containing the criteria and guidelines that the regions should follow to prepare the reclamation plans, as well as DM 30 December 1989, on the procedures for State financing of reclamation works.

308. In the meantime, the introduction of the term 'reclamation' in Italian environmental law was consolidated by Law No. 257 of 27 March 1992 (*Norms on elimination of the use of asbestos*). The law qualifies an object containing asbestos as a special and toxic-harmful waste (currently the term 'hazardous' is used) when it has lost its intended use and might lose fibres in the environment (Article 2, paragraph 1, clause *c*; Article 12, paragraph 6), and it regulates *decontamination and reclamation measures for asbestos contaminated areas* (Article 1, paragraph 1).

In this case, reclamation is linked to the presence of a specific type of waste, asbestos and most likely this is the reason why in 1997 norms on the reclamation of contaminated sites were included in the 'Ronchi' decree that reformed the general waste management regime.

Some legal scholars treated this choice as unconstitutional: in their opinion, the norms included in Legislative Decree No. 22 of 1997 (Article 17) delineated an organic regime for an entirely autonomous phenomenon with respect to waste management, beyond the power granted to the government by the relative enabling law, Law No. 146 of 1994 (which led to Legislative Decree No. 22 of 1997), above all, in consideration of the strong impact of the new norms on the owners of a contaminated sited. Effectively, the 'reclamation' contemplated by the Ronchi decree is a concept precisely identified by legal prerequisites, procedures, obligations and liabilities that has almost nothing in common, except for the name, with the interventions evoked by Law No. 441 of 1987 and those regulated by Law No. 257 of 1992.

309. Specifically, the prerequisites and objectives of reclamation, as governed by Legislative Decree No. 22 of 1997, and by the implementing regulation DM No. 471 of 25 October 1999 (*Regulation containing criteria, procedures and terms for security measures, reclamation and environmental cleanup of contaminated sites, in accordance with Article 17 of Legislative Decree No. 22 of 5 February 1997*), can be summarized as follows:

- the *prerequisite* for reclamation is when limit values for specific concentrations of pollutants in the soil or subsoil or underground waters are exceeded (or when there is the concrete and current danger that they will be exceeded). The reclamation obligation, therefore, relates to the rigid application of criteria indicated in a table (the limits are specified by DM No. 471 of 1999 and are differentiated on the basis of whether the site is used for manufacturing or residential purposes);
- at the same time, the *objective* of reclamation is to restore the site to contamination levels that are lower than the legal limit values. Prior to reclamation, which can be complex and often requires a lengthy period of time, *emergency security measures (MISE)* must be taken, aimed at impeding the propagation of pollutants in the soil or the worsening of the resource's impairment.

310. Legislative Decree No. 152 of 3 April 2006 significantly modified the reclamation regime in terms of the prerequisites and objectives of intervention, liability and the hierarchical structure of competence of the different levels of government. Two elements remain, however, which characterized its origin: (1) the norms on reclamation are contained in Part IV of Legislative Decree No. 152 of 2006, which also regulates waste management; (2) the reclamation regime is linked to the environmental damage regime, above all, after implementation of Directive 2004/35/EC.

§2. Objective Scope of Application and Principal Features of the Regime

I. The Relationship between the Reclamation Regime and the Waste Regime

311. The contents of the norms on reclamation are effectively summarized in the first paragraph of Article 239: section V of Part IV of Legislative Decree No. 152 of 2006:

regulates environmental reclamation and cleanup actions of contaminated sites and defines the procedures, criteria and manner in which the necessary operations to eliminate the sources of pollution are carried out, or in any event to reduce the concentrations of polluting substances, in compliance with Community principles and norms, with particular reference to the principle the polluter pays.

Paragraph 2 of said article delineates the applicative scope of the reclamation regime with respect to other laws in the sector (*see* section 1 *supra* on the problematic relationship with the rules on environmental damage). In particular, the provisions on reclamation do not apply:

(a) to the abandonment of waste;
(b) to reclamation activities provided by special laws, except within the limits of what is expressly stated therein or whatever remains unregulated.

In the case in point (a), the reclamation procedure can only be initiated when, subsequent to the removal of waste from a site, the presence of pollutants that exceed the legal threshold is confirmed. In other words, it is necessary first of all to remove abandoned waste, and only subsequently verify whether the soil, subsoil and underground waters are so degraded that they must be reclaimed. The reasoning is that the object of reclamation is not the waste itself, but rather the environmental resources (soil, subsoil and waters) that came in contact with waste. It is not always possible, however, to distinguish these two phases: waste removal (Article 192, Legislative Decree No. 152 of 2006) and reclamation, in particular, when the abandoned waste has lost its autonomous consistency with respect to the soil, for example, because liquid waste was poured, or because powdered waste was abandoned which mixed with the soil. This position was confirmed by the new Waste Framework Directive 2008/98/EC, which excludes from the category of waste *land (in situ), including non excavated contaminated soil and buildings permanently connected to the land* (Article 2, paragraph 1, clause *b*).

The case in point (b) is a provision originating from the regime in effect prior to Legislative Decree No. 152 of 2006, which provided for a specific type of reclamation as part of the regime regulating water pollution control (Article 58 of Legislative Decree No. 152 of 1999).

II. Attenuation of the Criteria Set Forth in the Tables by the Introduction of Risk Analysis

312. One of the most qualifying features of the new reclamation regime is the attenuation of the criteria set forth in the tables. Article 17 of Legislative Decree No. 22 of 1997 associated reclamation with exceeding (or the concrete danger of exceeding) limit values for the concentration of pollutants which were pre-established by law and valid for eternity, regardless of the actual ability of the substances found in environmental resources to cause damage (there were two alternative limits for each parameter, depending on whether the site was intended for residential use or manufacturing purposes). Legislative Decree No. 152 of 2006, implementing the guidelines provided by enabling Law No. 308 del 2004, gave a more flexible criteria to the system of legal limit values, based on an analysis of the concrete risk present in the site to be reclaimed.

An *analysis of the health and environmental site-specific risk*, means a *site-specific analysis of the effects on human health deriving from prolonged exposure to the action of substances found in contaminated environmental resources* (Article 240, paragraph 1, clause *s*). The analysis criteria are described in Annex 1 to Part IV of Legislative Decree No. 152 of 2006, while waiting for new technical standards to be approved by a decree of the Ministry of the Environment, together with the Ministry of Health and Ministry for Economic Development (Article 242, paragraph 4).

It should be specified that the legal limit values have not been abolished, but if they are exceeded, instead of a reclamation obligation there is an obligation to control the extent of the risk to human health found in the site (as well as an obligation to provide urgent measures to prevent further contamination).

On the basis of the controls, which are concentrated on the nature and scope of the risk related to the presence of pollutants, further limit values are identified (site-specific limit values), which are at the same time the prerequisite and objective of reclamation activities (due to their being acceptable levels of residual contamination).

The two types of limit values, legal (or *standard*) and site specific, are respectively known as 'CSC' (threshold concentrations of contamination) and 'CSR' (threshold concentrations of risk).

The CSC indicate the contamination levels of environmental resources that are attention levels; if exceeded, site characterization is required and it is necessary to perform a site-specific risk analysis. The CSC are linked to the definition of a *potentially contaminated site,* that is, a site in which one or more concentration levels of pollutants found in the environmental resources exceed the CSC, while the characterization and site-specific health and environmental risk analysis, necessary to determine whether or not the site is contaminated, are being completed.

The CSC values are indicated in Annex 5 to section V of Part IV of the Decree and repeat, with minimum variations, the acceptable limit concentration values in the soil, subsoil and underground waters set forth in DM No. 471 of 25 October 1999.

The CSR are defined as:

> the contamination levels of the environmental resources, to be determined on a case by case basis applying the site specific risk analysis according to the principles set forth in Annex 1 to Part IV of this Decree and the results of the characterization plan, which require security measures and reclamation if they are exceeded. The concentration levels defined above constitute acceptable levels for the site.

The site is considered to be a 'contaminated site' only if the CSR are exceeded. In addition to the concepts of 'potentially polluted site' and 'contaminated site', the decree also introduces the concept of an 'uncontaminated site', referring to a *site in which the contamination found in the environmental resources is lower than the threshold concentrations of contamination (CSC) or, if in excess, is in any event lower than the threshold concentrations of risk (CSR) found after analyzing the site-specific health and environmental risk* (Article 240, paragraph 1, clause *f*).

In some cases, application of the risk analysis is tempered, as in small areas (no greater than 1000 m^2): the responsible party can decide whether the reclamation should restore the site to levels that are lower than the CSC levels or reclaim the site according to the CSR levels, after a risk analysis has been prepared (Article 249 and Annex 4).

A partial return to the tabular system was made by the introduction of a simplified procedure for land reclamation by Law Decree No. 91 of 24 June 2014, converted, with modifications by Law No. 116 of11 August 2014.

The new Article 242*bis* provides that an operator interested in carrying out, at its expense, land reclamation with the reduction of contamination to a level that is equal to or lower than the threshold concentrations of contamination, can present a specific project to the competent administration with the scheduled interventions based on the data of the state of the contamination of the site, as well as the time schedule for the work. The characterization and relative reclamation project are not subject to the ordinary approval procedure established by Articles 242 and 252 (*see infra*), but instead to a control verifying compliance with the threshold concentrations of contamination in land having a specific intended use.

The ordinary procedure continues to apply to the containment and reclamation of groundwater. The simplified procedure allows a more rapid use of the site (depending on the intended use provided by outstanding urban planning instruments), without prejudice to the assessment of any health risks for the users of the site deriving from volatile contaminants in the groundwater.

III. The Liability Regime

313. Legislative Decree No. 152 of 2006 also changed the liability regime, both for whoever causes the potential contamination of the site, and for the mere manager or owner of the contaminated area.

Article 17 of Legislative Decree No. 22 of 1997 required reclamation to be carried out by anyone who caused, *even accidentally,* the limit values to be exceeded (or danger that they would be exceeded). On the basis of such clause, the majority of case law interpreted the polluter's liability as *objective liability*, exclusively based on whether the conduct was capable of causing the contamination, even though it recognized that the rule in the Italian legal system is one of subjective liability, in which even the psychological factor of fault or negligence is significant. Consistent with such rule, Legislative Decree No. 152 of 2006 eliminates the reference to 'accidental' pollution, and administrative law courts have found liability and ordered reclamation by recourse to the concept of extra-contractual liability.

An order that a site be reclaimed can, therefore, be issued against anyone who has contaminated the site only when the behaviour is at least found to be negligent.

Such regime is not very different from that of the directive on environmental damage In general, the operator, that is, the party carrying out a professional activity on site, does not have to sustain the cleanup costs when opportune security measures have been taken; Member States can, however, associate liability for such costs with behaviour found to be at fault or negligent (Article 8, Directive 2004/35/EC).

The EU Court of Justice, urged by the Council of State (Plenary meeting, Order No. 21 of 25 September 2013) ruled on these issues.

By means of the judgment of 4 March 2015 (issued in case C-534/13), the Court of Luxembourg confirmed its orientation (already expressed in its judgment of 9 March 2010, C- 378/08), according to which 'Directive 2004/35/EC of the European Parliament and of the Council of 21 April 2004, on environmental liability for the prevention and remedying of environmental damage, must be interpreted as meaning that it does not preclude national legislation (…) which, if it is impossible to identify the party responsible for the contamination of the site or to obtain remedial measures from such party, do not allow the competent authority to require the owner of such site who has not contributed to that pollution to carry out preventive and remedial measures, and the sole obligation imposed is the reimbursement of expenses related to the measures undertaken by the competent authority, within the limit of the market value of the site determined after such measures have been performed' (on this subject *see*, recently, Council of State, section VI, judgment No. 502 of 25 January 2018).

Legislative Decree No. 152 of 2006 contains some novelties with respect to the pre-existing regime, including in relation to the treatment of the innocent owner of a contaminated site.

Modification of the kind of liability, from objective to subjective, was balanced by providing obligations of notice and intervention, even for parties who are not liable for the contamination (Article 240, paragraph 1, clause *i*). In compliance with the principle of prevention, without prejudice to the obligations of the party responsible for the potential contamination, the owner or manager of an area where the CSC are exceeded, or where there is a concrete and present danger that they will be exceeded, must notify the territorially competent region, province and municipality and implement preventive measures (Article 234, paragraph 2).

The innocent owner must bear the economic costs for decontaminating the site, even if not responsible for carrying out the site reclamation. If the polluter does not do so or cannot be identified, the work is done ex officio by the public authority (municipality or region), and the relative costs constitute a legal encumbrance, guaranteed by a special lien on the property. This special lien on the real property remains even in the case of a sale to third parties; the presence of the lien is indicated on the Certificate of Urban Planning Destination for the site. The lien results in a pre-emption right granted by law to the creditor in consideration of the particular nature of the credit. In the case of enforcement against the debtor's assets, the privileged creditor will be paid in a preferential manner with respect to any other creditors (the real estate lien even prevails over a credit guaranteed by a mortgage).

The lien is special, and only extends to the proceeds of the sale of the polluted site that is party to reclamation (Article 253).

In relation to recovery of the costs of land reclamation with respect to the innocent owner, Legislative Decree No. 152 of 2006 provides that:

- the lien and the division of costs require a reasoned measure issued by the competent authority specifying, among others, that it is impossible to verify the polluter's identity, or impossible or fruitless to exercise a right of action against the polluter;
- the innocent owner can be required to reimburse expenses, however, only within the limit of the market value of the site determined after the reclamation has been completed (according to a general rule of proportion between limitation of ownership and pursuit of a public interest, T.A.R. Tuscany, judgment No. 8 of 8 January 2010).

IV. The Different Kinds of Interventions in Potentially Contaminated and Contaminated Sites

314. The interventions carried out in a contaminated site can be based on different premises and have various objectives:

- *Environmental characterization*: all of the activities that allow the contamination of the environmental resources to be reconstructed, in order to obtain information on the basis of which realizable and sustainable decisions on security measures and/or site reclamation can be taken.
- *Preventive measures*: initiatives to block an event, act or failure to act that has created an imminent threat to health or the environment, understood as being a sufficiently likely risk that damage will occur in the near future from a health or environmental standpoint, in order to prevent or minimize the occurrence of such threat; preventive measures must also be taken prior to discovering whether or not the CSC have been exceeded.
- *MISE* (Annex III refers to urgent security measures): immediate or short-term interventions, to be implemented in the case of emergency subsequent to any kind of sudden contamination, aimed at containing the spread of the primary sources of contamination (mitigation measures), prevent their contact with other resources at the site and remove them, while waiting for any other reclamation activity or ad interim or permanent security measures. In the lack of specific data, said interventions are determined on the basis of precautionary criteria. According to case law, the *proprium* for the MISE are the prerequisite of sudden contamination (T.A.R. Tuscany, judgment No. 762 of 6 May 2009), and the objective of avoiding that contamination in course spreads to the soil or groundwater while waiting for the definitive reclamation of the site (T.A.R. Friuli Venezia Giulia, judgment No. 837 of 17 December 2009).
- *Operative security measures* (MISO): all interventions at a site where operating activities are in course, that guarantee an adequate security level for persons and for the environment; MISO are realized pending permanent security measures or reclamation to be carried out after the activity has ceased.

- *Reclamation measures*: the entirety of interventions aimed at eliminating the sources of pollution and pollutants, or reducing their concentration in the soil, subsoil and underground waters to a level that is the equivalent of or lower than the risk threshold concentration values (CSR).
- *Permanent security measures*: these are definitive measures intended to reduce risk to beneath the CSR values the same as reclamation, but which are distinguished from reclamation because the sources of pollution are only isolated with respect to potentially sensitive areas, due to the impossibility of removal at supportable costs (T.A.R. Sardinia – judgment No. 549 of 21 April 2009).
- *Environmental restoration and cleanup*: landscape and environmental requalification, in addition to reclamation or permanent security measures, which restore the site to its effective and definitive use in conformity with urban planning instruments.

There are multiple technical solutions for site reclamation or permanent security measures.

Annex III clarifies that the choice of the best type of intervention in a specific case of pollution requires various interests to be balanced in the presence of many variables, both general and, above all, site-specific variables, such as: (a) the level of environmental protection that would be desirable to achieve; (b) whether there are reliable techniques capable of achieving and maintaining such levels of protection; and (c) the costs for planning, implementation, management, monitoring and so on that have to be sustained during the various phases of the intervention. Equilibrium is ensured by use of the *best available techniques* as defined by Article 5 of Legislative Decree No. 152 of 2006, which also indicates the parameter of 'supportable costs' (on balancing interests *see*, recently, T.A.R. Tuscany, judgment No. 3973, 18 December 2009; T.A.R. Tuscany, judgment No. 1540 of 14 October 2009; T.A.R. Lombardy-Brescia, judgment No. 1738 of 9 October 2009, also with reference to the principle of proportion). With reference to measures regarding groundwater, Article 243, paragraph 2, specifies that recourse to physical barriers is only allowed if hydraulic containment and treatment of the pumped groundwater is ineffective.

In the case of reclamation or safety operations (operative or permanent) that are particularly complex due to the nature of the contamination, the measures to be taken, the necessary equipment or the size of the area subject to such measures, the project can be articulated in separate design phases so that it is possible to implement the measures in individual areas or in subsequent stages.

§3. Planning and Programming Instruments

315. The widespread presence in Italy of contaminated sites has rendered the provision of planning measures indispensable, ever since the first laws on reclamation (*see* Law No. 441 of 1987).

316. The regional reclamation plan is an essential instrument for obtaining an overall view of the interventions to be prepared and for effectively implementing them.

The plan, which is an integral part of the waste plan, contains (Article 199):

- the identification of the sites to be reclaimed and the general characteristics of the pollutants present;
- environmental reclamation and cleanup procedures, which privilege, above all, the use of materials originating from the recovery of urban wastes;
- an estimate of financial costs (approval of the regional plan is a necessary prerequisite to obtain State financing); and
- the manner in which materials to be removed from the site are disposed of.

Further, the plan establishes an order of priority for interventions, based on risk evaluation criteria prepared by ISPRA. On the basis of such order, if the polluter does not act or cannot be identified, and if the competent municipality does not act as a substitute, the region shall reclaim the polluted site ex officio, and can use other public or private parties, identified at the outcome of special procedures that are open to the public (Article 250, Legislative Decree No. 152 of 2006).

The regions are responsible for preparing a census of the sites to be reclaimed (based on technical criteria prepared by ISPRA), which is functional to programming activity. The register of sites, in addition to indicating the areas to be reclaimed and the relative interventions, must also indicate the details of the responsible parties and the public or private operators that the region intends to use in the case of reclamations that it carries out ex officio (Article 251, Legislative Decree No. 152 of 2006).

§4. Authorization Procedures

317. The reclamation procedure is very complex and articulated and is developed by means of the approval of a series of acts that differ among themselves due to their objective and degree of thoroughness. The procedure can be initiated in different ways:

(i) upon the initiative of the polluter who, upon the occurrence of an event that could potentially contaminate the site, in addition to implementing the necessary preventive measures also notifies the competent public authorities (municipality, province and region, Article 242);

(ii) upon an order of the public administration, and, in particular, the province which, upon becoming aware of an episode of potential contamination, carries out the controls required to identify the polluter and issues a warning to remediate the situation (Article 244);

(iii) upon the initiative of any interested party not responsible for the pollution (such as an innocent owner), who has been granted the right to voluntarily intervene at any time to implement reclamation measures required in a site owned by or available to him (Article 245);

(iv) by the public administration (municipality or region, exercising substitute power), if the polluter does not provide directly or cannot be identified, and neither the owner of the site nor other interested parties intervene (Article 244, paragraphs 4 and 250).

318. Only the case in point (i) will be reviewed in detail below, however the procedural process is the same in the other cases as well. It is further noted that with respect to land reclamation, Article 242*bis* also provides for a simplified regime in which subsequent control activities are preferred to approval procedures of the characterization and reclamation project:

(a) Article 242 provides that *upon verification of an event that is potentially capable of contaminating the site, the polluter must take the necessary preventive measures within twenty-four hours and give immediate notice in accordance with and following the procedures set forth in Article 304, paragraph 2* (paragraph 1). The subsequent paragraph provides that *once the necessary preventive measures have been taken, the polluter must conduct a preliminary control of the contamination parameters in the contaminated areas*:
   (i) If it is determined that the level of CSC have not been exceeded, the responsible party must restore the contaminated site, advising the territorially competent municipality and province, by means of a special form of self-certification, within forty-eight hours from the above notice that initiates the procedure. The self-certification concludes the procedure, without prejudice to verifications and controls by the competent authority (the province), which must be carried out within the following fifteen days.
   (ii) If, instead, the controls reveal that the values of the parameters exceed the CSC, the responsible party must secure the site and provide the competent authority with a characterization plan (section 2, d).
(b) The characterization plan is party to approval by the region, which must convene a special conference of services. The regional authorization is consent for all of the work related to the characterization, substituting all other authorizations, permits, agreements, undertakings and approvals by the public administration. A site-specific risk analysis is conducted on the basis of the results of the characterization plan; the results must be presented to the region within six months from approval of the characterization plan.
(c) The risk analysis (which determines the site-specific CSR), is party to approval within the following sixty days, in the presence of the proponent, during a conference of services:
   (i) If the outcome of the risk analysis demonstrates that the concentration of contaminants at the site is lower than the CSR, the conference of services, by its approval of the risk analysis document, declares that the procedure has reached a positive conclusion, and can require a monitoring plan (that the responsible party must submit to the approval of the conference of services).
   (ii) If the outcome of the risk analysis procedure demonstrates that the CSR have been exceeded, the responsible party, within six months subsequent to approval of the document, must submit the operative reclamation

project, operating and permanent security measures, and, if necessary, additional environmental remediation and cleanup measures to the region.

(d) The operative project is approved by the region (again by means of a special conference of services). The regional measure substitutes to all effects authorizations, permits, agreements, *nulla osta*, opinions and approvals provided by outstanding law for interventions, inclusive of an EIA, approvals for the management of soil and rocks originating from excavations within the area, and authorization for the discharge of waters drained from the groundwater (regulated by Article 243). The approval of the project also constitutes an urban planning variant, considered to be a declaration of public utility, urgency and work that cannot be deferred for purposes of expropriation. The measure also establishes the timeframe for the interventions and the amount of the performance bonds that must be provided to the region for the proper execution and completion of the works (in an amount that does not exceed 50% of the estimated cost of the work).

§5. Specific Protection and Management Instruments

319. It has been emphasized that the site-specific risk analysis is a central and decisive instrument for the legal qualification of the contamination of a site and consequent obligation to take security and reclamation measures (*see*, Constitutional Court, judgment No. 214 of 2008).

Risk analysis has a clear Community matrix. Directive 2004/35/EC on environmental damage links the remediation of land damage to the elimination of a *significant risk of human health being adversely affected* (Article 2, paragraph 1, clause *c*), and specifies that the presence of such risk must be verified through *risk assessment procedures that consider the characteristics and function of the soil compared with the type and concentration of substances, preparations, and harmful organisms or micro-organisms, and their relative risks and possibility of dispersion* (Annex II, page (2).

Risk analysis involves a study of the harmful effects that contamination, or better, the exposure to a specific contaminant, can have on the final receptors. The components that must be considered are the contaminants index, sources, manner of exposure and final receptors. The identification and analysis of the potential course of exposure and targets, and definition of the reclamation objectives, must consider the intended use of the site provided by the territorial programming instruments. Legislative Decree No. 152 of 2006 does not conceal the probabilistic nature of each risk assessment, but refers, in addition to site-specific aspects (based on site controls), to the criteria of 'conservatism', because *the principle of caution is intrinsic in the risk analysis procedure* (Annex 1).

320. Another noticeable feature of legislation on reclamation is the use of different forms of agreement.

Article 246, paragraph 1, in general, grants parties who are obliged or interested in the reclamation the right to determine the manner and time within which the work will be carried out, in accordance with special programme agreements stipulated with the competent administrations within six months of approval of the risk analysis document. Specific applications are indicated in the subsequent paragraphs, in the case in which the same party must or intends to intervene in more than one site located in different regions or even throughout the entire national territory (e.g., fuel distributors), or more than one party must or intends to reclaim the same site of national importance. The instrument of a programme agreement is also used to intervene in sites of pre-eminent public interest for industrial reconversion (Article 252*bis*).

Alternatively, even though it still refers to an agreement, parties responsible for contaminating sites of national interest can reach a settlement with respect to the amount and quantification of the reclamation costs. In this case, the settlement occurs in the context of a controversy in course or potential, and its objective is to accelerate reclamation in areas that are particularly polluted that require costly and technically complex interventions (*see* Article 306*bis*, for which reference is made to the chapter on environmental damage).

§6. Control System

321. The principle of cooperation among all levels of government, expressly referred to by the waste management regime (Article 178, paragraph 4, Legislative Decree No. 152 of 2006), also applies to reclamation, in particular the obligation that all public administrations, during the exercise of their functions, must identify any sites where they have verified the presence of pollutants that exceed the CSC and notify the competent region, province and municipality (Article 244, paragraph 1).

Without prejudice to such notice obligation, for which all public administrations are responsible, the primary role in carrying out the control function rests with the province.

According to what is provided by Legislative Decree No. 152 of 2006, upon receipt of the above notice, the province must identify the polluter and order, by means of a reasoned measure, the work to be performed at the site (Article 244, paragraph 2).

The province also exercises control power with respect to proper compliance with reclamation obligations, using the technical support of the ARPA (Article 248). The full documentation relative to the characterization plan of the site and operative project, inclusive of remediation measures, monitoring to be carried out, limitations on use and any restrictions that might have been decided by the Conference of Services must be transmitted to the province and to ARPA in order to control the conformity of the work to the approved projects.

The province is also responsible for certifying the completion of the reclamation or security measures for the site (on the basis of a technical report prepared by ARPA); the certification attests the conformity of the work performed to the project, and allows the performance bonds to be released that whoever performed the work had to pay to guarantee completion of the works. The region has substitute power if the province does not act (Article 242, paragraph 13).

With the implementation of the Law No. 56 of 2014, many of these functions were transferred to other levels of government, most often to the region (e.g., *see* Tuscan Regional Law No. 22 of 2015 and subsequent modifications and integrations).

§7. Administrative and Criminal Sanctions

322. The reclamation regime is only supported by criminal sanctions. No administrative fines are provided, nor disqualification penalties such as, for example, the suspension of production, which instead would act as a strong deterrent with respect to industrial practice.

Article 257 of Legislative Decree No. 152 of 2006 punishes *whoever causes pollution of the soil, subsoil, surface waters or underground waters by exceeding risk threshold concentrations … unless reclamation is carried out in conformity with a project approved by the competent authority.*

Law No. 68 of 2015 inserted the clause 'unless the act constitutes a more serious offense' to coordinate the special criminal act with the crimes of environmental pollution and environmental disaster introduced by the same law in the Italian Criminal Code.

With respect to the provisions of Legislative Decree No. 22 of 1997 (Article 51*bis*) that have been repealed, the Italian legislator mitigated the severity of the incriminating law. Only damage from pollution caused by exceeding the CSR is punished and not, as was the case in the past, the concrete and present danger of pollution (which was determined by the mere danger of exceeding legal limits that were the equivalent of the current CSC). Further, criminal liability only arises if the competent authority approves the reclamation project and the polluter does not comply with the restrictions; in the case of failure to approve the project, which occurs in an advanced phase of the reclamation procedure, the party that caused the contamination of the site cannot be held criminally liable.

The failure to reclaim a contaminated site is punished by an alternative sanction: a fine (ranging from EUR 2,600 to EUR 26,000) or detention (from six months to one year). The crime becomes cumulative and the amount of the fine increases if the contamination derives from hazardous substances; in this case the sanction consists of detention ranging from one to two years and a fine ranging from EUR 5,200 to EUR 52,000.

Article 257 also punishes the failure to provide the notice required by Article 242 with an alternative sanction of detention, ranging from three months to one year, or a fine ranging from EUR 1,000 to EUR 26,000.

The objective of the sanction regime is the practical result of site reclamation, as seen from two provisions: (1) the conditional suspension of the sanction can be made subordinate to the reclamation work and environmental cleanup; and (2) implementing the reclamation project results in an exclusion from punishment for all integrated environmental crimes arising from the behaviour that caused the pollution (e.g., water discharge that exceeds legal limits, waste abandonment, etc.).

§8. Economic Instruments

323. The reclamation regime for contaminated sites starts with a reference to Community principles, *with particular reference to the principle the polluter pays.* The party responsible for the contamination reclaim the polluted site, even though an innocent owner can suffer the economic consequences of the site's contamination. In this case, the needs of environmental protection result in a derogation from the Community principle in favour of economic liability (within the limits of the value of the site). Moreover, the innocent owner, if the contaminated site is reclaimed spontaneously, has a right of recourse against the polluter for the costs sustained, as well as any potentially greater damages.

A problematic aspect of reclamation is represented by the so-called orphan sites, those sites for which it is not possible to identify the party responsible for the contamination, or the polluter cannot be required to sustain the costs of the interventions.

In said cases, unless an interested party acts (including the innocent owner), the public authority must reclaim the site, with all that this implies with respect to the economic resources required. Moreover, amounts paid in advance by the public administration are normally not entirely recoverable by resort to a lien and the forced sale of the asset, because the value of the cleaned up site is often less than the cost of the work performed.

For these reasons, Italian law provides that the regions create a special fund in their balance sheets so that these costs can be advanced (Article 250, Legislative Decree No. 152 of 2006), and also provides the possibility that the reclamation work can be partially paid for by a public loan that covers up to one-half of the expenses, if there are overriding public interests connected to hygienic-health, environmental or occupational protection needs (Article 253, paragraph 5).

§9. Summary Framework of Competence

324. The reclamation regime for contaminated sites is within the scope of environmental protection pursuant to Article 117, second paragraph, clause *s*) of the Constitution, and subject to the exclusive legislative competence of the State (most recently by the Constitutional Court, judgment No. 126 of 2018). State legislation is, therefore, *a limit on the regime that the regions and autonomous provinces can choose in other areas for which they are competent, and they therefore cannot derogate in any way from the level of environmental protection established by the State* (Constitutional Court, judgments No. 214 of 2008 and No. 247 of 2009). The Constitutional Court has held that a regional regime would conflict with the division of legislative power established by the Constitution, even if it introduced a more rigorous regime than the State regime, because the State has exclusive power with respect to reclamation in order to determine the point of equilibrium between conflicting interests.

In accordance with the Constitution, regulatory power rests with the State in matters of exclusive State competence. Specifically, the Ministry of the Environment (MATTM) regulates land reclamation, environmental cleanups and emergency, operative and permanent security measures for areas to be used for agricultural production and breeding. The regulations are approved upon the joint approval of the Ministry of Agricultural, Food and Forestry policies, the Ministry of Health, and the Ministry of Economic Development.

325. The distribution of administrative functions is described elsewhere, but the following brief summary of the powers of the different levels of government might be useful.

I. State

326. The State's role, by means of MATTM, in the land reclamation regime is traditionally associated with interventions in *sites of national interest* ('SIN', Article 252 of Legislative Decree No. 152 of 2006).

SIN are sites in which, due to the characteristics of the area, the quantity and hazardous nature of the pollutants present, the importance of the impact on the surrounding environment in terms of health and ecological risk, as well as the damage to cultural and environmental resources, the interventions to be carried out extend beyond local and regional interests and the uniform action of the State is required (Constitutional Court, judgment No. 247 of 2009).

SIN are identified by a decree of MATTM, together with the interested regions; local administrations are also heard with respect to the precise delimitation of the sites, as well as the responsible parties and owners of the areas involved.

The reclamation procedure for SINs is attributed to the competence of MATTM, upon consultation with the Ministry of Economic Development. The Ministry can also rely on ISPRA, the Regional Agencies for Environmental Protection of the relative regions, and the National Health Institute (*Istituto superiore di sanità*), as well as other qualified public or private parties. The ministry is also responsible for interventions when the polluter cannot be identified, does not act or there is nobody else interested in the reclamation. It should be noted that according to case law, ministerial competence for the reclamation procedure does not remove sites of national interest from the power of the province to order polluters who do not act spontaneously to intervene in contaminated sites (T.A.R. Puglia, judgment No. 372 of 7 February 2008).

The reclamation procedure regime repeats what is established in ordinary situations by Article 242 of Legislative Decree No. 152 of 2006, including with reference to the effects of approval of the project (Article 252, paragraphs 6 and 7).

Pending completion of the approval measure, after the technical appraisal has been completed MATTM may temporarily authorize, upon the request of the party involved – if there are reasons for urgency and without prejudice to obtaining the positive assessment of environmental compatibility, if envisaged, the commencement of the relative reclamation work, in accordance with the project that was favourably evaluated, with any restrictions, by the Conference of Services convened by MATTM.

State intervention is also provided for another type of site, those *of preeminent public interest for industrial reconversion* (Article 252*bis*).

The provision, introduced by Legislative Decree No. 4 of 2008 (modified by Law No. 9 of 2014), regards areas affected by historical contamination (contamination that occurred prior to 30 April 2007, in which the need for environmental cleanup accompanies the intent to implement industrial reconversions and economic-productive development programmes. The regime on sites of overriding interest for industrial reconversion is characterized by the use of a programme agreement to coordinate actions aimed at determining the time, procedures, financing and every other related and functional requirement to implement integrated safety or reclamation projects, industrial conversions and economic development.

II. Region

327. Briefly, the region is responsible for:

- approving the reclamation plan, which is an integral part of the regional waste management plan;
- preparing a register of the sites to be reclaimed;
- receiving notices regarding a potential contaminating event from the party responsible for the pollution, or from another public administration or party interested in the reclamation;
- approving, during the course of the reclamation procedure by means of a special conference of services, the characterization plan, the risk analysis document, the monitoring plan and the reclamation project;
- reclaiming the site when the polluter does not intervene, or cannot be identified, and the territorially competent municipality remains inactive;
- certifying that the reclamation has been completed when the province fails to act;
- participating in proceedings relating to sites of national interest or industrial reconversion in the manner set forth in Articles 252 and 252*bis*, Legislative Decree No. 152 of 2006.

III. Provinces and Municipalities

328. The province is primarily competent for control functions.

The municipality, which receives notices regarding the existence of an event of potential contamination from the responsible party or from another public administration or party interested in the reclamation, must reclaim the site whenever the responsible party fails to act or cannot be identified. The mayor is responsible for waste removal and public health emergencies.

IV. Environmental Protection Agencies (ISPRA and ARPA)

329. The regime for the reclamation of contaminated sites confirms the role of ISPRA (previously the National Environmental Protection Agency), and the ARPA as important technical-scientific consulting agencies. Both the regional agencies and the institute have operative control and investigative functions in the context of reclamation procedures (ISPRA, above all, with reference to the SIN). Different from the regional agencies, ISPRA's role is characterized by its participation in technical rule-making proceedings to determine standards that are valid throughout the national territory.

§10. Conclusions

330. The existence of ad hoc rules on the reclamation of contaminated sites, added to those on waste management and the regime on environmental damage, definitely represent a strong point in the Italian legal system. Italy has, thus, anticipated the Community legislator from this standpoint, even if the multiplication of rules does not necessarily ensure effective substantive protection and risks being detrimental to the certainty of the law.

The reclamation regime that first appeared in the Italian legal system (in 1997) was unable to combine rigorous protection with the flexibility of operative solutions. With respect to the first aspect, the peculiar features of eminently objective liability and the use of criteria indicated in a table to define the prerequisites and objectives of the reclamation should be noted. Precisely the latter characteristic, however, does not allow interventions to be measured in relation to the effective risk at a site, and such rigidity has led to a multiplication of lawsuits.

The introduction of risk analysis (in 2006) allows operative solutions to be adjusted to site-specific conditions: what is important is not that the presence of pollutants be decreased to concentration levels that are lower than general and abstract limits predetermined by law, but that the concrete risk of contamination, determined on the basis of the characteristics of the site and the contamination, be reduced to acceptable residual values.

In practice, however, the procedure based on a risk analysis has proven to be unsuitable for quickly returning the site to the use for which it was intended, so that with respect to the reclamation of the soil matrix, there has been a return to an approach based on the application of tabular pollution values.

Implementation of the norms on reclamation is also subject, more clearly than other sector regimes, to some structural difficulties regarding environmental protection in Italy, such as the insufficient level of control exercised throughout the territory, and the inadequacy of the amounts allocated for site cleanups (especially for 'orphan sites', which the public administration must provide for in the absence or failure to act of the responsible party).

Chapter 6. Noise Pollution

by *Marcello Cecchetti*

§1. Evolution of the Italian Legal System

331. The Italian legal system incorporates two major categories of laws aimed at protecting the environment from noise pollution:

(1) acts that refer to the general regulation of noise pollution;
(2) acts that contain special regimes on sound emissions originating from some of the principle sources of noise.

Similarly, as in the case of atmospheric pollution, prior to the introduction of a general regime specifically aimed at containing noise pollution, protection against sound emissions was obtained by reference to two norms respectively contained in the Civil Code and in the Criminal Code. Above all, Article 844 of the 1942 Civil Code regulates 'emissions', on the basis of which protection is granted to a property owner against noise disturbances originating from neighbouring property which exceed acceptable limits, 'also considering the condition of the places', with the clarification, in the second paragraph of the cited provision, that its concrete application must balance 'production needs with ownership rights'. In this respect, legitimacy case law has offered a constitutionally oriented interpretation of the provision in question, stressing that the legislator intended to protect the right to health and the right to a healthy environment through this provision.

Second, Article 659 of the Criminal Code, on the disturbance of the activities and rest of human beings, punishes whoever disturbs the work or rest of human beings or their performances, meeting places or public entertainment by means of a racket or noise, or abuse of sound instruments or acoustical signals. In addition, Article 659 punishes whoever exercises a profession or trade whose sound emissions violate the existing law or specific restrictions issued by public authorities.

332. DPCM of 1 March 1991 was the first act containing a general regulation of noise pollution: it established maximum exposure limits to noise in both residential and external environments.

Said decree required the municipalities to identify six distinct zones within their own territory: areas entitled to particular protection; areas destined to prevalently residential use; mixed areas; areas of intense human activity; areas that are prevalently industrial; and areas that are exclusively industrial. The decree also established maximum noise limits for each of these separate areas, differentiated into a day limit and a night limit (which are absolute limits of permissible sound levels) in consideration of each area's diverse purpose.

In addition, some 'differential' limits were provided for areas that are not exclusively industrial, consisting of a day limit and a night limit determined on the basis of the differential between residual noise and environmental noise. Annex A of the decree specified that 'residual noise' is 'the constant level of weighted sound pressure ("A") revealed when specific disturbing sources are excluded'. 'Environmental noise' was instead defined as 'the continuous level of weighted sound pressure ("A") produced by all of the sources of noise existing in a given place and during a determined amount of time. Environmental noise consisted, therefore, of the totality of residual noise. and the noise produced by a specific disturbing source'.

The 1991 decree also provided for a temporary regime, having more bland absolute limits but identical differential limits to those of the final regime, to be applied to sources of noise, while the municipalities proceeded with the subdivision of the territory into the various areas indicated by the law. The decree also provided both the criteria and the manner of measuring noise levels, and allowed industry the possibility of gradually aligning their existing situations with the established limits, upon presentation to the region of a special compliance plan, to be completed within a maximum of thirty months.

The last provisions of the decree, containing, in particular, the provisions of general compliance plans (to be prepared by the regions and municipalities), also required requests for issuance of building permits relating to new industrial plants or licences and authorizations for the exercise of such activities to contain as an annex suitable documentation of an acoustical impact forecast; these provisions were annulled by the Constitutional Court (judgment No. 517 of 30 December 1991) on the ground that appropriate legislative coverage was lacking.

333. The Framework Law on noise pollution was only definitively approved in 1995 (Law No. 447 of 26 October 1995), which was recently modified by Legislative Decree No. 42 of 17 February 2017. The Framework Law deals with the problem of noise pollution from a global standpoint by providing limit values, requiring preparation of compliance plans, confirming the obligation that the municipalities classify their territory into distinct areas, and by introducing the obligation of annexed documentation of an acoustical impact forecast to the request for a licence or authorization to perform determined activities. In addition, it creates an apparatus of administrative sanctions for violations of the new regime and provides explicit regulation of control activities.

334. The principal problem of the 1995 Framework Law, which currently persists notwithstanding the modifications made by cited Legislative Decree No. 42 of 2017, is the complex tiered system provided for it to definitively enter into effect, which was simultaneously entrusted to further acts of the State, regions and municipalities. The principal implementing acts within the competence of the State that have been issued as of today are the following:

- DM of 11 December 1996, on differential criteria for plants having a continuous manufacturing cycle;
- DM of 31 October 1997, on the containment and measurement of airport noise;
- DPCM of 14 November 1997, which contains emission limit values, input limit values, warning limit values and quality limit values with reference to the six areas of classification of the municipal territory already provided by DPCM of 1 March 1991;

- DPCM of 5 December 1997, on the determination of passive acoustical requisites for buildings;
- DPR No. 496 of 11 December 1997 on the reduction of noise pollution from civil aircraft;
- DM of 16 March 1998, which establishes the techniques and manner of data gathering and the measurement of noise pollution;
- DPR No. 459 of 18 November 1998, on noise pollution deriving from train traffic;
- DPCM No. 215 of 16 April 1999, which contains the regime on the acoustic requirements for sources of noise in places of public entertainment (including discotheques) and in places open to the public;
- DM of 20 May 1999, on determining the criteria to plan monitoring systems for levels of noise pollution near airports, as well as criteria for airport classification in relation to the level of noise pollution;
- DM of 3 December 1999, on anti-noise procedures and special areas in airports;
- DM of 29 November 2000, which establishes the criteria for the preparation by operators of public transportation services and the relative infrastructures of plans to contain and lower noise;
- DPR No. 304 of 3 April 2001, on the regulation of sound emissions produced by motor vehicles; and
- DPR No. 142 of 30 March 2004, on the limits and measures to contain and prevent noise pollution deriving from vehicular traffic in relation to road infrastructures.

335. The general regime of the Framework Law was flanked by the regime contained in Legislative Decree No. 194 of 19 August 2005, by means of which the Italian legislator implemented Directive No. 2002/49/EC of the European Parliament and of the Council on the assessment and management of environmental noise. Such law has a very clear triple objective:

(1) to enhance the assessment of exposure to environmental noise by 'noise mapping' and the preparation of 'strategic acoustical maps' in relation to specific places considered to be at greater risk, based on methods common to all Member States of the EU;
(2) to ensure and improve public information with respect to environmental noise and its related effects;
(3) to require the adoption of 'action plans' on the basis of the results of the noise mapping, in order to avoid and reduce environmental noise when necessary, in particular, when exposure levels can have harmful effects on human health, as well as preserve the acoustical quality of the environment when it is good.

Special legislation intended to regulate individual mobile sound sources was introduced in Italy almost exclusively on the impulse of Community law and international conventions. In particular, special regimes are provided for motor vehicles and motorcycles, aircraft and for domestic appliances, as well as a vast series of machinery and equipment to be used outdoors (motor-driven compressors, power generators, pneumatic drills, excavators, bucket loaders, lawnmowers, etc.).

These special regimes are specifically aimed at establishing the technical and functional characteristics of such sources of noise, including, above all, the maximum permissible sound levels.

§2. Contents of the Framework Law

336. Law No. 447/1995, as noted, regards the phenomenon of noise pollution in its entirety, and has recently undergone significant modifications due to Legislative Decree No. 42 of 2017, adopted in implementation of the delegation contained in Article 19, paragraph 2, clauses *a–h* of Law No. 161 of 30 October 2014.

In particular, the Framework Law defines noise pollution in the following terms: 'the introduction of noise in the residential and external environment that provokes annoyance or disturbs rest and human activity, danger for human health, deterioration of ecosystems, of material goods, of monuments, of residential or external environments or which interferes with the legitimate enjoyment of the same environments'.

337. The law provides, above all, an articulated system of planning instruments. Among them is a noise compliance plan, mandatory in some cases, whose preparation and approval is entrusted to the municipalities on the basis of procedures and criteria specified by the regions. Article 7, paragraph 2 of the law identifies the necessary contents of compliance plans, which must be coordinated with the urban traffic plans provided by Article 36 of Legislative Decree No. 285 of 1992, 'The New Code of the Road'. Moreover, following the replacement of paragraph 5 of the cited provision due to Legislative Decree No. 42 of 2017, for the purpose of coordinating with the action plans referred to in Legislative Decree No. 194 of 2005, it is mandatory for the Council of municipalities with a population that exceeds 100,000 inhabitants to provide the municipal council with a five-year report on the acoustical state of the municipality. This report 'shall be approved by the City Council and sent to the region at least within 31 March 2020, and subsequently every five years, also in order to allow the region to assess the need to insert the above municipalities among the urban centres identified pursuant to Legislative Decree No. 194 of 19 August 2005. The municipalities identified by the regions as urban centres for purposes of the presentation of the strategic acoustical maps referred to in Article 3, paragraph 3, of the above Decree' No. 194 of 2005 shall be exempted from the presentation of the report.

In view of the above, the noise compliance plan must contain the following:

- identification of the typology and extent of present sources of noise, including mobile sources, in areas to be reclaimed;
- identification of the subjects responsible for the intervention;
- identification of the priorities, manner and time frame for compliance;
- estimate of financial costs and necessary means;
- eventual urgent precautionary measures necessary for environmental protection and public health.

The Framework Law further provides for adoption of *multi-year plans to contain noise emissions* produced by essential public services such as trains, subways systems, highways and State roads. The adoption of such plans is entrusted to the State (Article 3, paragraph 1, clause *i*), or is imposed on operators of public transportation services and the relative infrastructures, which must present them to the municipality when they are not essential public services and emission and input limit values have been exceeded (Article 10, paragraph 5).

In addition to such plans are the *three-year regional plan for the cleanup of noise pollution*, which are entrusted to the regions and are binding on the municipalities' cleanup plans (Article 4, paragraph 2).

No new and specific authorization procedure is provided for activities that produce noise emissions. The preventive evaluation of the acoustical impact of a series of activities expressly indicated in Article 8 is inserted in the context of EIA proceedings. Article 8 also provides that requests for issuance of building permits and licences and authorizations must contain annexed documentation regarding acoustical impact forecasts. It should also be noted that Legislative Decree No. 42 of 2017 inserted paragraph 2*bis* in cited Article 8, which provides that for purposes of assessing the acoustical impact of linear, airport and maritime transport infrastructures, it is necessary to consider, in the design phase, the plurality of infrastructures which contribute to noise input, as provided in Article 10, paragraph 5, first clause of the decree.

The principal specific instruments provided by law for noise pollution control are limit values, differentiated in emission limit values, noise input limit values and specific input limit values (the latter introduced by Legislative Decree No. 42 of 2017), warning limit values and quality limit values. Noise input limit values are, in turn, distinguished into absolute limit values, determined with reference to the equivalent level of environmental noise and differentiated limit values (the difference between environmental noise and residual noise). 'Emission limit value' means 'the maximum value of noise that can be emitted by a sound source, measured in proximity to the source itself'. 'Noise input limit value' means 'the maximum value of noise that can be introduced by one or more sound sources in the residential environment or external environment, measured near receivers', whereas *specific noise input limit value* means the 'maximum value of the contribution of the specific sound source measured in an external environment or on the façade of the receiver'. Legislative Decree No. 42 of 2017 redefined warning values as the input value, independently of the type of source and territorial acoustical classification of the area to be protected, which if exceeded require acoustical mitigation and, when the prerequisites are met, require implementation of the actions set forth in Article 9', and quality limit values as 'noise values to be achieved over a short, medium and long period of time using the technologies and methodologies available, in order to achieve the objectives of protection' against noise pollution. The above kinds of limit values – except the specific input limit values, which are more recent – have been concretely identified by means of DPCM of 14 November 1997, which establishes a day value (between 6 a.m. and 10 p.m.) and a night value (between 10 p.m. and 6 a.m.). Municipalities having significant landscape, environmental or tourism interests have the right to set limit values of exposure to noise that are more severe than those determined by the State, in accordance with guidelines and criteria established by the relevant region (Article 6, paragraph 3). In determining noise disturbance, the emission levels are defined by the Framework Law and its implementing decrees, in particular DPCM of 14 November 1997. These levels were re-evaluated in view of paragraph 746 of Article 1 of Law No. 45 of 30 December 2018.

Article 6*ter* of Law 13/2009, as modified by the above paragraph, establishes that in determining the normal tolerability of noise emissions in accordance with Article 844 of the Italian Civil Code, the provisions of outstanding laws and regulations governing specific sources and the priority of a specific use must be safeguarded and must refer to the acceptability criteria for noise levels set forth in Law No. 447 of 26 October 1995 and the relevant implementing rules.

338. The control system is essentially differentiated at a provincial and municipal level (Article 14). The provinces are responsible for control and supervision – also with reference to compliance with the implementing regulations set forth in Article 11 of the Framework Law and the State and regional provisions provided to apply the latter (paragraph 2, clause d*bis*, added by Legislative Decree No. 42 of 2017) – in the territorial environments falling within the territory of more than one municipality, to be exercised utilizing the technical structures of the ARPA. The municipalities are responsible for administrative control functions of sound emissions produced by motor vehicle traffic and fixed sources, or by the use of noisy machinery and outdoor activities. The personnel entrusted with performing the controls and the personnel of the ARPA have a right of access to the installations and the site of activities that constitute sources of noise, and can request all data, information and documents necessary to perform their supervisory functions.

The regime of administrative sanctions (Article 10) revolves around three principal types of cases which trigger application of a fine: violations of urgent ordinances adopted on the basis of Article 9; exceeding emission limit values as well as noise input limit values; and, in a residual manner, violation of implementing regulations and the provisions dictated by the State, the regions, the provinces and the municipalities in the application of the Framework Law. Further, in accordance with paragraph 4 of Article 10, modified by Legislative Decree No. 42 of 2017, 70% of the revenue received from the administrative fines set forth in paragraphs 1–3, paid to the State, is reallocated to a specific budget item of the Ministry of the Environment, to be donated, by decree of such ministry, to the municipalities to fund the acoustical remediation plans and to the Environmental Protection Agencies competent by territory to implement the relevant controls.

The sanctions system is supplemented by the new paragraph 5*ter* of Article 10 of the Framework Law, which provides that 'In the event of breach by the companies and entities operating public transportation services or the relative infrastructures to what is set forth in paragraph 5 with regard to the preparation and presentation of the plan or its implementation within a predetermined timeframe, paragraphs 1– and 3 of this Article shall apply'. In this way, the system of sanctions has also been extended to the specific case of failure to comply, by the operators of the public transportation services or the related infrastructures, with the rules on the presentation and implementation of acoustical remediation plans, or paragraph 5 of Article

10 which is expressly referred to and the regime set forth in DM 29 November 2000 on the timeframe for those specific activities.

Finally, the competent acoustics technician should be mentioned, already provided by the Framework Law in paragraphs 6–8 of Article 2, in part substituted (paragraphs 6 and 7) and in part repealed (paragraph 8) by Legislative Decree No. 42 of 2017, which established a new regime with reference to the above professional figure. The competent acoustics technician is the suitable person 'to take measurements, verify compliance with the values defined by applicable law, prepare the acoustical remediation plans, and carry out the related controls' (Article 2, paragraph 6, as modified by Legislative Decree No. 42 of 2017), after inclusion in the list of competent technicians (Article 2, paragraph 7, as modified by Legislative Decree No. 42 of 2017). Articles 20 et seq. of Legislative Decree No. 42 of 2017, as well as Annexes 1 and 2 of the same Decree, contains the regime on such registration – including the structuring and provision of training courses for competent acoustics technicians – as well as for the exercise of such profession.

§3. Legislative Decree No. 194 of 2005

339. Legislative Decree No. 194 of 2005 implemented the first general law on noise pollution in Italy of Community matrix, consisting of Directive No. 2002/49/EC. The Italian legislator, however, did not coordinate the new regime in a sole text with the regime already contained in the 1995 Framework Law, but limited itself to 'overlapping' legislation, which certainly did not contribute to rendering the overall system of protection from noise pollution clearer or facilitate its implementation. Not by chance, Article 19 of Law No. 161 of 2014 provides that 'To ensure the complete harmonization of national rules on noise pollution with Directive 2002/49/EC of the European Parliament and of the Council of 25 June 2002 on the assessment and management of environmental noise, and Directive 2000/14/EC of the European Parliament and of the Council of 8 May 2000 on noise emissions in the environment by machinery and equipment for use outdoors, the Government is delegated to adopt within twenty-four months from the date of entry into effect of this law one or more legislative decrees to reorganize outstanding legislative measures on protecting the outdoor environment and residential environment from noise pollution produced by fixed and mobile sound sources, defined in Article 2, paragraph 1, clauses *c* and *d* of Law No. 447 of 26 October 1995', specifying that among the guiding principles and specific criteria of the delegation, those aimed at guaranteeing:

a) [the] consistency of containment and noise reduction plans provided by the Decree of the Ministry of the Environment 29 November 2000, published in the Official Bulletin No. 285 of 6 December 2000, with the action plans, acoustical maps and strategic acoustical maps provided by Directive 2002/49/EC and set forth in Article 2, paragraph 1, clauses o), p) and q), 3 and 4 as well as Annexes 4 and 5 of Legislative Decree No. 194 of 19 August

2005, as well as with the criteria provided by the decree issued pursuant to Article 3, paragraph 1, clause f) of Law No. 447 of 1995, and subsequent modifications;

b) [the] implementation in national law, as provided by Directive 2002/49/EC and by Legislative Decree No. 194 of 19 August 2005 of the acoustical descriptors other than those regulated by Law No. 447 of 1995 and introduction of the relative methods for making the relative assessments in order to complement and supplement those introduced by such law;

c) [the] harmonization of national law on the regime of noise sources of transportation infrastructures and industrial plants and related updating pursuant to Law No. 447 of 1995 […].

In implementation of the above delegation, however, only Legislative Decrees No. 41 and No. 42 of 2017 have been adopted, the latter of which also amended Legislative Decree No. 194 of 2005.

The latter decree entrusts the regions, among its primary functions, with: (a) identifying 'urban centres', that is, the urban areas consisting of one or more contiguous residential centres and whose overall population exceeds 100,000 residents; (b) determining which authority must prepare the 'strategic acoustical maps' relative to the previous solar year, for urban centres with more than 250,000 inhabitants. The responsibility for preparing the 'acoustical map' of the major roads and railways as well as major airports is entrusted directly to the entities that operate public transportation services or the relative infrastructures; (c) determining the authority that must prepare the 'action plans' for urban centres with more than 250,000 inhabitants. The task of preparing such plans, with reference to major roads and railroads as well as primary airports is entrusted directly to the entities operating public transportation services or the relative infrastructures; (d) verifying that the strategic acoustical maps and acoustical mapping satisfy the requirements set forth in paragraph 5 of Article 3; (e) verifying that the action plans satisfy the requirements set forth in paragraph 5 of Article 4.

The same parties responsible for mapping must also adopt 'action plans' within the term of 18 July 2018, and, subsequently, within 18 April 2023 and every five years starting from such date, which must regard all urban centres, all major roads and railways and all major airports. The action plans are complex and articulated, and must at least indicate:

(a) a description of the urban centre, the major roads and railways or primary airports and other sources of noise to be considered;
(b) the competent authority;
(c) the legal context;
(d) any limit value in effect in accordance with Article 5;
(e) a summary of the results of the acoustical mapping;
(f) an assessment of the estimated number of persons exposed to the noise, identification of the problems and the situations to be improved;
(g) a report on the public consultations organized in accordance with Article 8 of Legislative Decree No. 194 of 2005;

(h) the anti-noise measures already implemented, and projects in course of preparation;
(i) the work planned by the various competent authorities for the following five years, including the measures aimed at the preservation of quiet areas;
(j) the long-term strategy;
(k) financial information, if available: the funds allocated, cost-effectiveness and cost-benefit analysis;
(l) instruments to evaluate the implementation and results of the action plan (Annex 5).

A further element of complexity is the extremely difficult relationship between these 'action plans' and noise planning instruments provided by the 1995 Framework Law. In this regard, Article 4, paragraph 8, of Legislative Decree No. 194 of 2005 only provides, even after the change made by Legislative Decree No. 42 of 2017, that the action plans 'implement the plans to contain and reduce noise produced by public transportation services or the relative infrastructures adopted in accordance with Article 10, paragraph 5, of Law No. 447 of 26 October 1995, the multiyear plans to contain sound emissions produced by essential public services, the three-year regional plans for the remediation of noise pollution, the municipal plans for acoustical remediation, approved, respectively in accordance with Article 3, paragraph 1, clause *i*, Article 4, paragraph 2, and Article 7, paragraph 1 of the above Law'. Article 4, paragraph 9, adds that 'the provisions relating to the procedures, criteria and terms for approval of the plans remain unchanged' in accordance with Law No. 447 of 1995.

§4. SPECIAL LEGISLATION

340. In the context of the regimes aimed at containing sound power levels of specific sources, the first sector to consider is without question that relating to motor vehicles. Reference is made to the legislative sources already considered in the chapter on air pollution, in particular, with respect to the provisions of the Code of the Road (Legislative Decree No. 285/1992), which provides for the preparation at the municipal and provincial levels of urban traffic plans and traffic plans for extra-urban road networks (Article 36), as well as to other legislative sources that establish characteristics and specifications for the construction and functioning of motor vehicles (Articles 71 et seq.). In addition, the Code of the Road contains specific provisions regarding limitations of noises and the use of acoustical signals (Articles 155 and 156). The provisions related to permissible sound levels and to the exhaust systems of motor vehicles in general, which derive entirely from Community law, are set forth in DM of 5 August 1974, which has been updated various times (most recently by DM of 14 December 2007), whereas analogous rules specifically concerning the sound levels of noise emitted by two or three wheel vehicles are contained in DM of 23 March 2001, recently updated by DM of 3 June 2014.

341. The second context where special legislation is applied regards the containment of noise emissions produced by aircraft. DM of 3 December 1983 provided that starting from 31 December 1984, the use of any civil subsonic jet aircraft or civil propulsion aircraft, registered in the national aeronautic register and falling within certain categories that are peremptorily identified, is allowed only if the aircraft possesses an acoustical certificate in accordance with the Navigation Code. Subsequently, as implementation of the Convention on International Civil Aviation stipulated in Chicago on 7 December 1944 as well as some Community directives, some ministerial decrees were issued (DM of 19 December 1994, DM of 28 March 1995, and DM of 29 October 1999), containing rules for sound levels of noise emissions of subsonic jet aircraft. The cited decrees were recently substituted by Legislative Decree No. 66 of 2009, which implemented EC Directive 2006/93.

342. A law was added to this regime aimed at completing the strategy based on limiting noise emissions of individual aircraft while at the same time containing and monitoring noise in airports and neighbouring areas. DM of 31 October 1997 (supplemented by DM of 3 December 1999), containing norms on methodologies to measure airport noise and define anti-noise procedures, to determine the airport areas and activities subject to restrictions, as well as to classify airports in relation to the level of noise pollution, and the characteristics of monitoring systems; DPR No. 496 of 11 December 1997, which contains provisions on the violation of anti-noise procedures, activities to lower and contain airport noise, and limits on night-time aircraft traffic; and DM of 20 May 1999, which regulates the characteristics of monitoring systems to control noise pollution levels near airports, as well as their classification system on the basis of such levels, were supplemented by Legislative Decree No. 13 of 2005, which establishes a specific regime for the introduction of operative restrictions (among which the reduction or prohibition of access of aircraft to a specific airport) in order to contain noise in Community airports, as implementation of Directive 2002/30/EC.

343. The regulation of noise pollution produced by aircraft has been supplemented by a tax instrument: Law No. 342 of 2000 (Articles 90–95) created a regional tax on the sound emissions of civil aircraft, which substituted the previous taxes provided by Article 10 of Law Decree No. 90 of 1990 and Article 18 of Law No. 449 of 1997.

The tax, which Article 8, paragraph 1 of Legislative Decree No. 68 of 2011 qualifies as a regional tax, is calculated based on the sound emission of aircraft as indicated in the rules on international noise certification, is borne by any party operating civil aircraft and is due, on a quarterly basis, to each region for each takeoff and landing in non-military airports. The tax proceeds must be used on a priority basis to complete the acoustical monitoring system, for noise cleanup and any indemnity given to the residents of areas neighbouring the airport. Each region must divide the amounts received on the basis of the restoration and noise cleanup programs presented by municipalities that are affected by the airport. The regions can increase the tax by means of a regional law by up to 15% if the aircraft takeoff or landing occurs during the times of peak demand. The amount of the tax can also be varied from year to year by a regional law within the limits of the Italian Cost of Living

Index (ISTAT), and can also be differentiated on a territorial basis up to a maximum of 10%, in relation to the residential density of the areas neighbouring the airports.

Law Decree No. 145 of 2013 intervened on such tax, which provides in Article 13, paragraph 15*bis* that 'To avoid distortive effects of competition among airports and to promote the attractiveness of the Italian airport system, including with reference to the events linked to EXPO 2015, in determining the amount of the regional tax on sound emissions from civil aircraft (IRESA), set forth in Articles 90 et seq. of Law No. 342 of 21 November 2000, the maximum value of the parameters of the IRESA tax cannot exceed EUR 0.50. Without prejudice to the maximum value set forth above, the calculation of the tax shall be reformulated to that it also considers the additional criteria of the distinction between daytime and nocturnal flights and the urban characteristics of the geographic areas overlooking the individual airports'.

344. A further sector of special legislation concerns setting maximum sound power levels for certain machinery and equipment characterized by particularly high noise levels destined to be used in homes (domestic appliances) or outdoors (motor compressors, power generators, pneumatic drills, excavators, cranes, lawnmowers, etc.). The regulation of these sources of noise derives entirely from Community law and is characterized by the requirement of certification with respect to the sound power levels of each type of machinery; certification is mandatory prior to commercialization of the product. Further, each of these products must bear a label indicting its sound power level in a visible and lasting manner.

The regime currently applicable to domestic appliances remains that set forth in Legislative Decree No. 134 of 1992, even if it is destined to be superseded by the implementing measures regarding Directive No. 2009/125/EC of the European Parliament and Council of 21 October 2009, related to the creation of a framework for the preparation of specifications for the eco-design of energy-related products. The regime applied to machinery and equipment to be used outdoors is contained in Legislative Decree No. 262 of 2002, which implemented Directive No. 2000/14/EC of the European Parliament and Council of 8 May 2000. In this respect, in implementation of the delegation contained in Article 19, paragraph 2, clauses *i*, *l* and *m* of Law No. 161 of 30 October 2014, Legislative Decree No. 41 of 17 February 2017 was adopted which, through the technique of new provisions, intervenes precisely on cited Legislative Decree No. 262 of 2002.

Finally, after the modifications made by Legislative Decree No. 42 of 2017 to the Framework Law on noise pollution, a sector to be governed by a special regime is that of noise produced by wind farms. Article 3, paragraph 1, clause m*bis*) of the cited law entrusts to a decree of the Minister of the Environment, together with the Ministers of Economic Development, Health and Infrastructures and Transportation, with 'determining [...] the criteria to measure noise emitted by wind farms and to contain the relative noise pollution'. This has also been confirmed by Article 11, paragraph 1 of the Framework Law, as modified by Legislative Decree No. 42 of 2017, which establishes that by means of 'one or more decrees of the Minister of the Environment, together with the Ministers of Health, Infrastructures and Transportation, Defence, Cultural Heritage and Tourism and Economic Development, according to their respective competences, pursuant to Article 17, paragraph 3, of

Law No. 400 of 23 August 1988, one or more regulations have been adopted, distinguished by sound source with regard to the regime on noise pollution originating from maritime traffic, vessels, boats of any kind, cableway and rack lifts, heliports, live shows, as well as from wind farms'.

§5. Conclusions

345. The problem of noise pollution was not adequately dealt with by the Italian legislator for too many years. Only during the 1990s, with the approval of the 1995 Framework Law, was an overall strategy imposed to protect the environment from noise pollution. Notwithstanding the approval of a large number of implementing acts relating to the Framework Law, a concrete and efficient system of protection has not yet been created. The tiered implementation system provided by the Framework Law, based on an extremely complex division of responsibilities among all territorial levels of government, has not yet allowed more than an extremely laborious 'transition' period, characterized by episodic protection limited to individual noise emissions, even though twenty years have passed. Throughout a large part of the national territory, even where the responsible entities have formally complied with the obligations imposed by the national legislator (however not always, and almost never in a timely manner), an ordered and logical planning system of the objectives, the programming of interventions, ongoing monitoring of the phenomenon to be dealt with and the results progressively obtained is still lacking.

346. In addition to the particular intrinsic complexity of its content, three critical elements of the Italian legal framework that has been summarized above should be mentioned.

The first critical element that characterizes the legislation reviewed is the already noted lack of coordination among the various regimes, and in particular, between the two general regimes issued in 1995 and 2005. The Italian legislator is fully aware of such problem; in fact, Article 11 of Law No. 88 of 2009 provided for a special legislative delegation of power to the Government 'for the reorganization and reform of outstanding provisions on the protection of the external environment and the residential environment from noise pollution, acoustic requirements for buildings and the determination and management of environmental noise'; such legislative delegation remained, however, unimplemented due to the expiration of the term, notwithstanding the additional six-month extension provided by Article 15 of Law No. 96 of 2010. The above legislative delegation provided by Article 19 of Law No. 161 of 2014 has not led to significant results from the standpoint of the overall rationalization of the outstanding regime, in implementation of which only Legislative Decrees No. 41 and 42 of 2017 have been approved, regardless of the provision, in the context of such legislative delegation, of specific guiding principles and criteria aimed at rationalizing outstanding internal regulations and harmonizing them with European legislation.

The second critical element that characterizes the legislation reviewed is the total lack of allocation of the specific financial resources required to comply with the new functions imposed on the various territorial public entities. It is extremely significant, for example, that with respect to noise mapping and the action plans, Legislative Decree No. 194 of 2005 actually prohibits the competent entities from providing for 'new or increased charges for public finance', requiring them to implement the new regime exclusively 'within the limits of the financial resources already available under existing legislation' (*see* Article 3, paragraph 9, and Article 4, paragraph 11).

Finally, the third critical element regards the main instrument of protection of the population from noise pollution: the plans for the containment and the reduction of noise, the regulation of which is dictated by the Framework Law and by DM 29 November 2000. The regime concerning these instruments, in fact, at the time of concrete application, has proved to be entirely inadequate to achieve the objectives of acoustic remediation established both by legislation as well as by the plans themselves. Specifically, a number of gaps have emerged in relation to the identification of the parties entrusted with specific powers, such as that of approval of the above plans, powers related to the preliminary review prior to such approval, powers to determine the timeframe for achieving acoustic remediation in derogation of the terms established by the provisions of DM 29 November 2000, as well as with respect to specific procedural issues. With respect to the latter, the regime established by the above decree has been unsuitable in almost all cases of supporting the concrete development, in terms of procedures, of the preliminary process, approval and realization of the plans in question.

Chapter 7. Radiation

by *Antonio Borzì*

§1. Principal State Sources and Objective Scope of Application of the Regime

347. Until 2001, the legal regime on protection from electromagnetic radiation was essentially contained in three acts:

(1) DPCM of 23 April 1992 (*Maximum limits of exposure to electric or magnetic fields generated by low industrial frequency (50 Hz) in residential and external environments*), issued upon a proposal of the Ministry of the Environment, together with the Ministry of Health in accordance with the law creating the Ministry of the Environment (Law No. 349 of 1986), essentially due to the need to establish limits for the exposure of the population to electric and magnetic fields generated by power lines (implemented by DPCM of 28 September 1995).
(2) DM No. 381 of 10 September 1998 (*Regulation containing rules for determining maximum radio frequencies compatible with human health*), issued by the Ministry of the Environment together with the Ministry of Health and the Ministry of Communications, based on Law No. 249 of 1997, created by the Communications Regulatory Authority, to establish exposure limit values for electromagnetic fields related to the functioning and operation of fixed telecommunications and radio-television systems operating in the frequency range included between 100 kHz and 300 GHz.
(3) Law No. 615 of 12 November 1996 (*Implementation of Directive 89/336/EEC of the Council of 3 May 1989, on the reconciliation of the legislation of the Member States on electromagnetic compatibility, modified and integrated by Directive 92/31/EEC of the Council of 28 April 1992, by Directive 93/68/EEC of the Council of 22 July 1993 and by Directive 93/97/EEC of the Council of 29 October 1993*), which sets forth the requirements to place in commerce apparatus capable of generating electromagnetic emissions, or whose functioning could be altered by electromagnetic disturbances in the environment.

By means of Law No. 36 of 22 February 2001 (*Framework Law on protection from exposure to electric, magnetic and electromagnetic fields*), the Italian legal system now has a general and organic regime on electromagnetic pollution, which is applied to all installations, systems and apparatus for civil and military use and for use by the police, which might result in the exposure of workers and the general public to electric, magnetic and electromagnetic fields with frequencies included between 0 Hz and 300 GHz; in particular, the law applies to power lines and radio installations, including installations for mobile telephones, radar and radio broadcasting stations (intentional exposure to fields generated by diagnostic equipment is excluded, Article 2).

By means of the Framework Law, Italy complied with the exhortation of the EC to adopt *specific rules on sources and activities that result in exposure to electromagnetic fields* contained in the Council Recommendation of 12 July 1999, 1999/519/EC, *on the limitation to exposure of the general public to electromagnetic fields ranging from 0 Hz to 300 GHz*. The EC did not intervene in this sector with a binding act, but left the Member States free to introduce, by means of binding or voluntary rules, a framework of exposure limits to electromagnetic fields that use the values indicated in the Recommendation as a reference point (determined on the basis of a study of the International Committee for Protection against Non-Ionizing Radiation). The underlying reason for the choice of a general regime regulating to electromagnetic fields based on a non-binding act, justified by a reference to the principle of proportionality of the intervention of Community institutions (Article 5, paragraph 4 of the TEU), is the need to balance the protection of health with *the other benefits in the field of health and safety, which the devices that emit electromagnetic fields bring to the quality of life in sectors such as telecommunications, electrical energy and the safety of the general public* (Recital No. 7), all in a framework of uncertainty of the indications originating from the scientific community regarding the level of harmfulness of electromagnetic emissions.

348. Differently, the EC legislator intervened in a more decisive manner in the specific sector of the protection of the health and safety of workers, for example, by means of the following acts:

- Council Directive No. 90/270/EEC of 29 May 1990 on the minimum requirements for safety and health relating to occupational activities performed using display screen apparatus.
- Council Directive No. 92/85/EEC of 19 October 1992 concerning the implementation of measures aimed at promoting the improvement of the safety and health of pregnant workers, new mothers or during the period they are breast feeding.
- European Parliament and Council Directive No. 2004/40/EC of 29 April 2004, on the minimum safety and health requirements related to the exposure of workers to risks deriving from physical agents (electromagnetic fields) substituted by European Parliament and Council Directive No. 2013/35/EU of 26 June 2013;
- European Parliament and Council Directive No. 2006/25/EC of 5 April 2006 on the minimum safety and health requirements relative to the exposure of workers to risks deriving from physical agents (artificial optical radiation).

349. Framework Law No. 36 of 2001 serves a triple function:

(1) ensure the protection of the health of workers and the general public from the effects of exposure to electric, magnetic and electromagnetic fields;
(2) promote scientific research to assess the long-terms effects and implement precautionary measures for risks related to exposure to electromagnetic fields;
(3) ensure protection of the environment and the landscape and promote technological innovation and cleanup activities aimed at minimizing the intensity and effects of electric, magnetic and electromagnetic fields according to the best available technologies.

Three types of instruments provided by the law correspond to these objectives to ensure protection from electromagnetic pollution: exposure limits, attention values and quality objectives, which the State is primarily competent for determining, together with the regions.

350. Specifically, as implementation of Law No. 36 of 2001 two decrees of the President of the Council of Ministers were issued on the same date (8 July 2003), determining the exposure limits, attention values and quality objectives: (1) for protection from low-frequency fields (50Hz) generated by power lines; (2) for protection from high-frequency fields ranging from 100 kHz to 300 GHz (for which the exposure limits provided by DM No. 381 of 1998 for fixed telecommunications and radio-television systems are still in effect).

The Framework Law is the first Italian legislative text that explicitly refers to the principle of precaution (Article 1, paragraph 1, clause *b*). In essence, protection from the harmful effects of electromagnetic radiation is one of the backbones of the precautionary approach, which requires the public Authority to intervene to avoid potential danger to health or the environment, particularly in view of the lack of definitive scientific information on the dangerous nature of a human activity, thus, taking highly discretional measures for the political management of a risk to society.

351. At present, in fact, there is no scientific certainty as to the type and extent of damage provoked by electromagnetic waves, above all, in the case of prolonged exposure (*see* the *Report of the Commission on the application of Recommendation No. 1999/512/EC*, Com. No. 532 of 2008 Final, Chapter 4); the Scientific Commission on Emerging and Newly Identified Health Risks is of the opinion that: (a) for radio frequencies (RF: ranging from 100 kHz to 300 GHz), it is unlikely that exposure results in tumours, even if, especially with respect to the fields produced by mobile phones, the duration of exposure is less than the term of induction for some types of cancer (and thus studies are required that analyse a time period that exceeds ten years); and no effect on sensory or cognitive functions has been found, whereas an influence on sleep and on EEG traces has been noted; (b) for intermediary frequencies (IF: ranging from 300 Hz to 100 kHz), the clinical and epidemiological data is quite limited, so that it is necessary to increase research activity, especially regarding long-term exposure connected to work activity; (c) for extremely low frequencies (ranging from 0 kHz to 300 kHz), epidemiological studies reveal that electromagnetic fields are possible carcinogens, especially for childhood leukaemia, but there are no confirmations based on clinical trials (*see* Report on the health effects of exposure to electromagnetic fields of 19 January 2009).

352. The overview of State legislative sources includes the provisions of Legislative Decree No. 259 of 1 August 2003 (*Electronic Communications Code*); in particular, Articles 87 and 88, which deal with the authorization procedure for electronic communications infrastructures, as well as the provisions on the location of radio-television installations contained in cited Law No. 249 of 1997 and Legislative Decree No. 177 of 31 July 2005 (*Uniform Text on Audiovisual Media Services and Radio*) (specifically Articles 28 and 42).

353. Another aspect regards the construction characteristics of devices to mitigate electromagnetic emissions. The principal laws consist of:

- Legislative Decree No. 194 of 6 November 2007 *Implementation of Directive 2004/108/EC on the reconciliation of the legislation of Member States on electromagnetic compatibility, which repeals Directive 89/336/EEC,* modified by Legislative Decree No. 80 of 18 May 2016, implementing Directive 2014/30/EU.
- Legislative Decree No. 128 of 22 June 2016, *Implementation of Directive 2014/53/EU on the harmonization of the laws of the Member States relating to the making available on the market of radio equipment and repealing Directive 1999/5/EC.*

It is necessary to clarify that the decrees are intended to ensure the electromagnetic compatibility of products in order to avoid 'electromagnetic disturbance'. The primary interest pursued is that of standardizing technical standards for devices placed in commerce which, by means of the production of electromagnetic waves, might alter the functioning of other devices (or be subject to malfunctioning as a result of magnetic fields); the protection of health and the environment is, therefore, an indirect and secondary effect.

354. Further, Italy has implemented Community laws, cited above, on the safety and protection of the health of workers, most recently by means of Legislative Decree No. 81 of 9 April 2008 *Implementation of Article 1 of Law No. 123 of 3 August 2007 on the protection of workplace health and safety*; Title VII on apparatus with display screens and Title VIII on physical agents (in particular, Chapter 4 on the protection of workers from risks of exposure to electromagnetic fields and Chapter 5 on the protection of workers from risks of exposure to artificial optical radiation). Such regime and that on the protection from ionized radiation (i.e., radiation originating from the decay process of the nucleus of an atom, radioactivity, whether of artificial or natural origin, capable of modifying the structure of the materials with which they interact) are not the object of this chapter.

§2. Programming and Planning Instruments

355. The Framework Law provides for the gradual adjustment of radio installations and power lines to exposure limits, attention values and quality objectives, by means of recovery plans that are approved, depending on the power generated by the installations, by the Ministry of the Environment or by the regions (or the provinces, upon a delegation of power set forth in a regional law), upon a proposal of the managers (with the substitute intervention of the public authority in the case of the failure to act).

356. Article 9 of Law No. 36 del 2001, and the regional laws implementing it, regulate the timeframe, procedures and content of the plans, as well as the effects of the lack of approval:

(a) *Recovery plan for radio installations* (defined by Article 4, paragraph 1, clause *h*, and which include, in accordance with Article 2, paragraph 1, installations for mobile telephones, radar and radio broadcasting stations). The plan must be presented by the installation's manager within one year from the date the decree determining exposure levels, attention values and quality objectives enters into effect. The region (or province, if delegated by regional law) is competent to approve the plan, having heard the municipalities involved. If the manager fails to act or is non-compliant, the plan is approved by the region, which also controls the recovery work to be carried out by the manager, who must also bear the economic costs involved. With respect to content, the plan must also provide for the relocation of radio broadcasting stations to sites conforming to relevant planning instruments or different kinds of installations in suitable sites; in any case, it must provide for a gradual adjustment to be made over the course of twenty-four months subsequent to approval of the plan.

(b) *Recovery plan for power lines* (defined by Article 4, paragraph 1, clause e of the Framework Law). The plan must be presented by the managers of power lines within one year from when the State decree that establishes the criteria for its preparation is issued (Article 4, paragraph 4). The owners of portions of the national transmission network or anyone who in any case can use it must timely provide the manager of the national transmission network with a proposed recovery plan for the lines for which they are competent, as well as all of the information required to present the proposed recovery plan.

The plan must indicate the projects that it intends to implement in order to comply with exposure limits and attention values and to achieve quality objectives; it must also indicate the chronological implementation programme, adjusting itself to the priorities established by the cited decree, considering as a priority situations subject to the highest levels of electromagnetic pollution, closeness to residential, scholastic and healthcare buildings, or buildings to be used for prolonged periods of at least four hours, with particular reference to the protection of children.

(i) The plan related to power lines of more than 150 kV must be presented to the Ministry of the Environment, which approves it, with the necessary modifications, integrations or requirements, together with the Ministry of Productive Activities and the Ministry of Infrastructures, after hearing the Ministry of Health as well as the regions and municipalities involved. If the manager fails to act or is non-compliant, the plan is proposed by the region.

(ii) The recovery plan for power lines that are less than or equal to 150 kV is presented to the region which approves it, with the necessary modifications, integrations or requirements, within sixty days, having heard the municipalities involved. If the manager fails to act or is non-compliant, the plan is adopted by the region.

357. Article 11 of the Framework Law extends the provisions of the general law on administrative procedures, Law No. 241 of 1990, with respect to participation in the administrative procedure, to the recovery plans for power lines, that is, in derogation of what is established, in general, by such Law No. 241 of 1990 for the approval of planning acts. Case law has specified that Article 9 of Law No. 36 of 2001 expresses a dual need: that of initiating a dialogue with the managers, and considering, in relation to the work to be done to the installations, the operative needs of the public service (telecommunications or the distribution of electrical energy, T.A.R. Umbria, judgment No. 269 of 12 May 2005; *Ibid.*, judgment No. 333 of 12 May 2003).

358. The law provides for the completion of the recovery of the power lines over a period of ten years from the date it enters into effect (with intermediary stages in 2004 and 2008). It will be difficult to comply with this term given the delay that accumulated with respect to the presentation and approval of the plans.

The failure to cleanup the power lines, radio installations and systems, systems for mobile phones and radio broadcasting stations according to the requirements of the plan, due to the manager's failure to act or non-compliance, in addition to pecuniary sanctions, will also result in the deactivation of the station for a period of up to six months, as in any case the rights of users to use the public utility service must be guaranteed. Deactivation is ordered (Article 9, paragraph 6):

(a) for power lines with more than 150 kV, by the Ministry of the Environment;
(b) for power lines of less than 150 kV and for radio systems (excluding the categories of installations set forth in the following clause), by the President of the regional council;
(c) in the case of mobile phones and radio systems and fixed telephone installations, as well as radio stations for the transmission of data, by the Ministry of Communications, which must ensure the uniform application of the regime throughout the national territory.

359. With respect to the latter issue, it should be noted that the Communications Department of the Ministry for Economic Development has the power to order, upon the request of the regions, the relocation of radio-television installations that exceed exposure limits (Article 28, Legislative Decree No. 177 of 2005). The transfer is made at the expense of the owner of the installation in one of the sites provided by the National Plan for the Allocation of Frequencies.

Such plan is approved by the Communications Regulatory Authority and established the number of networks and programs broadcast nationwide and locally, indicating the various emission sites (Article 2 of Law No. 249 of 1997; Article 42 Legislative Decree No. 177 of 2005).

§3. Specific Instruments for Direct Regulation

360. The principal instrument that the Framework Law uses to ensure the protection of the health of the general public and of workers, safeguard the environment and the landscape and reduce as much as possible the intensity and effects of electromagnetic fields consists of exposure limits, attention values and quality objectives for installations (Article 3, paragraph 1, clauses b–d):

(a) exposure limit is defined as 'the value of the electric, magnetic and electromagnetic field, considered as an emission value, which must not be exceeded in any manner, determined to protect health from acute effects of exposure of the general public and workers'; and serves the purposes set forth in Article 1, paragraph 1, clause *a*: ensure the protection of the health of workers and the general public, especially from the acute effects of electromagnetic fields;

(b) *attention value* means *the value of the electric, magnetic and electromagnetic field, considered as an emission value, which must not be exceeded in residential and scholastic environments and in places used for prolonged periods*, and serves the purposes set forth in Article 1, paragraph 1, clauses *b* and *c*. The attention value is a precautionary measure to protect against the possible long-term effects of exposure to electromagnetic fields, and must be achieved with the timeframe and in the manner provided by law;

(c) the Framework Law considers two types of quality objectives:
   (i) the values of electric, magnetic and electromagnetic fields, defined by the State according to the provisions set forth in Article 4, paragraph 1, clause (a), in view of the progressive mitigation of exposure to such fields;
   (ii) the location criteria, urban planning standards, restrictions and incentives for the use of the best available technologies, indicated by the regional laws according to the competences defined in Article 8 of the law.

361. The procedure for the State to determine exposure limits, attention values and quality objectives, in terms of field values, is set forth in Article 4, paragraph 2, of the Framework Law (the same procedure is applied to determine detection and measurement techniques for electromagnetic pollution and the parameters for determining the buffer zones for power lines). The law identifies the proponent administration according to whether the measures are aimed at the general public or workers:

- The exposure limits, attention values and quality objectives for the general public are determined by a decree of the President of the Council of Ministers, upon a proposal of the Ministry of the Environment, together with the Ministry of Health, after hearing the opinion of the Inter-ministerial Committee for the prevention and reduction of electromagnetic pollution (an organ created by Article 6 of the Framework Law) and the competent parliamentary commissions, after agreement during the Unified Conference set forth in Article 9 of Legislative Decree No. 281 of 29 August 1997 (an organ made up of representatives of State, regional and local administrations).
- The exposure limits, attention values and quality objectives for workers are also established by a decree of the President of the Council of Ministers, but upon the proposal of the Ministry of Health, having heard the Ministry of the Environment and the Ministry of Labour and Social Policies, the Committee set forth in Article 6 and the competent parliamentary commissions, after agreement during the Unified Conference. Such decree was never issued: the exposure limits for workers are set forth in Legislative Decree No. 81 of 2008 and repeat those established by Directive 2004/40/EC.

In both cases, it is possible to bypass the opinion of the Unified Conference when it is not issued within the established deadlines. This was the case of DPCM of 8 July 2003, which established the exposure limits, attention values and quality objectives: (a) for protection from low-frequency fields (50Hz) generated by power lines; and (b) for protection from high-frequency fields included between 100 kHz and 300 GHz.

Law Decree No. 179 of 10 October 2012, converted with modifications in Law No. 221 of 17 December 2012 (Article 14, paragraph 8), established that, without prejudice to outstanding provisions contained in DPCM 8 July 2003 setting exposure limits, attention thresholds and quality objectives to protect the public from exposure to electrical, magnetic and electromagnetic fields generated on frequencies ranging between 100 kHz and 300 GHz:

(a) the attention thresholds indicated in Table 2 of Annex B of the cited decree are precautionary measures to protect against possible effects, including long-term effects, that may be related to exposure to the fields generated by the above frequencies in the following cases:
   (i) within buildings used for residential purposes with permanence of at least four hours a day;
   (ii) only in the case of use with permanence of at least four hours a day: in external areas with habitable dimensions as defined in the guidelines set forth in clause *d* below such as balconies, terraces and courtyards (excluding roofs even if there are skylights and flat roofs having the primary function of a roof covering, independently or whether or not there are balustrades or anti-fall protection and finished flooring, that are the common property of the condominium owners);
(b) in the case of exposure to installations that generate electric, magnetic and electromagnetic fields with a frequency between 100 kHz and 300 GHz, the exposure limits provided for in table 1 of Annex B of the cited decree, considered as effective values, cannot be exceeded. These values must be measured at a height of 1.50 m from the flooring and averaged over any six-minute interval. The values referred to in clause *a* must instead be measured at a height of 1.50 m from the flooring and considered as the average of the values during a twenty-four-hour period;
(c) for purposes of the progressive minimization of exposure to electromagnetic fields, the input values of electric, magnetic and electromagnetic fields generated at frequencies ranging between 100 kHz and 300 GHz, calculated or measured in open air areas that are intensively frequented must not exceed the values indicated in Table 3 of Annex B of the cited decree, measured at a height of 1.50 meters from the flooring and considered as the average of the values during a twenty-four-hour period;
(d) the techniques of measurement and detection of the exposure levels to be used are indicated in standard CEI 211-7 or in specific standards enacted subsequently by CEI (Italian Electrotechnical Committee). For control purposes to determine that the attention threshold and quality objective have not been exceeded, reference can also be made to extrapolation methodologies based on

the installation's technical and historical data to identify the average values during a twenty-four-hour period. The techniques for the forecast calculation to be used are those indicated in the standard CEI 211-10 or in specific standards enacted subsequently by CEI. For purposes of verifying the attention threshold and quality objective through the forecast calculation, the requirements provided by Legislative Decree No. 259 of 2003 will be based on the average values during a twenty-four-hour period, measured on the basis of the reduction of the maximum power to the antenna connector with specific factors that consider the temporal variability of the installation's emissions during the twenty-four-hour period. These power reduction factors are to be identified in specific guidelines prepared by ISPRA and ARPA/APPA. Such guidelines will be approved by one or more decrees of MATTM, after hearing the competent Parliamentary committees. To date the following have been enacted:

(i) guidelines for the provision of data and forecast estimates for the installations (DM 2 December 2014);
(ii) guidelines on the absorption value of the electromagnetic fields by the building structures (DM 5 October 2016);
(iii) guidelines for the definition of the external areas of buildings so operators can provide data on the installations (DM 7 December 2016).

362. With respect to quality objectives that are the competence of the regions, the Constitutional Court, in the context of the controversy between the State and regions subsequent to modification of Title V, Part II of the Constitution on territorial autonomies (2001), defined the limits of the power of the regions to determine location criteria, urban planning standards and restrictions for installations that produce electromagnetic fields.

363. Above all, the regions cannot establish threshold values that are more rigorous that those established by the State, because the latter are considered *the point of equilibrium between the opposing needs to avoid as much as possible the impact of electromagnetic emissions and to build installations that are necessary for the Nation*, which it is the State's duty to identify. With respect, instead, to location criteria and urban planning standards, the regions must act in compliance with the national planning needs for installations and cannot adopt measures which, in substance, might unjustifiably impede or hinder communications or energy infrastructures (Constitutional Court, judgment No. 307 of 2003; *see also* judgment No. 103 of 2006). In other words, in order to be lawful, location criteria must not be transformed into 'limits on location', that is, which impede de facto the location of the installations (as in the case of the provision of minimum distances, even in places that are highly urbanized), but must always allow a possible alternative location (as in the case of the prohibition of installations in correspondence with sensitive areas such as hospitals or nursery schools, Constitutional Court, judgment No. 331 of 2003, or in limited areas of the territory, Constitutional Court, judgment No. 303 of 2007).

364. Other instruments provided by the Italian legal system are directly linked to the principle of information in the environmental sector, in its dual meaning of the need for the public administration to obtain data and information for efficient protection, as well as the obligation of the authority to provide information to the public that is clear, updated and transparent on the state of the environment, the factors that might damage it and the measures that have been taken to guarantee its protection.

From the first viewpoint the creation of a national registry for fixed and mobile sources of electrical, magnetic and electromagnetic fields is noted, which, in coordination with the regional land registries, detects ambient field levels (Law No. 36 of 2001, Article 4, paragraph 1, clause *c*) and 7; DM 31 March 2017).

With respect to public information, Article 12 of the Framework Law provides for a decree issued by the MATTM that determines the information that the manufacturer of devices and apparatus, in particular, for domestic, individual or occupational use, that generate electrical, magnetic or electromagnetic fields must provide to users and workers by means of special labels or information sheets. The information must specifically regard the exposure levels produced by the device or apparatus, the distance of use advised to reduce exposure to the electric, magnetic and electromagnetic field, and the principal safety measures. The same decree identifies the types of devices and apparatus for which there is no emission of electric, magnetic and electromagnetic fields, or for which such emissions are considered to be so low that they do not require any precautions.

Such decree was never issued, and this is particularly indicative of how the communication of risk and the determination of 'acceptable' risk in order to adopt precautionary measures are mutually influenced. The communication of the existence of a risk is in and of itself a precautionary measure (Communication of the Commission of 2 February 2000, with respect to precaution: *decisions to inform the public on the possible negative effects of a product or process can be acts based on the principle of precaution*), but it is clear that the perception that public opinion has of a risk influences the determination of an acceptable risk which rests with the public power, and consequently the choice of additionally further precautionary measures to be taken to manage the risk.

Legislative Decrees No. 194 of 2007 and No. 269 of 2001 should be noted on the conformity and electromagnetic compatibility of products, again noting that the primary interest that they protect is the unrestricted circulation of goods, so that the information required from the manufacturer (or whoever places the apparatus in commerce) essentially regards the proper use of the device.

Finally, Article 9, paragraph 7 of the Framework Law provides that each power line, radio installation or radio broadcasting station must have a clearly visible informational label indicating the voltage generated, the exposure values set forth in the relative authorization, the exposure limits and attention values prescribed by national and regional laws, and the buffer zone.

§4. Authorization Procedures

365. The Framework Law attributes the State with competence to determine the paths and authorize the construction and operation of high-voltage power lines greater than 150 kV, and entrusts the regions with the same responsibility for power lines whose voltage is equal to or less than such threshold (Article 4, paragraph 1, clause *g*); Article 5, paragraph 3; and Article 8, paragraph 1, clauses *b* and *c*.

366. On the basis of Article 5 of Law No. 36 of 2001, a government regulation must:

(a) identify specific measures related to the technical characteristics of the installations and the location of the paths for the planning, construction and modification of power lines and systems for mobile phones and radio broadcasting;
(b) introduce measures aimed at avoiding damage to environmental resources, including specific provisions for the planning, construction and modification of power lines in areas subject to restrictions imposed by State or regional law, as well as territorial and urban planning instruments, for the protection of historic, artistic, architectural, landscape and environmental resources;
(c) approve measures to contain the electric risk of the installations set forth in clause *a*, and in particular, the risk of electrocution and collision with birds;
(d) establish a new regime of authorization procedures for the construction and operation of high-voltage power lines greater than 150 kV, that combines administrative simplification with the preventive assessment of electromagnetic fields (*see* Article 5, paragraph 3).

Such regulation was never issued, but starting from 2003 (and with subsequent modifications and integrations in 2004 and 2009), specific laws were introduced with respect to the authorization of power lines that are part of the national transportation grid for electrical energy (licensed to a sole manager).

367. Specifically, Article 1*sexies* of Law Decree No. 239 of 29 August 2003, converted with modifications into Law No. 290 of 27 October 2003, which has subsequently been further modified, provides that the construction and operation of power lines, as well as the related works and infrastructures indispensable for their operation, are subject to a single authorization issued by the Ministry for Economic Development, together with the MATTM, upon agreement with the region or regions involved.

There is only one authorization because it substitutes authorizations, permits, approvals and any clearances, regardless of what they are called, provided by outstanding laws, and includes any work or action required to resolve interference with other existing infrastructures. It serves as a permit to construct and operate such infrastructures, works or installations and to pass through public property, in conformity with the approved project. The procedure is carried out in compliance with principles of simplification and in the manner set forth in Law No. 241 of 7 August 1990 (the general law on administrative procedures) and DPR No. 327 of 8 June 2001 (Uniform Text on expropriations).

368. The realization of power lines is also subject to an EIA (Legislative Decree No. 152 of 2006, Part II and relative Annexes):

- the State (MATTM) is competent for aerial high-voltage power lines greater than 150 kV and with paths longer than 15 km, and underground cable power lines with alternating current, with paths longer than 40 km;
- the regions are competent for power lines for the transportation of electrical energy whose voltage exceeds 100 kV with paths longer than 10 km (if the path is between 3 km and 10 km, a screening is necessary to *see* whether it is subject to an EIA).

369. Article 8 of Law No. 36 of 2001 attributes the regions with responsibility for determining the procedures to issue authorizations for installations regarding mobile telephones, radio installations and radio broadcasting stations, considering pre-existing electric, magnetic and electromagnetic fields (clause *c*). Approximately one year after the Framework Law entered into effect, however, by means of Legislative Decree No. 198 of 2002, the national legislator regulated the authorization procedure in a uniform manner throughout the national territory. The Constitutional Court found the decree to be unconstitutional, however (judgment No. 303 of 2003) because it was prejudicial to the sphere of autonomy granted by the Constitution to the regions. At present, the authorization procedure for radio installations, including telephone installations, is regulated by the Electronic Communications Code (Legislative Decree No. 259 of 1 August 2003, Articles 86 through 88).

370. The code guarantees the mandatory rights of individual liberty to use electronic means of communication, as well as the right of economic initiative and its exercise in conditions of free competition in the sector of electronic communications. This results in the need for uniform rules for activities that Legislative Decree No. 259 of 2003 qualifies are of *predominant general interest* (Article 3).

The installation is authorized upon verification by the technical organ entrusted with the control (ARPA) of the compatibility of the project presented with the exposure limits, attention values and quality objectives.

The procedure is characterized by its speed and the use of different instruments in view of procedural simplification:

(a) the conference of services among the interested administrations, with the approval of the majority of those present substitutes, to all effect, any acts for which the individual administrations are competent, and also serves as a declaration of public utility and urgency of the work which cannot be delayed (thus avoiding the need for an additional bureaucratic procedure to obtain a building permit, Constitutional Court, judgment No. 129 of 2006 and order No. 203 of 2006; State Council, judgment No. 4557 of 15 July 2010, section VI);
(b) the certified notification of the initiation of work for installations using UMTS (universal mobile telecommunications systems) or other technology with single antennas having power equal to or less than 20 W (without prejudice to compliance with exposure limits, attention values and quality objectives);
(c) silence amounting to assent, after ninety days have passed from the presentation of the project and relative application, except in the case of the justified dissent of an administration entrusted with environmental protection, the protection of health or protection of historic-artistic heritage.

For some types of plants (the installation of devices using UMTS technology, its development or other technologies on infrastructures for pre-existing radio-electric systems or modification of the transmission characteristics), a further simplified procedure is envisaged, based on reporting the initiation of activity which is consolidated after thirty days has passed without notice of a negative measure of the Municipality or ARPA (Legislative Decree No. 259 of 2003, Article 87*bis*).

In order to accelerate the realization of investments for completion of electronic communications networks, it has been established that in the case of modifications of the characteristics of systems that have already been authorized, which result in increases of height that do not exceed 1 m and increases of the surface areas of shape that do not exceed 1.5 m^2, self-certification is sufficient that describes the change in size and compliance with the limits, values and objectives set forth in Article 87, to be sent at the same time as the work to the same bodies that issued the authorizations (Article 87*ter*).

371. In some regions (e.g., Abruzzo, Emilia-Romagna, Liguria, Molise, Piedmont and Tuscany) the manager of the telephone service must notify the municipality on an annual basis of its programme to develop the network. Case law has held that such instrument is not unconstitutional in and of itself, *because it corresponds to criteria of rationality of administrative actions, the need to introduce minimum criteria of prior knowledge and planning for the construction of installations in order to provide guidelines for preventive administrative building, urban planning and environmental controls with respect to consent for the installation of radio stations*, but in the end conflicts with the fundamental principles of administrative speed and simplification expressed by the Electronic Communications Code, if the manager is not allowed to update its programme during the course of the year (*see* T.A.R. Tuscany, judgment No. 3236 of 26 July 2006; *see* Constitutional Court, judgment No. 303 of 2007 on the municipal plan provided by Friuli – Venezia Giulia regional law No. 28 of 2004).

§5. Control System

372. The administrative functions of health and environmental controls and supervision of the implementation of regulations on electromagnetic pollution are attributed to the provincial and municipal administrations, which use, as a technical-operative organ, the ARPA, in accordance with Law Decree No. 496 of 4 December 1993, converted, with modifications, by Law No. 61 of 21 January 1994 and Law No. 32 of 28 June 2016.

The personnel entrusted with the controls, who are issued an identity card by the entity for which they work, can have access to the installations that are the source of electromagnetic emissions and request the data, information and documents required to carry out their functions, in conformity with the provisions of Law No. 241 of 7 August 1990 and subsequent modifications.

373. The control activities carried out by ARPA in relation to the emission of radio installations, regulated by the Electronic Communications Code, cannot be performed by the managers, given the prohibition for public administrations, established by Article 93 of Legislative Decree No. 259 of 2003, to *impose, for electronic communications networks or services, charges or fees that have not been determined by* (State) *law* (in general, *see* Constitutional Court, judgment No. 336 of 2005, which found that the objective of Article 93 is to protect competition and guarantee equal treatment throughout the national territory and measures that are not aimed at hindering the entry of new subjects in the sector, as well as judgment No. 450 of 2006 and No. 272 of 2010 with respect to the costs of ARPA's activity, provided by regional laws). Law No. 221 of 2015 introduced the obligation to pay a contribution for the preliminary expenses related to the issue of the authorizations).

374. The State's central organs are also responsible for supervision. In particular, Communications Regulatory Authority is responsible for supervising the maximum radio frequencies that are compatible with human health (established by DM No. 381 of 1998) as well as for controlling that such maximum limits, even due to the combined effect of various electromagnetic emissions, are not exceeded. The agency uses peripheral organs of the Communications Department of the Ministry for Economic Development, previously the Ministry of Communications (Law No. 249 of 1997, Article 6, clause *a*, and Article 15.

§6. SANCTIONS

375.

(a) Crimes provided by the Framework Law (Article 15):
   - (i) Exceeding exposure limits and attention values. Article 15 of the Framework Law punishes, above all, whoever exceed the exposure limits and attention values when operating or using a source or installation that generates electric, magnetic and electromagnetic fields. There is a monetary fine that varies from a minimum of EUR 103,200 to a maximum of EUR 309,874,00. Whoever does not comply with the limits and timeframe provided by a recovery plan in course of implementation is subject to the same penalty; in this case, in addition to the fine the installation is deactivated, in accordance with Article 9, paragraph 6.
   - (ii) Violation of the protective measures set forth in Article 5, paragraph 1. Whoever violates the protective measures determined by the State in accordance with Article 5, paragraph 1 of the Framework Law, that is, the specific measures related to the technical characteristics of the installations and the location of the paths for the planning, construction and modification of power lines and systems for mobile phones and radio broadcasting, as well as the measures aimed at avoiding damage to environmental resources, including specific provisions for the planning, construction and modification of power lines in restricted areas, must pay an amount ranging from EUR 1,032 to EUR 10,329,100.

(iii) Violation of the restrictions contained in authorizations for installations. In the case of failure to comply with the restrictions imposed by the authorization to protect the environment and health for the construction and operation of installations, the sanction consists of the suspension of the authorization from two to four months. In the case of a new offence, the authorization is revoked.

(b) Crimes provided by other laws in the sector. The Electronic Communications Code provides a minimum sanction of EUR 50,000 for the installation or operation of radio installations in the lack of authorization (Article 98); the law refers, however, not to the authorization of the single installation, regulated by Article 87 (paragraph 4), but to the general authorization set forth in Article 25, that the manager must obtain to provide electronic communications networks or services, and which entitles it to request the specific permits to exercise the right to instalment of an installation (Article 26). In any case, the instalment of an installation in the lack of the necessary authorization constitutes the realization of an abusive construction, provided and punished as a crime by legislation on the construction industry (Article 44, DPR No. 381 of 6 June 2001, *see* Criminal Court of Cassation, judgment No. 32527 of 1 September 2010, section III).

(c) Article 674 of the Criminal Code. With respect to the regime of sanctions, Italian law with respect to electromagnetic pollution is characterized by the exclusive presence of administrative crimes, the major part punished with pecuniary sanctions. Most cast law, however, has applied the general provision set forth in Article 647 of the Criminal Code to electromagnetic emissions, which punishes 'the dangerous throwing of moveable things', that is, the behaviour of whoever *throws or pours in a place of public transit, or in a private place that is common or used by others, things that offend or dirty or harm people.* On the basis of the literal tenor of the norm set forth in paragraph 2 of Article 624 of the Criminal Code (*for the purposes of criminal law considers even electrical energy any other form of energy that has economic value to be a moveable thing*) and in consideration of the very broad meaning attributed to the verb 'to throw', case law, attentive to the needs linked to economic and social development, has extended Article 674 of the Criminal Code to the broadcast of electromagnetic waves (*see* Criminal Court of Cassation, judgment No. 214416 of 13 October 1999, section I, and Criminal Court of Cassation, judgment No. 39 of 14 October 1999, section I). There is no uniformity, however, regarding the elements of the crime: according to one part (minority) of case law, the crime exists regardless of whether the emission limits have been exceeded due to the sole fact of having caused offence or damage to the public (Criminal Court of Cassation, judgment No. 10475 of 31 January 2001, section I); whereas for a different orientation (the major part), the emission of electromagnetic waves falls within the scope of Article 674 of the Criminal Code when, in addition to verifying that the emission limits have been exceeded, there is certain and objective evidence of actual and concrete danger of harm to health and the tranquillity of the general public (Criminal Court of Cassation, judgment No. 1570 of 9 January 2009, section III; Criminal Court of Cassation, judgment No. 36845 of 26 September 2008, section III).

§7. DISTRIBUTION OF COMPETENCE AMONG TERRITORIAL LEVELS OF GOVERNMENT

I. State

376. The State is responsible, above all, for determining exposure limits, attention values and quality objectives as field values; the Framework Law links State competence to the *predominant national interest in determining uniform criteria and homogeneous regulations in relation to the objectives set forth in Article 1* (Article 4, paragraph 1, clause *a*).

The State is also competent to:

- adopt a new regime for authorization procedures for the construction and operation of high-voltage power lines greater than 150 kV;
- authorize high-voltage power lines greater than 150 Kv (the Ministry for Economic Development, State Council, judgment No. 4664 of 20 July 2010, section VI);
- determine the paths of high-voltage power lines greater than 150 kV and determine the parameters for buffer zones around the power lines so that they are not next to buildings used for residential, scholastic or healthcare purposes or for prolonged periods of more than four hours;
- adopt specific measures related to the technical characteristics of the installations and location of paths for the planning, construction and modification of power lines and installations for mobile telephones and radio broadcasting;
- determine general criteria for the installation of networks used to broadcast radio-television programmes (Communications Regulatory Authority);
- adopt specific measures intended to avoid damage to environmental and landscape resources and additional specific measures for the planning, construction and modification of power lines in restricted areas;
- provide containment measures for the electrical risk of installations, in particular, the risk of electrocution and collision with birds;
- create a national registry of fixed and mobile sources of electric, magnetic and electromagnetic sources and the territorial areas involved;
- determine the criteria for the preparation of the recovery plans set forth in Article 9, paragraph 2;
- approve recovery plans for high-voltage power lines greater than 150 kV;
- issue the order for deactivation due to failure to implement the recovery plan, in the case of high-voltage power lines greater than 150 kV;
- issue measures for the relocation of radio-television installations that exceed exposure limits (Ministry for Economic Development, Communications Department);
- identify the techniques for the detection and measurement of electromagnetic pollution;
- promote research activity and scientific-technical experiments (in particular, the Ministry of Health);

- determine the information that manufacturers of devices and apparatus, in particular, for domestic, individual or occupational use, that generate electric, magnetic and electromagnetic fields must provide to users;
- enter into programme agreements with the managers or owners of power lines or transmission grids, or whoever is entitled to operate them, as well as operators of radio-television broadcasting stations and mobile telephone systems, in order to promote technologies and building techniques for the construction of the installations that allow ambient emissions to be minimized and in order to protect the landscape;
- promote undertakings and programme agreements with the managers of public transportation that produce electric, magnetic and electromagnetic fields, in order to enhance and develop technologies that allow emissions to be minimized.

II. Regions

377. The responsibilities of the regions are set forth in Article 8 of the Framework Law; the regime on functions is supplemented by the regional laws that have implemented Law No. 36 of 2001.

The regions are competent to:

- identify the transmissions sites and installations for mobile phone systems, radio installations and radio broadcasting stations (ensuring the compliance of such installations with the National Plan for the Allocation of Frequencies);
- determine the paths of power lines that do not exceed 150 kV, providing for buffer zones according to parameters established in accordance with Article 4 and the obligation to report them;
- authorize power lines equal to or less than 150 kV;
- determine the authorization procedures to instal the above installations, in conformity with criteria of administrative simplification, considering pre-existing electric, magnetic and electromagnetic fields;
- create, in coordination with the national registry, a regional registry of fixed sources of electric, magnetic and electromagnetic fields, in order to detect the levels of such fields in the regional territory, with reference to the conditions of exposure for the general public;
- identify instruments and activities to achieve quality objectives;
- contribute to developing scientific knowledge related to the effects on health, in particular, long-term effects, deriving from exposure to electric, magnetic and electromagnetic fields.

III. Local Entities

378. The major part of the powers of municipalities and provinces are regulated by regional legislation. Article 8 of the Framework Law grants the regions the power to determine, within the scope of their powers, the responsibilities of the local administrations; thus, some regions entrust the provinces with the function of approving the recovery plan for power lines (e.g., Abruzzo, Emilia-Romagna, Piedmont) or planning the location of radio broadcasting stations (e.g., Abruzzo, Emilia Romagna).

The Framework Law expressly refers to provincial and municipal administrations with respect to supervision and control, and Article 8, paragraph 6 attributes the municipality with power to adopt a regulation to ensure the proper urban and territorial location of the installations and to minimize the exposure of the general public to electromagnetic fields.

Case law has clarified the regulatory power of local entities. In general, the municipality cannot have the objective (even if undeclared, but demonstrated by the content of the regulatory act) of preserving human health from electromagnetic emissions, as this is attributed to concurrent State-regional legislation (Council of State, judgment of 24 September 2010, section VI, No. 7128).

Following such approach, the municipality has the possibility of implementing rules, from an urban planning standpoint, to protect areas and resources having particular landscape-environmental or historical-artistic value, or, with respect to the minimization of exposure to electromagnetic fields, to identify sites which due to their use or type of user can be considered to be sensitive to radio emissions (Council of State, judgment No. 1017 of 3 March 2010, section VI). For the same reasons, the municipality can neither impose limitations and general prohibitions referring to homogeneous territorial areas, nor buffer zones with respect to residences and places used for prolonged periods, or in urban centres, when such power is aimed at regulating the compatibility of such installations with the protection of human health in order to prevent risks deriving from the exposure of the general public to electromagnetic fields, rather than just control compliance with the limits on radio frequencies established by State law and regulate matters that typically relate to the urban planning sector (Council of State, judgment No. 450 of 14 February 2005, section V; Council of State, judgment No. 5673 of 2 November 2007, section VI; T.A.R. Sicily, Catania, section I, judgment No. 407 of 11 February 2016).

Normally the municipality is competent to authorize the installation of plants according to what is established by Article 87 of the Code on Electronic Communications.

§8. Conclusions

379. Italy has had an organic regime since 2001 on the protection of health from exposure to electromagnetic radiation and the protection of the environment from the impact provoked by installations that generate electromagnetic fields. Italian law, based on a precautionary approach, not only imposes exposure limits to protect health from acute effects of radiation, but determines attention values aimed at avoiding the long-term effects of electromagnetic waves, as well as field values and location requirements (i.e., quality objectives) aimed at progressively reducing the effects of electromagnetic fields in accordance with the best available technologies (Framework Law No. 36 of 2001).

Some of the national measures proposed by the European Parliament in the *Resolution on health concerns associated with electromagnetic fields* of 2 April 2002 already exist in the Italian legal system, similar to the requirement of an authorization for the construction of installations or the use of agreements between authorities and managers to minimize the impact of electromagnetic fields.

The critical nature of the Italian situation essentially regards two issues: the implementation of the part of the Framework Law that requires the recovery of existing infrastructures, and information to the general public on the risks connected to the installations and devices that generate electromagnetic radiation, judged to be very poor since the survey conducted by Eurobarometer in June 2007. Under this second profile, the situation has improved due to the implementation of disclosure requirements with respect to the worker (but not the general public) provided by Legislative Decree No. 81 of 2008.

Chapter 8. The Prevention of Major Accidents

by *Marcello Cecchetti*

§1. Evolution of the Italian Legal System

380. The current Italian legal framework on the dangers of major accidents is the result of a progressive stratification of legal interventions that can be subdivided into six fundamental periods.

381. No specific regime existed prior to 1988: it was necessary to refer to a broad series of heterogeneous provisions regarding fire prevention, the use of toxic gas, the prevention of industrial accidents and unhealthy and dangerous industries.

382. In 1988, the Italian legislator implemented, with a few years of delay, the first Community directive, Directive No. 82/501/EEC (the 'Seveso Directive'), specifically aimed at regulating the 'risks' of major accidents connected with specific industrial activities. The formal Italian implementation of the directive is set forth in DPR No. 175 of 17 May 1988, which incorporates the contents of the Community law with only a few modifications, all of which are stricter than Community law. Definitive alignment with the European regime was subsequently reached by means of DPCM of 31 March 1989 and DM of 20 May 1991, the latter as implementation of Directive No. 88/610/EEC, which partially modified the 1982 directive.

Notwithstanding formal conformity to the Community legal system, Italian regulation of major accident risks was unsatisfactory. In particular, it was excessively complex and its procedures were scarcely functional due, above all, to the superimposition of competencies of the technical control organs and due to the lack of adequate organizational support, includingwith reference to political and administrative entities.

383. This situation constituted the basis for a reform process initiated by DPR No. 175 of 1988, which is characterized by the issuance of a lengthy series of law decrees by the government (twenty in all, starting from Law Decree No. 4 of 7 January 1992), all of which lapsed after sixty days due to the lack of conversion into law by Parliament. After the lapse of the last law decree (No. 461 of 6 September 1996), Law No. 137 of 19 May 1997 was promulgated, which attempted to remedy the effects of the decrees that had not been converted into law, and which introduced some new elements in order to improve the functioning of the pre-existing regime, above all, from the point of view of organizational efficiency and procedural speed.

384. With the approval by the EC of a new directive (Directive No. 96/82/EC – the 'Seveso II Directive') which entirely substituted the 1982 directive, the fourth phase initiated, in which the Italian legislator issued Legislative Decree No. 334 of

17 August 1999 as well as some implementing ministerial decrees, which incorporated the new formulation that had been affirmed at the Community level and that was based on two assumptions that were radically different than those of the 1982 Directive: the need to prevent the 'danger' rather than just the 'risk' of major accidents, and the relationship of the special regime on prevention with the simple presence or use of specific hazardous substances rather than just carrying out specific industrial activities.

385. The fifth phase is the one subsequent to modification of the 1996 directive due to Directive No. 2003/105/EC, which extended the scope of application of the regime, specifically including storage and processing in the mining industry, adding new substances to be considered hazardous, and significantly reducing the quantity limits which, if exceeded, require prevention. The Italian legislator adjusted to such modifications by issuing Legislative Decree No. 238 of 2005, which partially modified the regime contained in Legislative Decree No. 334 of 1999.

With the substitution at the European level of Directive No. 96/82/EC with Directive 2012/18/EU ('Seveso III Director'), which the Italian legislator implemented just with respect to Article 30 by Legislative Decree No. 48 of 14 March 2014, and for the rest by Legislative Decree No. 105 of 26 June 2015, the sixth and final phase initiated, characterized by the attempt, in view of experience, the ensure that the existing levels of environmental protection and human health are maintained and further strengthened, while at the same time making the legislation more effective and efficient, expanding information tools and public participation in decision-making processes and, where possible, reducing superfluous administrative requirements through the enhancement and simplification of procedures.

§2. Principal Contents of DPR No. 175 of 17 May 1988

386. The 1988 Law was based on the notion of 'industrial activity', 'operator', 'major accident' and 'dangerous substance', as defined by Directive No. 82/501/EEC.

'Industrial activity' was 'any transaction performed in the establishments specified in Annex I, which leads or can lead to the use of one or more dangerous substances and which can present major accident risks, as well as transportation within the establishment for internal reasons and warehousing connected to such operations within the same'. Some activities were explicitly excluded from the regime's scope of application: military and police establishments; manufacture and separate warehousing of explosives, ammunition and arms; mining and quarry activities; nuclear establishments and treatment establishments for radioactive materials and substances.

'Operator' was 'whoever is responsible for an industrial activity'.

'Major accident risk' was 'an event such as a major emission, fire or explosion resulting from uncontrolled developments in the course of industrial activity which leads to a grave, immediate or delayed danger to man or the environment, inside or outside the establishment, and involving the use of one or more dangerous substances'.

'Dangerous substances' were those specifically identified due to type and quantity in Annexes II, III and IV.

387. The system of protection against major accident 'risks' was centred on the provision of a series of obligations that were the operator's responsibility. To ensure compliance with such obligations, Article 21 provided for a series of administrative and criminal sanctions. Prevention requirements were distinguished from notification requirements.

Prevention requirements included: a general obligation to take all necessary measures to prevent major accidents and to limit their consequences, and to comply with laws on safety and work hygiene and the protection of the population and the environment; an obligation to identify risks; an obligation to adopt appropriate safety measures in order to be able to deal with any problems; an obligation to inform, train and equip employees and those who have access to the establishment (or 'industrial establishment') for reasons of work; an obligation to prepare emergency plans with a forecast of the work to be done inside of the establishment; and an obligation to stipulate specific insurance policies.

Among the notification requirements were, in particular: the obligation to provide notification or file statements; the obligation to present a special informative schedule which the mayors of the interested municipalities had to disseminate among the population that might have suffered negative consequences in the case of an accident; the obligation to periodically update the contents of the notification (safety report) or statement; and the obligation to provide timely information in the case of an accident.

In conformity with the Community directive, the alternative between the requirements of providing notification as opposed to a statement was raised in relation to the use of specific dangerous substances in determined quantities, indicated in the annexes.

388. Fulfilment of the notification requirement in cases in which the accident risk was held to be greater resulted in the operator preparing a safety report regarding the substances utilized, relevant risks connected with the industrial activity performed, the characteristics of the industrial establishments and procedures, and the safety measures and emergency plans that have been prepared. The notification, together with the safety report, had to be transmitted prior to the initiation of activity to the Ministry of the Environment and Ministry of Health, as well as to the territorially competent region and province. On the basis of the information received, the relevant Prefect (*Prefetto*) had to prepare an emergency plan for the areas outside of the industrial establishment, as well as inform the interested population of the risks connected to the exercise of the activity, the safety measures arranged in order to prevent major accidents, the work foreseen by the external emergency plan and the rules to be followed in the case of an accident.

The information that had to accompany a statement was, instead, more limited and only regarded identification of major accident risks, adoption of appropriate safety measures and the information, training and equipping of the establishment personnel. The statement had to be sent prior to the initiation of activity to the territorially competent region and province, as well as to the local prefect.

All of the documentation supplied by the operator had to be controlled and verified by a particularly lengthy and complex technical-administrative proceeding, with the exception that the operator could initiate the activity if the competent administration did not issue a decision within a specific term, upon presentation of a sworn expert report regarding the completeness and accuracy of the information provided. The complexity of these administrative procedures has constituted one of the principal reasons why the objectives of protection proposed at a Community level have not been reached.

This is the reason why the Court of Justice of the EC declared, in a judgment dated 17 June 1999 (case No. C-336/97), that Italy was non-compliant with respect to the obligations contained in Directive No. 82/501/EEC, noting, in particular, that not even the law issued subsequent to DPR No. 175 of 1988 was able to ensure implementation of Community provisions that required the designated national authorities to prepare and supervise external emergency plans, as well as organize inspections and other control measures according to the type of industrial activity identified. The data examined by the court significantly demonstrated that, until June 1999, with respect to 443 emergency plans that should have been prepared, only 110 had actually been adopted, and inspections had only been made in 179 establishments.

§3. Principal Contents of Legislative Decree No. 334 of 17 August 1999

389. Legislative Decree No. 334 of 1999 implemented Community Directive No. 96/82/EC, whose purpose is to ensure increasingly greater levels of protection of the quality of the environment and human health throughout the entire Community, by means of a more coherent and efficient system of prevention of major accidents.

Such decree was subsequently partially modified by Legislative Decree No. 238 of 2005, in order to adjust the Italian legal system to Directive No. 2003/105/EC. A special regime applicable to industrial and oil ports and which similarly implements Directive No. 96/82/EC was contained in DM No. 293 of 16 May 2001.

The new regime of 1999 decisively changed the approach to the problem of the prevention of major accidents. What was taken into consideration was no longer the performance of determined industrial activities, but rather the simple presence of substances or preparations identified on the basis of categories of risk and determined quantities. 'Dangerous substances' were defined as those 'substances, mixtures or preparations set forth in Annex I, Part I, or which fulfil the criteria set forth in Annex I, Part II, which are present as raw materials, products, by-products, residues or intermediary products, including those substances which it is reasonable to suppose may be generated in the event of an accident'.

390. Further, the concepts of 'danger' and 'risk' were specifically distinguished: the first consisted of the 'intrinsic properties of a hazardous substance or the physical situation of an establishment to provoke damage to human health or the environment'; the second, instead, consisted of the 'probability that a specific event occurs on a given date or in specific circumstances' (Article 3). The regime was based on providing prevention thresholds to avoid major accidents in 'dangerous' situations.

The scope of application of the decree expressly referred to 'establishments containing hazardous substances in quantities that are the same as or greater than those indicated in Annex I' (Article 2, paragraph 1); the 'presence of hazardous substances' meant 'their presence, current or expected, in the establishment, or those that it is deemed can be generated, in the case of the loss of control of an industrial process, in a quantity that is equal to or greater than those indicated in Annex I' (Article 2, paragraph 2).

391. The protagonist of the entire regime was the 'operator', defined as the 'individual or corporate body who operate or hold an establishment or installation'. 'Establishment' included 'the whole area under the control of an operator where dangerous substances are present in one or more installations, including common or related infrastructures or activities'. An 'installation', instead, was the 'technical unit within an establishment in which dangerous substances are produced, used, handled or stored. It includes all of the equipment, structures, piping, machinery, tools, private railway sidings, docks, unloading quays serving the installation, jetties, warehouses or similar structures, whether floating or otherwise, necessary for the operation of the installation'. 'Storage' was specifically defined as 'the presence of a quantity of dangerous substances for the purpose or warehousing, depositing in safe custody or keeping in stock'.

392. The system of prevention of the dangers of 'major accidents' – defined as 'an event such as a major emission, fire or explosion, due to uncontrolled developments that occur during the operation of any establishment in accordance with Article 2, paragraph 1, which results in a serious danger, whether immediate or delayed, to human health or the environment, within or outside of the establishment, involving one or more dangerous substances' – was based on a new system of safety management which is the responsibility of the operator and which is differentiated in notification, a prevention policy, and a safety report (Articles 6–8). Article 5 also specified some general obligations to be borne by all operators (paragraph 1), as well as some general obligations – with respect to identifying major risks, the use of suitable safety measures, information, education, training and outfitting of anyone working in the establishment – for which the operator of specifically identified establishments (Annex A) is responsible in which dangerous substances were present, even in minor quantities with respect to those triggering the specific requirements set forth in Articles 6–8 (paragraph 2).

Notification (Article 6) had to be made by all operators of establishments in which dangerous substances are present in quantities equal to or greater than those set forth in Annex I. The notice had to be sent to the Ministry of the Environment, the region, the province, the municipality, the prefect and the territorially competent Provincial Command of the Fire Department and regional or interregional Technical Committee of the National Fire Department within a specific time frame, together with an information sheet on major accident risks for citizens and workers (Annex 5). The principal information that the notice had to contain regarded: all of the information that allows determining the dangerous substances or categories of dangerous substances at the establishment; their quantity and physical form; the operation, in course or foreseen, of an establishment or deposit; the establishment's immediately surrounding environment; and, in particular, any factors that might have caused a major accident or aggravate its consequences.

The operators of establishments in which dangerous substances were present in quantities that are equal to or greater than those indicated in Annex I also had to prepare a prevention policy in which the major accident prevention policy was defined, and which had to include the programme adopted to implement a safety management system, prepared according to the guidelines established by DM 9 August 2000. The prevention policy did not have to be sent to any public authority but must simply be kept on file at the establishment, re-examined every two years and made available to the Regional Technical Committee and the region, which exercise control and inspection powers.

In addition to these requirements, the operators of establishments in which dangerous substances in quantities equal to or greater than those indicated in Annex I, parts 1 and 2, column 3 were present, Article 8 added the preparation of a safety report which incorporates the prevention policy and which described, among others, the safety management system adopted, the dangers of major accidents identified and the internal emergency plans prepared. On the basis of the modifications introduced by Legislative Decree No. 238 of 2005, Article 8, paragraph 3 provided that the safety report had, in any event, to contain at least the information that is specified in Annex II, as well as an updated inventory of the hazardous substances at the establishment.

The safety report had to be sent to the Regional Technical Committee for the assessment procedure regulated by Article 21. The operator had to re-examine the report, as well as upon the request of the Ministry of the Environment, at least every five years and whenever modifications are made to the establishment as specified in DM 9 August 2000.

The Regional Technical Committee had to issue a feasibility clearance (Article 21, paragraph 3) for new establishments, an indispensable prerequisite to obtain a building permit. For this purpose, prior to the initiation of construction of the establishments, a preliminary safety report had to be presented, to be completed and integrated prior to the initiation of the activity (Article 9). Decree No. 238 of 2005 eliminated the possibility of initiating work in the lack of a decision by the authority within specific deadlines.

393. The other obligation with which all operators of establishments required to file safety reports had to comply was that of preparing – upon consultation with the personnel working in the establishment, including the personnel of long-term subcontractors (*see* DM No. 138 of 26 May 2009) – an 'internal emergency plan' to be used in the establishment. This plan had to at least contain the information indicated in Annex IV, point 1, and is aimed at the following objectives:

(a) to control and circumvent accidents in such a way as to minimize their effects and limit damage to people, the environment and to things;

(b) to implement the measures required to protect people and the environment from the consequences of major accidents;
(c) to adequately inform workers and the competent local authorities;
(d) to restore and cleanup the environment after a major accident.

The 'external emergency plan' had the same objectives – but with the obligation extended (pursuant to Decree No. 238 of 2005) to all establishments subject to the notification obligations set forth in Article 6 –, which is prepared by the prefect together with the regions and interested local entities, upon consultation with the public, on the basis of the information provided by the operator and in conformity with the guidelines established by the Civil Protection (*see* DPCM of 25 February 2005 and DPCM of 16 February 2007).

The internal and external emergency plans had to be reviewed, tested and, if necessary, modified and updated at intervals that do not exceed three years.

394. Decree No. 334 of 1999 contained other important new elements with respect to the pre-existing regime. Among these, in addition to some norms on the simplification of the verification and control procedures, the following were noted:

– the provision for special regimes which bear in mind a domino effect (possible sequence of accidental events, even of a diverse nature, which, originating in a component of an establishment, also extend to neighbouring components) and the high concentration of installations in a specific area (Articles 12 and 13);
– the provision for a system of control of land use planning to be applied to areas of new establishments, modifications of existing establishments and new areas or infrastructures surrounding existing establishments; such system was based on a prior definition of minimum safety requirements with respect to land use planning, with reference to the destination and utilization of the land, which considered the need to maintain the necessary distances between establishments and residential areas, as well as the objectives of preventing major risks and limiting eventual consequences; the territorial entities – in particular, the provinces and municipalities – had to adjust their territorial and urban planning instruments to the above minimum requirements and, in any case, they were directly responsible for considering the needs to control urban planning while governing the territory (Article 14);
– the overall strengthening of instruments and procedures in order to guarantee the certainty, continuity, understanding and updating of information with respect to the interested population, which was also granted a special right to be consulted within the context of land use planning procedures and EIA procedures, with respect to new establishments, modifications of existing establishments and the creation of new areas or infrastructures surrounding existing establishments (Article 23).

395. The regime was completed by a decisive rationalization of the system of distributing legislative power, connected to the general transfer of administrative functions from the State to the regions provided by Article 72 of Legislative Decree No. 112 of 1998.

Consistently with such transfer, – which remains unimplemented due to its excessive operational complexity, as it is subordinate to the issue, by the regions, of 'specific regulations for connecting the parties entrusted with the preliminary review and the guarantee of the safety of the territory and the population', as well as the stipulation of a 'program accord between State and Region to verify the prerequisites to carry out the functions, as well as for the declaration procedure' – Article 18 of Decree No. 334 established the general rule according to which *the region regulates (...) the exercise of administrative competencies with respect to major accidents*. Specifically, the regions were attributed with the power to determine the competent authorities having administrative functions and the measures to be issued after the technical procedure; regulating the manner in which such acts are approved and coordinated among all of the parties and technical organisms involved with the technical procedure; regulating the manner in which control and supervisory powers are exercised; as well as for regulating the procedures to adopt all measures to protect the environment and territory in relation to the presence of establishments at risk of major accidents.

On the basis of Article 15 of Decree No. 334, the Ministry of the Environment retained the power to issue the technical safety standards for the prevention of major accident risks, as well as to establish the manner in which the operator had to identify such risks, the use of the appropriate safety measures, information, training and outfitting of anyone working in the establishment, the valuation criteria for safety reports, the reference criteria for the adoption of specific initiatives in relation to different types of accidents and the criteria to determine modifications of the industrial activities that might have implications for major accident risks.

§4. Modifications and The Most Significant Innovations of Legislative Decree No. 105 of 26 June 2015

396. As noted, the Italian legal system adjusted to the new European regime in this area, introduced by Directive 2012/18/EU by means of Legislative Decree No. 105 of 2015. The 2015 Decree repealed prior Legislative Decree No. 334 of 1999, as modified by Legislative Decree No. 238 of 2005, representing, however, substantially both the approach of the system for the prevention of major accidents as well as the contents and entitlements that characterized the previous legislation, although it was duly updated in accordance with the European Directive.

Among the main innovations of the new regime, some simplifications stand out.

The first – following the formalization contained in the EU Directive of the fundamental distinction between 'lower-threshold establishments' and 'higher-threshold establishments' (depending on whether, for the hazardous substances listed in Annex 1, the thresholds indicated respectively in column 2 and column 3 of such Annex 1 have been exceeded) – consists of the elimination of any obligation for 'lower-threshold operators', who are – for that matter – considered to be excluded from the scope of application of the legislation being reviewed. Therefore, without prejudice to general obligations borne by the operator of both types of establishment (Article 12), operators of 'lower-threshold establishments' are only subject to obligations of notification (Article 13) and preparation of the document containing the definition of the prevention policy, together with the programme adopted to implement the security management system (Article 14 and Annex B), whereas only operators of 'higher-threshold establishments' are subject to the obligation of preparing the safety report (Article 15 and Annex C).

The second important simplification instead regards alignment to the provisions of the EU Direction with respect to the possibility for the prefect not to prepare the external emergency plan in all cases where there are no reasonably foreseeable effects outside the establishment caused by major accidents related to the presence of hazardous substances (Article 21, paragraph 11).

Other important innovations with respect to prior legislation regard:

- strengthening the role of orientation and coordination carried out by the Minister of the Environment, Land and Sea through the establishment of coordination for the uniform application in the national territory of the legislation introduced, composed of representatives of the central and local administrations concerned and by technical bodies (Article 11);
- the introduction of unified forms at a national level, which can be used electronically by the operator for notification and other information (Annex 5);
- the 'derogation' mechanism, as provided by the EU Directive, for substances which, in certain conditions, are incapable of causing the release of matter or energy which could result in a major accident (Article 4);
- strengthening the control system through the planning and scheduling of inspections in the establishments (Article 27);
- strengthening the measures necessary to ensure more information to the public, as well as enabling more effective participation in decision-making processes, in particular in the planning and implementation phases of the work in sites where there are establishments at risk of major accidents (Articles 23 and 24).

With respect to the distribution of competence between the State and the regions, considering that the general transfer to the regions of administrative functions related to activities at risk of major accidents, already provided by Article 72 of Legislative Decree No. 112 of 1998, has not yet occurred and that such functions have until now been efficiently performed on a transitional basis by the State (Ministry of the Interior, through the National Fire Department and the Prefects' Offices), Decree No. 105 of 2015 generally confirmed the structure of the competences envisaged by Legislative Decree No. 334 of 1999. Article 1, paragraph 4 provides that until the transfer to the regions of the functions set forth in Article 72 of Legislative Decree No. 112 of 1998, preliminary enquiry and control functions on upper threshold establishments will be performed by the Ministry of the Interior through the Regional Technical Committees (CTR) created in each region, as well as functions regarding emergency planning outside of the establishments (entrusted to the prefects), as well as the domino effect and technical opinions on urban planning (Article 6), while the regions are entrusted with control functions on lower threshold establishments (Article 7).

Finally, Legislative Decree No. 105 of 2015 was also designed to resolve the problem of the time required to ensure full concrete application of the regime. Different from in the past, in fact, the Italian legislator found it opportune to simultaneously adopt all of the indispensable technical legislation required for the immediate application of the Decree, inserting among the technical annexes the entire implementing regime already provided by Legislative Decree No. 334 of 1999, suitably updated and including even provisions still waiting to be adopted (Annexes B through L), together, obviously, with the necessary technical rules to implement the parts of the regime that were entirely new (Annexes A and M).

Part II. Nature and Conservative Management

Chapter 1. Landscape Regulation

by *Antonio Borzì*

§1. Principal Sources of Law

397. The first Italian law on the protection of natural beauty was Law No. 778 of 11 June 1922, which specified that beautiful landscapes and buildings of particular historical interest were entitled to protection.

Law No. 1497 of 29 June 1939 subsequently offered four different types of environmental resources legal protection based on their public interest, divided into two categories: 'individual beauty' and 'the beauty of an entirety'.

The principal instrument used to protect natural beauty consisted of subjecting real property, or real property complexes, to administrative restrictions; landscape planning, while contemplated by the 1939 Law, was left to the discretion of the Public Administration and was essentially aimed at preventing the beauty of an entirety from being 'used in a way that would damage the beauty of a panorama'. Both the 1922 law and the 1939 one primarily used an aesthetic valuation aimed at overseeing definition of the concept of environmental 'resource', and landscape protection arose to the extent and if such resource had characteristics of particular beauty.

Law No. 431 of 8 August 1985, the so-called Galasso Law, was a turning point in landscape regulation. The law directly protects landscape without the need for any administrative measure, in addition to protecting specific types of areas covering a significant part of the Italian territory, and made adoption of a landscape plan mandatory.

The landscape regime was subsequently simplified and coordinated with the Law on Cultural Heritage by means of Legislative Decree No. 490 of 29 October 1999 (*Uniform Law on Cultural and Environmental Resources*), which reinforced planning as an instrument, attributing greater significance to landscape enhancement.

This sector is currently regulated by the Code on Cultural Heritage and Landscape, introduced by Legislative Decree No. 42 of 22 January 2004, which has been subsequently modified (the most relevant being the modifications made by Legislative Decree No. 157 of 2006 and Legislative Decree No. 63 of 2008). The European Landscape Convention is also of fundamental importance, signed in Florence on 20 October 2000 and ratified by Italy by Law No. 14 of 9 January 2006, whose influence is due to the introduction in the Italian legal system of an explicit definition of 'landscape'.

§2. Scope of Application

398. Article 9(2) of the Constitution attributes the Italian Republic with responsibility for the protection of Italy's landscape and historic-artistic heritage. The first paragraph of such article provides that the Republic shall promote cultural development and scientific and technological research.

Legal scholarship concurs that the most proper significance of Article 9 derives from an overall reading of the two paragraphs together, in the sense that they describe a common context represented by an aesthetic-cultural value, which manifests the need to ensure the cultural progress of the individual and society as a whole; this value has been qualified as a 'primary' and 'absolute' value by the Constitutional Court (*see* judgments No. 367 of 2007, No. 180 of 2008, No. 272 of 2009, and recently No. 66 of 2018).

The constitutional regulation of landscape raises at least two types of problems: one regarding definition of the object entitled to constitutional protection, and the other the limit of the scope of jurisdiction of the different levels of the governmental hierarchies of the Italian Republic.

It is necessary to refer to the general part of this volume with regard to this second aspect, noting that interpretative difficulties arise from the fact that subsequent to constitutional revision in 2001, the State has exclusive legislative competence in matters regarding 'environmental protection, protection of the ecosystem and cultural heritage', whereas the regions retain legislative jurisdiction both with regard to the 'enhancement of culture and the environment' and 'territorial governance'. No less complicated is the *rebus* of the division of administrative jurisdiction, since the entity holding legislative power is also competent to determine the allocation of functions among various levels of government in accordance with the principles set forth in Article 118 of the Constitution. As clearly appears from what is set forth in the following pages, the Italian legislator's most recent tendency has been to centralize most of the administrative functions regarding landscape and, above all, landscape protection. At the same time, however, constitutional case law has found that national landscape legislation expresses a limit on the protection of other public interests, assigned to the concurrent jurisdiction of the regions with regard to territorial governance and the enhancement of cultural and environmental resources (specifically, *see* Judgment. No. 367 of 2007).

I. The Landscape

399. An equally complex operation, from which the Constitutional Court has abstained, is a precise understanding of the term 'landscape'. It is certainly a concept that has changed over time due to the Italian legislator's diverse levels of awareness.

Initially, the concept of landscape essentially coincided with 'natural beauty' protected by Law No. 1497/1939 as a reference to the exegetic criteria of 'the law set in stone', which required that constitutional provisions be interpreted in view of outstanding legislation at the time the Constitution was enacted.

A broader concept of landscape subsequently emerged, which does not revolve around the aesthetic quality of the resources entitled to protection, but refers to the form of the territory or environment, shaped by the continuous interaction of man and nature. This concept of landscape emerged on a legislative level upon the enactment of Law No. 431 of 1985, which extended protection to territorial areas not on the basis of their intrinsic aesthetic quality, but rather their specific morphological characteristics or location, determined to be worthy of interest at an environmental landscape level. The same interpretation was followed by Legislative Decree No. 112 of 31 March 1998, which defined 'environmental resources' as *those resources identified on the basis of law that provide significant testimony of the natural and cultural characteristics of the environment.* As a result of legislative development, even the Constitutional Court has referred to landscape as an *aspect of the territory, due to the environmental and cultural content that it contains* (judgment No. 367 of 2007, but see first, among many, judgments No. 39 and No. 151 of 1986) and, more recently, to landscape and cultural assets as being those assets 'suitable for distinguishing in an original, unique and unrepeatable manner a specific geographic and territorial area' (judgment No. 66 of 2018).

The Code on Cultural Heritage and Landscape (Legislative Decree No. 42 of 2004), influenced by the European Landscape Convention of 2000 (ratified by Italy by means of Law No. 14 of 2006), introduced the first legislative definition of landscape in the Italian legal system. Landscape is identified as *a homogeneous part of the territory whose characteristics derive from nature, human history or their reciprocal interaction,* with the specification that *the protection and enhancement of landscape safeguards the values that it expresses as perceptible identifying characteristics* (Article 131).

History confirms the concept of landscape as the form of a nation resulting from human-nature interaction and enhances its identifying characteristics, in the sense that the landscape values to be protected are found in the environment's external aspects that a community considers to be a qualifying expression of the relationship created with the territory.

Subsequent to some modifications of the code made in 2006 and 2008, the current definition of landscape refers to *territory that expresses identity, whose nature derives from the action of natural and human factors and from their interaction,* protected *with respect to those aspects and characteristics that constitute material and visible representations of the national identity, in that they are an expression of cultural values.*

In essence, there are two new elements with respect to the original version: the lack of reference to the 'perception' of manifestations of identity that constitute the landscape, together with the specification that protection regards representations of national identity that express cultural values. Thus, on the one hand landscape would appear to have become objective, in that it is a concept of territory that is expressive of cultural values independently of its relationship with the local community; on the other hand, however, only manifestations of national identity would be capable of expressing those values, to the detriment of the kinds of territory that refer to local identities.

These are very significant modifications whose content, as noted by legal scholarship, risks conflicting with the Landscape Convention, which expressly links the object of protection with public perception, and does not identify it with the territory as such, but – by using the noun in the plural – as inclusive of ordinary and degraded landscapes as well. The issue of the relationship between the code's approach and the Convention's philosophy is of decisive significance with respect to whether or not the Italian law will remain in force, due to the fact that the Italian legislator is bound by obligations assumed on an international level and conflicting national laws are unconstitutional (Constitution, Article 117, paragraph 1).

The approach to this issue that must undoubtedly be shared tends to reduce the distance between the two arguments by means of interpretation, so that landscape is considered to be a quality of the overall territory, always and fully part of the conflict between public and private interests that must be addressed and resolved by institutions and communities.

The code seeks to reconcile traditional interpretations of the landscape as an expression of aesthetic-cultural value using innovative approaches which tend to be based on the subjective profile of the public perception of places, which involves heterogeneous territories. The result of this attempt at synthesis is seen in the distinction between 'landscape' and 'landscape resources', even more prominently in the latest version of the code (after the modification contained in Legislative Decree No. 63 of 2008). Landscape as contemplated by Article 9 of the Constitution corresponds to the entire national territory, distinguished by homogeneous contexts corresponding to the same number of 'landscapes' referred to in the plural; in this context, specific areas or buildings that can be characterized as 'landscape resources' are selectively identified or identifiable (since they express cultural landscape values in terms of particular quality). This distinction is currently also appreciated in terms of the distribution of jurisdiction among different levels of government, as landscape planning regarding landscape resources must necessarily be the result of an agreement between the State and the regions.

II. Landscape Resources

400. Landscape resources are entitled to specific protection in the Italian legal system. They consist of buildings or areas identified by a law or based on a law that express historic, cultural, natural, morphological and aesthetic values of the territory (Article 2, paragraph 3 of the Code) which, together with cultural resources, constitute the Republic's cultural heritage (Article 2, paragraph 1 of the Code).

As a rule, it is only possible to modify these resources upon authorization by the administrative authority.

401. The code provides for three kinds of landscape resources (Article 134 of the Code):

(i) buildings and areas included in the kinds of natural beauty set forth in Article 136, whose use is restricted by means of an ordinance;
(ii) the areas indicated in Article 142, which are directly protected by law;
(iii) typical buildings and areas, as well as some other buildings and areas specifically identified by Article 136 that are entitled to be protected by landscape plans.

402. Sub (i). The first type of landscape resource consists of buildings and areas of significant public interest, listed in Article 136 of the Code:

(a) real property having conspicuous characteristics of natural beauty, geological uniqueness or historical significance, inclusive of monumental trees;
(b) villas, gardens and parks that are distinguished by their uncommon beauty;
(c) all characteristic real property having aesthetic and traditional value, inclusive of historic centres and villages;
(d) panoramic beauty accessible to the public, inclusive of lookout areas or viewpoints, from which the spectacle of such beauty can be enjoyed.

The protection of these resources is prevalently linked to the aesthetic characteristics of quality that they express; the reference, in fact, is to natural beauty, differentiated among individual beauty, the beauty indicated in clauses *a* and *b*, and beauty of an entirety as indicated in clauses *b* and *c*.

Natural beauty is entitled to protection subsequent to an administrative measure known as a 'declaration of public interest', whose effect is to restrict the use of said resources. Thus, no work can be done to them unless previously authorized by the public administration, and they are subject to specific restrictions on their use.

403. Sub (ii). The second kind of landscape resource consists of the areas specifically protected by the law, currently listed in Article 142 of the Code of Cultural Heritage and Landscape:

(a) coastal territories included within a strip of 300 m from the shoreline, including land elevated above sea-level;
(b) land abutting lakes included in a strip of 300 m from the shoreline, including land elevated above sea-level;
(c) rivers, streams and courses of water registered in the lists provided by the Uniform Text on Water and Electrical Installations, approved by Royal Decree No. 1775 of 11 December 1933 and the relative banks or embankments for an area of 150 m each;
(d) mountains for the part exceeding 1,600 m above sea-level for the Alpine chain and 1,200 m above sea-level for the Apennine chain and the islands;
(e) glaciers and glacial circles;
(f) national and regional parks and reserves, as well as protected areas outside of the parks;
(g) forests and woodland, including trails or fire-damaged areas, and those subject to reforestation requirements, as defined by Article 2, paragraphs 2 and 6, of Legislative Decree No. 227 of 18 May 2001;

(h) areas assigned to agricultural universities and areas subject to 'civic uses' (easements on public land and customary use of public and private land);
(i) wetlands included in the list referred to in Presidential Decree No. 448 of 13 March 1976;
(j) volcanoes;
(k) areas of archaeological interest.

These are areas which, due to the characteristics regarding their type and location, have been recognized as being expressive of interests that are particularly worthy of protection, starting from Law No. 431 of 1985.

Different from natural beauty, which is protected by an administrative measure that declares it to be of public interest, the restriction on these resources is imposed directly by the law.

Article 143, par. 1, clause (c) of the Code includes among the necessary content of the landscape plan 'delineation and representation in scale suitable for identification' *of areas protected by the Law, as well as* 'the determination of restrictions on use aimed at ensuring conservation of the distinctive characteristics of said areas and, compatibly with them, their enhancement'. *The legislative origin of the restriction does not exempt the Public Administration from determining and limiting the territory of the areas in question, more or less complex depending on the case, and said responsibility must be carried out in the form of the landscape plan.*

In lack of a planning instrument, these areas are protected in any event by periodic interventions related to the issue of permits; once the restrictions of a plan have been introduced, protection and enhancement acquire the necessary concreteness.

404. Sub (iii). The third kind of landscape resource contemplated by Article 134 of the Code, which represents a novelty with respect to pre-existing legislation, consists of real property and areas protected by landscape plans.

A review of the law reveals that the typological profile regards both resources that are abstractly included as part of the entirety of natural beauty (in accordance with Article 136), and any 'additional' *buildings and typical areas identified* by the plan.

This means that on a planning level it will be possible not only to recognize the particular landscape significance of some areas of the territory or individual resources, on a case-by-case basis and independently of any kind of assessment, but also to determine new categories of landscape resources, specifying morphological characteristics and locations. It is clear that the 'determination of a type' must be accompanied by 'specification', that is, – according to the language of Article 143 (*see* clause *d*) – the recognition of areas and buildings within the territory that can be assimilated to the 'types'.

When the resources can instead be included in one of the categories set forth in Article 136 (natural beauty), the issue is raised of how to guarantee the owner, possessor or holder of the resource a way to participate in the planning process, which is the procedural equivalent of what is allowed in proceedings for a declaration of public interest.

§3. PLANNING INSTRUMENTS: THE LANDSCAPE PLAN

405. The Code on Cultural Heritage and Landscape requires the State and region to ensure that the entire territory is adequately known, protected and managed based on the different values expressed by its diverse contexts (Article 135, paragraph 1).

For such purpose, the regions can choose whether to subject territory to specific laws by means of the use of landscape plans, or whether to integrate the consideration of landscape values in zoning-territorial plans. The uniqueness of the planning instrument tends to guarantee the effectiveness of coordination between policies related to territorial layout and those on the protection and enhancement of regional landscape, as required by Article 145 of the Code. Otherwise, the multiplication of the planning, zoning-territorial and landscape instruments inherent in dedicated planning might render the necessary integration among the different choices that affect the territory more difficult.

In both cases, the administrative act is called a 'landscape plan'.

406. Above all, the plan has a mandatory content. The landscape plan must at least contain the following:

- recognition of the territory that is the object of the plan by means of an analysis of its landscape characteristics;
- recognition of the buildings and areas subject to restriction by means of an administrative measure, and determination of the specific restrictions on use;
- recognition of the areas protected by the law, and determination of the restrictions on use aimed at guaranteeing conservation and, compatibly, enhancement;
- an analysis of the dynamics of the transformation of the territory aimed at identifying the risk factors and elements of the landscape's vulnerability, as well as the comparison with other programming, planning and soil protection acts;
- determination of the reclamation and requalification of the areas that have been significantly compromised or degraded and other acts of enhancement compatible with the needs of protection;
- determination of the measures necessary for the proper insertion, in the landscape context, of work that transforms the territory, in view of the sustainable development of the affected areas.

407. The plan also has an optional content, which can include:

- identification of additional buildings or areas to be considered landscape resources with respect to those subject to restriction by means of a measure or *ex lege*, and determination of the relative restrictions on use;
- identification of eventual additional areas which are not subject to the landscape resources regime, but which are, nevertheless, regulated by specific measures for their protection and use;
- identification of areas, among those protected by the law, in which the assessment of landscape compatibility with the contemplated work is made during the procedure to grant a building permit, rather than during an autonomous proceeding for landscape authorization;

- identification of gravely compromised or degraded areas in which land reclamation is exonerated from the obligation to obtain landscape authorization;
- priority guidelines for conservation projects and projects for the reclamation, requalification, enhancement and management of regional areas, with an indication of implementation instruments, including economic incentives;
- coordination of measures with sector and land use planning instruments, as well as with national and regional economic development plans, programmes and projects (Article 145, paragraph 2).

408. As noted, the content of the landscape plan reflects the distinction, which appears rather evident from the norms of the code, between landscape and landscape resources, because the idea of protection of landscape resources, which can be considered conservative and static, is flanked by a dynamic concept of landscape which, as the result of the ongoing historical relationship between man and nature, is open to urban planning and construction transformations of the territory according to the principle of sustainable development (from a landscape viewpoint).

An initial characteristic that qualifies planning is, in fact, that of the gradual nature and differentiation of landscape regulation, as seen from the missions of the landscape plan, indicated in Article 135, paragraph 4.

The hierarchical criteria of landscape planning are enunciated according to a growing trend, so that maintenance of what already exists (conservation of fundamental elements and morphologies of landscape resources) is followed by the reclamation or requalification of compromised or degraded areas, as well as by developmental planning compatible with different levels of recognized landscape values. Thus, landscape resources that are still intact are not compromised, the errors of the past are amended by restoring pre-existing resources or by realizing new ones that are coherent and integrated with them, and such resources are subject to sustainable development.

409. The gradualness and differentiation of land use interventions also impact another aspect of landscape planning regarding the definition of territorial contexts that include, but which are not identified as, landscape resources.

Article 143 of Code, in addition to the regime intended to protect and enhance the 'Galasso areas' (including measures to preserve their distinctive characteristics), provides management criteria for areas and buildings declared to be of significant public interest, and specific regulation of the use of new landscape resources. The plan must contain general and operative regulations for the protection and use of land included in the areas that have been identified, even if such land does not have the legal characteristics related to the restriction. This results in a differentiated regime, whose primary distinctive feature consists of the lack of a need for a work permit in areas not subject to restriction. Landscape regulation is, however, required for these areas and is expressed in other forms, in particular, by enhancing the orientation function of the plan with respect to urban and sector planning, as well as by means of binding restrictions aimed at land use planning.

410. A second fundamental characteristic of landscape planning regards its essentially regional scope.

Article 135 expressly attributes the region with responsibility for adopting a planning instrument, thus, identifying the regional government as the most suitable administrative level for the protection of the interests at play.

Landscape planning and its regional dimension, implemented by uniform methodology throughout the national territory, is considered by national legislation to express 'essential values', and is binding on the regional legislator (Constitutional Court, judgment No. 182 of 2006).

411. The third fundamental characteristic of landscape planning is the *global nature* of the action, understood as a necessary consideration of all of the territory within the region.

With respect to the code, the formulation of Article 135, modified in 2008, should be noted, which requires the State and the regions to ensure that *all of the territory is adequately planned,* as well as the provision of Article 155, paragraph 2*bis* which establishes that *all urban or territorial planning instruments must conform to the principle of safeguarding the landscape characteristics of the various contexts,* favouring landscape planning that is not only aimed at landscape resources, but at the entire territory (Constitutional Court, judgment No. 51 of 2006).

Above all, it is the European Convention on Landscape of 2000 that determines the global nature of landscape planning. The landscape, in fact, is *an important element of the quality of life of the population* present *in every place ... in urban areas and in the countryside, in degraded territories, as well as those of great quality, in areas considered to be exceptional, as in those of daily life* (considering No. 5), as long as they contribute in a decisive manner to *individual and social well-being* (considering No. 8); consequently, this approach requires that landscape protection and enhancement must regard all of the territory, that is, *natural, urban and suburban areas* (Article 2).

It is clear, therefore, that according to this approach (which is constitutionally required by Article 117, paragraph 1, of the Constitution), the landscape is not a brief and summary form of 'landscape resource', not only if emphasis is placed on the environmental aspect (the form of the territory and the environment), but also if its 'cultural' component is considered, because territories 'lacking culture' or which have been 'ignored by culture' are excluded, and their form, exterior appearance and relationship to the community living within said territories are not subject to any consideration by public powers in both static and dynamic terms (such as a project to be realized).

412. Another fundamental aspect of landscape planning regards constitutional cooperation and coordination.

Ever since the first version of the Code (2004) entered into effect, the national legislator's intention was that the preparation of the plan based on an agreement between the State and region would be the ordinary procedure used to adopt the planning instrument, whereas the choice of a plan that was not joint but instead exclusively regional, while possible, was intended as the exception. In 2008, the code was modified to require joint preparation of the plan with respect to the recognition, determination and limitation of landscape resources, as well as to determine the relative restrictions on use. With respect to the other objects of the plan such as, for example, specification of protective measures for territorial areas that are not considered landscape resources, even if particularly appreciable for the landscape values that they express, the joint preparation by the State and region remains optional.

The Constitutional Court has clarified that the obligation of the joint preparation of the landscape plan, with reference to the restricted property indicated directly by Article 135 of the code, is an imperative principle of national legislation, which is in turn a reflection of the uniform approach to landscape planning aimed at establishing a uniform methodology in compliance with legislation on the protection of cultural heritage and landscapes throughout the national territory (judgment No. 66 of 2018; in the same sense *see* judgment No. 64 of 2015; No. 210 of 2016, No. 197 of 2014, and No. 211 of 2013).

Collaboration among the different levels of government is not limited to the State and region, but also involves subregional entities: Article 144, paragraph 1 requires that proceedings for the approval of landscape plans must ensure institutional coordination, participation of the interested parties and associations created for the protection of collective interests, and broad forms of public notice. The regional legislator is, therefore, required to define a procedure for the preparation of the landscape plan which, even though it concludes with a sole regional act, has mechanisms that guarantee the broadest consent possible between the region and territorial entities, or which at least enhances an effective search for that consent, if it is true, as has been argued, that 'coordination' differs from mere institutional 'consultation'.

413. The final issue that merits attention is the relationship between the landscape plan and other planning instruments.

Article 145, paragraph 2 of the Code requires the landscape plan to be coordinated with land use planning instruments and with national and regional plans, programmes and projects for economic development. It is apparent that this necessary coordination is best implemented if the region decides to opt for directed landscape planning, that is, to integrate landscape protection and enhancement in the territorial governance regime, since in this case they can use all of the guarantee mechanisms that regulate the interaction of the regional and subregional plans.

A similar situation regards the principle of the hierarchy or prevalence of the landscape plan with respect to municipal, provincial and metropolitan urban planning instruments (see the Constitutional Court, judgment No. 180 of 2008).

Above all, the municipalities, metropolitan cities, provinces and entities that manage protected natural areas must conform and adjust their own land use and urban planning instruments with the provisions and the term established by the landscape plan (and in any case within two years from its approval), which must also contain the protective measures applicable during the period of adjustment.

The provisions of the landscape plans (new, or which in any event conform to the Code) are compulsory with respect to the urban planning instruments of municipalities, metropolitan cities and provinces, and they immediately prevail over any conflicting provisions contained in urban planning instruments. The same effect, limited just to the provisions on landscape protection, is verified with respect to sector planning instruments that impact the territory (inclusive of those of entities managing protected natural areas), whose norms must cede to planning regulations (Article 145, paragraph 3 and Article 143, paragraph 9, of the Code).

§4. Landscape Authorization

414. Landscape authorization is the instrument of preventive consent used by the public administration to verify compatibility between protected landscape interests and the planned action, assessing conformity between the restrictions contained in the act of declaration of public interest (the restriction) and the landscape plan.

The landscape plan regime and authorization regime are, thus, intertwined, both because the former's articulated content avoids arbitrary decisions to be made related to the episodic nature of the latter, and because, under certain conditions, the landscape plan can provide derogations from the cases for which authorization is required.

I. Activities Subject to Authorization

415. In accordance with Article 146 of the Code, prior authorization is required before any work can be done to the following:

(1) buildings and areas subject to restriction by an ordinance (natural beauty);
(2) areas protected *ex lege* ('Galasso areas');
(3) buildings and areas protected by provisions of the landscape plan (pursuant to Article 143, paragraph 1, clause *d*, of the Code).

Not all kinds of work, however, require authorization, as seen by Article 149 of the Code, which excludes the following from the prior authorization requirement:

(a) ordinary or extraordinary maintenance work, static consolidation and conservative restoration that does not alter the state of the places involved and the exterior aspect of the buildings;
(b) work related to agricultural-forestry-pastoral activity that does not result in permanent alterations to the current state of the places involved due to building construction and other civil engineering works, and as long as these activities and work do not alter the hydrogeological layout of the territory;
(c) forestation, reforestation, land reclamation, fire prevention and conservation of woodlands and forests, as long as authorized in accordance with the relevant laws.

The ordinary landscape authorization regime can be modified by a landscape plan approved as the result of an agreement between the State and region; in particular, the following must be specified:

(a) the areas protected on the basis of law which are not subject to a restrictive ordinance, in which work and activities can be performed upon verifying, in the context of the ordinary procedure for the issue of building permits, their conformity to the provisions of the landscape plan and municipal planning instrument;
(b) the areas that have been seriously compromised or degraded, in which work effectively aimed at reclamation and requalification does not require authorization.

These are cases of a 'relaxed' regime (which is not permitted for areas that are subject to restrictive ordinances), and cases of exclusion from the need to obtain authorization for reclamation and requalification work in degraded and compromised areas, which only become effective after the urban planning instruments have been adjusted to the landscape plan (Article 143, paragraph 5).

Further, subsequent to the 2008 modification of the code, it is possible to establish simplified authorization procedures for minor work, determined by means of a government regulation (Article 146, paragraph 9). Such regulation was approved two years later (DPR No. 139 of 9 July 2010).

Subsequently, Article 25, paragraph 2, of Law Decree No. 133 of 12 September 2014 ('Urgent measures for the opening of worksites, the realization of public works, the digitalization of the country, bureaucratic simplifications, the emergence of hydrogeological instability and the resumption of productive activities'), converted, with modifications, in Law No. 164 of 11 November 2014, entrusted to a 'deregulation' the determination of the 'types of work for which landscape authorization is not required, in accordance with Article 149 of the Code of Cultural Heritage, both in the context of minor works already included in Annex 1 to the above regulation set forth in Article 146, paragraph 9, fourth clause of the Code of Cultural Heritage, as well as through the determination of further minor works that lack landscape relevance'.

DPR No. 31 of 13 December 2017 was enacted as implementation of cited Article 25, which is the regulation that identifies the works excluded from the need for landscape authorization or which are subject to simplified authorization (and which repealed the prior DPR No. 139 of 2010).

The exclusion of landscape authorization for the works set forth in Annex A to DPR No. 31 of 2017 prevails over any conflicting provisions in the authorization regime for the works contained in landscape plans or in planning instruments adjusted to them, without prejudice to specific restrictions on the use of landscape assets provided in accordance with Articles 140, 141 and 143, paragraph 1, clauses *b–d*), of the code (Article 14 of DPR No. 31 of 2017).

There are particular rules regarding the placement of billboards or other advertising materials near landscape resources (Article 153), and the colour of building facades (Article 154), as well as for the installation or modification of electronic communications systems (in some cases excluded from the authorization requirement (Article 6, paragraph 4, Legislative Decree No. 133 of 2014, cited).

II. The Competent Administration for Landscape Authorizations

416. Starting from 2006, the Italian legislator has adopted measures to avoid having the same entity that decides whether or not to issue landscape authorization be the same authority that is competent to issue building permits. The law is based on the distrust of landscape management functions carried out in a municipal context, deemed too small to avoid having landscape interests succumb to the conflicting interests that emerge in a local setting. Further, with regard to monitoring the granting of landscape authorizations, the separation of competence avoids having greater consideration paid to urban planning compatibility and construction projects than to an assessment of the effects that the realization of the work could produce on the landscape.

The region is the authority competent to grant landscape authorization, utilizing offices having adequate technical-scientific skills and instrumental resources. The specification is important because it suggests that only by means of a competent and well-equipped bureaucracy, modelled after the State Superintendence, is it possible to ensure adequate protection of landscape interests, which are truly an object of primary representation and do not succumb when balanced with other public interests.

This is demonstrated by the fact that the region can delegate authorization functions to the province, to forms of associations and cooperation among local entities, park authorities, or to the municipalities as long as the entities that receive the delegation of authority have structures that are able to ensure an adequate level of technical-scientific skill, as well as guarantee differentiation between landscape protection and administrative functions regarding urban planning (Article 146, paragraph 6).

III. The Procedure

417. The owners, possessors or holders of any kind of building or area of landscape interest must file a project indicating the work that they intend to perform with the competent administration, together with the required documentation, and they must refrain from initiating work until they have received authorization.

Upon receipt of the request from the interested party, the administration competent to grant landscape authorization must first control whether it falls within one of the categories of work that is excluded from the authorization obligation.

If the prerequisites provided by Article 149, paragraph 1 are lacking, the administration must verify whether the request is supported by the necessary documentation and control the conformity of the proposed intervention with the restrictions contained in the declarations of public interest and in the landscape plan.

For such purpose, the competent administration must obtain the opinion of the Superintendence (a peripheral organ of the Ministry for Cultural Heritage), which is mandatory and also binding, at least until the requirements for the use of the landscape resources (set forth in the declarations of public interest or in the plans) have been approved and the urban planning instruments have been adjusted to such restrictions (control performed by the ministry upon the request of the relative region). The opinion is binding until this double condition has been met, and, thus, the decision on the request for authorization is basically performed by a peripheral organ of the State.

If competence to issue landscape authorization is delegated to subregional entities, local landscape commissions must be created, composed of persons with specific, multi-year and qualified experience in landscape protection; unlike the Superintendence, these commissions have merely advisory functions.

The Code provides a strict timeframe for the procedure: Within forty days from receipt of the application, the administration shall assess the conformity of the proposed work with the restrictions set forth in measures containing declarations of public interest and in the landscape plans and must transmit the documentation filed by the interested party to the Superintendence, together with an illustrative technical report and a draft measure; it shall also notify the interested party of the initiation of the procedure and the transmission of the documentation to the Superintendence in accordance with outstanding law on administrative procedure.

The Superintendence shall issue its opinion limited to the landscape compatibility of the planned work as a whole and its conformity to the provisions contained in the landscape plan or to the specific regime set forth in Article 140, paragraph 2, within forty-five days from receipt of the documentation. In the case of a negative response, the Superintendence shall notify the interested parties of such negative opinion in accordance with Article 10*bis* of Law No. 241 of 7 August 1990. The administration shall act accordingly within twenty days from receipt of the opinion.

After sixty days have passed from the Superintendence's receipt of the relative documentation without the necessary opinion, the competent administration shall nevertheless issue its decision on the request for authorization.

IV. The Landscape Authorization Regime

418. By means of the landscape authorization, the public administration discretionally assesses the compatibility of the intervention that the applicant intends to realize with the landscape.

The parameter for such assessment is represented by the restrictions contained in the landscape plan and in the declarations of public interest, which are 'dynamic' rather than 'static' because they are not limited just to conserving what already exists by requiring protection in a strict sense, but orient territorial development in view of improving and enhancing landscapes.

The need manifested by the legislator is to avoid having landscape protection be episodic or left to the arbitrary actions of the individual competent administrations. All of this influences the characteristics of the authorization power, whose scope of discretion is reduced by the overlapping effect of the declarations of public interest with landscape plans. In any event, the importance of the values involved requires the authorization to be specifically and adequately justified (Constitutional Court, judgment No. 1205 of 2001), in such a way that the review made of the significant factual circumstances clearly appears and that the choice to give prevalence to a value that conflicts with another value entitled to constitutional protection is not manifestly unreasonable (Constitutional Court, Ad. pleno. No. 9 of 2001). If authorization is denied, the Administration, in its justification of the measure, cannot limit itself to expressing stereotypical and apodictic judgments but must specify the reasons for the denial, or explain the reasons of conflict between the work to be realized and the motives for the protection of the area subject to the restriction (Council of State, judgment No. 634 of 2018, and judgment No. 5108 of 2016).

Article 146, paragraph 4 specifies that the landscape authorization 'is an autonomous act and prerequisite for a building permit or other form of authorization that legitimizes building construction'. *The prevalent orientation of case law confirms the reciprocal autonomy and independence of the two measures; consequently, the landscape authorization constitutes a mere prerequisite of the effectiveness (and, thus, not the constitutionality) of the building permit. An eventual refusal to grant landscape authorization can, therefore, be the grounds of a court ruling that the permit that had previously been granted is ineffective (rather than unconstitutional). What has been established by the Court, however, appears to substantiate another argument that has also been made, which tends to be reinforced by administrative case law, that is, that landscape authorization is a condition for the building permit to be considered legitimate, and defects of the authorization negatively influence the legitimacy of the permit (Council of State, judgment No. 5371 of 2013; T.A.R. Lombardy, Milan, judgment No. 3062 of 2014).*

Landscape authorization can be appealed to the Regional Administrative Court or to the President of the Republic by means of an extraordinary appeal, by any interested public or private party: such party must have a differentiated subjective right, appearing from a stable relationship that is significantly connected to the areas that are affected by the measure.

Environmental associations that represent collective interests recognized according to Article 13 of Law No. 349 of 8 July 1986 can also file an appeal.

As noted, Legislative Decree No. 42 of 2004 introduced a prohibition against the issuance of authorization after the work has been realized, unless the work is modest in accordance with Article 167 of Code.

The impossibility of obtaining 'posthumous' landscape authorization has effects which, with all probability, also reverberate on the scope of the building permit issued 'in sanatoria' (i.e., after the construction work has been performed) in areas protected by restrictions, given the nature of the authorization as a prerequisite with respect to the building permit.

V. Simplified Procedure for Minor Works

419. DPR No. 31 of 2017 governs a simplified procedure for the issue of landscape authorizations, which mostly regards minor works that are indicated in Annex B of the decree.

It obviously regards works that result in an alteration of the exterior areas or aspect of the buildings, because otherwise their realization does not require landscape authorization.

The simplified procedure also applies to requests for the renewal of landscape authorizations, including those issued following the ordinary procedure, that have expired for less than one year and which relate to works that were not executed in all or in part, on the condition that the project conforms to what was previously authorized and to any specific supervening protection requirements.

The simplifications introduced by the regulation regard the documentation to be annexed to the application; the procedural requirements when a building permit is also requested or when it is necessary to obtain other authorizations; the duration of the procedure (established to be sixty days), as well as the procedural simplification (especially in relations with the Superintendence). In the simplified authorization procedure, the opinion of local landscape commissions is not mandatory (in accordance with Article 148 of the Code), unless otherwise provided by regional legislation.

§5. Specific Instruments: The Declaration of Public Interest

420. Since 1939 natural beauty, falling within the types of beauty currently referred to in Article 136 of the Code, is entitled to particular protection if subject to restriction by means of a specific measure of the administrative authority.

421. With respect to pre-existing legislation on natural beauty, the most significant innovation introduced by the code is represented by the substitution of registration in special registers with a declaration of significant public interest, an ordinance that applies not only to individual beauty but also to the beauty of an entirety.

The essential features of the regime of restrictions on use can be summarized as follows:

(a) the declaration of significant public interest can be issued both by the region, upon the proposal of special regional commissions, and by the Ministry for Culture upon the proposal of the Superintendence (*see* Article 138, paragraph 3 and Article 141*bis*);
(b) the draft measure is prepared in view of the historical, cultural, natural, morphological and aesthetic values expressed by the special aspects and characteristics of real property or the areas considered and the importance of their identity in relation to the territory in which they are located, and it contains proposals for restrictions on use aimed at ensuring the preservation of the values expressed; in other words, as noted by legal scholarship, the code 'has embellished' the restriction, which is not limited to determining the perimeter of the building or area that is protected, but provides the specific rules for its use;
(c) the draft measure is subject to special forms of public notice (publication in the Preatorian Register, notice in daily newspapers and on the internet sites of the entities involved as well as notice to the owner or holder of the property if an individual natural beauty is involved), intended to increase public participation in the procedure, which is guaranteed not only for the owner, possessor or holder of the property but also for local entities, environmental associations and anyone who is interested. The proceeding can take place in the form of a public hearing;

(d) the declaration of significant public interest, whether regional or State, indicates a specific regulation aimed at ensuring preservation of the values expressed by the specific features and characteristics of the territory in question. It is an integral part of the landscape plan and cannot be eliminated or modified during the course of the procedure in which such plan is drafted or revised. This confirms the approach that considers the restriction imposed by a declaration of significant public interest to be hierarchically superior to the landscape plan.

§6. CONTROL

422. Article 155 of the Code regulates heterogeneous institutes under the heading *supervision.*

It is necessary to clearly distinguish between supervising the proper exercise of administrative functions regarding landscape by the administrations identified by the region (paragraph 2), from supervising landscape resources, understood as a control action intended to prevent buildings or areas entitled to protection from being damaged (paragraph 1). Understood in this second sense, the supervisory function for landscape resources is attributed to the region and to the Ministry of Culture.

With regard to the first meaning of the term 'supervision', Article 155, paragraph 2 specifies that *non-compliance or persistent inertia in exercising said authority results in activating the Ministry's power of substitution.* Both the supervision of the activity of the competent administrations and the exercise of substitute power must be based on the principle of loyal collaboration (Constitutional Court, judgment No. 43 of 2004). Above all, in the case of substitution, the ministry's intervention cannot consist of the brusque adoption of measures that the competent authority failed to issue, but must be developed through a procedural sequence in which the competent authority is warned to comply, is enabled to act when it cannot take action, and is ultimately substituted in the case of persistent inaction.

Article 155 was supplemented by two other provisions in 2008: paragraph 2*bis*, which provides that all urban and territorial planning acts must conform to a conscious use of the territory and protection of the landscape characteristics of the various territorial contexts; and paragraph 2*ter,* which, in referring to Article 146, paragraph 12, grants recognized environmental associations the right to contest urban or territorial plans that include landscape resources.

§7. SANCTIONS

423. Landscape regulation is supported both by administrative and criminal sanctions.

The violation of legal obligations and provisions on landscape protection can result in an order to demolish any work built or the assessment of a monetary fine, calculated based on the larger amount between the damage caused and the profit obtained by the offender.

424. In 2006, the legislator clarified the cases in which a monetary fine is applied rather than an order of demolition: those cases involving minor abuses for which a 'posthumous' assessment of landscape compatibility is made by the competent authority. Specifically, those cases involve:

(a) work performed without landscape authorization or which is non-compliant, which has not resulted in the creation of useful surface areas or volumes or an increase of those that had been lawfully created;
(b) use of non-compliant materials with respect to the landscape authorization;
(c) work which, nevertheless, can be considered ordinary or extraordinary maintenance in accordance with Article 3 of Presidential Decree No. 380 of 6 June 2001.

If one of the above cases exists, the owner, possessor or holder of any kind of building or area where the work was performed can present a specific request to the authority entrusted with managing the restriction on use to verify whether the work is compatible with the landscape. Therefore, the prohibition of a 'posthumous' landscape authorization is limited to abuses that cannot be classified as one of these types of intervention.

The competent authority must decide the request within the mandatory term of 180 days from receipt of the binding opinion of the Superintendence, which must be issued within the mandatory term of ninety days.

In the event the work is found to be compatible with the landscape, the offender must pay an amount equivalent to the larger amount between the damage caused and the profit obtained by means of the infringement. The amount of the fine is determined by an expert appraisal. Otherwise, if the request be denied, the sanction of demolition is applied.

Article 168 of the Code punishes *anyone who places billboards or other means of advertising in violation of the provisions set forth in Article 153*, with reference to the sanctions set forth in Article 23 of the Code of the Road, which provides for the payment of diverse amounts in addition to the reparatory measure of the removal of the unauthorized billboard.

With respect to landscape protection offered by criminal law, the Code punishes *anyone who performs any kind of work on landscape resources without the required authorization, or in a manner that does not conform to said authorization* (Article 181).

In the event the abuses are minor (the same as Article 167), and the competent authority issues an ordinance of landscape compatibility, the abuse is not subject to criminal sanctions and only an administrative fine is applied. The request for verification of landscape compatibility filed for purposes of criminal law (in conformity with Article 181, paragraph 1*quater*) is understood as also having been presented in accordance with and for the effects of Article 167.

Finally, the offender's restoration of the areas or buildings subject to landscape restrictions to their original condition before being ordered to do so independently by an administrative authority, or in any event prior to a court ruling, extinguishes the crime.

Landscape protection is completed by Article 734 of the Criminal Code, which punishes 'whoever, by means of constructions, demolitions, or in any other manner, destroys or alters the natural beauty of places entitled to special protection'.

§8. Summary Framework of Competence

425. Even in the new Code, the administrative regulation of landscape revolves around the traditional institutes of the landscape plan, authorization and measures of restriction on use.

With regard to the first, it is necessary to note two aspects: the cited regional dimension of the plan, and the requirement that, at least in relation to the regulation of landscape resources, the plan is the result of an agreement between the region and the Ministry of Cultural Heritage and Activities and Tourism (hereinafter, the Ministry).

The ministry is also responsible for determining the fundamental outline of the layout of the national territory with respect to landscape protection, aimed at orienting planning.

426. The landscape authorization regime has at least two interesting novelties from the standpoint of the distribution of competence:

(1) the change of the Superintendence's role in the procedure;
(2) the State legislator's disapproval of the attribution of jurisdiction to the municipalities.

In accordance with the Code on Cultural Heritage and Landscape, the State level of government no longer has the power to annul the authorization, but intervenes in the procedure with a mandatory and binding opinion, at least until restrictions on the use of the landscape resources have been determined (by the landscape plans or declarations of significant public interest), and the ministry has verified, upon the region's request, whether the urban planning instruments have been adjusted.

The Code is aimed at the supra-municipal level (region, province or association of municipalities) with respect to the choice of which authority is competent to issue the authorization, which can be derogated to a lower level only if the relative bureaucratic apparatus has adequate technical know-how that allows it to guarantee differentiation between landscape protection and the exercise of administrative functions in urban planning – building matters. In the case of default by the competent Administration, the intervention of the governing body of the higher territorial level is foreseen (the Superintendence in the case of inertia by the region; and the region in the case of authorization functions delegated by it to a subregional entity; Article 146, paragraph 10).

With respect to the declaration of public interest, it should be noted that as a result of the 2008 modification of the code, the ministry no longer intervenes as a substitute in the case in which the region does not act, as still occurs for landscape authorization, but has instead been given autonomous jurisdiction that flanks that of the region.

Jurisdiction also rests both with the Ministry of Culture and with the regions with respect to the supervision of landscape resources.

§9. Conclusions

427. It clearly appears from a review of the landscape regime that the evolution of the manner in which landscape is conceived in the Italian legal system involved two different issues: all of the resources to be protected, and the breadth of instruments of intervention.

428. The 1939 legislation primarily considered landscape protection to be the protection of natural beauty by means of restrictions applied to buildings and areas of prestige, whereas preparation of the landscape plan was left to the discretion of the public administration. By means of Law No. 431 of 1985, the restriction on use in the form of an ordinance (the declaration of significant public interest) was flanked by the restriction imposed ex lege on a much broader panorama of resources whose management is also entrusted to the landscape plan, which became mandatory.

429. Legislative Decree No. 490 of 1999 subsequently reinforced the planning instrument, attributing greater significance to the planning of landscape enhancement, while the definition of 'environmental resource' as a 'significant testimonial of the natural or cultural characteristics of the environment', introduced by Article 148 of Legislative Decree No. 12 of 31 March 1998, accentuated the landscape's cultural dimension.

Similar considerations hold true for the Code of Cultural Heritage and Landscape. The first legislative definition of landscape (Article 131) is accompanied by an extension of the categories of landscape resources entitled to protection and enhancement, and, above all, by development of the potential of the landscape plan. It is important to note both the principle of the prevalence of the plan over urban planning instruments and sector planning, and the express provision requiring the plan to identify the restrictions on use of landscape resources and measures on the use of other appreciable landscape contexts.

The modification of the regime on restrictive ordinances (the declaration of significant public interest), moves in the same direction, which should not be limited to determining the perimeters of the protected resource, but must include specific regulations aimed at ensuring preservation of the values expressed by the unique features and characteristics of the territory in question.

The legislator's intent was to remove landscape protection from the episodic nature of individual landscape authorizations, issued in a legal context that granted excessive discretion to local administrations, with the risk that economic interests could prevail over landscape interests. By means of the code, restrictive ordinances and planning instruments have been activated in order to create a network of regulations on landscape protection, to be used as a parameter of the validity of the authorization power. In addition, there is the desire to create a highly specialized and adequately equipped local bureaucracy which, using the Superintendence as a model, can avoid alterations of the state of places in a manner that is incompatible with landscape values.

The trend towards higher levels of administrative functions should also be noted, above all, with respect to the protection of landscape resources, which occurred by means of the 2008 modifications to the code: authorizations issued by supra-municipal entities are preferred; planning that regards landscape resources must be the result of an agreement between the State and region; and the ministry no longer acts as a substitute, but has the direct power to impose restrictions, thereby flanking regional power and accentuating a counter-trend with respect to the principle of the proximity of administrative action to the public, ratified by Article 118 of the Constitution.

Chapter 2. Protected Areas

by *Alessandro Andronio*

§1. Nature and Objectives of the Regime

430. The object of nature protection is the protection of individual ecosystems, that is, the totality of the relationships that are created in a particular area between the biotic community (flora and fauna) and the non-living environment. It is performed primarily by means of public intervention intended to identify and preserve particular portions of territory entitled to protection because they have an intact 'ecological equilibrium', or which must be reconstructed intact.

These particular portions of territory are defined as 'protected areas', subject to a differentiated regime of use under the control of a public authority. Within these areas, the conservation and recovery of the natural environment and the landscape is given primary importance, followed by scientific research, environmental education and the sustainable socio-economic development of the populations residing within protected areas or in neighbouring areas.

§2. Framework of the International and EC Regime

431. After the 1972 Stockholm Conference on Conservation and Development, which constitutes one of the fundamental passages for the normative evolution on nature protection, Italy ratified the Ramsar Convention on Wetlands Protection of 2 February 1971, which Italy implemented by means of Presidential Decree No. 448 of 13 April 1976, subsequently modified by Presidential Decree No. 184 of 11 February 1987 (*see*, with respect to such Convention, *infra*, *Wetlands*).

The EC intervened in this area by means of the Fourth Action Programme, which explicitly emphasizes the necessity of creating an 'overall structure' of protection of natural habitats of Community interest. It is, however, above all, the Fifth Action Programme entitled 'Lasting and Sustainable Development', that marked a decisive turning point in the objectives and instruments of Community action.

Adopting the orientations of the Rio Declaration and the Convention on Biodiversity, the Community provided for a specific objective entitled 'Nature Protection and Biological Diversity', which maintains biological diversity in Europe by means of the protection of natural habitats and the sustainable management of the territory (*see infra*, Biodiversity).

A network of ecological protection denominated 'Natura 2000' was created as implementation of the Community directives issued in this area (Directive 79/409 of 2 April 1979 on the Protection of Wild Birds and Directive 92/43 of 21 May 1992 on 'Nature Protection').

The sites included in the ecological network are subject to a transitory regime of protection intended to avoid the degradation of the habitat as well as the disturbance of the species for which the areas were designated. The protection regime is essentially characterized by norms specifying its purpose and only in party by norms setting forth the details that are directly applicable in the domestic legal system of the States, even without a precise implementing act. Some of these details regard assessment of the impact of projects on the environment within the area designated as a conservation area.

432. Directive No. 43/1992 was implemented in the Italian legal system by DPR No. 357 of 8 September 1997.

§3. Development of the Domestic Legal System: The Role of the Regions and the Institutional Framework

433. The principal characteristics common to the first national parks created in Italy are: (1) creation by means of legislation; (2) management entrusted either to an autonomous entity or to the State Forestry Agency; (3) a legal regime characterized by an absolute prohibition against performing certain activities and by a general regime of authorizations to which other activities are subject; (4) the objective of protection: to 'conserve fauna and flora and preserve special geological formations, as well as the beauty of the landscape'.

434. The first overall protection of an important nature area was given by RDL No. 1584 of 3 December 1922, converted into Law No. 1473 of 17 April 1925, which provides for the creation of the National Park of the Gran Paradiso in the Graie Alps. Four other parks followed: the National Park of Abruzzo (created by means of RDL No. 257 of 11 January 1923, converted into Law No. 1511 of 12 July 1923); the National Park of Circeo (created by Law No. 285 of 25 January 1934); the National Park of Stelvio (created by Law No. 740 of 24 April 1935); and the National Park of Calabria (created by Law No. 503 on 2 April 1968).

The Park of Abruzzo and the other two subsequent parks have, in addition to the conservatory purposes, also that of the 'development of tourism and the hotel industry'. The National Park of Calabria was created 'for the conservation of environmental characteristics and the education and recreation of citizens'.

Regardless, it was only by means of the creations of the ordinary regions in 1970 that 'nature protection' assumed specific importance. At the time that the administrative functions of the central State were transferred to the new regional entities, the first questions were raised regarding the division of competence on nature protection.

435. The evolution of nature protection by means of the creation of protected areas and parks in Italy essentially coincides with evolution of the division of legislative and administrative competence between the State and the regions, with the essential interpretative contribution of the Constitutional Court.

The regions, created in 1970, are among the public subjects to whom the Constitution attributes choices relating to land use and, among these, the eventual protection of existing ecosystems.

The creation of the regions, having autonomous legislative and administrative powers, provoked a decisive centralist reaction by the State at the beginning of the

1970s, as many matters for which it had previously been competent were transferred to the regions. Article 117 of the Constitution contained a list of matters in which the regions exercised concurrent legislative powers with the State. In particular, regional legislative power was exercised within the general limits of national interest and the fundamental principles established by the laws of the State (framework laws). The scope of such limits determined the effective scope of application of regional legislation.

436. Law No. 281 of 16 May 1970 and DPR No. 11 of 15 January 1972 inaugurated a long phase of initial centralist formulation of the division of competence between the State and the regions.

During this period, on the basis of Article 4 of DPR No. 11 of 1972, the regions created their own protected natural areas, that is, 'interventions that do not conflict with those of the State', and they acted utilizing the sphere of powers that are constitutionally guaranteed with respect to the use and layout of the territory (such as urban planning, agriculture, forestry, hunting and fishing, mining activities, tourism, water within their territory, transportation). In this phase, case law confirmed the legitimacy of the definition of the topics set forth in Article 117 of the Constitution used by the State legislator and the substantial curtailment of the transfer of functions in favour of the State (*see* the Constitutional Court, judgment No. 79 of 26 April 1971; judgment No. 79 of 4 May 1972; judgment No. 142 of 24 July 1972; judgment No. 219 of 20 December 1972; judgment No. 175 of 14 July 1976).

437. Constitutional case law starting from this period developed, however, some principles that would become the basis of an evolution of the division of competence in a less centralist sense: (1) definition of 'national parks' as a sector extraneous to agriculture and forestry (*see* Constitutional Court, judgment No. 142 of 24 July 1972); and (2) definition of 'nature protection' as an activity of national interest, whose performance must be based on organic programming valid for the entire national territory, whose details are left to the local authorities (*see* Constitutional Court, judgment No. 175 of 14 July 1976, which recognizes the interface between regional competence and State competence).

438. The entry into effect of DPR No. 616 of 24 July 1977 opened a new phase in the State-region relationship, overturning the previous formulation (*see* Articles 66, 68, 78, 80 and 83).

The principal features of this decree are the transfer of nature protection from State competence to regional competence (this competence is concurrent with that of the State to establish the fundamental principles for legislation and issue orientation and coordination acts for administrative functions), and introduction of the concept of interregional parks.

The principle of the regionalization of interventions, intended to protect nature as opposed to a de facto freezing of the competence exercised by the State to existing national parks and state reserves and government intervention on the basis of the Ramsar Convention (*see infra, Wetlands*), must be seen in the context of the State's compliance with international obligations, which constitute a limit on the legislative and administrative powers of the regions.

439. Subsequent to issuance of DPR No. 616/1977, the Italian regions created more than ninety protected areas with respect to five existing national parks. The surface area of the national territory affected by protected regional areas is approximately 5,019 km^2, as compared to 2,685 km^2 of national parks and 1,444 km^2 of national reserves.

Starting from this period, regional legislation generally shares the following characteristics:

- the park is a territory subject to a particular regime, but it is also a legal entity guided by its own representative organism having management powers, administrative competence and regulatory power. All of the regional parks have an entity that represents them: the prevalent choice is that of a consortium among the local entities involved, whereas in other cases there is a public entity or direct management by the municipalities or mountain communities;
- the protected area's legal regime is governed at diverse levels by: general regional laws on protected areas, laws creating individual areas, area plans, regulations and social-economic programmes;
- the standards and objectives of sustainable development are indicated.

The Constitutional Court also implemented the changed legislative orientation by means of judgment No. 223 of 25 July 1984, which annulled three decrees of the Ministry of Agriculture that had attempted to create three natural reserves, declaring that subsequent to DPR No. 616/1977, the State no longer had the power to create them.

In its judgment, the court confirmed the regionalization of the entire subject matter of national parks, and expressed the need that the legislator provide by means of a Framework Law for the definitive regulation of this area.

440. At the end of the 1980s, the State administration reacquired a role of primary importance with respect to nature protection.

The reasons for this change derived from an 'environmental emergency', which led to extraordinary interventions.

For the purposes of nature protection, the principal legislation that characterized this phase is the following:

- Law No. 349 of 8 July 1986, 'Creation of the Ministry of the Environment and Rules on Environmental Damage'.
- Law No. 59 of 3 March 1987, 'Temporary and Urgent Measures for the Functioning of the Ministry of the Environment', which empowers the Ministry of the Environment to adopt necessary protective measures in the areas destined to become national parks and natural reserves.
- Law No. 67 of 11 March 1988, Article 18, which attributed CIPE, upon the proposal of the Ministry of the Environment, with the power to approve the annual programme for 1988 of urgent interventions for environmental protection. Such programme provided for the creation of three new national parks, thus, modifying Article 83 of DPR No. 616/1977, and provided for the possibility of increasing the number of new parks 'in agreement with the interested regions'; and –

Law No. 305 of 28 August 1989, 'Regime of Three Year Environmental Protection Programmes', with which Parliament rationalized what it had established on an emergency basis by means of Law No. 67/1988: it confirmed the choices made by the CIPE resolution, and provided for the creation of other new national parks, to be created using the procedure set forth in Article 5 of Law No. 349/1986 (*see, infra,* on the Three-Year Programmes).

441. At the end of the 1980s, the Constitutional Court reviewed its own prior interpretation of Article 83, DPR No. 616/1977, elaborating the following principles: (1) a framework law is required (Constitutional Court, judgment No. 1029 of 15 November 1988); (2) nature protection is a regional matter in which the region exercises legislative power concurrently with the State (Constitutional Court, judgment No. 1029 of 15 November 1988); (3) the State can deviate from the latter principle in the presence of a 'national interest'; (4) all public subjects involved in nature protection are subject to an obligation of loyal cooperation (Constitutional Court, judgment No. 1031 of 15 November 1988, No. 1031; judgment No. 344 of 29 October 1989; judgment No. 337 of 15 June 1989; judgment No. 346 of 20 July 1990; judgments No. 151 and 153 of 27 June 1986); and (5) a national interest cannot be generically affirmed: it is necessary to demonstrate the naturalistic importance for the entire national society of the area under consideration (Constitutional Court, judgment No. 346 of 20 July 1990; T.A.R. Lazio, section II, No. 1900 of 25 September 1992, in *T.A.R.,* 1992, I, 3820).

The principles elaborated by the court with reference to the division of competence between the State and the regions prior to the constitutional reform of 2001 still constitute the basis of the present Framework Law.

§4. State and Regional Laws

I. General Principles

442. The legal evolution described above eventually led to the approval of Framework Law No. 394 of 6 December 1991 on protected areas, which despite having been modified several times remains outstanding. It is an organic attempt to incorporate and implement the constitutional principle of environmental protection and protection of the ecosystem in the Italian legal system.

The objective of the framework law is that of 'guaranteeing and promoting the conservation and enhancement of the nation's natural patrimony in a coordinated manner'.

443. 'Conservation' indicates the overall activity aimed at protecting biotic and abiotic factors present in a specific area, both individually and relationships existing among them, and, in particular, the equilibrium that is created in these relationships (the framework law refers to 'ecological equilibrium'). Enhancement constitutes the dynamic aspect of protection by means of 'the application of methods of environmental management or restoration suitable to integrating man and the natural environment (Article 1, paragraph 3, clause b)' and 'the experimentation of compatible manufacturing activities (Article 1, paragraph 4)'.

444. The other fundamental principle of the framework law is the principle of loyal cooperation among diverse territorial levels of government (Article 1, paragraph 5), reaffirmed by the Constitution Court (judgment No. 302 of 15 July 1994), which was subsequently formulated in Title V of the second part of the Constitution (*see supra* judgments No. 339 of 2005, No. 21 of 2006, No. 437 of 2008, and No. 315 of 2010).

445. The principles developed by the court with reference to the division of competence between the State and the regions prior to the constitutional reform of 2001 have substantially been reiterated by subsequent constitutional case law. Specifically, the court held in judgment No. 108 of 2005 that the regional legislator cannot lower the levels of protection established by the State with reference to national protected areas; the regions have broad legislative discretion with respect to regional protected areas, as long as they are compliant with national legal principles, in particular, those set forth in Articles 22 and 23 of Law No. 394 of 1991 (*see* judgments No. 241 of 2008, No. 44 of 2011, No. 212 of 2014, No. 38 of 2015, and No. 74 of 2017).

More recently, constitutional case law has peremptorily reaffirmed the State's exclusive legislative competence with regard to protected areas, with the exception of regional regimes that offer greater environmental protection (judgments No. 180 of 2008; judgments No. 12 and No. 272 of 2009, No. 234 of 2011, and No. 36 of 2017).

II. Specific Instruments of Nature Protection: Protected Areas, Parks and Reserves

446. The legal instrument used to protect natural resources is the creation of a 'protected area', which is a territory subject to a special legal regime.

Within the uniform category of protected areas, the law proposes four different kinds of creation classification: parks (national and regional), reserves (national and regional), protected marine areas (*see infra, Marine protection*) and natural protected areas of local interest.

Article 2 provides that: 'national parks are made up of land, rivers, lakes or seas containing one or more intact ecosystems or ecosystems partially altered by anthropic interventions, one or more physical, geological, geomorphological, or biological formations, of international or national importance due to their natural, scientific, aesthetic, cultural, educational and recreational values that require State intervention to conserve them for present and future generations' (paragraph 1); 'Regional nature parks consist of land, rivers and lakes as well as stretches of sea overlooking the coastline, having natural and environmental value, which, within one or more neighbouring regions, constitute a homogeneous system identified by the natural appearance of the places, by landscape and artistic values and cultural traditions of local populations' (paragraph 2); 'Nature reserves consist of land, rivers, lakes or seas containing one or more significant natural species of flora and fauna, or which have one or more ecosystems that are important due to biodiversity or the conservation of genetic resources. Nature reserves can be State or regional based on the significance of the interests they represent' (paragraph 3).

Aside from the formulation of the law, the various types of protected areas are only differentiated on the basis of the level of interest that is protected (international, national, regional or local). In this regard, the Constitutional Court, already by means of judgment No. 366 of 27 July 1992, specified that in the event the interest of the resource that is the object of protection is held to be of national importance, competence to identify the relative area and the creation within it of national parks or reserves rests with the State.

The framework law provides that each protected area shall have a management organism.

447. With respect to national parks, the model of a public entity has been chosen (park entity, regulated by Article 9), whereas for State natural reserves a management organism is provided that is regulated by the individual decree that establishes the reserve (Article 17). The law indicates a public entity or mandatory consortium among local entities or associative organisms as the possible institutional figures to manage regional protected areas (Article 23).

The organizational structure of national parks is that typical of public entities. The park organs are:

- the president, who is the legal representative of the entity and responsible for its internal coordination. In cases of urgency, he exercises the powers of the park's executive council. He also exercises the responsibilities that have been delegated to him by the executive council and adopts the relative ordinances; – the executive council, which is competent for all general issues: the park's by-laws, balance sheets, regulations draft park plans and so on;
- the board of auditors, which is entrusted with the internal control of the park's accounting system;
- the park director, competent with respect to all acts of extraordinary administration: this is the organ responsible for the concrete management of the park; and
- the park community, a consultative organ empowered to make independent proposals: all of the presidents of the interested regions and the highest representatives of the local entities (provincial and municipal) are included in the park community.

Law No. 394/1991 imposes numerous rules of principle, but also rules setting forth details on the internal legal regime of protected areas.

All of the acts creating the individual protected areas are issued at decreasing hierarchical levels: a DPR for national parks; a regional law for regional parks; and a ministerial decree for national reserves. These sources define protected areas and establish the fundamental principles of their internal discipline and organization.

At an even lower hierarchical level are the individual regulations for national parks, which are legal acts that regulate in detail the activities allowed within the parks. The regulations govern activities which, even though allowed in principle because they are capable of harmonic integration with the natural equilibrium, must be limited. In addition, there is a general prohibition against activities and works that could compromise safeguarding protected landscape and natural environments, with particular attention paid to protected flora and fauna and their respective habitats.

III. Institutional Framework

448. As affirmed by the Constitutional Court in judgment No. 302 of 15 July 1994, the provisions of Law No. 394/1991 have a direct impact on the division of competence that was previously made on a temporary basis by Article 83 of DPR No. 616/1977 (with regard to the evolution of the division of Framework Law No. 394/1991 represents a synthesis with the prior regime and constitutes a structural division of powers between the State and regions that configured in a different manner according to the type of protected area involved. The model is concurrent with respect to protected areas of regional and local interest. The plan provides for the State to exercise active powers for protected areas of international or national interest, whereas the regions have competence of a participatory and legislative nature, according to a dual management model.

Such model is compatible with the elastic criteria for the division of administrative competence among different territorial levels of government contained in the new Article 118 of the Constitution and is based on principles of subsidiarity, differentiation and adequacy (*see* Constitutional Court, judgment No. 422 of 18 October 2002).

449. The Framework Law provides for the creation of two new bodies:

- a Committee for Natural Protected Areas, composed of national and regional representatives, which has the task of formulating the orientation for the preparation of the Nature Charter and, on the basis of this, identifying the fundamental outlines of the land's layout. In addition, it is responsible for adopting a three-year Plan for natural areas and an Official List of protected areas (the Committee's functions have currently been transferred to the State-Regional Conference); and
  – a technical Advisory Board for protected natural areas, a consultative organ responsible for expressing opinions of a technical-scientific nature (Article 3).

A. *Competence with Respect to Protected Areas of International and National Importance*

450. The State has legislative and administrative powers for international and national protected areas, which, however, in the actual exercise of such powers must consider the participation of the regions.

The identification, classification and 'temporary' delineation of protected areas rest with the Committee for Natural Protected Areas. In the event, it is not possible to obtain majority approval; the Ministry of the Environment places the question before the Council of Ministers (Article 3).

The Minister of the Environment is generally attributed with substitute powers in the case of delays or omissions.

National parks are created by means of presidential decree; natural reserves are created by a decree of the Minister of the Environment.

The decrees establishing the above are issued after consultation with the regions having an ordinary charter, or else after agreement with the regions having a special charter.

Article 6 provides that, by means of the decree creating the protected area or by means of a subsequent ordinance, protective measures can be approved which are applied through adoption of the park plan and regulations and which regulate the activities that can be performed in the various areas of the park. On the basis of such measures, the following activities are prohibited outside of residential areas:

> new development and the transformation of existing buildings, any change of land use other than agricultural use, and anything else that might impact the area's topography, ecological, hydraulic and hydrogeothermal equilibrium, or the institutional purposes of the protected area. In cases of necessity and urgency, the Minister of the Environment can waive the protective measures at issue, prescribing the manner in which work is carried out and the works that are suitable for safeguarding the integrity of the places and the natural environment. It is possible, however, to perform ordinary and extraordinary maintenance. If there is a violation of protective measures, the transgressor is required to restore the places to their pre-existing state and eventually recreate damaged plant and animal species.

451. With respect to the principal normative and planning acts relating to individual protected areas, competence is subdivided between the State and the regions.

The regulation must be approved by the Minister of the Environment, upon consultation with the local entities and agreement with the regions involved (Article 11); the park plan, prepared by the managing entity, is instead approved by the region (Article 12). The park community, after a binding opinion of the park's executive council, approves the multi-year economic and social plan; in addition, its opinion is mandatory with respect to the park regulation, the park plan, the budget and its final balance sheet (Article 10).

452. In conclusion, in protected areas of international and national interest, the framework law provides that the regions must cooperate with the State administration: the model of the division of competence has, thus, evolved in a regional sense.

B. Competence with Respect to Regional and Local Protected Areas

453. In the case of regional areas, the division of competence is based on a concurrent model.

The underlying principle for regional legislation is found in the 1991 framework law, independent of their self-qualification. In particular, Article 22 of the framework law establishes the principles that the regions must observe in regulating regional protected areas: (a) the classification and creation of protected areas of regional and local interest rests with the regional (or provincial) law; (b) the participation of local infra-regional entities must be ensured with respect to the creation and management of regional protected areas; (c) the public dissemination of the acts relating to the creation of the protected area and the definition of the park plan must be guaranteed.

The regions must create an organ for the management of the area: each area's charter must provide for a differentiated organizational form on the basis of its specific nature. The park's management organ must adopt the park plan, which must then be approved by the regions; such plan has value also on a landscape and urban planning level. The multi-year economic-social plan is adopted by the park entity, in consideration of the opinion expressed by local entities and approved by the region, and can be updated annually (Articles 24 and 25).

In substance, the legal regime of individual protected areas uses the national parks as a model, even if the two regimes are not totally analogous.

On the basis of Article 32, the regions can specify and delineate areas that are adjacent to protected areas in order to safeguard the latter more effectively. They can adopt environmental protection measures in such adjacent areas, in particular, with regard to hunting, fishing and mining.

With regard to competence for protected marine areas *see infra, Protection of the Sea.*

IV. Planning and Programming Instruments

454. The framework law originally created two distinct planning levels.

455. The first level included the Three-year Programme for natural protected areas, abolished by Article 76 of Legislative Decree No. 112 of 31 March 1998, in implementation of Chapter 1 of Law No. 59 of 15 March 1997.

456. At a second level – the only planning level that has remained – two other kinds of plans are contemplated, with the objective of 'compatible economic development':

1) the park plan, prepared by the park's managing entity and adopted by the region, is the instrument for the protection of natural and environmental resources: it has the 'effect of a declaration of public interest and the interventions provided in it are considered to be urgent and cannot be delayed, and it substitutes landscape plans, territorial or zoning plans, and every

other planning instrument at all levels' (Article 12, paragraph 7, Law No. 394/1991). In addition, it is immediately binding on both private as well as public parties (*see* T.A.R. Campania, No. 950 of 10 December, in *Riv. giur. ambiente,* 1997, 726). Article 12 of Law No. 394/1991 provides that the park's territory is differentiated 'in areas or parts characterized by differentiated forms of use, enjoyment and protection' and provides for four kinds of areas characterized by the presence of increasingly intense human activity: areas that are entirely reserves, areas that are generally oriented as reserves, areas of protection and areas of economic promotion. The plan, however, does not only regulate the use of the territory, but also establishes the orientation and criteria for interventions that protect flora and fauna;

2) the multi-year economic-social plan for the promotion of compatible activities (Article 14), which is prepared by the park community upon the binding opinion of the park entity's executive council, and which is approved by the regions. It promotes initiatives intended to favour the economic and social development of the society residing within the territory of the park and in neighbouring areas, and is substantially a financial instrument that directly provides economic resources for the performance of the activities set forth in Article 14, paragraph 3 of Law No. 394/1991. These initiatives regard agricultural tourism types of building construction, the revitalization of historic centres, the creation of campgrounds and cooperatives for activities connected with tourism, the creation and management of faunal areas, the training and use of nature guides, the encouragement of artisan and gastronomic activities, and the support of agricultural-forestry-pastoral activities.

V. Authorization Procedures

457. Article 13 of the framework law creates a legal instrument of *nulla osta*, on the basis of which the managing entity can control human activity capable of altering or compromising the environmental equilibrium inside of a protected area. The *nulla osta* is a preventive permission, on which the issuance of all permits or authorizations relating to 'interventions (including on work already existing inside of the area, *see* Council of State, section VI, judgment No. 1019 of 7 December 1992, in *Giust. Civ.*, 1993, 1687), installations and work to be done inside of the park' are subordinated.

On the basis of Article 13, permission is considered to have been granted when no denial is issued within the term of sixty days from presentation of the relative request. The Council of State (section VI, judgment No. 6591 of 29 December 2008, in *Dea*) has specified that this special form of silence amounting to assent was not implicitly abolished after Law No. 80/2005, which amended Law No. 241/1990, entered into effect.

VI. Powers of Management Organs

458. The self-protection system of protected areas is regulated by Article 29 of the framework law, which attributes the managing organs of protected natural areas with substantive powers of an administrative nature to oppose the activities of third parties that conflict with relevant regulations, plans and the preventive permission obtained.

The first paragraph of Article 29 attributes powers of enjoinment to the legal representative that he is obliged to exercise (*see* Council of State, section IV, judgment No. 816, 21 May 1994, in *Ambiente*, 1994, 82), ordering the immediate suspension of illegal activity and the restoration or recreation of vegetable or animal species at the expense of the transgressor. In the case in which the illegal activity consists of the construction and transformation of work projects, the owner of the company and director of the works are jointly liable with the person who ordered the works to be performed.

In the event that the transgressor remains non-compliant after a suitable period of time has passed from an order of restoration, Article 29, second paragraph, provides that the area's legal representative must provide for 'the performance of the obligations according to the procedure set forth in the second, third and fourth paragraphs of Article 27 of Law No. 47 of 28 February 1985 (currently the Uniform Text on Building Construction, DPR No. 380/2001), and can recover the relative expenses by means of an administrative injunction', issued in accordance with the Uniform Text on Recovery of State Revenue (RD 639 of 14 April 1910).

The third paragraph of Article 29 specifies that the entity entrusted with managing the protected natural area has standing to sue.

It 'can participate in legal actions regarding negligent or intentional facts that can compromise the integrity of the protected area's natural heritage, and has the right to appeal to administrative jurisdiction, requesting the annulment of illegitimate acts that are harmful to the objectives for which the protected area was created'.

An action requesting the compensation of damages according to Article 2043 of the Civil Code can be brought in the case in which, in addition to the harm to the environmental resource, individual subjective positions for which the managing entity is responsible might also be harmed.

VII. Regime of Sanctions

459. The regime of sanctions set forth in Article 30 is centred on the punishment of behaviour that conflicts with the fundamental regulation of the protected area; it lacks, however, an explicit norm that punishes the alteration or the compromising of natural heritage as such. In any event, it should be noted that Article 30, paragraph 3, refers to Articles 733 and 734 of the Criminal Code: the distinction between violation of the park's management instruments, the alteration of natural beauty and the alteration of the individual components of the overall heritage that constitute the protected area are explicit. Further, the crime defined in Articles 13 and 30 (failure to obtain prior permission) does not substitute what is provided by Article 1*sexies* of Law No. 431/1985 (currently Article 181 of Legislative Decree

No. 40 of 2004), as the object of protection is different as well as the procedures to be followed to obtain permission from the park entity or from the authority entrusted with supervising the restriction.

460. Article 30 provides differentiated protection for each of the various phases of the creation of the area, in relation to the obligations that it imposes:

- a phase prior to the creation of the protected area: such phase is set forth in Articles 4–6 of Law No. 394/1991, and ranges from identification of the area entitled to protection through the creation of the protected area. Article 6 provides for the effectiveness of measures of protection: the violation of such measures is punished by Article 30, paragraph 1 by means of detention of up to twelve months and a fine ranging from EUR 103 to EUR 25,822; – a phase ranging from the creation of the area to the adoption of management instruments: in accordance with Article 6, paragraph 4, the prohibitions set forth in Article 11 are applicable. The violation of such measures is also punished by Article 30, paragraph 1 by detention of up to twelve months and a fine ranging from EUR 103 to EUR 12,911;
- a definitive phase: the law provides that violation of the provisions set forth in Article 13 regarding preventive permission is a crime punished by detention of up to twelve months and by a fine ranging from EUR 103 to EUR 25,822; as well as violation of the provisions set forth in Article 11 in matters regarding the park's regulations and violation of the provisions of Article 19 regarding marine reserves.

461. With reference to the first of the three violations, the absence of preventive permission from the park entity had not been found to constitute a crime in accordance with Article 13, paragraph 1 unless the plan and park regulation had been adopted, whose terms constitute the parameters for verification of the work that is to be performed (*see* Court of Cassation, Criminal, section III, 18 October 1995, Di Felice, in *Diritto penale e processo*, 1996, 722).

More recently, case law has affirmed the opposite principle, according to which the lack of approval of the plan and regulation is not an obstacle to the exercise of the authorization power, because a different interpretation would introduce an unconstitutional limit on the obligatory nature of criminal law, which would only be applied in areas governed by the more diligent administrations (i.e., those that have approved the plan and regulation), but not in those governed by negligent administrations (which have not approved the plan or regulation) (Court of Cassation, Criminal section III, judgment No. 14183/2007 of 13 April 2006).

In the lack of a plan and regulation, the decision as to whether or not the authorization should be issued must be made considering the principles emerging from the laws of reference (*see* Council of State, section V, judgment No. 4469 of 20 August 2001; Court of Cassation, Criminal section III, judgment No. 5863 of 14 January 2004).

VIII. Restrictions and Indemnification: Economic Instruments and Incentives

462. Article 15 of the framework law regulates activities and resources existing inside of protected areas.

In order to pursue the objectives of conservation and enhancement of Italy's natural heritage, it is necessary to subject areas and property located within protected areas that are privately owned to a regime of restrictions, to ensure that their use is compatible with that of the protected area.

The limitations placed on property located inside of a protected area, provided for and imposed by the park plan, differ as they can regard both prohibitions of changes of the state of a place and restrictions on all other forms of use of the resources determined to be compatible with the purposes of the park (such as grazing, breeding and cultivation). The zoning of the park determines the diverse intensity of the reduction of the property owner's rights.

463. The principal problem raised relating to park restrictions is that of indemnification. The limitations placed on use of the park are the equivalent of landscape restrictions imposed by Law No. 431 of 1985; such equivalency has led to the position that no indemnification is provided (a consolidated orientation in such sense has been expressed by the Constitutional Court in judgments No. 56 of 29 May 1968; No. 9 of 20 February 1973; No. 202 of 4 July 1974).

464. Restrictions relating to agricultural-forestry-pastoral activities, unlike landscape restrictions, are regulated by Article 15, paragraph 2, and the Italian legislator has provided that they can be indemnified. The regime relating to indemnities is approved by means of a decree of the Ministry of the Environment. The procedures for the payment of indemnities are provided by the park regulation. Case law has clarified that no indemnity is due for the sole inclusion of the property within a natural park, even in the lack of the above regulation or on the basis of Community law, which provides a regime of assistance aimed at sustaining agricultural activities for the use of production methods that are compatible with the needs of environmental protection, or on the basis of Article 15, paragraph 2 of the framework law on protected areas. Such restrictions are not considered to be expropriations, as an expropriation deprives the *ius aedificandi* of theoretical income from buildings (whereas land classified as agricultural land is not to be used for building development). Further, the environmental objective of the restriction justifies its constraint on use, which is not entitled to indemnification (Court of Cassation, section I, judgment No. 10803 of 10 May 2006; section I, judgment No. 18963 of 16 September 2011).

Actual expropriations, for which indemnification is always required in accordance with Article 42, paragraph 3, of the Constitution, are different from situations regarding restrictions placed on property located within a park.

465. Article 7 of the framework law provides that incentives can be granted to municipalities, provinces and to private parties with respect to activities falling within a protected area.

In particular, with respect to private parties, the reference is to manufacturing or service activities as long as they are compatible with the specific purposes for which the park was created. The order of priority established by the legislator aims at the enhancement and recovery of already existing property, historic centres, resources of aesthetic-cultural value and rural residential centres.

Article 16 provides sources of financing for park entities (ordinary and extraordinary State contributions, revenue from activities in which the entity collaborates with other subjects, donations, etc.) and a beneficial tax regime.

Chapter 3. Biodiversity

by *Alessandro Andronio*

§1. The International Legal System

466. The Italian legal system on biodiversity arises in large part from the necessity of domestic implementation of the international agreements to which Italy is a party and of relevant Community directives.

In the context of international law, the Convention of Rio de Janeiro on Biological Diversity of 5 June 1992 (ratified by Italy by means of Law No. 124 of 14 February 1994, which entered into effect on 15 April 1994, and integrated in 2000 by the Protocol of Cartagena and in 2010 by the Protocol of Nagoya), is the international treaty that attempts to regulate the entire subject matter in an organic manner.

Article 1 sets forth the Convention's general objectives: the conservation of biological diversity; the use of biological components; just and equitable division of the benefits deriving from the utilization of genetic resources.

Article 2 of the Convention includes a legal concept of biodiversity, defined as 'the variability between living organisms of every origin, including, *inter alia*, terrestrial, marine and other aquatic ecosystems, and the ecological ecosystems of which they are part, including diversity of and among the species of the ecosystems'. The same article also specifies the concept of sustainable development, defining 'sustainable' as 'the use of the components of biological diversity according to a manner and rhythm of use that does not lead to long-term impoverishment, thus protecting their potential to satisfy the needs and expectations of present and future generations'.

The treaty entrusts biodiversity protection to the States at a national level by means of the preparation of specific strategies and adoption of measures intended to implement its basic principles (Article 6). The preamble specifies that the 'States have sovereign rights over their own biological resources' and they are 'responsible for the conservation of their own biological diversity and for the sustainable use of their own biological resources'. It is, therefore, up to each contracting party to adopt a series of measures for the conservation of genetic resources, ecosystems and natural habitats.

Among the conservation instruments of biological resources, the treaty identifies, in particular, protected areas considered as 'geographically identified areas, selected, regulated and managed for the purpose of achieving specific conservation objectives' (Article 2).

The responsibility for creating such areas is left to individual nations, which must adopt special measures in order to preserve biological diversity both within and outside the protected areas; protect ecosystems and natural habitats; promote sustainable and ecologically healthy development in areas adjacent to protected areas; and restore threatened flora and fauna and degraded ecosystems. The treaty does not, however, contain specific lists of endangered animal and vegetable species.

467. In addition to the Treaty of Rio, Italy has ratified other international multilateral agreements intended to protect biodiversity:

(a) the International Convention for the Protection of Birds (Paris, 18 October 1950), which entered into effect on 6 September 1979 (Law No. 812 of 24 November 1978), and which regulates fundamental protections, such as the specification of the species that can be hunted;
(b) the Convention on Wild Life and Natural Environment Conservation in Europe (Berne, 19 September 1979), which entered into effect on 1 June 1982 (Law No. 503 of 5 August 1981), whose annexes, containing the lists of protected species, have been amended on various occasions by the Conference of the Parties;
(c) the Convention on the Conservation of Wild Migratory Species (Bonn, 23 June 1979), which entered into effect on 1 November 1983 (Law No. 42 of 25 January 1983), and its following agreements: (a) the Agreement on the Conservation of Populations of European Bats; (b) the African-Eurasian Migratory Waterbird Agreement; (c) the Agreement on the Conservation of Small Cetaceans in the Baltic and North Seas (ASCOBANS); (d) the Agreement on the Conservation of Cetaceans in the Black sea, Mediterranean Sea and contiguous Atlantic Area; (e) the Agreement on the conservation of seals in the Wadden sea; (f) and the Conservation of Albatrosses and Petrels.

The first two conventions were implemented by means of specific legislation, as well as by Law No. 157 of 25 January 1992 (Article 1, paragraph 4, *infra*), which contains an explicit reference to them.

§2. The Community Legal System

468. At a Community level, Directives No. 79/409/EEC of 2 April 1979 (the 'Bird' Directive) and No. 92/43/EEC of 21 May 1992 (the 'Habitat' Directive) are particularly important.

469. The first directive creates specially protected geographical areas that are considered to be the most suitable territories due to location and surface area for the conservation of the species listed in the first three annexes, bearing in mind the necessity of protecting such species in both maritime and land contexts. Member States must identify and classify such protected areas in order to create a coherent network throughout of the territory of the EU.

Specifically, Article 9 provides that, as long as there are no other satisfactory solutions, Member States can derogate from the measures of protection for the following reasons: (a) in the interest of public health and safety, in the interest of the safety of the area, to prevent serious damage to cultivations, crops, livestock, forests, fish and water, or for the protection of flora and fauna; (b) for research and teaching, repopulation and reintroduction, as well as for breeding relating to such activities; (c) to allow in rigidly controlled conditions and in a selective manner the capture, detention or other limited uses of specific birds in small quantities.

The directive has been modified on various occasions and supplemented, and currently consists of a codified text set forth in Directive 2009/147/EC.

470. The second directive, which has also been modified on various occasions, amplifies the first directive's scope of application by instituting an organic system intended to create special conservation areas (ZSC) on the basis of their natural characteristics. In particular, Article 2 and Annex III emphasize the purposes of promoting biodiversity protection by means of maintaining or restoring natural habitat and species of wild flora and fauna of Community interest indicated in the annexes.

471. Among the numerous programming acts adopted by Community bodies, the Communications of the Commission to the European Council and Parliament of 27 March 2001 (containing the Action Plan to enhance biodiversity in different sectors) and the Commission's Report on the 2010 assessment of the implementation of the Action Plan (8 October 2010) are particularly important.

§3. Implementation of the International Regime

472. Turning to the Italian legal system, Article 1 of the framework law on protected areas (Law No. 394 of 1991) contained an express (although redundant) reference to the 'respect of international agreements'.

Legislative Decree No. 112 of 31 March 1998 makes the State responsible for the protection of biological diversity as well as of flora and fauna specifically protected by international agreements and Community law.

The Rio Convention on Biodiversity contains norms which may or may not be directly applicable, leaving each State with the choice of the means for concrete implementation. Mere implementation by means of implementing decrees in accordance with Law No. 124 of 14 February 1994 is, therefore, insufficient to create effective protection.

473. To remedy such situation, the strategic lines for implementation of the Rio Convention and the preparation of a national biodiversity plan were approved by CIPE by means of a resolution dated 16 March 1994, which utilizes the instrument of protected areas to pick up the orientation that already emerged in the 'National Plan for Sustainable Development as Implementation of Agenda 21' (CIPE Resolution, 28 December 1993).

The 1994 resolution identifies the following guidelines for the preparation of an implementation plan referring to biodiversity: completion of a cognitive analysis in matters of diversity; identification of an international framework of protection with particular reference to programmes of collaboration with other countries; verification of national conservation programmes with respect to ecosystems and their reinforcement and integration in biodiversity programmes; verification of conservation programmes of species with reference to various populations; the strengthening of genetic resources and their inclusion in the policies of sustainable development; identification of strategies to integrate protective measures for biodiversity in all sectors of human activity, training and educational programmes; as well as implementation of measures to identify and periodically verify strategies at an institutional level.

The resolution also identifies the following areas that must be examined in view of preparation of the national biodiversity plan: knowledge of the Italian biodiversity patrimony; monitoring the state of diversity; on-site training and education; present state of conservation (protected areas, unprotected areas and environmental recovery); promotion of sustainable activities, containment of risk factors; on-site conservation; and international cooperation.

474. The Ministry of the Environment has recently (October 2010) prepared a Biodiversity Strategy, an extensive document that identifies three strategic and complementary objectives to be achieved within 2020. They are rather generic objectives: (a) the protection of biodiversity and ecosystem services; (b) the substantive reduction of the impact of climactic changes on biodiversity and human wellness; (c) the integration of the conservation of biodiversity in economic and sector policies. Such objectives must be realized in the context of fifteen working areas:

> 1. Species, Habitat, Landscape; 2. Protected Areas; 3. Genetic Resources; 4. Agriculture; 5. Forestry; 6. Domestic Waters; 7. Marine Environment; 8. Infrastructures and Transportation; 9. Urban Areas; 10. Health; 11. Energy; 12. Tourism; 13. Research and Innovation; 14. Education, Information and Communications; 15. Italy and Biodiversity in the world.

475. With respect to implementation of the Convention of Paris of 1950 and the Berne Convention of 1979, Law No. 157 of 25 January 1992, 'Norms for the Protection of Wildlife and Hunting', which implements Directive No. 79/409/EEC of 2 April 1979, provides that 'wildlife is the absolute heritage of the State and is entitled to protection in the interests of the national and international Community' (Article 1) and that protection regards 'all other species that Community directives or international conventions or special DPCM indicate are threatened with extinction' (Article 2, paragraph 1, clause *c*). With respect to this issue, the Convention of Paris does not specify the kinds of birds that can be killed, captured or maintained in captivity (Articles 8 and 9). The Berne Convention, instead, does contain lists of species of wild flora and wildlife as well as the relative natural habitats entitled to protection, and sets forth a series of specific obligations for the States relating to the wildlife species listed in Annexes II and III, even if the Constitutional Court, by means of judgments No. 830 of 1988 and No. 124 of 1990, has specified that, in general, the norms of such Convention are not self-executing, but are simply intended to direct national policies (*see also* judgment No. 165 of 2009).

476. Implementation of the Bonn Convention of 1979 instead took place by the sole implementation law (Law No. 42 of 1983); this is sufficient to create an adequate protection for the species listed in Annex I but not for the other species, for which the Convention is not self-executing and notes the necessity of executing special international agreements.

§4. The National Regime on Hunting and Implementation of Community Law

477. In the Italian legal system, the protection of biodiversity is placed between hunting, which is the exclusive residual legislative competence of the regions, and environmental protection and protection of the ecosystem, which is the exclusive legislative competence of the State (Article 117, second paragraph, clause *s* of the Constitution).

Specifically, according to what has been indicated by constitutional case law, the State is responsible for determining minimum and uniform standards of protection for fauna throughout the entire national territory, in particular, from the standpoint of limiting the period within which hunting is allowed as well as from the standpoint of specifying the species that can be hunted; the regions are instead responsible for the administrative and operative hunting regime. The general principle also applies to the field of hunting, according to which the State environmental regime can be modified by the regions and autonomous provinces in the exercise of their primary or residual legislative powers exclusively to raise the level of protection (judgments No. 227 of 2003, No. 392 of 2005, No. 272 of 2009, No. 233 of 2010, No. 191 of 2011, No. 278 of 2012, and No. 139 of 2017).

478. The general regime implementing the 'Birds' directive is, as noted, contained in State law No. 157 of 1992, which also implements, as noted, the Paris and Berne Conventions.

It specifically provides that: (a) hunting is allowed as long as it does not conflict with the need to preserve wildlife and does not cause actual damage to agricultural productions (Article 1, paragraph 2); (b) the regions issue the rules on managing and protecting all species of wildlife in conformity with State law, international conventions and Community directives (Article 1, paragraph 3); (c) the regions must create, along bird migration routes, areas of protection aimed at maintaining and providing, in conformity with ecological needs, habitats within such areas and in nearby areas, restoring biotopes that have been destroyed and creating biotopes; in the case of the regions' failure to act, the Minister of Agriculture and Forestry and the Minister of the Environment act jointly by means of a substitute control (Article 1, paragraph 5); (d) the regions must adopt conservation measures also for habitats that are outside of ZPS (Article 1, paragraph 5*bis*); (e) the National Wildlife Institute works as a scientific research and consulting technical body on behalf of the State, regions and provinces, with the responsibility of preparing a census of environmental resources consisting of wildlife, preparing action projects, collaborating with analogous foreign bodies and, in particular, with those of the countries in the EEC and with universities and other research institutes, to express technical-scientific opinions requested by the State and regions (Article 7); (f) the regions have to adopt wildlife-hunting plans, to programme hunting and protect wildlife (Article 10), specify the areas where hunting can take place (Article 14) and the periods in which different species can be hunted (Article 18); (g) hunting can take place in accordance with a permit which the State issues to citizens (Article 12) and that the regions can subject to the payment of a tax (Article 23); (h) the regions can create wildlife-hunting and hunting-agritourism businesses (Article 16); (i) the regions can consent to the derogations set forth in Article 9 of the 'Birds' directive, in compliance with the prerequisites established by such article (Article 19*bis*); j) hunting is subject to controls (Articles 27–29), with criminal and administrative sanctions for transgressors (Articles 30–32).

479. With respect to implementation of the 'Birds' directive, Italy has been condemned on various occasions by the ECJ for its violation of Community law.

An initial judgment was issued against Italy due to its lack of complete implementation by 6 April 1981 of Directive No. 79/409/EEC (Court of Justice, EC 8 July 1987, case 262/85).

Two other judgments were issued against Italy on 17 January 1991 (judgment No. 157/89), for violation of obligations deriving from the directive and lack of implementation of the modifications made by Directive No. 85/411/EEC (judgment No. 334/89).

480. In further relation to implementation of the 'Bird' Directive, DPCM of 27 September 1997 set forth a regime of derogations regarding the species that can be hunted in accordance with Article 9 of the same directive. The criteria for such derogation must be provided by precise national provisions in accordance with a judgment of the Court of Justice of 7 March 1996. Such orientation was confirmed by the Constitutional Court by judgment No. 272 of 22 July 1996, which reiterated judgment No. 1002 of 1998 according to which the regions are supposed to modify the list of species that can be hunted in the sense of 'limiting and not amplifying the number of exceptions to the general prohibition against hunting', as implementation of a principle of major protection, if compatible with the environment (*see also* Constitutional Court, judgments No. 168 of 1999, No. 387 of 2008 and No. 266 of 2010).

By means of its judgment of 15 July 2010, C-573/08, the Court of Justice affirmed that:

> since the law of transposition in the Italian legal system of the directive […] does not completely conform to such directive and the implementation of Article 9 of the latter does not guarantee that the derogations made by the competent Italian authorities comply with the conditions and pre-requisites provided by such article, the Republic of Italy is non-compliant with the obligations or which it is responsible pursuant to Articles 2-7, 9-11, 13 and 18 of the cited directive.

Specifically: (a) Article 4, No. 4, second sentence, according to which Member States must seriously follow the objective of protecting habitats, even outside of special areas of protection, was violated because the provisions of Laws No. 394/1991 and No. 157/1992 contain generic measures that are unsuitable for the specific protection of ornithological interests; (b) Article 9, which establishes the prerequisites for any derogations from the restrictive hunting regime approved by the competent authorities, was violated because regional legislation provides for derogations that do not consider such prerequisites (in a conforming sense *see* the Court of Justice, 15 May 2008, C-503/06; Constitutional Court, judgments No. 168

of 1999, No. 387 of 2008 and No. 266 of 2010); (c) Italy had already acknowledged the violation of the other mentioned articles of the directive, and meantime modified the relevant law in the direction indicated by the Commission by means of Article 42 of Law No. 96 of 2010. Similar violations were found, with reference to regional legislation, in judgments 11 November 2010, C- 164/2009; and 3 March 2011, C-508/2009.

481. Implementation of the 'Habitat' Directive was supposed to have taken place by 5 June 1994 but it was finally done after approximately three years of delay through DPR No. 357 of 8 September 1997, which was later modified significantly by DPR No. 120 of 12 March, 2003, at the time Italy was condemned by the Court of Justice (judgment of 20 March 2003, C-143/02; with respect to the interpretation of the directive, *see also* the judgment of 13 January 2005, C-117/03; and the judgment of 20 September 2007, C-304/ 2005).

482. The Ministry of the Environment had in any event, by means of the 'Bio-Italy' project, already identified SCI in June, 1995, and supplied the European Commission with an initial list of sites that has subsequently been updated.

483. DPR of 1997 regulates the procedures aimed at ensuring the maintenance or restoration in a satisfactory state of conservation, of natural habitats and species of wildlife and wild flora of Community interest, reproducing the Habitat Directive; it refers to the principal definitions (Article 2) and the standards for the creations of ecological networks, consisting of ZSC and ZPS, already provided as implementation of the 'Birds' directive, by Law 157/1992 (Article 1, paragraph 5).

The Constitutional Court intervened in this area (judgments No. 425 of 1999, 378 of 2007, No. 104 of 2008, No. 329 of 2008, and No. 151 of 2011), to delineate the boundaries between State and regional competence, recognizing that the obligation to implement Community law rests with all national levels of government. It has also been established that the communication of the countervailing measures necessary to ensure the overall global consistency of the European Ecological Network Natura 2000, provided by Article 4 of the Habitat Directive, is up to the State pursuant to Article 1, paragraph 5, of Law No. 349 of 1986 and Article 5 of Law No. 131 of 5 June 2003, in accordance with the principle enshrined in the third and fifth paragraphs of Article 117 of the Constitution.

Specifically, the court repeated, including with specific reference to DPR No. 357 of 1997, that 'the regions, in deciding the rules for the use of environmental resources, or in any event in carrying out its other responsibilities, must adapt to State law, however, if they deem it opportune, in exercising their legislative power they can establish limits of environmental protection that are more rigorous than State levels' (judgments No. 30 and No. 316 of 2009).

§5. Special and Criminal Legislation

484. The general regime of biodiversity protection in Italy essentially consists of laws, already analysed above, to implement international and Community law as well as, more or less indirectly, the norms set forth in the law on protected areas.

To complete the regulatory framework: (a) DM 3 April 2000, modified on various occasions, approved the list of ZPS in accordance with Directive 79/409/EEC and the SCI prepared in accordance with Directive 92/43/ EEC; (b) DM 25 March 2004 and the subsequent DM 26 March 2008, approved the list of SCI for the alpine biogeographical region in Italy, in accordance with Directive 92/43/EEC, which list was subsequently updated by DM 30 March 2009 and DM 2 August 2010; (c) by means of various ministerial decrees (the most recent being DM 2 August 2010), the lists of SCI for the continental biogeographical region and Mediterranean biogeographical region in Italy were approved and subsequently updated, in accordance with Directive 92/43/EEC.

485. The following are among the areas subject to special forms of biodiversity protection unrelated to protected areas:

(a) repopulation and capture zones for non-migratory wild game, in accordance with Article 6 of Law No. 991 of 25 July 1952;
(b) protected oasis, repopulation and capture zones, and public and private centres of reproduction, in accordance with Article 10, paragraph 8, of Law 157/92;
(c) areas of biological protection for the preservation of marine biodiversity in accordance with Article 98 of DPR No. 1639 of 2 October 1968;
(d) 'protected areas' defined in accordance with Articles 31–33 of Legislative Decree No. 214 of 19 August 2005 and Article 2 of DM 31 January 1996 containing 'Protective Measures Against the Introduction and Diffusion within the Territory of the Italian Republic of Organisms Harmful for Vegetables and Vegetable Products'.

As closure of the regime on habitats, Article 1, paragraph 1, clause *b* of Legislative Decree No. 121 of 7 July 2011, which implements Law No. 96 of 4 June 2010, which had delegated the government to adopt one or more legislative decrees in order to transpose the provisions set forth in Directive No. 2008/99/EC of 19 November 2008 on criminal protection of the environment and in Directive No. 2009/123/EC of 21 October 2009, introduced in the Criminal Code the new Article 733*bis* (Destruction or deterioration of habitats within a protected site), which provides that 'Anyone, except in permitted cases, who destroys a habitat within a protected site or otherwise deteriorates it by compromising its state of conservation, shall be punished by detention up to eighteen months and with a fine of not less than 3,000 Euro'.

This contravention is aimed at protecting the conservation of ideal environmental conditions for plant or animal life, identified in Article 1, paragraph e, of Legislative Decree No. 121 of 2011, which establishes that 'for purposes of the application of Article 733*bis* of the Criminal Code, "habitat within a protected site" means any habitat of species for which an area is classified as a ZPS by Article 4, paragraph 1 or 2, of Directive No. 79/409/EEC of 2 April 1979, or any natural habitat or habitat of species for which a site is designated as a ZPS pursuant to Article 4, paragraph 4, of Directive No. 92/43/EEC of 21 May 1992'.

The drafting technique used by the legislator does not seem entirely adequate, because it is based on reference to various provisions, some of which, in turn, make further references to other provisions. The first part of the definition requires that the conduct regard a habitat of species, consisting of an environment defined by specific abiotic and biotic factors in which the species lives during one of the phases of its biological cycle, and that such environment be in a place that the State has classified as a ZPS. The second part adds natural habitats to habitat of species, consisting of land or water areas that are distinguished due to their geographic, abiotic and biotic characteristics, and which are entirely natural or semi-natural and which are located in a place designated as a ZSC.

Consequently, the concept of 'natural protected areas' is broader than that including the categories of national parks, State nature reserves, interregional natural parks, regional natural parks and regional nature reserves, because it also includes wetlands, ZPS, ZSC and other protected natural areas (Criminal Court of Cassation, section III, judgment No. 14488 of 28 September 2016).

Chapter 4. Water Resource Management and Soil Conservation

by *Marcello Cecchetti and Antonio Borzì*[4]

§1. Principal Sources of National Law

486. The expression 'water resource management' refers to the 'quantitative protection of water', which aims at ensuring the proper utilization of all water resources in such a way as to guarantee different uses made by society as a whole in accordance with a rational scale of priorities. Rational water resource management also includes issues relating to the protection of soil from water, that is, protection from the destructive effects of water: river control and the battle against flooding; protection against erosion; agricultural and forestry water systems; control, defence and cleanup of land vulnerable to rockslides; and control of soil subsidence (*see* the Communication of the European Commission to the European Council and European Parliament 'Towards Sustainable Water Management in the European Union', of 22 July 2007, as well as the Communications of 14 November 2012 'Report on the Review of the European Water Scarcity and Droughts Policy' and 'A Blueprint to Safeguard Europe's Water Resources').

Unlike the water pollution control regime, the water resource management system was only introduced at the end of the 1980s, with significant delay with respect to the effective needs of protection. A timid reference on water pollution was contained in Article 2, paragraph 1, clause *d* of Law No. 319/1976.

487. The first attempt in Italy to impose an organic water policy was Law No. 183 of 18 May 1989, 'Law on the Administrative and Functional Reorganization of Soil Conservation', which made soil conservation the legal sector implementing the substantive and organizational regime on water resources. Some orientation and coordination acts were subsequently issued, aimed at the regions, as implementation of this Law: DPCM of 23 March 1990, DPR of 7 January 1992 and DPR of 18 July 1995.

488. The reform plan inaugurated by Law No. 183/1989 was completed by Law No. 36 of 5 January 1994, 'Provisions on Water Resources', which contains, in addition to some general principles on water use, fundamental norms for the efficient management of water resources. DPCM of 4 March 1996 is the most important act implementing this law.

In addition to the above two laws, reference must be made to some provisions of RD No. 1775 of 11 November 1993 'Uniform Text on Water and Electrical Systems' as regards individual users.

4. This chapter reflects the joint efforts of its two authors: Marcello Cecchetti wrote ss 1, 4, 6, 8 and 10, while Antonio Borzì wrote ss 2, 3, 5, 7 and 9.

The legislation on hydro-geologic risk control inaugurated by Law Decree No. 180 of 11 June 1998 should also be noted, promulgated after the tragic flood in Sarno and Quindici in the province of Campania, followed by Laws No. 226/1999 and No. 365/00.

489. By means of Legislative Decree No. 152 of 11 May 1999, the Italian legislator overcame the net separation between the quantitative and qualitative aspects of water protection. It also attempted, by means of modifications and integrations to Law No. 183/1989, Law No. 36/1994 and the Uniform Text of 1933, to coordinate the legal system, which must regulate different aspects of water protection, that must, nevertheless, remain 'closely interrelated' (*see*, Constitutional Court, judgment No. 232 of 2009).

490. Water protection is currently regulated by, in addition to the Uniform Text of 1933, Part III of Legislative Decree No. 152 of 3 April 2006, entitled the 'Environmental Code', promulgated with the intent of reorganizing, coordinating and integrating pre-existing environmental law. By means of this Legislative Decree, Italy implemented European Parliament and Council Directive No. 2000/60/EC of 23 October 2000, 'establishing a framework for Community action on water'.

In particular, section I of Part III of Legislative Decree No. 152 of 2006 (Articles 53–72) regards soil conservation and the battle against desertification, reintroducing many of the provisions set forth in Law No. 183/1989. Articles 141 through Article 176 of section III contain the water resource management regime and reconfirm most of Law No. 36/1994.

Articles 95–99 of the decree contain additional provisions on quantitative water resource protection and water savings.

491. The most significant change with respect to the integrated water service regime, is the transfer to an independent administrative authority of 'water service regulation and control functions' (Article 21, paragraphs 13 and 19, of Law Decree 201 of 2011).

The provisions on hydrogeological risk should be noted that are contained in the 2010 Budget Law (Law No. 191 of 23 December 2009) and Law Decree No. 195 of 31 December 2009, converted into Law No. 26 of 26 February 2010, which allocate funds and establish organizational rules for work to be done based on extraordinary plans.

By means of Legislative Decree No. 49 of 23 February 2010, Italy implemented Directive 2007/60/EC of 23 October 2007 of the European Parliament and Council on the assessment and management of flood risks (the decree was modified several times, among which the modification made by Law No. 97 of 6 August 2013 to avoid an infringement procedure).

Provisions on hydrogeological risk mitigation are set forth in Article 10 of Law Decree No. 91 of 24 June 2014, converted with modifications in Law No. 116 of 11 August 2014, and Article 7 of Law Decree No. 133 of 12 September 2014, converted with modifications into Law No. 164 of 11 November 2014.

A fund to plan the actions required to contrast hyrdrogeological instability was created at MATTM by Law No. 221 of 28 December 2015 to allow the speedy preparation of the national plan against hydrogeological instability (Article 55; *see also* DPCM 14 July 2016 on the rules that determine the operation of the fund).

More recently, with respect to the planning and realization of the actions required to mitigate damages related to drought and to promote the strengthening and adjustment of water infrastructures, a national action plan in the water sector was prepared, articulated in two sections: 'aqueducts' and a section on 'water basins' (Article 1, paragraphs 516 et seq., Law No. 205 of 27 December 2017, the 2018 Budget Law).

§2. Objective Scope of Application

492. Article 54, paragraph 1, clause *u* of Legislative Decree No. 152 of 2006 introduced the first legislative definition of 'soil conservation':

> a combination of actions and activities that relate to the protection and preservation of land, rivers, canals and manifolds, lakes, lagoons, coastlines, and underground waters, as well as the land connected to them, that serve to reduce water risk, stabilize geological risks, optimize water use and water resource management, and enhance related environmental and landscape characteristics.

It is undoubtedly a broad definition, similar to the related definition of 'soil' ('land, soil, subsoil, residential areas and infrastructures').

In fact, in order to understand the concept of soil conservation, it is necessary to recognize the most important modifications that effect the relative programming, planning and implementing activities (currently Articles 56 and 65). With respect to the provisions of Law No. 183 of 1989 (Articles 3 and 17), the provisions that are the most directly related to the qualitative protection of water bodies and the organization and management of integrated water services are missing; they are related but distinct regimes.

Soil conservation regards all activity performed on land and in surface and underground bodies of water, whose purpose is to reduce hydrogeological risks, prevent upheavals and stabilize their effects on a long-term basis (different from emergency interventions for civil protection). Further, soil conservation enhances water resource management, but excludes anything more directly related to integrated water services. Landscape enhancement is not an autonomous objective of soil conservation, but is a 'filtered' objective, to be pursued in the context of interventions on land intended to mitigate hydrogeological risks and instability.

Such interventions must, above all, be determined by a series of planning and programming instruments aimed at the rational utilization of water resources, which constantly maintain an integrated vision of the diverse aspects of soil conservation and water resource management.

493. The most important novelty introduced by Law No. 183/1989 was without doubt the identification of the 'water basin' as a geographical reference area. The water basin is the basis of both the organizational model, which is centred on the

Basin Authorities, and the planning regime for the basin plans, true pillars of the regulation of soil and water. The water basin represents the geographical and institutional dimension that is best suited to create an organic and uniform management of the water environment, precisely because it is in such context that the natural water cycle exists in its entirety.

In accordance with Law No. 183/1989, the entire national territory is divided into water basins, classified as basins of nation, interregional and regional importance (the latter are determined by the regions).

494. Legislative Decree No. 152 of 2006 significantly modified the soil conservation regime with respect to pre-existing legislation, giving greater importance to the 'geographic district' as the 'principal unit for water basin management', consisting of one or more water basins (Article 54, paragraph 1, clause *t*).

Thus, while Law No. 183 of 1989 had many limits in the applicative phase, it defined the administrative level of intervention, depending on the natural dimensions of the water basin. The 2006 legislator appears to have been more concerned with finding an efficient organizational system for water resources than with the status of those resources.

The entire national territory has been subdivided into eight water districts, with the creation of a Basin Authority for each district (Articles 64 and 65, as modified by Law No. 221 of 2015).

495. The Constitutional Court, by means of judgment No. 232 of 2009, found the legislative choice of organizing soil conservation 'by districts' to be constitutional, among others in consideration of the fact that Community law on water has specified 'the district (broader than a water basin) as the territorial unit within which activities intended to protect aquatic ecosystems and land directly dependent on them should be concentrated'.

The regime on the assessment and management of flood risks, set forth in Legislative Decree No. 49 of 2010, must be inserted in this framework. Its objective is to reduce the adverse consequences of floods on human health, the territory, property, the environment, cultural heritage and economic and social activities (Article 1). The decree articulates public intervention assessing and managing flood risks in three separate means of protection: a preliminary flood risks assessment, mapping flood hazards and risks, and a flood risk management plan, which must be prepared considering the information and data developed during the planning phase of a basin that has already been realized.

496. Law No. 36/1994 implemented the second phase of the overall reform of water resource management. Its provisions were incorporated, with some modifications, in section III of Part III of Legislative Decree No. 152 of 2006.

Article 144, paragraph 1, establishes that 'all surface and underground water, even if not extracted from the subsoil, is State property'. With respect to Law No. 36 of 1994, which affirmed the principle of the public nature of water ('all water ... is public'), the 2006 Decree affirms that it belongs to the State, whereas Law No. 166 of 20 November 2009 (Article 15, paragraph 1*ter*) explicitly refers to the 'exclusive public ownership of water resources'. Regardless, the principle remains that water 'is a resource entitled to protection and utilization in accordance with criteria of solidarity'. All water resources must, therefore, be used considering the rights of future generations (Article 144, paragraph 2), which explains why such use must avoid waste and enhance the renewal of resources, in order not to damage water resources, the liveability of the environment, agriculture, aquatic fauna and flora, geomorphologic processes and water equilibrium (Article 144, paragraph 3).

497. To achieve these objectives, Legislative Decree No. 152 of 2006 regulates two fundamental aspects of resource management: different kinds of water utilization and the reorganization of water services.

Current legislation does not restate the explicit affirmation of Law No. 36 of 1994 that 'the use of water for human consumption is a priority with respect to other uses of a water body' (Article 2). The priority of use of water resources for human consumption derives from the system of outstanding laws, in particular, Article 144, paragraph 4, and, thus, different uses are only allowed 'to the extent that there are sufficient water resources, on the condition that they do not prejudice the quality of such resources', as well as by the norm that requires, the priority of agricultural use must be ensured during periods of drought or when water resources are scarce, but only after the indispensable resources required for human consumption have been guaranteed (Article 167, paragraph 1). Articles 98, 99 and 146 contain general norms to encourage water savings and the reuse of wastewater, while Articles 166–168 contain greater details on the uses of water for irrigation and land reclamation, for agricultural and industrial purposes, and for the production of electrical energy.

Article 167 (paragraphs 3–5) specifies the only two cases in which the use of water is unrestricted: rainwater collected in containers and cisterns for agricultural land or for individual buildings and the use of underground water for domestic use, such as 'watering flower and vegetable gardens used directly by the owner and the owner's family, and as drinking water for animals'.

498. With regard to the second issue, the reorganization of water services, Legislative Decree No. 152 of 2006 confirms pre-existing legislation, in particular, the 1994 Law, which introduced integrated water services (currently defined in Article 141, paragraph 2 of Legislative Decree No. 152 of 2006). It is a sole regulatory and management model for aqueduct services (the reception, conduction and distribution of drinking water), sewage systems and water treatment in ATO, in order to overcome the fragmentation of pre-existing management services entrusted to parties at a municipal level.

499. Law Decree No. 133 of 2014 introduced the principle of the unity of management: management of the service not only must be coordinated, i.e., integrated in the various phases of adduction, water distribution, sewerage and purification, but must be performed, in general, by a single subject for each ATO. At the local level, management of the service rests with the ATO Authority, in which the local entities that are within the same ATO must participate (Article 147). At the national level, an independent administrative Authority performs water service regulation and control functions.

500. The legal framework is completed by:

- some provisions of Uniform Text No. 1775/1933, which still contains the norms on the administrative permit regime to which all forms of use of public waters are subject;
- the regime of hydrogeological restrictions and forestry constraints (RD Law No. 3267 of 30 December 1923, entitled 'Reorganization and reform of legislation on woodlands and mountain terrain', and its implementing regulation, RD No. 1126 of 1926, as well as subsequent regional laws).

§3. Planning and Programming Instruments

I. The Basin Plan

501. The basin plan is the 'fundamental planning instrument for soil conservation, the battle against desertification and water protection' (Constitutional Court, judgment No. 232 of 2009), and it is indispensable to achieve those objectives:

(i) Principal characteristics and content. The basin plan is explicitly qualified as a 'territorial plan in the sector'. Such qualification, inherited from Law No. 183/1989, establishes that the restrictions imposed by the basin plan are immediately binding on public administrations and public entities (State and regions), which must observe them and act accordingly (Constitutional Court, judgment No. 85/1990). Even though it is defined as a sector plan, the basin plan is considered to be a general and all-inclusive instrument, both due to the evident breadth of the sector involved and to its contents. Article 65, paragraph 1 of Legislative Decree No. 152 of 2006 defines it as a 'cognitive, normative and technical-operative instrument by means of which the actions and guidelines intended to promote soil conservation and soil enhancement and the direct utilization of water are planned and programmed on the basis of the physical and environmental characteristics of the territory involved'.

The contents of the plan can, therefore, be distinguished in three general components, all of which are necessary and strictly interrelated: a cognitive component, which relates to the overall recognition of factual situations (Article 65, paragraph 3, clauses *a*, *b*, and *p*); a rule-making component, which relates to the preparation of restrictions, directives and prohibitions, including of a programmatic nature (Article 65, paragraph 3, clauses *f*, *e*, *m* and *n*); and a technical-operative component, which relates to definition of the measures and works in different sub-sectors, with specific reference to the identification of the work to be performed according to a specific order of priorities and the relative financial resources (Article 65, paragraph 3, clauses *f*, *g*, *o*, *s* and *t*). In particular, Legislative Decree No. 152 of 2006 requires the basin plan to define the principal orientations of water use policy; that a complete survey of current water derivations be compiled, specifying their relative purposes such as energy production, drinking water, irrigation or other use, as well the relative capacity; that a survey be compiled of diverse uses for fishing, navigation and other purposes; and that a plan of future use be prepared both in view of derivations and for other purposes, distinguishing among types of use and the quantities of water involved (Article 65, paragraph 3, clauses *c*, *e*, *p*, *q* and *r*).

The basin plan also considers the directives to which soil conservation, hydrogeological layout and hydraulic systems must conform; it specifies the restrictions, measures and works aimed at soil and environmental conservation (necessary to prevent or reduce the effects of rockslides, landslides, floods, draughts, coastal erosion, ground subsidence and desertification). It also contains mechanisms offering benefits to property owners in agricultural areas or woodlands, so that any work that they perform is suitable for preventing hydrogeological instability (Article 65, paragraph 3, clauses *d*, *f*, *g*, *h*, *o* and *i*).

The contents of the basin plan are particularly complex and diversified because they embrace, from a cognitive, normative and operative perspective, both the regime on water utilization and soil conservation actions to protect against the risk of hydrogeological instability, subsidence and desertification, in order to choose among different types of governance and management. It is, therefore, necessary to perform a preliminary assessment of the cost-benefit relationship, environmental impact and financial resources for the principal interventions (Article 65, paragraph 3, clause *l*).

Upon implementation of Directive 2000/60/EC, the contents of the basin plan were integrated with those set forth in Annex IV to Part III of Legislative Decree No. 152 of 2006, which are the *proprium* of the management plans (*see infra*, above as well as the chapter on water pollution).

(ii) Approval procedure. The basin plan is prepared and adopted by the district Basin Authorities (*see* section 9 *infra* for the internal organization of the Authority). Pursuant to Article 66 of Legislative Decree No. 152 of 2006, the plan is adopted by the institutional Conference of the Basin Authorities by a majority vote (with the requirement that sufficient reasons have to be provided for dissenting opinions). The conference intervenes well before the formal adoption of the plan, defining the criteria and methods for the preparation of the plan, and specifying the terms and procedures required to adopt it (Article 63, paragraph 6). The preparation of the plan requires the joint efforts of the State and regional administrations that make up the Basin Authorities. If one of the regions involved does not adopt the acts that are required to prepare the plan (above all, the parts of the plan that are of exclusive interest to individual regions), the President of the Council of Ministers, upon the request of the Ministry of the Environment, can act as a substitute power and can appoint a Commissioner *ad acta* (Article 66, paragraph 4).

Once adopted, the basin plan, together with the related environmental report, is subject to a SEA (Part II of Legislative Decree No. 152 of 2006).

Upon the conclusion of the SEA procedure, depending on the judgment of environmental compatibility expressed by the competent authority, the plan is approved by a decree of the President of the Council of Ministers, upon a proposal of the Ministry of the Environment and after consulting the State-Regional Conference. It is published in the Official Bulletin of the Italian Republic and in the Official Bulletins of the territorially competent regions.

Basin Authorities promote the active participation of all of the subjects interested in the preparation, review and updating of the plan: for each hydrographic district, a temporary overall assessment of the principal water management problems, a calendar and programme of activities for the presentation of the plan, and the draft plan are made available to the public. A minimum period of six months is allowed for written comments to be filed by the public (*see* Article 66, paragraph 7 with regard to the terms of publication).

It is important to note that the basin plan can also be prepared and approved for sub-basins, or excerpts of the plan related to functional sectors, which must in any event be part of sequential and interrelated phases with respect to the contents described above, and the systematic consideration of the territory must be guaranteed (Article 66, paragraph 8). The district hydrogeological risk exposure plan ('*Piano di Assetto Idrogeologico*' or Hydrogeological Plan – PAI, Article 67 of Legislative Decree No. 152 of 2006) and the district management plan (Article 117, Legislative Decree No. 152 of 2006) are among the most important planning instruments.

(iii) Effects of the Basin Plan. The scope of its contents indicates why the basin plan tends to be placed in a superimposed position with respect to other urban or sector planning instruments, almost as a sort of 'super plan', and all actions within the territory must conform to it. Legislative Decree No. 152 of 2006 expressly requires that urban planning instruments, as well as numerous other specific plans and programmes, be adjusted to the basin plan (Article 65, paragraphs 4 and 6). The regions must issue the implementing provisions of the plan in the urban planning sector within ninety days from publication of the basin plan in the Official Bulletin. Once said term has expired, the entities that are territorially subject to the plan must comply with its restrictions in the urban planning sector.

The provisions of the basin plan also apply to private parties as well as public administrations and entities, if the requirements are declared to be effective by such basin plan.

The importance attributed to the planning instrument is confirmed by the laws on water resource management, which refer to the obligation of the Basin Authorities to adopt 'measures to ensure the planning of water economy based on the intended uses of the resources', in order to 'ensure equilibrium between resources and needs' (Article 145, paragraph 2, Legislative Decree No. 152 of 2006). From this standpoint, a fundamental role is attributed to the 'water balance', the instrument prepared by the Basin Authorities when they prepare the basin plan that is 'intended to ensure equilibrium between the available resources that can be found or activated in the area of reference and the needs of different uses' (Article 145, paragraph 1).

502. The water protection plan must provide measures to ensure the equilibrium of the water balance, as defined by the Basin Authorities (Article 95, paragraph 2, Legislative Decree No. 152 of 2006).

II. Other Planning and Programming Instruments

503.

(i) The Management Plan, the Flood Risk Management Plan and the Water Protection Plan: Additional planning and programming instruments flank the basin plan, such as the management plan (Article 117 of Legislative Decree No. 152/2006), the flood risk management plan (Legislative Decree No. 49/2010) and the water protection plan (Article 121 of Legislative Decree No. 152 of 2006).

If there is a significant man-made impact from diffuse sources, the management plans provide measures that prohibit discharges of polluting substances into water, or which establish prior permit or registration requirements based on general and binding rules.

The management plan contains a water basin management programme, in order to combine flood risk prevention with the protection of river ecosystems.

The water basin management plan must be reviewed and updated every six years (Article 117, paragraphs 2*bis*, 2*ter*, 2*quater*).

The flood risk management plan regards all aspects of managing flood risks, specifically prevention, protection and preparation, including flood forecasts and systems to warn the population. The plan can also include the promotion of sustainable land use practices, improvement of water retention, as well as the controlled flooding of certain areas in the case of a flood (Article 7, Legislative Decree No. 49/2010). The flood management plan is prepared by the Basin Authority (and by the regions with respect to the warning system) and is implemented through the action programmes set forth in Articles 69 et seq. of Legislative Decree No. 152 of 2006.

The management plans define the flood risk management objectives for the areas at risk, and specifically indicate the reduction of the potential adverse effects on human health, the territory, property, the environment, cultural heritage and economic and social activities through the priority implementation of non-structural actions and to reduce harmfulness. The flood risk management plan must also be reviewed every six years.

The water protection plan is defined as a specific sector plan and regards an individual water basin, different from the management plan. It must conform to the management plan (and the basin plan) as well as to the orientations and objectives determined by the Basin Authorities at a district level (*see* Constitutional Court, judgment No. 254 del 2009 as well as the chapter on water pollution control).

(ii) The Three-Year Management Programmes and the National Management Programme: three-year management programmes must be prepared to implement the basin plans, which must consider the orientation and purposes of the plans. The management programmes are prevalently economic in nature, referring to the allocation of the financial resources required to realize the works and activities contained in the basin plans.

The three-year programmes are adopted by the Permanent Institutional Conference of the Basin Authorities, and must designate at least 15% of their allocations to: (a) ordinary maintenance for works, installations and resources; (b) carrying out water policing services, internal navigation, as well as full and prompt interventions; and (c) preparing and updating the basin plan and drafting projects, feasibility studies and EIAs of the works.

The activities provided by the Three-year programme are normally implemented by conventional instruments, such as programme agreements signed by all of the competent entities (State, regional and local).

The activities are financed entirely by the State but the regions, provinces, municipalities, mountain communities and other public administrations can also assist with their realization by means of their own financial allocations (Article 72, paragraph 1, and Article 69, paragraphs 3 and 4).

In order to coordinate the works provided by the different Three-year Programmes for individual districts and to divide the State allocations required to realize them, the Committee of Ministers drafts a National Works Programme, after consulting with the State-Regional Conference. It is subsequently approved by a decree of the President of the Council of Ministers, after consulting with the Unified Conference (Constitutional Court, judgment No. 232 of 2009. The Unified Conference is an organ that includes representatives of the State, regions and local autonomies, *see* Legislative Decree No. 281 of 18 August 1997).

(iii) PAI, Extraordinary Plans for High Risk Situations, and Programmes of Urgent Measures: Programming and implementing interventions in areas of highest hydrogeological risk are difficult to reconcile with the time required to prepare and approve the water basin plan.

For this reason, while waiting for the basin plans to be approved, the Basin Authorities adopt plans to create hydrogeological districts (PAI), which identify areas at hydrogeological risk, delineate areas subject to protective measures and determine such measures (Article 67, paragraph 1). The protective measures have the same nature and function as the activities provided for in general by the basin plan, but they are precautionary measures because they are intended to protect soil and water conditions until the basin plan has been approved (Article 65, paragraph 7 and Constitutional Court, judgment No. 232 of 2009).

The PAI also specifies the infrastructures and buildings that create hydrogeological risk. On that basis, the regions:

- define the incentives that owners can obtain in order to adjust infrastructures and relocate productive activities and private residences outside of the area at risk;
- prepare, after consulting the local entities involved, a plan to adjust the infrastructures and establish a congruous deadline to provide and grant financial incentives to relocate productive activities and private residences in conformity with zoning laws or amnesties.

If the subjects involved do not use such incentives, they forfeit any benefits to which they might otherwise be entitled for damages deriving to facilities they own consequent to natural disasters (Article 67, paragraph 6).

PAI projects are adopted following the same procedure used to approve as the basin plans, but they are not subject to a SEA. Due to urgency they must be adopted, on the basis of available documentation and opinions, within and no later than six months from the date the relative draft plan is approved (Article 68, paragraphs 1 and 2).

In order to eliminate situations of high hydrogeological risk, the Basin Authorities can also approve extraordinary basin plans (this instrument was introduced in Italian legislation after a natural disaster in Sarno, Campania, Law Decree No. 180 of 1998, converted into Law No. 267/1998 and modified on various occasions). Such plans, which can also be prepared on the basis of proposals from regions and local entities, must include as a priority hydrogeological risk areas for which a state of emergency has been declared in accordance with Article 5 of Law No. 225 of 1992 ('Creation of a National Civil Protection Service'); recently substituted by Legislative Decree No. 1 of 2 January 2018, the 'Civil Protection Code'; special protective measures are adopted for such areas. If the Basin Authorities fail to act, the President of the Council of Ministers, upon a proposal of the Committee of Ministers for soil conservation interventions, can adopt the relative acts to identify, delineate and protect such areas (Article 67, paragraph 2).

Urgent measures can be adopted in order to implement extraordinary plans; if necessary, they can be adopted by means of civil protection ordinances (Article 67, paragraph 3).

The 2010 Budget Law allocated EUR 1 billion for extraordinary plans intended to remove the highest hydrogeological risk situations determined by the responsible Directorate-General of the Ministry of the Environment, after consulting the Basin Authorities and the Department for Civil Protection of the Presidency of the Council of Ministers (Article 2, paragraph 240, Law No. 191 of 2009). The implementation of these extraordinary plans was initially referred to extraordinary commissioners (Article 17 of Law Decree No. 195 of 2009 converted into Law No. 26 of 2010).

Law Decree No. 91 of 2014, converted into Law No. 116 of 2014, provided that the functions of the commissioners be taken over by the Presidents of the regions.

The president oversees all activities for which the public administrations are responsible, that are needed to carry out the measures provided by the extraordinary plans, in compliance with international obligations and those deriving from membership in the EU.

The authorization issued by the president substitutes all endorsements, opinions, permits, clearances or any other licence needed to implement the action, results in a declaration of public utility and is considered, if necessary, a variant of the urban planning and territorial instruments.

In exercising their powers, the Presidents of the regions can request the assistance, based on specific conventions regulating the relative relationships, of any public or private party, in compliance with the public procedures provided by the Code on Public Contracts (Law Decree No. 133 of 2014, Article 7, paragraph 4).

§4. Authorization Procedures

504. As is the case for water pollution control and the rational management of water resources, the public administration, pursuant to its power to issue permits, can allow water to be drawn and used, upon preventive verification. The most important of such instruments is without doubt the power to grant a right of derivation and use of public waters, regulated by Uniform Text No. 1775/1933, which has remained the principal source of regulation of uses for public water for more than fifty years.

The provisions of the Uniform Text were progressively adjusted (first by Legislative Decree No. 275/93, then Legislative Decree No. 152/1999 and, more recently, by Legislative Decree No. 152 of 2006) in order to utilize the permit regime to achieve the objective of the organic and rational management of all water resources. The instrument of the granting permit, in fact, on the basis of its recognition of the public nature of all water introduced by Article 1 of Law No. 36/1994, confirmed by Legislative Decree No. 152 of 2006, can by now be considered as having been extended to all cases involving the utilization of water, with the exception of those cases already mentioned in section 2, in which the collection, removal and use of water resources is 'unrestricted' and, thus, not subject to limitations (Article 167, paragraphs 3– and 5 of Legislative Decree No. 152 of 2006, as well as Article 17 of Uniform Text No. 1775 of 1933).

505. The uses of public water are distinguished as major and minor derivations, on the basis of fundamental quantitative criteria. This distinction is important due to the division of competence relative to the granting of permits for derivations. By means of the reform of the organization of administrative functions contained in Legislative Decree No. 112 of 1998, and after the promulgation of Legislative Decree No. 79 of 16 March 1999, implementing Directive 96/92/EC ('Common Rules for the Internal Energy Market'), the regions are responsible for major derivations, whereas normally the provinces are responsible for minor derivations (*see* Constitutional Court, judgments No. 1 of 2008 and No. 28 of 2014).

506. On the basis of what is provided, above all, by Articles 7–21 of the 1933 Uniform Text, whoever intends to collect and utilize water must file a request for a permit with the competent authority, which must request the opinion of the territorially responsible Basin Authority 'regarding the compatibility of use with the provisions of the water protection plan, in order to control water equilibrium or hydrological balance, even while waiting for such plan to be approved' (Article 7). The opinion of the Basin Authority is binding on the granting authority. Article 9 establishes that in the case of more than one concurrent request, the applicant must be preferred who, alone or together with other uses already granted or requested, presents the most rational use of water resources in relation to the following criteria:

(a) the present level of satisfaction of the applicants' essential needs, also in view of the public aqueduct services or irrigation, avoiding all waste and preferentially qualified resources destined for human consumption;

(b) the effective possibility of a better use of the resources in relation to utilization;
(c) the quantitative and qualitative characteristics of the body of water;
(d) the quantity and quality of the water that is returned with respect to the water that is drawn.

It also established that preference should be given to the request that guarantees, with respect to the same kind of use, the greatest restitution of water in relation to the quality standards of the relative bodies of water, and well as which guarantees that the lower levels of withdrawal required are integrated by the water volumes deriving from recovery and recycling activities.

507. The permit, which is accompanied by specifications containing all of the restrictions that the operator undertakes to respect (Article 40), in particular, an indication of the quantity and qualitative characteristics of the water that is restituted, is issued only if the following conditions are satisfied (Article 12*bis*, paragraph 3):

– maintenance or compliance with the quality standards defined for the interested watercourse is not prejudiced;
– the minimum vital flow is guaranteed (*see also* Article 95, paragraph 4 of Legislative Decree No. 152 of 2006);
– there is no possibility to recycle treated wastewater or rainwater, or recycling would be economically unsustainable.

In any case, the quantity of water granted must be proportional to the possibility of saving, reusing and recycling the resource.

508. Specific limitations of the authorization regime are provided in relation to the various types of water use:

– the use of resources reserved for human consumption can only be allowed for a different purpose in those cases in which such resources are widely available or in cases of an ascertained qualitative and quantitative lack of alternative sources of supply (Article 12*bis*, paragraph 3);
– permits for hydroelectric use are forbidden when the installations are connected to aqueducts (Article 12*bis*, paragraph 4);
– permits for major derivations for industrial use can be conditioned on the implementation of water savings by the recycling or reuse of water, in quantitative terms and within the time period established when the permit is granted, considering the best available technology for the specific case (Article 21, paragraph 2);
– permits for irrigation must consider the types of cultivation on the basis of the availability of the water resource, as well as the minimum quantity needed for the cultivation itself, requiring, if necessary, a specific manner of irrigation. Such permits can only be issued or renewed when it is impossible to satisfy the request for water through use of one of the cleanup and irrigation consortiums already operating in the territory (Article 21, paragraph 4).

All of the permits are issued for a limited period of time and are generally renewable, upon verification that the purposes of the derivation still exist and that there are no prevalent public interest needs (Articles 28 and 30). A maximum duration of thirty years is established for all permits, with the exception of those regarding large hydroelectric derivations; such period can be extended to forty years for permits for irrigation use and is instead limited to fifteen years for permits allowing major derivations for industrial use (Article 21, paragraphs 1 and 2).

509. Legislative Decree No. 152 of 2006, in addition to directly amending the provisions of the 1933 Uniform Text as noted above, also contains additional rules on the management of the permit regime. In particular, Article 95, paragraphs 4 and 5, establishes that the granting authority must regulate derivations of water already in course, imposing restrictions on the party receiving the permit intended to guarantee the minimum vital flow of water; it must also revise the current utilization of such water body, imposing restrictions or time and quantitative limitations.

In addition to the system of permits for derivations, the 1933 Uniform Text provides for the issuance of a particular authorization (at present the competence of the regions, due to the delegation of power contained in Article 90, paragraph 2, clause *d* of DPR No. 616/1977) for research activities regarding underground water and the excavation of wells (Articles 92–106). The request for authorization must include the outline plan of extraction and utilization that the applicant proposes to perform. The authorization cannot be issued for a period of time that exceeds one year and can be renewed, including more than once, for periods that do not exceed six months. If the underground water that has been discovered has the necessary characteristics so that it is subject to the permit regime for derivations, the party discovering such source has a preferential title to obtain the authorization for the use indicated in the plan annexed to the request (Article 103).

510. The system is completed by the final norm introduced by Article 10, paragraph 1, of Legislative Decree No. 275/1993. By means of this norm, the Italian legislator has established that the owners, possessors or uses of all existing wells, independent from the type of use and even if unutilized, must notify their existence to the territorially competent region and province within twelve months, in order to allow the public administration to comply with Article 103 of the Uniform Text of 1933.

§5. Specific Management and Protection Instruments

511. The principal instrument specifically intended for rational water resource management is without doubt the integrated water service regime, which unifies 'all public services for the reception, conduction and distribution of drinking water, sewage and water treatment' (Article 141, paragraph 1).

The integrated water service attempts to achieve the objective of bypassing inefficiencies due to fragmentation among the diverse reception, conduction and distribution services, as well as sewage and water treatment systems, by means of three fundamental mechanisms:

(1) creation of a sole water system in an ATO larger than the municipal dimension;
(2) identification of a sole subject entrusted with managing the service;
(3) preparation of a sole tariff system.

Water services are organized based on the ATO defined by the regions or, as a substitute, by the State.

If the ATO coincides with the entire territorial region, if necessary to achieve greater management efficiency and a better quality of service for users, the integrated water service can be entrusted to ATO that correspond at least to the territorial areas of the provinces or metropolitan cities.

From a subjective standpoint, there is a distinction between the organization and actual management of the service (Article 148).

512. Organizational responsibility is entrusted to the ATO Authority, a legal entity to which local entities included in the territorial areas must belong.

The ATO Authority is responsible for preparing (and updating) the ATO Plan, which must provide for the following (Article 149):

(a) the reorganization of the infrastructure: the state of the infrastructures to be entrusted to the integrated water service manager, indicating their operating status;
(b) the works programme: an indication of extraordinary maintenance work and new works to be realized, including the adjustment of existing infrastructures required to achieve at least minimum services levels, as well as satisfaction of the overall demand of users. The action plan, proportionate to overall management, is specific with respect to the objectives to be achieved, indicates the infrastructures planned for such purpose and the time required to realize them;
(c) the management and organizational model;
(d) the financial business plan: the plan forecasts operating and investment costs. It is integrated by the annual budget of projected earnings from tariffs, extended to the entire period in which the service is entrusted. The plan must guarantee financial and economic balance, and must comply with principles of effectiveness, efficiency and cost management, including with respect to programmed investments.

The ATO Authority decides the basic tariff and sends it to the National Regulatory Authority for approval.

The Basin Authority, in compliance with the water basin plan set forth in Article 149 and the principle of coordinated management for each ATO, deliberates the type of management from among those provided by the European legal system, and as a result entrusts the service in compliance with national legislation on the organization of economically significant local network public services. A direct award can be made to purely public companies having the prerequisites provided by the European legal system for in house management, with the participation of the local entities within the ATO.

The relationship between the manager and the ATO Authority is regulated by a special service agreement (and annexed specifications), based on a framework agreement prepares by the National Regulatory Authority. Among the most important obligations assumed by the manager are: achievement of economic-financial balance; adoption of a service charter; realization of the Works Programme provided by the ATO Plan; and suitable insurance and financial guarantees.

The integrated water service regime is completed by the provision of a tariff system that follows the full cost recovery principle, including environmental costs, based on the principle 'the polluter pays'.

513. Other specific instruments for the rational management of water resources can be found in these provisions, such as Articles 99 and 146 of Legislative Decree No. 152 of 2006, which aim at developing water savings and recycling. Among the activities intended to reduce consumption and eliminating waste, for example, Article 146, paragraph 1 expressly requires:

- the creation of dual networks for water conduction in new areas of significant dimensions, in order to allow the use of lower quality water for compatible activities;
- the installation of meters for water consumption in every individual residential unit, as well as differentiated metres for manufacturing activities and service activities that are performed in an urban context;
- the creation of differentiated collection systems for rainwater and wastewater in new areas.

These provisions are reinforced by the subsequent paragraph, which requires urban planning instruments to provide for the creation of dual networks (if compatible with the existing territorial layout and available financial resources) and makes the issuance of building permits conditional on the requirement that the projects provide for the installation of meters for each individual residential unit and the connection to dual networks, if already available.

With respect to the reuse of water, Article 99, more generically, is limited to a reference to the issue of technical standards by the Ministry of the Environment, as well as the adoption by the regions of measures aimed at encouraging water recycling and the reuse of treated wastewater.

514. The integrated water service system and measures to save and reuse water resources do not exhaust the specific instruments of protection.

Hydrogeological restrictions and forestry constraints should also be noted. The first subject portions of the territory to controls which, due to the effect of specific forms of utilization (grazing, creating clearings and changes of cultivations) might be subject to stripping, the loss of stability or the undermining of the water regime, to the public harm. Differently, the forestry constraint regards woodlands 'which, due to their special location, defend lands or buildings from landslides, rockslides, movements of sand dunes and strong winds, and those deemed useful for local sanitary conditions' (RD No. 3267 of 1923, RDL No. 1126 of 1926 and subsequent regional laws). Similar to landscape restrictions, the establishment of a restriction does not result in an absolute prohibition against modifying an area, but authorization is required from the competent authority (usually the province).

§6. Control System

515. Regulation of water resource management is rather poor with respect to specific provisions regarding controls, and this determines the application, in general, of ordinary powers of supervision belonging to the competent authorities (in particular, those responsible for the issuance of derivation permits or authorizations).

516. Specific norms are instead contained in Articles 105 and 106 of the Uniform Text of 1933, which attributes to the administration's technical organs control powers over the reception and use of underground waters, as well as, in particular, responsibility for controlling that the relative works respond to the purpose for which they are intended and do not prejudice the water system. To these control powers is added the possibility of issuing 'all measures held appropriate for the protection of general interests and the region's water system', among which an order of suspension of activities performed and the closure of wells, as well as revocation of authorizations and permits by the administrative authority entrusted with their issuance.

Controls of the proper management of the integrated water service are more articulated.

Controls are also carried out at a local level, above all, by the ATO Authority with respect to the manager of the integrated water service.

The ATO Authority has the right of access and control of water infrastructures, including during the construction phase. The ATO Authority must intervene promptly, exercising all of the powers granted to it by law and by the service agreement, in order to guarantee compliance if the manager's breach of obligations imposed by law or by the service agreement compromises water resources or the environment, or results in a failure to achieve minimum service levels. Should the manager's breach not be cured, without prejudice to any criminal sanctions to which he may also be subject, in addition to the power of termination and revocation, the ATO Authority, after a warning, has substitute power with respect to the manager and can entrust the works to third parties, complying with the law on public procurements. The region has substitute power if the ATO Authority does not intervene, and the Ministry of the Environment has substitute powers should the region also fail to act (Article 152, Legislative Decree No. 152 of 2006).

517. The law also provides for forms of self-control by the manager. In particular, each water service manager (directly or by means of an agreement with other service managers) must have an adequate territorial monitoring service and a testing laboratory for quality controls of water, to ensure good water quality and the control of discharges in water bodies, without prejudice to the public control functions provided by laws on water pollution control (Article 165, paragraph 1, Legislative Decree No. 152 of 2006).

The National Regulatory Authority's supervisory and control powers should also be mentioned regarding compliance by the managers with its regulatory measures, in accordance with what is provided by Law No. 481 of 1995.

The manager must have a service charter for users, and must comply with the quality levels established by the National Regulatory Authority.

§7. Administrative and Criminal Sanctions

518. A system of administrative penalties is only provided in the Uniform Text of 1933 and in Legislative Decree No. 275 of 1993.

519. In general, Article 219 of the Uniform Text establishes that violations of the provisions of the decree, unless provided otherwise, are punished by an administrative fine ranging from EUR 10.33 to EUR 516.46 (converted from Lire into Euro in accordance with Article 51, Legislative Decree No. 213 of 1998). The subsequent Article 221 provides that, whenever an alteration of the 'state of things' is provoked by such violation, the public administration can order restoration to its original state, and can even provide on its own that such work be performed at the transgressor's expense.

520. The provisions of Article 17 (entirely substituted by Legislative Decree No. 152/2006) must be added to these general rules, which establishes that in the case of derivations or water use without a permit or authorization (except for the 'unrestricted' uses already noted in section 2 *supra*), the responsible administration must order the immediate cessation of the abusive use and the offender must pay an administrative fine ranging from EUR 3,000 to EUR 30,000. This amount is reduced (by a minimum of EUR 200 to a maximum of EUR 1,500) in cases of petty offences, but it can never be less than the amount of the unpaid charges.

A permit holder can have such authorization to create a derivation and utilize water revoked in a number of cases listed in Article 55, among which:

- non-use for a consecutive period of three years;
- abuse of the stated purposes of the utilization of water;
- non-compliance with the essential conditions of the derivation and utilization; or
- habitual negligence and lack of compliance with the law.

As noted in section 6 above, specific control powers provided by Articles 105 and 106 can be exercised for the overall protection of the proper regulation of water in the case of revocation of a permit or authorization issued to research underground water, and an order to close wells.

521. Further, Article 10 of Legislative Decree No. 275 of 1993 establishes that failure to report existing wells shall be punished by an administrative fine ranging from EUR 103.29 to EUR 619.75 as well as the closure of the well as the expense of the transgressor once the order applying the sanction becomes final.

522. Finally, Article 165 of Legislative Decree No. 152 of 2006 should be mentioned, by which the legislator intends to circumscribe the criminal liability of the water service manager with respect to the supply of drinking water. After having established that each water service manager must be equipped with an adequate territorial monitoring service and a testing laboratory to control water quality, paragraph 3 provides that the sanctions provided by Article 19 of Legislative Decree No. 31 of 2001 (which establishes the regime for the quality of water destined to human consumption) 'are applied to the party responsible for the management of an aqueduct only in the case in which, after communication of the outcome of the analysis, he has not adopted measures to adjust water quality or prevent the consumption or distribution of non-potable water in a timely manner'. Article 19 *supra* imposes an administrative fine on whoever supplies water for human consumption that does not meet the quality standards established by the Decree (for an overview of the sanctions provided by Legislative Decree No. 31 of 2001 *see* the chapter on water pollution control).

523. Prior to 2001, similar conduct was punished by a criminal sanction (Article 21 of DPR No. 236 of 1988), and the reference made by Law No. 36 of 1994 (Article 26), analogous to what is contained in Article 165, *supra*, was the only reference to criminal sanctions (which was later removed) in the entire regulation of rational water resource management.

Law No. 481 of 1995 attributes the National Regulatory Authority with the power to issue fines ranging from EUR 2500 to EUR 154,937,069.73 (and nevertheless within the maximum amount of 10% of the company's invoiced sales) in the case of the breach of its measures or failure to comply by the subjects performing the service with requests for information or requests related to controls, or if the information and documents acquired are untruthful.

§8. Economic Instruments

524. The principal economic instruments for rational water resource management consist of the tariff of the integrated water service, presently regulated by Articles 154–156 of Legislative Decree No. 152 of 2006, and by the charges for the use of public water, provided by Articles 35 et seq. of Uniform Text No. 1775/1933 and Article 154, paragraph 3, of Legislative Decree No. 152 of 2006.

One of the most important characteristics of an integrated water service is the provision of a sole tariff system in substitution of the previous system, which distinguished the tariff for drinking water services from charges for sewage and treatment services (Articles 16 and 17 of Law No. 319 of 1976).

525. Legislative Decree No. 152 of 2006 explicitly provides that the tariff 'is compensation for the integrated water service' (Article 154, paragraph 1); different from a tax, which is a fiscal obligation, it is only due based on the actual use of the service (Constitutional Court, judgement No. 335 of 2008, and subsequent judgment No. 246 of 2009).The tariff is calculated taking into consideration the quality of the water source and service supplied, the work and necessary adjustments, total management costs for the works, and management costs for protected areas, as well as a share of the costs of the functioning of the ATO in such a way that the entire coverage of the investment and operating costs is ensured in accordance with the full cost recovery principle and the principle of 'the polluter pays' (Article 154, paragraph 1, Legislative Decree No. 152 of 2006 as well as Article 119; Article 2 of DPCM 20 July 2012. In the European context *see* Article 9 of Directive 2000/60/EC that creates a framework for Community action on water).

The tariff ensures the economic-financial equilibrium of management and the efficiency and trustworthiness of the service through a tariff method aimed at guaranteeing the coverage of costs, while at the same time avoiding that the concessionaire, i.e., the sole manager, abuse its dominant position (Council of State. judgment No. 2481 of 26 May 2017, section VI).

The method used to calculate the tariff is established by the National Regulatory Authority, which approves the proposed tariffs adopted by the ATO or other competent subjects (e.g., the municipalities that still manage the service directly).

The tariff varies on the basis of groups of uses and territory and must provide benefits for essential domestic consumption as well as for the consumption of specific categories according to pre-established income brackets. Increases of the tariff are permitted for secondary residences and for seasonal facilities, in order to allow an equitable redistribution of costs (Article 154, paragraphs 6 and 7).

526. There are specific norms for industrial use aimed at providing incentives for in-house water treatment as well as the reuse and recycling of water. Paragraph 5 of Article 155 of Legislative Decree No. 152 of 2006 provides a mechanism for reduction of the tariff as an incentive for users who treat water directly and who utilize the public sewage system. Subsequent paragraph 6 states that:

> in order to motivate the reutilization of wastewater or water already used in the manufacturing cycle, the tariff for industrial users is reduced on the basis of the use in the manufacturing process of wastewater or used water. The reduction is determined applying a corrective to the tariff that takes into consideration the quantity of reutilized water and the quantity of primary water utilized.

527. Articles 35 through 39 of the Uniform Text of 1933 regulate the application of an annual charge for all users of public water. Such regulation was subsequently integrated and updated by Article 18 of Law No. 36 of 1994 which, after having defined the charges as 'compensation for the use of the water drawn', provided for its re-quantification in relation to the diverse forms of use to which the water was destined (and the amounts were periodically updated to the inflation rate by a decree of the Ministry of Finance). The Uniform Text of 1933 provides for variations in the amount of the tariff, such as a one-half reduction in the case of derivations for irrigation, if the leakage and residue are returned to the underground stratum.

528. Legislative Decree No. 112 of 1998 innovated the pre-existing regime, attributing the regions with responsibility for determining the charges for the use of public water (Article 89, paragraph 1, clause *i*). Article 154, paragraph 3, of Legislative Decree No. 152 of 2006, to ensure homogeneous regulation throughout the national territory, provides that the Ministry of the Economy and Finance, together with the Ministry of the Environment, shall establish the general criteria to determine the charges, 'considering environmental costs and the costs of the resource, further providing for the reduction of the charges if the licensee reuses water by reutilizing water originating from the manufacturing process or part of it, or by returning wastewater having the same qualitative characteristics as the water that was drawn'.

529. Among the economic instruments for water resource management, in addition to charges for the use of public water and the tariff for integrated water services, are contributions from owners of resources located in an area to be reclaimed must pay to the Reclamation Consortium for the implementation, maintenance and operation of any drainage or other land reclamation works (this is regulated by the Civil Code, Articles 857 through 865, RD No. 368 of 1904, RD No. 215 of 1933, Articles 62, 63, last paragraph, and 166 of Legislative Decree No. 152 of 2006, as well as by regional legislation). In this context the term 'reclamation' refers to activities that create land from lakes, ponds, marshes, wetlands or uneven mountain terrain that can be used for manufacturing or residential purposes; the 'cleanup of contaminated sites' is a different concept.

530. Further, anyone not associated with the Reclamation and Irrigation Consortium, but who utilizes the consortium's channels or irrigation system for the discharge of wastewater, even if treated and compatible for irrigation, that originates from any kind of installation must also contribute to the expenses sustained by the consortium on the basis of the flow of discharged water (Article 166, paragraph 3, Legislative Decree No. 152 of 2006). Both the ordinary contribution and the contribution due by parties not associated with the consortia are tributary in nature (*see*, most recently, Constitutional Court, judgment No. 246 of 2009).

§9. Institutional Framework

531. An attempt shall be made to provide a brief schematic overview of the various responsibilities belonging to the principal entities and organisms involved in water resource management and soil conservation, also bearing in mind the general laws on the transfer of administrative responsibilities from the State to the regions (in particular, Legislative Decree No. 112 of 1998), as well as the regulation of this sector set forth in Legislative Decree No. 152 of 2006, on which the Constitutional Court has ruled many times.

The Constitutional Court has found the regulatory scope of soil conservation to be included in the concept of 'environmental protection', for which the State retains exclusive legislative competence (Article 117, paragraph II, clause *s*, Constitution). The soil conservation regime, to the extent related to 'protection of the intrinsic conditions and quality of the soil and not to its utilization', intends to 'guarantee a certain state of the soil, the same as the norms on water pollution aim at guaranteeing a specific qualitative standard for bodies of water, those on air pollution a specific qualitative level for air, etc.' (judgment No. 232 of 2009); thus justifying Legislative Decree No. 152 of 2006's referral to State competence.

The provisions on water resource management follow similar reasoning, with exclusive State legislative competence with respect to 'the protection of competition' (in particular, with reference to the integrated water service regime, judgment No. 246 of 2009; and more recently judgment No. 93 of 2017).

532. The court's corrective intervention regarded cases in which the regime appears more capable of producing indirect effects on regional legislative competence (especially in matters of 'territorial governance'), and consists of introducing suitable connective mechanisms between the State and the regional system during the approval phase of some State acts, in the form of an opinion or in agreement with the State-Regional Conference (or Unified Conference, when the decision also involves the competence of local subregional authorities). The conference's intervention is already provided for by Legislative Decree No. 152 of 2006 (to which a specific provision, Article 59, is dedicated), and has been reinforced by constitutional case law.

533. The specific competence of the diverse levels of government is briefly outlined below.

I. State

534.

(a) President of the Council of Ministers. The President of the Council of Ministers has important deliberative powers with respect to soil conservation, as well as responsibility for policy-setting and substitute powers. In particular, after an affirmative vote of the Council of Ministers, he approves by means of a presidential decree (Article 57, Legislative Decree No. 152 of 2006):
  (i) upon the proposal of the Minister of the Environment (MATTM):
    - resolutions relating to the methods and criteria, including technical methods and criteria, for carrying out the cognitive, planning, programming and implementation activities set forth in Articles 55 and 56, as well as those relative to the verification and control of basin plans and works programmes;
    - basin plans, after consulting the State-Regional Conference;
    - substitute measures after a warning has been issued, in the case of persistent inactivity of the subject having the responsibilities set forth in section I of Part III of Legislative Decree No. 152 of 2006 (e.g., relative to regional requirements for the preparation of the basin plan, Article 66, paragraph 4), and in the case in which the Basin Authorities do not identify high risk hydrogeological areas or provide protective measures (Article 67, paragraph 2);
    - any other orientation and coordination measure in the sector regulated by section I, Part III of Legislative Decree No. 152 of 2006;
  (ii) the national works programme, upon the proposal of the Committee of Ministers, after obtaining the opinion of the Unified Conference (Constitutional Court, judgment No. 232 of 2009).

The criteria and procedures for attributing or transferring personnel and economic and financial resources to the district Basin Authorities are determined by means of a decree of the President of the Council of Ministers, upon the proposal of the MATTM, jointly with the Minister of the Economy and Finance and the Minister for Public Functions, which is issued after obtaining the opinion of the permanent State-Regional Conference (Article 63, paragraph 2).

(b) Committee of Ministers. With regard to soil conservation, a Committee of Ministers has been established within the Presidency of the Council of Ministers, presided over by the President of the Council of Ministers, or, upon a delegation of power, by the Minister of the Environment, Land and Sea. The Committee is composed of the Minister of the Environment, Land and Sea, the Minister of Infrastructures and Transportation, the Minister of Productive Activities, the Minister of Agricultural and Forestry Policies, the Minister for Regional Affairs, the Minister for Culture and the person delegated by the President of the Council of Ministers in matters of civil protection.

The Committee of Ministers is responsible for supervising the functions for which State bodies are responsible (Constitutional Court, judgment No. 232 of 2009), adopting orientation and coordination measures for their activities. Among the Committee's most important responsibilities is that of proposing an outline of the national works programme to the President of the Council of Ministers and controlling its implementation. The Committee also ensures coordination between the national programme and district programmes.

The Committee of Ministers also integrates environmental policies, proposing the orientation of State policies in the sector that are, directly or indirectly, related to the objectives and contents of district planning.

(c) Ministry of the Environment. The principal responsibilities of the Minister of the Environment with regard to soil conservation are set forth in Article 58 of Legislative Decree No. 152 of 2006. Specifically, the ministry:
   (i) makes proposals, after receiving the opinion of the State-Regional Conference, for the adoption by the President of the Council of Ministers of the orientation and criteria for water policing services, internal navigation and the creation, management and maintenance of works and installations and the preservation of resources;
   (ii) prepares a report on the use of soil and conditions of the hydrogeological structure, annexed to the report on the state of the environment required by the law that established the ministry (Law No. 349 of 8 July 1986), as well as the report on the state of implementation of the three-year programmes for soil conservation;
   (iii) ensures the coordination of soil conservation at every planning level, with interventions for the protection and use of water and environmental protection.

The following are among the ministry's principal functions:

- programming, financing and control of activities regarding soil conservation (after obtaining the opinion of the Unified Conference, Constitutional Court, judgment No. 232 of 2009);
- mid and long-term forecasts, prevention and conservation of the soil from landslides, flooding and other hydrogeological instabilities in order to guarantee permanent and homogeneous environmental conditions, without prejudice to the competence of the Department of Civil Protection of the Presidency of the Council of Ministers in cases requiring urgent measures;
- identification of the basic outline of national spatial planning, with reference to natural and environmental resources and soil conservation, as well as with respect to the environmental impact of infrastructural networks, works for which the State is competent and territorial transformations (after obtaining the opinion of the Unified Conference, Constitutional Court, judgment No. 232 of 2009);
- orientation and coordination of the activities of the ministry's representatives at the district Basin Authorities;
- assessment of the effects due to implementation of the plans, programmes and projects on a national scale of works in the sector of soil conservation;
- determination of the criteria, methods and standards for the collection, processing (by ISPRA) and consultation of data; definition of the coordination and collaboration procedures among public subjects operating in the sector, as well as guidelines for the assessment and study of elements of the physical environment and general conditions of risk;
- coordination of mapping systems.

In general, the MATTM carries out the functions and responsibilities belonging to the State with respect to water resource management (Article 142, paragraph 1, Legislative Decree No. 152 of 2006). In particular, the Ministry of the Environment:

- exercises substitute power for the ATO when it does not intervene to ensure that the integrated water services manager complies with his obligations, or does not exercise substitute power in the case of an inactive region (Article 152, paragraph 3);
- establishes, together with the Ministry of the Economy, the general criteria for the regions to determine charges for permits to use public waters (Article 154, paragraph 3);
- ensures public notice of projects for hydraulic works that result in or require major derivations, the creation of barriers and channels, or the drilling of wells (Article 162, paragraph 2);
- issues a special regulation on the utilization of water for hydroelectric purposes, in accordance with Article 168 of Legislative Decree No. 152 of 2006.

In accordance with DPCM 20 July 2012 MATTM:

- adopts the guidelines to ensure coordination at all planning levels of the functions related to the use of water resources, identifying general and priority measures;

- adopts the guidelines and establishes quality standards for the resource in accordance with Part III of Legislative Decree No. 152/06 and the Community Directive in this sector;
- defines criteria and guidelines to enhance water savings, efficiency in the use of water resources and for the reuse of wastewater;
- defines the criteria to determine the environmental cost and the cost of the resource for the various sectors where water is used;
- defines the criteria to determine the coverage of costs related to water services other than the integrated water service and each of its component individual services (which are regulated by the National Regulatory Authority);
- determine the general quality objectives for the integrated water service throughout the national territory, having heard the regional managers and consumer associations;
- defines the guidelines to achieve, through differentiated tariffs, equalization among areas that have different supplies of water resources.

(d) ISPRA. The Italian Geological Service, which is within ISPRA, conducts purely technical-scientific activities for knowledge and information. Specifically, the Service (Articles 55 and 60, Legislative Decree No. 152 of 2006):

(i) collects, processes, archives and disseminates data, and is responsible for the creation of a sole informational system and a national monitoring and surveillance network;
(ii) carries out controls, experiments, research and studies of the elements of the physical environment and general conditions of risk;
(iii) prepares and updates thematic maps of the territory;
(iv) performs assessments and studies of the effects of implementation of plans, programmes and projects regarding soil conservation;
(v) provides data, opinions and consulting to whoever requests it, in accordance with a fee schedule established every two years by a decree of the President of the Council of Ministers.

II. Basin Authorities

535. The Basin Authority is a non-profit public entity created in each geographical district (the districts are specified in Article 64 of Legislative Decree No. 152 of 2006).

In compliance with principles of subsidiarity, differentiation and adequacy, as well as efficiency and cost reduction, in the hydrographic districts whose territory coincides with the regional territory, the regions, in order to adjust their legal systems with the principles of this decree, shall create an ATO that performs the tasks and functions provided by Article 63 of Legislative Decree No. 152 of 2006. The ATO are also attributed with competence for the regions set forth in this part. The Ministry of the Environment, including through the involvement of ISPRA, shall assume the guideline functions of the district Basin Authority and coordination functions with the other district Basin Authorities.

For the Basin Authorities of water districts whose territory exceeds the regional territory, the following are required: the permanent institutional conference, a general secretary, an operational conference, an operational technical secretary and Board of Auditors.

The permanent institutional conference is a political-representative body and the Authority's decision-making centre. The Presidents of the regions and the autonomous provinces in whose territory the water district is located participate, or the council members delegated by them, as well as the Minister for the Environment and the Minister for Infrastructures and Transportation, or the Undersecretaries of State delegated by them, the Head of the Department of Civil Protection of the Presidency of the Council of Ministers, and, in cases in which their respective areas of competence are involved, the Minister of Agriculture, Food and Forestry Policies and the Minister of Culture and Tourism, or the Undersecretaries of State delegated by them. Two representatives of agricultural organizations that are the most representative at the national level and a representative of ANBI-National Association of consortium for the management and protection of the territory and irrigation water, can be invited in a consultative role for issues related to soil conservation and the management of irrigation water.

The Basin Authority prepares and adopts the district basin plan (subsequently approved by a decree of the President of the Council of Ministers). The Authority approves eventual extracts of the basin plan (such as the PAI and the management plan), the extraordinary plans set forth in Article 67, and the Programmes of Activities (Article 70), as well as the Flood Risk Management Plans (Legislative Decree No. 49 of 2010, Article 7). The Basin Authorities also define the objectives on a district level to which the water pollution control plans must conform (Article 121, paragraph 2).

The Authority is also responsible for:

- expressing its opinion on whether the objectives of the basin plan conform to Community, national, regional and local plans and programmes on soil conservation, the battle against desertification, water protection and water resource management;
- preparing an analysis of the district's characteristics, a review of the impact of human activities on the state of surface and underground waters, and an economic analysis of water use;
- coordinating and supervising the activities of the Reclamation Consortia.

With respect to water resource management, the Authority is primarily responsible for determining the water balance. The Basin Authorities, in fact, define and periodically update the water balance to ensure equilibrium between the availability of resources located in the reference area, or which can be activated therein, and the needs for diverse uses. To ensure equilibrium between resources and needs, the Authority adopts, to the extent it is competent, measures to plan water economy based on the intended uses of the resources (Articles 145 and 95, Legislative Decree No. 152 of 2006).

With respect to permits regarding public water (Uniform Text of 1933), the public administrations entitled to grant permits and entrusted with supervisory responsibilities must provide information and transmit data to the Basin Authorities (Article 5*bis*, paragraph 2). The Basin Authorities also have consulting power with respect to requests for new permits and water uses, in view of their compatibility with the provisions of the basin plan and the equilibrium of the water balance (Article 7, paragraph 2). Additional consulting powers are provided with respect to water management in protected areas (Article 164, Legislative Decree No. 152 of 2006), the use of irrigated water and water resulting from reclamation (Article 166) and the use of water intended for hydroelectric purposes (Article 168).

III. Regions

536. Legislative Decree No. 112 of 1998 transferred many functions from the State to the regions and local entities. This reform process was completed by the entry into effect of special regional laws implementing Legislative Decree No. 112 of 1998, by means of which each region established which of these functions has to be exercised by the regional government and which are instead exercised by the province or municipality.

The role of the regional entity has also been defined by subsequent legislation in the changed constitutional framework of State-region relations, which grants the latter concurrent legislative power in matters of 'territorial governance' (*see* the express reference contained in Article 142, paragraph 2 of Legislative Decree No. 152/2006).

With respect to soil conservation, the regions (Article 61):

- collaborate with sampling and the preparation of basin plans for hydrographic districts in accordance with the guidelines of the permanent Institutional Conference;
- propose programmes as well as studies and projects relating to the hydrographic districts;
- to the extent of their competence, prepare, approve and implement projects, interventions and work to be performed in the hydrographic districts, establishing common management when required;
- provide, to the extent of their competence, for the organization and functioning of water policing services, services for the management and maintenance of works and installations, and the preservation of resources;
- provide for the organization and functioning of internal navigation, without prejudice to the residual competence that rests with the Ministry of Infrastructures and Transportation;
- prepare an annual report on the use of the soil and conditions of the hydrogeological layout of the territory of competence and the status of implementation of the three-year programme in course, which must be transmitted to the MATTM.

The above functions are performed by the ATO for water districts whose territory falls entirely within one region.

The regions also prepare the part of the Flood Risk Management Plans relating to the system used to warn the population for purposes of civil protection (Article 7, paragraph 3(b) of Legislative Decree No. 49/2010).

The following regional powers are particularly important with respect to water resource management:

- initiatives to ensure water savings (Article 146);
- functions relating to integrated water services, such as delineation of the ATO; the choice of the institutional form of the ATO Authority; substitute power with respect to the latter;
- establishing the charges for the use of public water.

It should also be noted that the regions contribute to the formation of State acts not only individually but also as a 'system', by means of the State-Regional Conference (or the Unified Conference), which has consulting or co-decision-making responsibilities when, in matters subject to regional competence, choices made by the State involve areas that cross the territorial boundaries of an individual region.

IV. Local Authorities

537. What has been noted for the regions also holds true for subregional local entities, such as provinces and municipalities: the structure of competence is defined by regional laws implementing Legislative Decree No. 112 of 1998 and subsequent legislative provisions.

The importance of regional legislation in this sector is confirmed by Article 62 of Legislative Decree No. 152 of 2006: the municipalities, provinces, their consortia or associations, mountain communities, reclamation and irrigation consortia, mountain consortia and the other public and public law entities located in the hydrographic district participate in exercising regional functions regarding soil conservation in the manner and forms established by the regions, individually or in agreement among themselves.

The National Association of Italian Municipalities (ANCI – Associazione Nazionale Comuni Italiani, a private association) has a recognized ability to contribute to cognitive activities regarding soil conservation and the spread of environmental information by means of the collection and processing of the data required to monitor environmental costs (Article 55, paragraphs 4 and 5).

With respect to water resource management, local entities carry out their functions primarily due to their participation in the ATO Authority, which has the following functions: organization of the integrated water service; choice of the management form; entrusting management and the relative controls; preparation of the tariff proposal.

The reclamation and irrigation consortium should be mentioned, which have powers to realize and manage networks whose purpose primarily regards irrigation, installations for the use of wastewater in agriculture, rural aqueducts and other installations functional to irrigation and reclamation systems. Upon request to the competent authorities, supported by the project for the works to be performed, they can utilize water flowing in channel and cable consortia for uses that result in the restitution water compatible with subsequent uses, including the production of hydroelectric energy and water supplies to manufacturers (Article 166).

V. The Italian Regulatory ARERA

In 2011 the Italian legislator attributed regulatory and control functions for water services to an independent administrative authority (Article 21, paragraphs 13 and 19 of Law Decree 201 of 2011).

The choice was made of the Authority for Electrical Energy and Gas, created by means of Law No. 481 of 14 November 1995, which was renamed the Authority for Electrical Energy, Gas and the Water System.

Recently, such Authority was attributed with regulatory and control functions related to waste recycling, including differentiated, urban and assimilated waste (Article 1, paragraphs 527–530, Law No. 205 of 2017) and the Authority was renamed ARERA – the Regulatory Authority for Energy, Networks and the Environment.

In accordance with the 1995 Law that established it, the Authority is responsible for protecting consumer interests and promoting competition, efficiency and the distribution of services with adequate quality levels, through regulation and control. It acts autonomously using its independent judgment and assessment. To ensure the independence of its members (five after Law No. 205 of 2017), they are appointed by a procedure that provides for an opinion expressed by a qualified majority of two-thirds of the members of the competent Parliamentary Commissions. For the same reason, the Authority is financed through a mandatory contribution that rests with the regulated subjects.

In addition to what is provided by the law that established it, the Authority's specific powers in the water service sector are set forth in detail in DPCM 20 July 2012.

The following are ARERA's main powers:

- determine the minimum levels and quality objectives of the integrated water service, or for each of its component individual services, providing for bonus and penalty mechanisms;
- prepare in accordance with Article 151 of Legislative Decree No. 152 of 3 April 2006, one or more standard conventions for the regulation of relationships among authorities with the power to contract the service and the managers;
- determine the cost components – including the financial costs of the investments and management – in order to calculate the tariff for the integrated water service;
- prepare and periodically review the tariff method to calculate the integrated water service tariff, or for each of its component individual services;
- approve the tariffs of the integrated water service, or for each of its component individual services, usually proposed by the ATO based on the water basin plan set forth in Article 149 of Legislative Decree No. 152 of 6 April 2006;
- adopt directives for accounting transparency and for accounting and administrative separation for managers of the integrated water service or its segments;

- protect the rights of users, including by evaluating complaints, petitions and reports in accordance with Article 2, paragraph 12, clause *m*) of Law No. 481 of 14 November 1995, and determining, if possible, automatic indemnity obligations on behalf of such users.

§10. Conclusions

538. The overall judgment of the Italian legal system on water resource management and soil conservation must necessarily be articulated.

The current regime has clearly positive aspects, among which the following are noted:

- an interdisciplinary approach to problems of soil conservation and overall water resource management;
- programming logic, which requires acts of a planning nature, and, in particular, the basin plan, prior to the use of legal instruments such as permits and authorizations, with the basin plan substituting diverse existing sector plans;
- the creation of specialized technical entities (the Basin Authorities), entrusted with the most important functions;
- the provision of specific instruments so that public authorities have complete and updated knowledge of the situations that have evolved;
- the provision of a precise scale of priorities, which should guide choices regarding the diverse kinds of use of water resources in relation to their effective availability; and
- reform of the water service management system, on the basis of efficiency and cost savings.

These aspects cannot, however, hide the limits and contradictions that characterize the regulation of this sector, which contributed in the past in large part to slowing its effective implementation.

539. The principal limits can be summarized as follows:

- the complexity and scarce clarity of the organizational framework, due, above all, to the superimposition of functional entities (the Basin Authorities) and territorial entities (State, regions and local authorities), on which action was taken in 2015;
- the compromise of certain basic choices in the distribution of competence, particularly at a central level. The net dualism that existed in the past between the Ministry of the Environment and the Ministry of Public Works has been alleviated by the creation of a collegial body, the Committee of Ministers, for the orientation and coordination of State functions, whose effective ability to act, however, has not yet been determined;
- the excessive complexity of planning instruments, from both a substantive and procedural standpoint, which has recently prompted, due to the proliferation of hydrogeological risks, reinforcement of the instrument of extraordinary plans according to an emergency logic, applied ever since 1998 after the flood in Sarno, which risks being totally ineffective unless followed by structural interventions;

- implementation mechanisms that follow a 'waterfall' regime (an aspect related to the previous point), which imposes a rigid chain of actions that often lead to the total paralysis of the system, so that emergency protection actions are required to remedy situations that have degenerated due to the lack of preventive programming; and
- insufficient financial and technical resources have been made available to the competent subjects.

Chapter 5. Wetlands

by *Alessandro Andronio*

§1. The International Legal System

540. The term 'wetlands' includes particular habitats (ponds, swampland, peat bogs, natural and artificial permanent basins with stagnant or running fresh or salt water, low-lying maritime areas, lagoons, small and large lakes, plains and pastures subject to seasonal flooding, flooded forests, estuaries, delta and other areas), whose true environmental nature has been re-evaluated in its totality, in particular, due to the presence and nesting of waterfowl species.

541. Due to their aviary-faunal importance, the major wetlands of many countries were the object of the Ramsar Convention of 2 February 1971, ratified by Italy by DPR No. 448 of 13 July 1976, later amended by the Protocol of Paris of 3 December 1982, implemented in Italy by DPR No. 184 of 11 February 1987.

In brief, the primary objective of the Convention is the protection of the particular ecosystems created by wetlands, imposing on signatory States two different types of obligations: (1) identification and insertion of at least one area in the list of wetlands of international importance maintained by a permanent office established by the Convention; (2) promotion of wetlands protection 'whether they are included in the list or not' by creating special nature reserves.

It is, therefore, a framework convention that establishes obligations of an extremely general nature, which have been reworked and specified over the course of the years by means of the recommendations adopted by the Conference of the Parties. In this context, the guidelines aimed at orienting the policies of the States, in the version approved by the Fifth Conference of the Parties of 1993, are largely inspired by principles of sustainable development. They identify, in fact, the enhancement of economic and social factors as the central aspect of national conservation policies and policies regarding the management of wetlands.

542. The Sixth Conference of the Parties, which was held in Brisbane in March, 1996, signalled further progress in this direction. The principle acts that it adopted were the Twenty-Fifth Anniversary Declaration and the 1997–2000 Action Plan, which specify the general objectives of the Ramsar Convention in relation to the environmental priorities identified by UNCED (the Conference of the United Nations on Environment and Development of 1992). These priorities consist, in particular, in the integrated and sustainable management of water resources and in the conservation of biodiversity. They were further specified in subsequent conferences, up through the last one held in Changwon in 2008, which concluded with the Declaration on Human Well-Being and Wetlands.

543. Italy and the EU are also parties to the Agreement on the Conservation of African-Eurasian Migratory Waterbirds concluded at The Hague on 15 August 1996 (which Italy implemented by means of Law No. 66 of 2006). The agreement provides general conservation measures (unfortunately rather generic) that the States must adopt.

§2. Protection of Wetlands in the Mediterranean Basin

544. The Ramsar Convention provides a regional model of implementation of wetlands protection. In the Mediterranean basin, of which Italy is part, this trend is translated in the Mediterranean Wetlands programme (MEDWET), an international initiative born out of the 1991 Conference of Grado on Mediterranean Wetlands, in which the organs established by the Ramsar Convention, the EC (represented by the Commission), the Mediterranean Member States of the EU (France, Greece, Italy, Portugal and Spain) and some non-governmental organizations participate.

The programme focuses on: (a) providing technical tools and ensuring the sustainable management of wetlands and their natural resources; (b) creating stakeholder networks and partnerships between and within Mediterranean countries on issues pertaining to wetlands; (c) promoting and disseminating information on the wise use of wetland resources; (d) putting into practice best practices of wetland management with hands-on projects in Mediterranean wetlands.

The acts adopted in the context of the MEDWET programme cannot impose judicially enforceable obligations on the Member States. Therefore, said States are not directly obligated to adopt corresponding measures. In any event, however, protection policies and national judicial instruments more or less tend to adapt themselves to internationally accepted standards.

§3. The Marginal Role of EU Law

545. The non-binding nature of international law on wetlands protection is also true for the EU which, however, is not a party to the Convention, although it participated in the MEDWET programme.

This is the reason why there are no specific juridical norms in EU law relating to wetlands, but only EU acts that do not have juridical effect, such as:

(a) the Communication of the European Commission to the European Council and Parliament of 29 May 1995 on the rational use and conservation of wetlands and the Report of the European Parliament on the same Communication dated 10 July 1996;
(b) Articles 3 and 6 of the Sixth EC Action Programme on the Environment;
(c) Council Decision No. 2005/923/EC of 2 December 2005 related, among others, to the 'Soil Protection' Protocol, which provides that 'drainage schemes in wetlands and moors shall be limited to the upkeep of existing networks, unless there are sound reasons for exceptions' (Article 9);
(d) the Protocol of 21 January 2008 on the integrated management of coastal areas of the Mediterranean, which mentions wetlands among particular coastal ecosystems (Article 10).

546. EU law indirectly protects wetlands, however, by means of general environmental laws.

In this context, in addition to directives concerning water quality and the prevention of industrial and agricultural pollution, Directives No. 79/409/EEC of 2 April 1979 concerning the conservation of wild birds, and No. 92/43/EEC of 21 May 1992 relating to the conservation of natural and semi-natural habitat and wild flora and fauna (*see* the chapter on Protected Areas), whose scope of application partially coincides with that of the Convention, assume particular importance. The 1979 Directive in fact provides that the Member States protect wetlands, especially those of international importance (Article 4, paragraph 2), whereas the 1992 Directive provides for the protection of Mediterranean lagoons and ponds (Annex i).

In such manner, many of the wetlands situated within the territory of the States that are members of the EU, and which are protected by the Ramsar Convention, are part of the ecological network of sites entitled to special protection, created by the 1992 Directive 'Nature 2000'.

The EU contributes, however, in the more general framework of programmes that promote the environment or, in the MEDWET context, that protect Italy's wetlands, including by locating financial resources. In addition, the possibility of classifying Ramsar sites as 'specially protected areas' for the protection of wild birds and as 'ZSC' and natural habitats introduced by Directives No. 79/409 and 92/43 and adopted in the Italian legal system by means of the Resolution of the Committee for Natural Protected Areas of 2 December 1996, constitutes a useful instrument to reinforce protection.

§4. Implementation of the International Regime

547. The adhesion of Italy to the Ramsar Convention and its implementation in the Italian legal system by means of DPR No. 448 of 13 March 1976 has inverted a tendency of Italian legislation, which up until then had been directed at wetlands reclamation.

548. The Constitution does not contain any provision for the protection of such sites; instead, it accepts the orientation of pre-existing legislation (according to Article 44, 'in order to pursue the rational exploitation of the soil, the law promotes and imposes the reclamation of land').

549. The law subsequent to Italy's adhesion to the Ramsar Convention is instead aimed at knowledge of the ecological, scientific and economic value of wetlands and prepares instruments to counteract their deterioration and progressive disappearance, also for the purpose of protecting aquatic birds that live there. At the time of its adherence to the Convention, Italy had already prepared a list of eighteen sites to be registered in the list of wetlands of international importance.

550. But considering that adhesion to the Convention took place by means of a DPR, which is a secondary legislative source, and that for a long period of time this was the only instrument having as its purpose the conservation and management of wetlands, protection has not turned out to be particularly adequate. Articles 42 and 44 of the Constitution, in fact, reserve the possibility of setting limits and restrictions on private property to primary normative sources.

551. In the fifteen years between the implementation of the Ramsar Convention and the framework law on protected areas, Law No. 431 of 8 August 1985 (subsequently substituted by Article 142 of Legislative Decree No. 42 of 22 January 2004, and modified in 2006) guaranteed partial protection of wetlands, subjecting them to landscape restrictions (*see* Article 1, clause *i*), even though such restrictions have turned out more often than not to be inadequate with respect to the needs of protection that contemplates the necessities of use of the sites in relation to parameters of sustainable development. From the point of view of effectiveness, the imposition of a landscape restriction is, however, a very important innovation because it provides an instrument with which to impose sanctions against transformations and alterations of the territory, even though it leaves the more general problem of protection from other damaging activities such as poaching, waste disposal and other forms of pollution unresolved.

552. With respect to the division of legislative power between the State and regions, Constitutional Court judgment No. 164 of 2009 clarified that Article 142 of Legislative Decree No. 42 of 2004 does not distinguish, for purposes of landscape protection, between natural and artificial lakes, and, therefore, even artificial lakes are covered by it, as they can be significant factors from a natural, aesthetic and cultural standpoint. Moreover, an implicit equivalency between natural and artificial lakes for environmental protection purposes can be inferred from a variety of legal sources, among which Article 1 of DPR No. 488 of 13 March 1976 (Implementation of the International Convention on Wetlands of International Importance, especially as Waterfowl Habitat, signed at Ramsar on 2 February 1971), and Article 54 (included in the section dedicated to soil conservation and the fight against desertification) and Article 74 (included in the section related to water pollution protection) of Legislative Decree No. 152 of 3 April 2006 (Environmental Regulations).

553. True and proper wetlands were subsequently identified on the basis of Law No. 394/1991 by the Committee for Protected Natural Areas (*see* Article 2, paragraph 5) and were included in the official list of 1 December 1993 that has been updated several times. It would have been opportune in this case as well to directly utilize acts having the force of law in that, as noted, only such acts can place limits and restrictions on private property.

From a substantive viewpoint, however, the notion of wetlands adopted by the Italian legal system by formal reference to international law perfectly coincides with that of the Convention, even if only 51 of the 200 wetlands existing in Italy (with a total surface area of 60,052 hectares) have been registered in the Convention's list.

554. The connection of the domestic concept of wetlands with the international concept is also guaranteed, in addition to the formal nature of the reference to international law, by Italy's adherence to the Protocol of Amendment of the Ramsar Convention, adopted in Paris on 3 December 1982 (implemented by DPR No. 184 of 11

February 1987) which, by broadening the powers of the Conference of the Parties, facilitates further developments in the protective regime.

§5. The Italian Legal System: Secondary Norms

555. With respect to Italy's domestic legal system, the specific protection of wetlands remains theoretical because it is tied to a mere enunciation of principle, in that the identification of areas entitled to protection is unaccompanied by identification of concrete control and sanction mechanisms.

556. At a domestic level, the designation of what areas constitute wetlands occurs by means of a decree, presently within the responsibility of the Ministry of the Environment on the basis of Articles 1 and 5 of Law No. 349/1986 (reference is made, for example, to DM 28 June 2011 related to the designation of Ramsar areas in some municipalities in Sicily). These decrees constitute an order of implementation that is complementary with respect to DPR No. 448/1976. In substance, the regime of each Ramsar area is delineated by the indispensable decree of designation and by a plurality of concurrent instruments (State and regional laws, regulations, decrees and ministerial orders, administrative permits and other individual measures, instruments of private law, etc.), which are often left uncoordinated.

Even with respect to competence the regime remains rather diversified: the concrete management of the sites is entrusted from time to time to regions, municipalities, ad hoc authorities, environmental organizations and so on.

This non-homogeneous framework derives, at least in part, from the diversity of local situations and the multitude of parties involved in protection, which are characteristic and recurring issues with respect to wetlands, where the interest of providing protection conflicts with interests related to productive and recreational activities.

Territorial entities and local communities also participate in the conservation and management of the sites. In particular, the regions need to be consulted regarding the creation of Ramsar areas in relation to acts that decide matters of regional competence such as the regulation of hunting and fishing.

557. With respect to the division of competence between State and regions, wetlands protection was explicitly included in 'agricultural and forestry' matters by Article 66 of DPR No. 616 of 24 July 1977, which transferred the administration functions in such area to the regions.

558. In any event, the Constitutional Court adopted a restrictive orientation in the past, affirming the exclusive competence of the central organs with respect to the creation of Ramsar areas, in that the decrees of designation, which constitute a necessary condition for compliance with obligations arising from the system of the Convention, are based on the State's exercise of powers in matters of international law (judgment No. 123 of 23 July 1980 and No. 223 of 25 July 1984).

Part of legal scholarship has criticized this 'centralist' trend of the court and has sustained the requirement that all territorial levels of government participate, each according to its own area of competence, in the implementation of international obligations regarding wetlands protection.

Subsequently, the Constitutional Court partially overturned its previous orientation, affirming that the State must obtain the opinion of the region prior to imposing measures of protection inside of wetlands (judgment No. 464 of 13 December 1991).

The problem of the division of powers among the State and regions is a recurring issue in relation to all protected areas.

559. Even though it must be acknowledged that the Italian legal system has made progress in wetlands protection, it cannot be affirmed that Law No. 394/1991 has entirely filled the gaps of pre-existing norms. In relation to wetlands of international importance, in fact, it is limited to a provision of a programmatic nature, which defers creation of this particular category of protected areas to further acts, omitting to provide any substantive indication with respect to concrete mechanisms for their upkeep and protection.

560. The mere reference to the international regime, by means of the implementing act of the Convention, appears insufficient for the general, or actually generic, tenor of the provisions of the Convention (e.g., the obligation set forth in the Convention to create nature reserves within wetlands might be implemented in the Italian legal system by the creation of a national or regional park, with the use of wetlands or parts of them as a nature reserve, or, more generally, by the creation of any protected area).

The lack of homogeneity of protection analysed above is due to the normative gap provoked by Law No. 394/1991 and the lack of a specific law at the Community level.

In order to create a more homogeneous normative and institutional framework, a law aimed at establishing a uniform and sufficiently flexible management model is advisable, even if its goal is effective decentralization.

Chapter 6. Protection of the Sea

by *Alessandro Andronio*

§1. The International Framework

561. Italian legislation on protection of the sea against pollution developed starting from a series of international cooperation agreements signed at the end of the 1960s. Among these were two important conventions signed in Brussels on 29 November 1969 regarding the high seas and civil liability in the case of accidents involving pollution caused by oil spills, and the London Convention of 2 November 1973 on the prevention of marine pollution caused by ships.

562. The Convention that has had the greatest influence on the Italian legislator, however, was the one signed in Barcelona on 16 February 1976 for the protection of the Mediterranean Sea against pollution, which was ratified by Law No. 30 of 25 January 1979. The subsequent additional protocol on specially protected areas of the Mediterranean is also particularly important; it opened for signature in Geneva on 3 April 1982.

563. The protocol represents a scientific approach on a regional basis to problems regarding protection the marine environment, and is the fourth of the additional instruments that are inserted in the context of the general framework of the Barcelona Convention. It is aimed at the protection of marine areas that are particularly important for the purpose of safeguarding natural resources the landscape of the Mediterranean Sea, as well as protection of the region's cultural heritage (Article 1).

In accordance with Article 3 of the protocol, the Member States have undertaken to create protected areas within the confines of the territorial waters, in as much as possible; in addition, they must progressively adopt prohibitions or restrictive measures in relation to a series of activities exemplified in Article 7, that include, among others: waste discharge, fishing and hunting and exploitation of the marine bed or sub-bed.

Cooperation undertakings among coastal States, institutionalized by means of the mechanism of periodic meetings of the parties, arise from various provisions of the protocol: for example, it provides for reciprocal assistance programmes, and, in particular, assistance to be given to developing countries (Article 15).

564. The Geneva Protocol was substituted by a new protocol relating to specially protected areas and biological diversity in the Mediterranean, signed in Barcelona on 10 June 1995. Clearly influenced by the Montego Bay Convention of 10 December 1982, which entered into effect in 1994 (*see*, in particular, Article 194, paragraph 5), and the consolidation of the principles that emerged from the 1992 Conference of Rio de Janeiro on environment and development, the new Barcelona Protocol provides for the creation of a list of specially protected areas of interest in the Mediterranean.

The most important innovations, however, consist of broadening the scope of territorial application which, according to Article 2 of the new Protocol, coincides with that of the Barcelona Convention, and the possibility of creating protected areas within exclusive economic areas of the contracting parties (Article 5), including, with respect to specially protected areas of Mediterranean interest, in international waters (Article 9).

565. Even after the Protocol of Barcelona and additional protocols integrating the Convention, effective protection of marine and coastal areas of the Mediterranean will continue to depend in large measure on national implementing legislation, and the obligations of the parties are considered to be undertakings to achieve results.

§2. The EU Legal Framework

566. The EU has adhered to the Barcelona Convention of 1977 and to its subsequent protocols, and has dedicated growing attention to the protection of the marine environment, in particular, the Mediterranean area. The need for protection, already emphasized by the Third Action Programme in Environmental Matters (1982–1986) and, subsequently, by a series of programmatic acts, is contained in Directive No. 92/43/EEC of 21 May 1992, which includes Community protection of the marine and coastal areas of the Mediterranean in the more general protection relating to special habitat conservation areas.

567. Regulation No. 1973/92/EEC of 21 May 1992, which has been repealed, rationalized the regime for this subject matter, on the basis of which all Community appropriations aimed at environmental protection flow into a sole fund. The financing of environmental protection projects, including those regarding marine environmental protection, is currently regulated by Regulation No. 1293/2013/EU of 11 December 2013, which regulates the LIFE+ fund created by Regulation No. 2007/614/EC of 23 May 2007. The Community legislator also organized the management of coastal marine waters by means of Directive No. 2000/60/EC of 23 October 2000, which established a framework for Community action on waters and which has been amended several times.

568. The most important EU source on the protection of the sea is represented, however, by Marine Strategy Framework Directive No. 2008/56/EC of 17 June 2008 (whose Annex III was recently modified by Directive No. 2017/845/EU of 17 May 2017) on strategy in the field of the marine environment which, in line with the Sixth Community Action Environment Programme, provides for the sustainable use of the seas, conservation of the relative ecosystems and protected areas, the regulation of human activities having an impact on the marine environment and specific objectives of environmental protection to be achieved gradually over time.

§3. Implementation of the International Regime and the Evolution of the Domestic Legal Framework

569. The first legislative instrument in Italy aimed at regulating the protection of marine areas of particular naturalistic value was, prior to the adoption of the organic law on protected areas, Law No. 979 of 31 December 1982 entitled 'Provisions for the Protection of the Sea', which has been amended several times, even recently. Section V of the Law, dedicated to marine reserves, attributes a preponderant value to the preservation of the natural environment with respect to economic uses.

570. The timely adaptation of the domestic legal framework to international law was not followed, except in a limited measure, by the effective protection of marine areas according to applicable international and domestic laws. Law No. 979/1982 has, in fact, remained largely unimplemented. In turn, Law No. 394 of 6 December 1991 ('Framework Law on Protected Areas'), even though it introduced important innovations, did not repeal the pre-existing laws and raised various coordination problems. Law No. 426 of 9 December 1998, 'New Action in the Environmental Sector', while containing some appreciable provisions in this regard, only constituted a partial reform which was unable to ensure the necessary coherency of the applicable regulations in this sector.

571. Notwithstanding the time that has passed since Law No. 979/1982 was promulgated, the protection ensured in Italy to marine and coastal areas still appears to be inadequate with respect to the need to protect the immense heritage consisting of Italy's coastlines and numerous islands.

On the basis of Law No. 979/1982, the creation of marine reserves, provided by Title V in relation to 'marine environments, created by waters, depths and overlooking coastlines having significant interest due to their natural, geomorphologic and biochemical characteristics, with particular regard to marine and coastal flora and fauna, and due to the scientific, ecological, cultural, educational and economic importance that they have' (Article 25), are placed within the context of an overall environmental protection policy that utilizes as a primary operative instrument the general plan of defence of the sea and coastlines provided by Article 1 of the same law, has not yet been adopted.

The Ministry of the Merchant Marine was competent to create, by means of a decree, the marine reserves provided by Title V, on the basis of a general plan and upon the proposal of the Advisory Board for the defence of the sea against pollution, and after hearing the regions of the territorially interested municipalities. These reserves are considered state reserves, in that their creation responds to a national interest, and it has been held that differentiated regimes of protected property without impeding its use does not prejudice the competence of the regions (*see* Constitutional Court, judgment No. 1031 of 15 November 1988).

Although reserves were created, regimes of protection were lacking, by means of which prohibited activities or activities subject to restrictions or authorizations could be specified. In relation to the latter, in fact, the cited article only lists, as an example, a series of activities that can be prohibited or limited within the reserves (e.g., fishing, hunting or the introduction of extraneous species).

Therefore, in Italy, prior to the issuance of the Framework Law on Protected Areas, a paradox existed: there was a specific normative instrument, but it largely lacked concrete application.

572. Law No. 349/1986 transferred competence to issue decrees creating marine reserves to the Ministry of the Environment, together with the Ministry of the Merchant Marine (the latter was subsequently abolished, however, at the end of 1993).

573. Marine reserves, which have been included in the Three-Year Programmes for protected natural areas since 1991, are no longer missing a form of general programming the lack of adoption of a defence plan for the sea and coastlines, and notwithstanding the abrogation of the Three-Year Programmes in accordance with Legislative Decree No. 112 of 31 March 1998. Such regulation is not included in Legislative Decree No. 190 of 13 October 2010 (Articles 10–12).

574. The status of implementation of Italian legislation with respect to protected marine reserves has thus remained unsatisfactory, both due to the modest number of reserves that have been created, and due to the continuous conflicts among the State administration, regions and local entities with respect to their management (*see* Constitutional Court, judgments No. 12 of 2009, No. 21 of 2006 and No. 27 of 2004). In this context, cited Law No. 426 of 1998 contained a series of provisions relating to marine reserves intended to overcome, at least in part, the limits regarding application of pre-existing legislation, and incorporated some developments in international law.

Financial coverage for the creation of protected marine reserves was provided for the period 1998–2000 (Article 2, paragraph 13), and this represented a concrete attempt to end, within the limits of available resources, the lack of application of the cited norms that has been going on for years. The 1998 Law also transferred management of the reserves to Harbour-Master's offices, public entities, scientific institutions and environmental associations (Article 2, paragraph 37). It also provided for the creation of a 'Cetacean Sanctuary' in the Alto Tirreno – Ligurian Sea, as implementation of the joint Declaration of France – Italy – Monaco for the protection of marine mammals, signed in Brussels on 22 March 1993. Further, it also promoted sustainable economic activities in protected areas, including marine reserves (Article 2, paragraph 22), within a general legal framework that is more suitable to the needs of the greatest compatible protection.

575. Law No. 394/1991, Articles 18 and 19, specifically regulates the establishment and management of protected marine reserves (subsequently modified by Law No. 426/1998). Article 19 directly prohibits 'activities that may compromise the protection of the environmental characteristics that are the object of protection and the purposes for which the reserve was created', for example, the capture or collection of flora and fauna.

It also provides that:

(a) the achievement of the institutional purpose for each protected marine reserve shall be secured by a central Inspectorate for the defence of the sea. The Inspectorate shall use the competent Port Authority to manage protected marine reserves. By means of a specific Convention to be stipulated by the Ministry of the Environment, together with the Ministry of the Mercantile Marine, management of the protected marine reserve can be granted to public bodies, scientific institutions or recognized associations (paragraph 1);
(b) if a protected marine reserve is established in waters adjacent to land in a protected land, management is entrusted to the subject responsible for it (paragraph 2);
(c) a decree of the Ministry of the Environment shall approve a regulation that governs the prohibitions and any exceptions based on the degree of protection that is required (paragraph 5);
(d) the Port Authority and the local entities delegated to manage said protected areas are responsible for monitoring protected marine reserves (paragraph 7).

The law also requires a more detailed regime to be prepared for each marine reserve, including any exceptions, by means of a regulation approved by a decree of the Ministry of the Environment.

576. Other regimes intended to protect the sea are contained in Law No. 61 of 2006, entitled ‘Establishment of Ecological Protection Beyond the Outer Limit of the Territorial Sea’, transposed by DPR No. 209 of 27 October 2011, establishing the creation of Ecological Protection Areas in the north-western Mediterranean the Ligurian Sea and the Tyrrhenian Sea – and in the Environmental Code (specifically Articles 54, 56, 73, 104, 105 and 109).

Chapter 7. Mining

by *Alessandro Andronio*

§1. Legal Framework

577. The Italian legal system regulates mining activities in a complex and differentiated manner; the regime will, therefore, be examined only from the viewpoint of its most significant interactions with environmental protection.

578. The fundamental principles regarding mining activities are still those set forth in RD No. 1443 of 9 July 1927, 'Legislative norms regulating the research and exploitation of mines within the Kingdom'. On the basis of the 1927 RD, mining activities are subdivided into mines, mineral and thermal waters, quarries and peat bogs, depending on the materials extracted and independent of the systems used for the extractions. Article 2 provides, in fact, that the following belong to the category of mines:

(a) minerals that can be utilized for the extraction of metals, metalloids and their composites, even if said minerals are used directly;
(b) graphite, solid, liquid and gaseous fuels, asphalt and bituminous rocks;
(c) phosphates, alkaline and magnesium salts, alumite, mica, feldspar, china clay and bentonite, bleached earth, clay for porcelain and strong earthen-ware, earth having a fire-resistance level greater than 1630 degrees centigrade;
(d) precious stones, garnets, corundum, bauxite, leucite, magnesite, fluorine, barium and strontium minerals, talc, asbestos, cement marl, lithographic stones;
(e) radioactive substances, mineral and thermal waters, vapours and gas.

579. The following instead belong to the category of quarries:

(a) peat;
(b) materials for building, road and hydraulic constructions;
(c) coloured earth, ground fossils, quartz and siliceous sands, grindstones and whetstones;
(d) other materials that can be utilized by industry not included in the category of mines.

580. Mines, which include mineral and thermal waters in accordance with Article 2, paragraph 2, clause *e*, are subject to a permit regime since they do not belong to the owner of the ground, but are instead part of the non-transferable patrimony of the State or regions. Whereas a special permit is required for mining research activity, mining extractions or deviations of mineral and thermal waters require an exploitation permit (*see* Articles 4 et seq., RD No. 1443/1927; the public authority is responsible for carrying out the necessary controls over the research and exploitation activity).

581. Article 45 of RD No. 1443/1927 makes quarries and peat bogs available to the owner of the ground. When the owner does not exploit the quarries or peat bogs or does not adequately develop them, the public administration can establish a term for the initiation, resumption or intensification of the work. After such term has passed without any action being taken, the quarry or peat bog can be granted in concession by the State to third parties.

582. Prior to the 2001 constitutional reform, legislative and the administrative competence in matters regarding mines rested in general with the State (with the exception for mines located within some of the regions having a special charter), whereas the competence for quarries and peat bogs, as well as mineral and thermal waters, rested with the regions in accordance with the previous Article 117 of the Constitution. The new Article 117 of the Constitution does not mention mines, quarries and peat bogs, or mineral and thermal waters as being among the matters attributed to State legislative power or to concurrent regional legislative power. All mining activity must, therefore, be presumed to be attributed to the exclusive legislative power of the regions. Such legislative power has strong 'transversal' limitations, however, because the legislative regime on mining activities is also partially linked to 'environmental protection and protection of the ecosystem', set forth in Article 117, paragraph 2, clause *s* of the Constitution (*see* Constitutional Court, judgments No. 66 of 2018, No. 210 of 2016, No. 199 of 2014, No. 246 of 2013, No. 145 of 2013, No. 112 of 2011, No. 345 of 2010, and No. 108 of 2005), as well as the 'civil law regime' set forth in Article 117, paragraph 2, clause *l* of the Constitution (such as the public ownership of mines and private ownership of quarries) (*see* Constitutional Court, judgment No. 228 of 2016).

Specifically, by means of its judgment No. 67 of 2010, the Constitutional Court significantly limited regional legislative power, providing that extensions of authorizations to open mines provided by regional law damage environmental protection, because they do not allow an EIA. By means of its recent judgment No. 176 of 2018, the Constitutional Court specified that the exploitation of quarries is also within the scope of application of Directive 2006/123/EC, implemented by Legislative Decree No. 59 of 2010, since the object of those sources is 'any entrepreneurial or professional economic activity carried out without any subordination restriction, aimed at the exchange of goods or provision of other services' (Article 1, paragraph 1, of Legislative Decree No. 59 of 2010). The above provision regards the specific case in which the number of 'authorizations' – as even concessions are qualified, because they are formal acts that must be obtained by whoever provides the services from the competent authorities in order to carry out an activity (considering No. 39 and Article 4, paragraph 6, of Directive 2006/123/EC) – is limited due to the scarcity of natural resources or available technical skills. In other words, regional legislative power is subject to the 'transversal' limitation of State legislative power on the protection of competition (Article 117, second paragraph, clause *e*) of the Constitution; *see also* Constitutional Court, judgment No. 199 of 2014).

583. Most State administrative competence with respect to mines has been transferred to the regions, and mines are, therefore, subject to regional legislation.

With respect to the sector of mineral and thermal waters, the regions have approved laws, in compliance with the fundamental principles established by the State 'mine law', that provide detailed and differentiated regimes for research permits and exploitation permits regulating the relative activities and fees. Such regimes, even when they deviate in part from the general mining regime contained in the 'mine law', have been found not to conflict with the constitutional division of legislative competence between the State and the regions (Constitutional Court, judgment No. 65 of 2001).

With respect to quarrying and peat-bog extractions, in the lack of a more detailed State legislative regime, the legal systems of the different regions have autonomously provided for diverse planning regimes and authorization regimes. The common characteristics of such regimes are briefly as follows:

(a) Many regions have already prepared and adopted plans for mining activities which establish restrictions and limits on said activities in compliance with water basin and landscape plans, as well as in conformity with special restrictions such as hydrogeological restrictions. The location of quarries and peat bogs, perimeters of the areas involved, and the effective scope of the mining restrictions are, in practice, determined by urban planning instruments. The plans, generally differentiated on two levels (regional and provincial), also contain an estimate of the need for different materials and a general indication of environmental cleanup measures for abandoned quarries.
(b) In a planning context, quarries and peat bogs can only be exploited after appropriate authorization has been obtained; in some regions, authorization is also required for research activity. Such activities in the absence of authorization, or in a manner that does not conform to the relative authorization, constitute an administrative infraction, subject to different sanctions depending on the region (the regions cannot, however, establish criminal sanctions).

A special permit regime is provided for the marble quarries located in the municipalities of Massa and Carrara in Tuscany (Tuscan Regional Law No. 35 of 2015, which amended and integrated prior legislation).

§2. The Environment and Mining: Authorization and Permit Regime for Quarries and Peat Bogs

584. Case law and legal scholarship have examined for years the problem of whether the exploitation of a quarry or a peat-bog, in addition to any authorization that may be required by regional legislation, also requires a building permit, provided in general for the entire national territory by Law No. 47 of 28 February 1985, 'Norms on the control of urban-building construction work, sanctions, recovery and amnesty relative to construction' (currently transformed into 'building permits' by the Consolidated Act of Laws and Regulations on the Building Industry, Law No.

380 of 2001). Quarries currently represent one of the most important factors of environmental deterioration because their impact on the territory is even greater than that of building construction, often damaging areas that are valuable from a naturalistic standpoint.

585. On a substantive level, it is, therefore, inappropriate that quarrying is only subject to regional authorization regimes that provide weak administrative sanctions, rather than a building permit regime, thus, subjecting them to the criminal sanctions set forth in Article 44, clause *b* of DPR No. 380/2001, which punishes whoever performs work without a building permit, or does not comply with the requirements of the permit.

586. On a formal level, however, the strict equivalency of mining to building construction has raised for years the issue of an overly broad interpretation of the norm that establishes sanctions. The two conflicting orientations can be summarized as follows:

(1) Quarrying results in a change of the territorial structure, and, therefore, it also requires a building permit, as do all building activities in a strict sense (*see* Court of Cassation, section III, 29 December 1994, Michetti); the need for a building permit is confirmed by the fact that quarrying is considered the equivalent of building construction, including from a landscape standpoint, in that both activities, if performed in areas subject to landscape restrictions, require the relative authorization (Court of Cassation, section III, 21 January 1992, De Luca).

(b) 'No building permit has to be requested from the mayor in order to open and cultivate a quarry, therefore the crime set forth in Article 20, paragraph 1, clause (b), of Law No. 47 of 28 February 1985 does not occur' (Court of Cassation, United Sessions, 13 October 1993, Antonelli). This reconstruction has been confirmed in numerous other judgments (among which see, in particular, Court of Cassation, section III, 9 September 1996, Scacco), according to which quarrying is not part of urban planning activity, which is strictly related to developed areas within the territory, even if it must be performed in accordance with territorial planning instruments. This has become the prevalent orientation, even after the transformation of the building concession into a 'building permit' after the Consolidated Act of Laws and Regulations on the Building Industry, Law No. 380 of 2001 entered into effect (Council of State, section VI, judgment No. 4342 of 11 September 2008; Criminal Court of Cassation, judgment No. 39056 of 26 August 2008, Criminal Court of Cassation, judgment No. 33162 of 26 February 2013).

Part III. Zoning and Land Use Planning

by *Stefano Grassi*

§1. Introduction

587. The Italian territory has a conformation and natural beauty that renders it particularly fragile with respect to urban planning and building construction.

The central role that the legislative regime on construction activity and transformation of the territory plays is, therefore, evident.

It is not possible to illustrate all of the complex problems that are raised by the relationship between urban planning laws and the environmental protection regime. The urban planning regime has been the object of numerous legislative and judicial interventions in Italy, and, therefore, requires a complex and broad review which is autonomous with respect to a review of the environmental protection regime.

In addition, for some time, legal scholarship and legislation have acknowledged that the management of interests related to the control and use of the territory constitutes an essential part of the environmental protection regime.

This chapter will, therefore, be limited to summarily illustrating: (a) the manner in which Italian legislation has developed urban planning, inclusive of the regulation of the environmental interests connected to it; (b) the general norms that regulate land use; and (c) which parts of the urban planning regime are particularly related to the environmental protection regime (other chapters in this volume contain more detailed discussions of these topics).

§2. The Development of Urban Planning Laws

588. Urban planning laws have not had a linear development in Italy, and even at present they give rise to a complex and uncoordinated legal regime.

It should also be noted that urban planning issues are conditioned on two basic choices of the legal system: a 'land regime' (i.e., the regulation of property rights in areas utilized for urban development and building construction), and the restrictive and authoritarian regime that the State, regions and local entities can impose in order to achieve the public interests connected with the development of urban areas and the activities that have an effect on and which transform the territory.

589. The normative evolution has seen an increasingly broadened and differentiated expansion of the urban planning regime, intended to adapt property rights to collective interests in order to achieve a rational and organized use of the territory.

Before the entry into effect of the Constitution of 1948, Law No. 1150 of 1942 (the 'urban planning law', whose principles remain in effect), provided that each Municipality have a general regulatory plan for its entire territory. It therefore established that property owners had to comply, with respect to construction works in their areas, not only with the construction methods indicated in building regulations and hygiene regulations, but also with zoning restrictions (i.e., identification of the functions attributed to the single areas) defined by the general regulatory plan. During its initial stage, only a few municipalities prepared general regulatory plans. Only after the entry into effect of Law No. 765 of 1967 did almost all of the municipalities approve their own regulatory plans. The new law established, in fact, that territories of municipalities lacking a regulatory plan would have to apply stringent limits on building construction. Such reform also provided that each regulatory plan must identify urban planning standards (i.e., a specific quantity of areas to be used for infrastructures and public services: for example, parking lots, green areas, athletic facilities, etc.). It further provided that private parties could develop subdivision projects in areas of urban expansion, provided that they undertake by means of special conventions to carry out the necessary urbanization works. Subsequent legislation developed further institutes aimed at imposing limits and guidelines for building development throughout the municipal territory, both urban centres as well as agricultural areas (in particular, the principle was introduced whereby building permits can only be issued after payment of contributions commensurate with the impact the new construction will have on the urban planning costs that the Municipality will have to sustain).

The legislator has been assisted by the provision set forth in Article 42 of the 1948 Constitution according to which 'private property is recognized and guaranteed by the law, which determines the manner in which it can be purchased and enjoyed, and its relative limits in order to ensure its social function and render it accessible to everyone'.

For a lengthy period of time, including after the 1948 Constitution entered into effect, urban planning was perceived of in a restrictive manner as only referring to activities concerning the structure and building construction of urban centres (*see* the Constitutional Court, judgment No. 141 of 1972). It is, therefore, a system aimed at the rational organization of cities and road networks; an ordered distribution of public installations, green areas and sports facilities; as well as the supervision and protection of environmental and cultural resources located within urban centres.

The complex network of urban planning restrictions relative to urban centres, with the consequences that the interrelations between urban centres and agricultural or industrial areas provoke within a territory, and even more the attempt to uniform and render less unjust the consequences that urban planning restrictions caused to land owners, forms the basis of the expansion of the urban planning regime to include the management and transformation of the entire territory. This expansion is the heart of the reform introduced by Law No. 10 of 1977 (Article 1 includes in urban planning 'all activity that leads to urban and construction transformation of the municipal territory, which as such is obliged to participate in the related costs, with the subordination of the execution of the works to a permit from the local authority').

A much broader definition of urban planning is derived from this diverse formulation, which also includes environmental interests such as those set forth in Article 80 of DPR No. 616 of 1977, according to which administrative functions relating to urban planning 'concern the regulation of land use, including all cognitive, legal and managerial aspects regarding the protection and transformation of land, as well as environmental protection'.

On the basis of this premise, even the case law of the Constitutional Court (keeping in mind further legislative innovations, such as the principles regarding protected areas set forth in Law No. 394 of 1991), has recognized that urban planning includes everything that regards land use, including water pollution and waste disposal, and has held that laws that subordinate construction work involving property of landscape or environmental interest to particular forms of authorization are coherent with constitutional principles (as was the case, for example, with respect to legislation that granted an amnesty for violations of urban planning laws, but which excluded from such amnesty violations relating to property protected by environmental legislation).

590. Expansion of the definition of the urban planning regime developed, in particular, starting from the 1970s after the regions began to function: Article 117 of the Constitution attributes the regions with legislative and administrative competence in this subject matter. National legislation broadened the concept of urban planning, partly in consideration of the evolution and interpretation that regional laws gave to regulation of the interests involved in this area. It is not by chance that the most recent regime intended to complete the transfer of administrative competence from the State to the regions (Legislative Decree No. 112 of 1998) specifies that regional laws must attribute to urban planning instruments the value and effects of protection plans in the sectors of nature protection, environmental protection, and the safeguarding of water, the soil and natural beauty (Article 57). This confirms, therefore, the evolution of the urban planning regime to the inclusion of environmental interests within its scope.

591. Most recently (after the revision of the Title V, of the Constitution, by Constitutional Law No. 3 of 2001), 'building construction' and 'urban planning' are matters included in the concept of 'land use control' (*governo del territorio*). 'Land use control' is attributed to the legislative power of the regions, in the framework of the fundamental principles established by State legislation according to the provision of Article 117, third paragraph, Constitution (Constitutional Court, judgments No. 245 of 2018; No. 314 of 2012; No. 309 of 2011; No. 362 and No. 303 of 2003). The urban planning powers of Municipalities can be subject to general prevailing interests related to the realization of infrastructures and public works of national or regional competence, provided that they guarantee adequate forms of participation of the municipalities involved in procedures that condition their autonomy (*see* Constitutional Court, judgments No. 126 of 2018, No. 46 of 2004, No. 478 of 2002, No. 378 of 2000, No. 357 of 1998, No. 286 and No. 83 of 1997 and No. 61 of 1994).

Land use control is a sector of a legislative regime that differs from the regime on landscape protection and the regime on environmental protection. In trying to determine the regimes related to 'land use control', 'landscape' and 'environmental protection', coordination and collaboration issues have arisen between the State and the regions (the case law of the Constitutional Court has clarified, however, that the State has exclusive legislative power in determining the levels of environmental protection and regarding the protection of landscape resources, while the regions have legislative power to implement the State's principles of protection, by controlling urban planning and building construction: *see* judgments No. 367 and No. 378 of 2007; and No. 225 of 2009).

592. The building construction regime was collected in a Uniform Text contained in DPR No. 380 of 6 June 2001, while the regime on land ownership and related expropriations was collected in the Uniform Text contained in DPR No. 327 of 8 June 2001. National law defines the type of different categories of building works and the relative types of authorization (Constitutional Court, judgments No. 102 and No. 139 of 2013; No. 259 of 2014). The regional law can 'exemplify the building works that are within the scope of the national definitions, provided that such exemplification is consistent with the definitions contained in the Consolidated Act of Laws and Regulations on the Building Industry' (Constitutional Court, judgments No. 49 of 2016 and No. 68 of 2018).

§3. General Norms Regulating Land Use

593. The regulation of land use, notwithstanding the broad attribution of competence to regional legislation, is still formulated in accordance with the orientation of State legislation, going back to Law No. 1150 of 17 August 1942 which defines urban planning instruments, on which the entire legal regime in this area is still based. Subsequent laws (starting from Law No. 765 of 6 August 1967, through Law No. 10 of 28 January 1977) have confirmed the orientation of this urban planning regime, strengthening the instruments of mutual consent between public and private interests by means of forms of contracts or urban planning agreements, in which property owners are authorized to develop land on the condition that they realize or at least finance the urbanization works and public interest works that are indispensable for rational urban development. The extension of the scope of intervention of the urban planning regime has led to a necessary and gradual adjustment of building construction activity to the principles established by the most recent legislation, which has raised numerous controversies regarding 'construction amnesty' (a form of amnesty for infractions committed by anyone who performed construction work without the required authorizations: it is required due to the intense building development that took place in Italy between the end of the 1950s and the 1960s when urban planning provisions had barely evolved and were not largely respected. The controversies and difficulties relating to application of the regime derived and still derive from the fact that in most cases, the construction work seriously compromised the landscape, and amnesty legislation excludes automatic application of the amnesty to whoever has damaged Italy's environmental and landscape heritage by means of construction).

594. On the basis of the State regime, land use is regulated by a complex mechanism of planning instruments, which are developed according to a hierarchical system:

(a) territorial coordination plans at a regional or subregional or provincial level (which contain directives regarding areas to be reserved for special uses or in which particular restrictions or legal limitations must be enforced; said directives also identify the location of new building clusters or installations of particular importance, as well as the network of the major roadways, railroad lines, electrical lines and navigational paths;
(b) inter-municipal development plans (which are the coordination instrument of the plans prepared by outlying municipalities, whose urban planning problems are strictly and necessarily related);
(c) general development plans or construction programmes (which define the restrictions and urban uses of the municipal territory, essentially indicating the network of the principal roadways; the subdivision of the municipal territory into areas destined for the expansion of urban centres, defining the restrictions and prohibitions to be observed in building development; and identification of the areas to be destined for public use, special rights of way, the creation of public buildings or buildings open to the public or else of interest to society. The development plan must also contain the restrictions to be observed in areas of a historic nature (there are specific regimes for historic centres) or of an environmental or landscape nature;
(d) implementing plans (which regulate, by means of detailed restrictions, the development of determined portions of the municipal territory according to the principles and directives established by the general development plan: there are public initiative implementing plans, whose procedures correspond to those for the realization of works of public utility, and private initiative implementing plans, in which the urban planning regime is agreed upon by means of special agreements with the owners who intend to perform the building development; it also provides for numerous implementing plans having specific purposes, such as recovery plans, intended to implement the provisions of zoning plans in already developed areas that require urban and building restrictions; low-income building construction plans, intended to guarantee housing rights to workers and low-income citizens; and plans for manufacturing areas, which tend to regulate the development of industrial, artisan or commercial areas that require specific infrastructures).

595. The urban planning regime is completed by the verification that must be made by the administrative authority with respect to each construction project: building construction can, in fact, only be performed after a permit has been issued by the municipal authority, and is subordinated to both a monetary contribution and a contribution in works and to further conditions that might be imposed, with specific reference to a guarantee of the respect of environmental interests.

Competence with respect to the adoption of the plans is defined by State legislation and by regional implementing legislation. In particular, the general zoning plan must be approved both by the municipality whose territory is to be regulated, and by the region.

596. The region is responsible for defining the contents of the plan in such a way that it is adjusted to the restrictions imposed by national and regional legislation (in particular, the region can modify the zoning plan on its own initiative, including, and above all, in order to guarantee respect of environmental and landscape interests). The implementing plans are generally approved at a municipal level. In all cases, the procedures to approve the plans guarantee forms of active public participation both in regard to the approval procedure and with respect to definition of urban planning choices.

597. Law No. 10 of 1977 provides for multi-year implementation programmes for the general zoning plan, in order to control the development over time of construction work and related works within the territory. Such provision has not been sufficiently implemented, however, and has led to controversies that have been reflected in subsequent and several laws' reforms. In addition, the tendency has been to allow programming to be phased over time, including urban and territorial development. The most frequently adopted solution has been that of providing for phased building development and infrastructure work in the implementation plans (which usually remain in effect for a period of ten years).

§4. Sectoral Laws

598. Urban planning and land use regulation are affected by numerous provisions of sectoral laws which insert restrictions and obligations aimed at protecting specific public interests in a broader planning context.

The need for a global vision and coordination of the interests involved in land use planning have not yet found an efficient normative framework. Therefore, in addition to urban planning of a general nature, regulated in accordance with Law No. 1150 of 1942, there are several sectoral plans and regimes aimed at restricting or prohibiting, in part or totally, use of the land or the territory in relation to particular interests entitled to legal protection.

This normative technique refers in a specific manner and in the most frequent cases to the protection of environmental and landscape interests.

599. Individual sectoral plans and restrictions or absolute prohibitions of building development have been proclaimed in the various sectors of environmental regulation discussed elsewhere in this volume. The major sectoral plans, restrictions and absolute prohibitions relating to environmental protection are summarized below:

(a) Sectoral plans: landscape plans (which, in accordance with Law No. 1497 of 1939 and the more recent Law No. 431 of 1985 – currently substituted by the Code of Cultural Heritage and Landscape, Legislative Decree No. 42 of 22 January 2004 – regulate the manner in which works can be performed in declared sites of natural beauty); land reclamation plans and water basin plans (which are intended, in accordance with RD No. 215 of 1933 as well as by Law No. 183 of 1989 and by the subsequent Law No. 253 of 1990, to programme actions and use aimed at conserving, defending and enhancing the soil and the proper utilization of water in water basins; as well as programme the public and private works to be performed in areas in which lakes, swamps, swampland or land ruined from a hydrogeological or forestry viewpoint are located); programmes of limitations for military needs (which define, according to what is set forth first by Law No. 898 of 1976 and Law No. 104 of 1990 and later by Legislative Decree No. 66 of 15 March 2010 (Code of the Military System), the manner in which military easements are formulated and regulated); and plans for mining activity (provided by regional laws, in order to regulate the exploitation of quarries and peat bogs, with specific reference to activation of the indispensable infrastructures to provide access for mining and the transportation of materials).

(b) Restrictions: restrictions regarding sites of natural beauty deriving from Law No. 1497 of 1939, and from Article 1 of Law No. 431 of 1985 (which subjects to landscape restrictions coastlines, land bordering lakes, rivers, streams, watercourses, mountains, glaciers, parks, reserves, woodlands, forests and areas subject to civic uses), laws that have been substituted by the Code of Cultural Heritage and Landscape set forth in Legislative Decree No. 42 of 22 January 2004 (*cultural resources* are real and personal property having artistic, historic, archaeological, and ethno-anthropological value, or are of archive and bibliographical interest, or which the law specifies are the material evidence of civilization; *landscape resources* are real property and areas that are expressions of the historic, cultural, natural, morphological and aesthetic value of the territory and the other resources specified by the law), which establish principles of protection and the use of such resources.

(c) The Code of Cultural Heritage and Landscape (Legislative Decree No. 42 of 2004) establishes the fundamental points of reference for landscape planning, entrusted jointly to the State and the regions. Specifically, Article 135 of the Code establishes that the State and regions shall subject the territory to specific regulations on land use by means of 'landscape plans', i.e., urban planning-territorial plans that consider the landscape values involved. Such plans are prepared jointly by the ministry and the regions, with reference to buildings and areas that have been declared to be of significant public interest in accordance with Article 136 ('natural beauties'), areas that are protected directly by the law in accordance with Article 142 (the 'Galasso areas', as well as coastal areas, rivers, streams, parks) and, finally, further buildings and areas of significant public interest (Article 143, clause *d*) (Constitutional Court, judgment No. 66 of 2018). The landscape plan prevails over planning acts with territorial impact provided by sector regulations (Article 145, paragraph 3, of Legislative Decree No. 42 of

2004), because 'in the regime on transformations of the territory, landscape protection assumes a prevailing value' (Constitutional Court, judgment No. 11 of 2016).

(d) Other restrictions regard national and regional parks (Law No. 394 of 1991 and the laws creating individual parks); and restrictions deriving from maritime and military property of public domain; acoustic zoning plans (Law No. 447 of 26 October 1995); seismic classification plans; water basin plans and coastal management plans (Legislative Decree No. 152 of 2006), and forestry plans (RD No. 826 of 1923, that requires authorization for the transformation of woodlands to another kind of exploitation, or of uncultivated land into land subject to periodic cultivation),

(e) Absolute prohibitions (and, thus, the impossibility to utilize land without an authorization or permit) are those placed on land located near roads and highways, airports, watercourses, railroads, cemeteries, national monuments and water destined for human consumption. These are restrictions that only regulate the territory indirectly, because their primary objective is to protect public or public interest property, or the functions that such property performs.

§5. Conclusions

600. In conclusion, it can be noted that with particular reference to the development of the concept of urban planning (which includes the protection of nature, the environment, water, soil and natural beauty), the entire environmental protection regime, in particular, with respect to protection against pollution, constitutes a restriction and an objective of land use within the Italian legal system.

Part IV. Civil Liability and Criminal Liability

Chapter 1. Civil Liability Questions

by *Gianni Taddei*

§1. General Introduction

601. Law No. 349 of 8 July 1986 created the first Italian legislative regime on environmental damage. The need to adjust that regime to the principles established at a Community level subsequently led to various legislation, the most significant of which is Legislative Decree No. 152 of 3 April 2006, Part VI, which is specifically dedicated to 'protection by means of compensation for environmental damage'.

602. Additional norms on environmental damage were introduced by Article 2 of Law Decree No. 208 of 30 December 2008 (on 'global' settlement agreements for environmental damage and responsibility for remediation and environmental cleanup), and Law Decree No. 135 of 25 September 2009 (which substantially modified the criteria used to quantify environmental damages), by Law No. 97 of 6 August 2013, (whose Article 25 made further modifications, above all with respect to the quantification of damage), as well as Law No. 221 of 28 December 2015 (which introduced a specific case of 'settlement' regarding compensation for environmental damage and the restoration of sites of national interest).

§2. Directive 2004/35/EC

603. The creation of a homogeneous Community regime on liability for environmental damage was characterized by a lengthy and difficult bureaucratic process, beginning with the European Commission's White Book on Environmental Liability (published in 2000).

The liability regime for environmental damage is currently based on the guidelines established by Directive 2004/35/EC of 21 April 2004 *Environmental liability with regard to the prevention and remedying of environmental damage* (published in the *Official Journal of the European Union*, No. 143 of 20 April 2004).

Article 19, paragraph 2, first clause of the Directive implements TFUE on environmental pollution, which, as is known, established that: 'the environmental policy of the European Union aims at a high level of protection, considering the diverse situations in the various regions of the European Union. It is based on the principles of precaution and preventive action, the principle of remediation, on a primary basis at the source, of damage caused to the environment, as well as the principle "the polluter pays"'.

The directive, which should have been implemented by Member States within 30 April 2007, essentially creates a sole regime for the prevention and remediation of environmental damage. The 30 April 2007 deadline also represents the initial date that the new liability regime became effective (Article 17 of the Directive provides that it does not apply to damage that occurred prior to such date or which, even though it occurred subsequent to 30 April 2007, derives from an activity that was previously carried out or completed).

The new directive dictates an extremely detailed liability regime for environmental damage. In particular, the directive establishes a threshold of significant environmental damage (the damage must be 'measurable and significant'), specifies the environmental resources entitled to protection, and identifies the actions to prevent and remedy environmental damage.

Annex II of the directive, with respect to the remediation of damage to water, protected species and protected natural habitat provides that the remedying of environmental damage be achieved by restoring the damaged environment to its original condition through measures of primary, complementary and compensatory remediation ('primary' remediation means any remediation measure that restores the damaged natural resource and/or services to or towards their baseline conditions; 'complementary' remediation means any remedial measure taken in relation to natural resources and/or services to offset the failure to completely restore the damaged natural resources and/or services; 'compensatory remediation' means any action to offset the temporary loss of natural resources and/or services from the date the damage occurs through the date when the primary remediation has achieved its full effect).

On a subjective level, the directive introduces objective liability, even in the absence of fault or negligence, in the case of environmental damage caused by certain specific 'professional activities'. The directive also extends environmental liability to other professional activities 'in the case of the operator's fault or negligence' resulting in damage to 'natural habitats or protected species' (Article 3). All operators liable for damages must assume 'the costs of preventive and remedial actions' (Article 8).

The principle of environmental liability, even without fault or negligence, is applied to activities included in a list of potentially polluting sectors prepared by the Member States of the EU (including, among others, the energy sector, refineries, coke ovens, chemical activities, mining, metal production and processing and waste management).

§3. Environmental Damage in the Italian Legal System: Article 18 of Law No. 349 of 1986

604. Prior to approval of Law No. 349 of 1986, case law referred to an 'environmental right', determined to be advantageous to society as a whole.

During the 1970s, the Court of Auditors (*Corte dei Conti*) continued the protection of environmental resources by qualifying the environment as a public resource. The exclusive competence of the Court of Auditors with respect to environmental damage was coherently based on this qualification, understood as pure and simple damage to the State treasury. The Constitutional Court confirmed, however, in judgment No. 641 of 1987 that ordinary courts have jurisdiction in matters regarding environmental damage, as the courts entrusted with protecting individual rights.

605. The perspective effectively changed on a systematic level after the Italian legislator intervened in 1986. Article 18 of Law No. 349 of 1986 establishes the right to compensatory damages for environmental damage independent of the violation of other individual rights, not in view of protecting a healthy environment but rather as protection of the environment as such.

With regard to the liability model dictated by Law No. 349 of 1986, the Italian legislator chose an intermediary route between the solution offered by the fundamental norm of the Civil Code on extra-contractual civil liability (Article 2043, a true general liability clause of the Italian legal system), and other solutions based on the polluter's strict liability.

The liability regime contained in Article 18 of Law No. 349 of 1986 is clearly based on the fundamental branch of tort liability, which is a form of liability based on fault: the beginning of the first paragraph of Article 18 ('any intentional or negligent act') intentionally corresponds precisely with Article 2043 of the Civil Code ('any intentional or negligent act that results in unjust damage to others obliges whoever who has committed the act to compensate the damage'). The Constitutional Court has confirmed that the liability for environmental damage established by Article 18 'is properly inserted within the scope and scheme of civil liability' (judgment No. 641 of 1987). Such court noted, however, that the 'type of civil liability' delineated by Article 2043 'can assume preventive and penalty functions over time', thereby allowing 'not only the reintegration of the damaged subject's assets, but also the prevention of the tort and the provision of penalties' (judgment No. 641, *supra*).

Article 18's provisions on the quantification of environmental damage leave broad interpretative space to the courts. The court has to order 'when possible, restoration of the status of the places involved at the transgressor's expense' (paragraph 8). When restoration is not materially possible, the court must determine the 'precise quantification' of the damage; and when even the 'precise quantification' of the damage is impossible, the court (paragraph 6) must determine the amount of environmental compensatory damages 'in equity'.

The criteria for quantifying damages provided by Article 18 for this type of equitable payment are, however, rather unique: the gravity of the transgressor's fault (which is a criminal law criteria that is substantially indeterminate, in line, however, with the indeterminate nature of the value of the environment); the transgressor's profit (a new criterion, difficult to define economically); and the cost of remediation (a contradictory criterion, since the quantification of damages in equity rather than at law presumes that it is impossible to establish in advance the cost to remedy the situation).

There have been rare and non-homogeneous judgments regarding the quantification of damages based on Article 18 ever since 1986. In effect, the distinctiveness of the criteria used to quantify environmental damage contained in Article 18 has also led to questioning the admissibility of 'punitive' environmental damages. The reference to substantially criminal law criteria, such as the degree of gravity of the fault and the need to consider the profit obtained by the transgressor, could technically result in a court order for compensatory damages that might actually exceed the environmental damage effectively provoked. In practice, however, the possibility that a court would order the payment of punitive damages is doubtful, since Article 18 of Law No. 349 requires the 'precise quantification of damages' as the first parameter for compensation.

The issue of penalties for having caused environmental damage has, however, had another consequence: the possibility of finding that environmental damage exists as such based on the simple violation of environmental protection laws, even without concrete damage to an environmental resource. This well-known theory, which has even been upheld by some courts, argues that even when the offence is 'formal' (e.g., the lack of authorization), the offender should, nevertheless, be required to pay compensatory damages, even if no specific or concrete deterioration of environmental resources can be objectively measured.

§4. Norms on Environmental Damage Set Forth in Part VI of Legislative Decree No. 152 of 2006

606. Legislative Decree No. 152 of 2006 implements Community Directive 35/2004/EC. It introduces new provisions on environmental damage, and cancels the pre-existing regime set forth in Article 18 of Law No. 349 of 1986.

Article 311, paragraph 2, which compares environmental damage to a 'tort' due to violation of laws or technical regulations, again places environmental liability within the classic liability model, punishing the violation of individual rights based on intentional misconduct.

607. Legislative Decree No. 152 of 2006 is definitely based on a 'centralized vision'. The Ministry of the Environment is primarily responsible for environmental protection. This is clear with respect to the issue of who has standing to bring an action seeking compensation for environmental damage. The repeal of Article 18 of Law No. 349/1986, contained in Article 318, paragraph 2, appears to formally restrain local entities from taking such action. The pre-existing form of concurrent standing for local entities has been substituted by the simple possibility for the regions, provinces and local entities to 'request State intervention' (Article 309, paragraph 1). The Ministry of the Environment evaluates these 'requests' for intervention and 'immediately informs' the subjects entitled to make such 'request'.

By means of judgment No. 126 of 1 June 2016, the Constitutional Court held that the constitutional challenge to the provisions of Legislative Decree No. 152 of 2016 that only recognize that the State has the standing to sue for the compensation of environmental damage was groundless because, in the court's opinion, such reservation of power is justified based on the need to guarantee the uniform nature of the management of the 'environmental' asset.

The right to request State intervention is granted (by Article 309, paragraph 1) to individuals or legal entities 'that are or which could be affected by environmental damage or which have an interest that entitles them to participate in proceedings relating to the adoption of precautionary, preventive or remedial measures', in accordance with Part VI of Legislative Decree No. 152 of 2006.

608. The definition of environmental damage (Article 300) consists of a general definition ('environmental damage is any significant and measurable deterioration, direct or indirect, of a natural resource or of its usefulness') (paragraph 1), and a series of particular cases, which have, however, the defect of providing different parameters for defining environmental damage (damage to species and natural habitats, as well as to inland waters and waters of the territorial seas, consists of simple 'deterioration', damage to inland waters presumes a reference to 'acts that have significantly adverse effects on the ecological, chemical and/or quantitative status or ecological potential of the waters concerned'; 'or to the environmental status of the marine water concerned (clause *b*, no. 2); damage to land presumes a 'significant risk of adverse effects, including indirect effects, on human health'.

On a practical level, it is clearly difficult to distinguish between acts that cause damage, which tend to 'blur' into simple, dangerous acts, from violation of the principle of certainty and specificity of the cause of damage.

609. The subjective qualification of liability for environmental damage represents one of the greatest problems the interpreter faces. In its original version, Legislative Decree No. 152/2006 provided for the negligent nature of liability for environmental damage, while Article 311, paragraph 2, linked environmental damage to the commission of a tort.

The latter norm was, however, modified by Article 5*bis*, paragraph 1, clause *a* of Law Decree No. 135 of 2009 and subsequently by Article 25, paragraph 1, clause *g* of Law No. 97 of 2013. In its current version, Article 311, paragraph 2 – using the analogous formulation of Article 298*bis* – imposes the obligation of adopting the necessary remediation measures by operators of the 'named' professional activities that are specified, based on a presumed criteria of hazardousness, set forth in Annex 5 to Legislative Decree No. 152 of 2006 and, in general, to 'anyone else who causes environmental damage negligently or maliciously'. Subjectively, Legislative Decree No. 152 of 2006 now fully implements the principle, established by Directive 2006/35/EC, of objective liability for activities considered to be of greater risk of environmental impact. With respect to 'unnamed' activities, the criteria remain that of the classic model of liability for negligence.

The legal framework does not allow the subject responsible for the environmental damage to be determined on the basis of the relationship existing between a specific party and the 'polluted resource', even in cases of objective liability. There is legal scholarship and case law, however, that vice-versa theorizes liability for environmental damage 'due to possession', based on the simple relationship between possession (or detention) and the polluted resource.

By means of two fundamental judgments on 9 March 2010 (issued in case C-378/08 and in the united cases C-379/08 and C-380/08), the Court of Justice of the EU provided important clarifications on the crucial issue of the proper determination of liability for environmental damage. Specifically, the court indicates the fundamental principles to be applied with respect to environmental damage (the search for the actual responsible party, on the basis of an ascertained causal connection between event and damage), and modification by the administration of reparatory measures already decided (an actual proceeding with the parties who are potentially liable).

The specific significance of the 'requirement of a causal connection between the operator's activity and the environmental damage' for purposes of applying the principle 'the polluter pays' was expressly emphasized by the ECJ even in its subsequent judgment of 4 March 2015 (issued in case C-534/13).

In judgment 13 July 2017 (issued in case C-129/16), the ECJ appears, however, to accept the argument that, independent from the causal connection, even the owners of the polluted site can be held liable jointly with the users of such site.

A recent judgment of the Italian Administrative Court (T.A.R. of Emilia Romagna, No. 125/2017) confirmed that the actual subject responsible for the pollution must bear the costs of remediation, unless a causal connection between the conduct of the owner of the polluted site and the contamination has been demonstrated. The cited judgment No. 125/2017, however, links liability for environmental damage to 'grave, precise and consistent evidence', which can also be inferred from the proximity of the facility to the pollution found 'certainly not understood as contiguity, but rather as belonging to the same area and with a distance that would allow the spillage'.

At a procedural level, Articles 311–316 of Legislative Decree No. 152 of 2006 design a binary system based on the alternative between legal proceedings (civil or criminal) and administrative proceedings, by means of the adoption of ordinances regarding damages. The two options are alternatives, as Article 315 provides that 'the Ministry of the Environment, Land and Sea that has adopted an ordinance in conformity with Article 313 cannot initiate or continue proceedings seeking compensation for environmental damage, unless it intervenes as the victim of a crime in criminal proceedings'.

610. With respect to the quantification of environmental damage, Article 311, paragraph 2 of Legislative Decree No. 152 of 2006 currently provides that the 'remedial measure' must to be accomplished 'within the congruous term' set forth in Article 314, paragraph 2 of Legislative Decree No. 152 of 2006 (not less than two months and no greater than two years, except for a justified extension in consideration of the work to be done).

When the adoption of the above remedial measure is lacking in all or in part, or is incomplete or differs from the prescribed terms and procedures, the Minister of the Environment will determine the cost of the necessary activities to completely and correctly implement it, and shall act with respect to the offender to obtain the payment of the equivalent damages. Article 311, paragraph 3, refers to a future decree of the Ministry of the Environment (not yet issued) to determine the 'criteria' and 'methods, including monetary assessment', to identify the scope of the complementary and compensatory remedial measures (this is not a novelty: Article 299, paragraph 5, of Legislative Decree No. 152 of 2006 provided for the adoption of a DM that was never issued, to establish the 'criteria for preliminary activity to assess environmental damage and to recover the amount due for an equivalent monetary value'). Such 'criteria' and 'methods' are 'also applicable to pending proceedings where a final judgment has not yet been issued' as of the date the DM set forth in Article 311, paragraph 3, enters into effect.

611. Article 5*bis* of Law Decree No. 135 of 2009 also reintroduced a principle that was contained in Article 18 of Law No. 349 of 1986: liability is not joint in environmental matters but is several, 'to the extent of the offender's personal liability'. The principle, as clarified by the Court of Cassation in judgment No. 14935 of 20 July 2016, serves to avoid liability for the acts of others.

612. There are numerous exclusions regarding the norms of Part VI of Legislative Decree No. 152 of 2006.

According to Article 303, Part VI of Decree No. 152/2006:

(a) does not apply to environmental damage or an imminent threat of such damage caused by:
    (i) armed conflicts, sabotage, hostilities, civil war or insurrection;
    (ii) natural phenomena that are exceptional, inevitable and uncontrollable;
(b) does not apply to environmental damage or to an imminent threat of such damage provoked by an incident in respect of which liability or compensation falls within the scope of application of any of the International Conventions listed in Annex 1 of Part VI of this decree to which the Republic of Italy has adhered;
(c) does not prejudice the operator's right to limit his liability in conformity with national legislation implementing the Convention on the Limitation of Liability for Maritime Claims, 1976, or the Strasbourg Convention on the Limitation of Liability in Inland Navigation, 1988;
(d) neither applies to nuclear risks relative to the environment nor to the imminent threat of such damage caused by disciplinary actions regulated by the Treaty establishing the European Atomic Energy Community, or caused by an accident or activity in respect of which liability or compensation falls within the scope of application of any of the international instruments listed in Annex 2 to Part VI of this decree;
(e) does not apply to activities carried out in conditions of necessity, whose exclusive purpose is national defence, international security or protection from natural disasters;
(f) does not apply to damage caused by an emission, event or incident that occurred prior to the date Part VI of this decree entered into effect;

(g) does not apply to damages in relation to which more than thirty years have passed from the emission, event or incident that caused them;
(h) does not apply to environmental damage or to an imminent threat of such damage caused by pollution of a diffused nature, if it is not possible to establish a causal connection between the damage and the activities of individual operators.

The exclusions set forth in clauses *b–h* were taken from Directive 2004/35/EC.

§5. Environmental Damage and Remediation

613. The concept of environmental damage must be coordinated with that of remediation (*see* the specific chapter on the concept of remediation).

It is sufficient to note with regard to this issue that in the current legal framework, environmental damage is subject to two different regimes: one of a general nature relating to compensation for environmental damage (introduced for the first time by Law No. 349 of 1986 and currently regulated in Part VI of Legislative Decree No. 152 of 2006); and another of a special nature relating to the remediation of contaminated sites (introduced by Legislative Decree No. 22 of 1997 and currently set forth in Part IV of Legislative Decree No. 152 of 2006).

The classic and fundamental distinction between the payment of compensatory damages in a specific form and equivalent damages raised by Article 2058 of the Civil Code is translated, in the sector of environmental protection, into a distinction between remediation and the payment of compensation for environmental damage.

In general, remediation is the restoration method for contaminated environmental resources, if there is a risk of harmful effects on human health; compensation for environmental damage is compensation for the damage caused to the environmental resource (or to the value ensured by such resource).

This reconstruction – unquestionably valid in relation to the first Italian law on environmental damage, Law No. 349 of 1986 – must however be reviewed, in consideration of the subsequent legislative modifications. Directive 2004/35/EC radically modified at a European level the approach to environmental damage, excluding any monetary compensation and only providing for compensation for environmental damage through 'remedial measures'. In 2008 the European Commission started an infraction procedure against Italy, precisely because various provisions of Legislative Decree 152/2006 allow the remedial measures to be substituted by the payment of a monetary equivalent (as stated in the notice of contestation of the European Commission to the Italian Government on 31 January 2008).

To overcome this infraction procedure, in 2009 the Italian legislator issued Article 5*bis* of Law Decree No. 135 of 2009, which imposed the obligation of compensation for environmental damage primarily by means of remediation ('primary remediation') or, in the lack thereof with 'complementary' and 'compensatory' remedial measures. Further, compensation by monetary equivalent was only admissible if the remedial measure is lacking in all or in part, impossible or excessively costly or implemented in an incomplete manner or which does not conform to what is required.

In 2012 the European Commission has again charged that Italy 'adopted and maintained laws (Articles 311, 313, paragraph 2, and 314, paragraph 3, of Legislative Decree 52/2006), which allow remedial measures to be substituted by monetary compensation, in violation of Articles 1 and 7 and Annex II of Directive 2004/35/EC' (*see* the justified opinion of the European Commission of 26 January 2012).

This led to the decision of the Italian legislator to again modify – by means of Article 25 of Law No. 97 of 2013 – the regime on the quantification of environmental damage, providing in Article 311, paragraphs 2 and 3 of Legislative Decree 152/2006 that 'when environmental damage occurs' the responsible operators are obligated to adopt the remedial measures set forth in Annex 3 of such Part VI (i.e., 'primary', 'complementary' and 'compensatory remedial measures'); only if the remedial measures for environmental damage are lacking in all or in part or have been implemented in an incomplete manner or different from what is prescribed, the Ministry of the Environment can request the transgressors to pay the 'costs' of the activities required to perform the remedial measures that are lacking or which were implemented in an incomplete or incompatible manner.

Such 'costs' are, however, not compensation for monetary equivalent, but only the monetary 'translation' of implementation of the remedial measures adopted by the administration.

The Court of Cassation, in the recent judgment No. 14935 of 20 July 2016, confirmed that currently environmental damage cannot in any case be compensated by 'monetary equivalent'.

The fact that at present compensation for environmental damage is based on the adoption of remedial measures, rather than on forms of restoration for monetary equivalent, results in the tendency that the regime on environmental damage is based on the adoption of remedial measures, rather than on forms of remediation for monetary equivalent, which results in the regime on environmental damage bending with the regime on remediation, following the approach of Directive No. 2004/35/EC.

An issue to be raised is whether, given the strong conceptual commingling that results in the boundary between remediation and compensation being blurred, the distinction between the two legal instruments remains relevant. It would therefore be useful to have, even at a national level, a uniform regime on remediation and environmental damage, in line with the sole Community source on this issue (Directive 2004/35/EC).

§6. Settlement Agreements and Environmental Damage

614. In a consultative opinion issued 18 May 2001, the Council of State confirmed the possibility of a settlement agreement whose object regards proceedings for environmental damage in accordance with Article 18 of Law No. 349 of 1896 'as long as the State is the subject entitled under substantive law to receive compensation for such damage'. In the Council of State's opinion, the fundamental consideration is that the environmental controversy must not regard the potential, future alteration of the environment *in pejus*, but only a civil action seeking compensatory damages based on a tort that has already been committed.

615. In 2003, the Court of Auditors also dealt with the issue of settlement agreements regarding environmental compensation. In the judgment issued 15 January 2003 by its central control section, the court found settlements regarding compensation for environmental damage to be 'within the scope of competence of the political-administrative leadership'.

616. Article 2 of Law Decree No. 208 of 30 December 2008 (converted by Law No. 13 of 27 February 2009), specifically introduced the possibility of 'global' settlements in the legal system that regard remediation, restoration and compensatory environmental damages, which could be stipulated by the companies involved on the basis of a framework contract approved by the administration following an extremely detailed procedure.

Article 306*bis* of Legislative Decree No. 152/2006 – introduced by Article 31, paragraph 1, of Law No. 221 of 28 December 2015 – currently provides for a new settlement regime related to the pollution of sites of national interest. Specifically, the party subject to remediation procedures or actions for environmental damage can formulate a 'settlement proposal' which:

(a) identifies the primary, complementary and compensatory remedial measures;
(b) if formulated for compensatory restoration, it considers the time required to achieve the objective of primary remediation or of primary and complementary remediation;
(c) if the resource-resource and service-service criteria are not applicable with respect to determining the complementary and compensatory measures, it includes compensation for the damage by means of an economic assessment;
(d) it nevertheless provides for a monitoring and control plan if the impossibility of primary remediation corresponds to residual pollution resulting in a risk to health and the environment;
(e) it contemplates remediation activities that have already been approved and implemented;
(f) in the case of the joint liability of various parties for having caused the damage and in remediation obligations, it can be formulated just by some of them with reference to the entire obligation, without prejudice to the right of recourse against the other transgressors;
(g) it contains an indication of suitable financial guarantees.

§7. Insurance and Environmental Damage

617. The possibility to insure environmental damage by means of a third-party liability policy has remained an outstanding issue.

The primary problem regards the difficulty of applying normal insurance techniques to environmental damage, due to the penalty component that characterizes compensation (which is not considered to be insurable). In addition to the penalty component, another obstacle exists – at least in view of the regime set forth in Article 18 of Law No. 349 of 1986 – due to the possibility of compensation determined in equity, or even punitive damages, for the environmental damage. This is the reason why the international markets felt that damage caused by pollution was uninsurable until the 1970s. Coherently with this orientation, normal third-party liability policies explicitly excluded such risk from coverage.

A pollution pool was established in 1980, which reassured the insurance companies. The pool's activity is based on a risk-selection procedure and a specific contractual instrument, structured in such a way as to provide the insurer with a precise picture of the insured risk. The policy is stipulated after a questionnaire has been compiled. Legislative Decree No. 152 of 2006 and Directive 2004/35/EC do not mention third-party liability insurance for environmental damage.

In general, this instrument is not yet widespread at a business level.

§8. Criminal Liability for Environmental Damage

618. This chapter is dedicated to civil liability for environmental damage, but for completeness it is opportune to note the significance that environmental liability can assume in criminal law as well.

It is known that in Italy environmental criminal law is late with respect to other European countries and is substantially developing through case law.

The situation changed, however, with Law No. 68 of 22 May 2015, which introduced in the Second Book of the Criminal Code the new section VI*bis*, which is entirely dedicated to 'environmental crimes'.

It is interesting to note that the new group of provisions dedicated to safeguarding environmental resources is modelled, even from a terminology standpoint, on concepts originating from Directive 2004/35 (e.g., the crime of environmental pollution, provided by Article 452*bis* of the Criminal Code which punishes whoever causes 'the compromising or significant and measurable deterioration' of the environmental resource).

Chapter 2. Environmental Crimes

by *Alessandro Andronio*

§1. European Union law

619. Criminal penalties in the field of environmental law were initially contained in the individual sector laws and later incorporated in Legislative Decree No. 152 of 2006, which collected them and kept the prior sectoral division without creating an organic regime. In May 2015, the Parliament finally approved a reform of environmental criminal law (Law No. 68 of 22 May 2015), which represents an initial attempt to establish the general principles and aggregate rules.

The law does not expressly refer to EU law, but in substance is linked to the requirements set forth in Directive 2008/99/EC of 19 November 2008 on the protection of the environment through criminal law (already partially implemented by Legislative Decree No. 121 of 7 July 2011).

Recital No. 5 of the Directive specifies that 'harmful activities, which typically cause or are likely to cause substantial damage to the air, including the stratosphere, to soil, water, animals or plants, including to the conservation of species' require criminal penalties with greater dissuasive power. Article 2 defines as 'unlawful' whatever infringes: (1) legislative acts adopted pursuant to the EC Treaty and listed in Annex A; or, (2) with regard to activities covered by the Euratom Treaty, the legislation adopted pursuant to the Euratom Treaty and listed in Annex B; or (3) a law, an administrative regulation of a Member State or a decision taken by a competent authority of a Member State that gives effect to the Community legislation referred to in the above clauses. Article 3 lists, by category of offences, which unlawful acts require a criminal penalty when they are committed intentionally or at least with serious negligence. The entire legislation is also based on principles of effectiveness, proportionality and deterrence (Articles 5 and 7), as well as the principle of the liability of legal entities for acts committed to their benefit (Articles 6 and 7).

These are very general indications, which necessitated, at the time of implementation in national law, a level of specification that complies with constitutional principles of legality and the level of offensiveness which governs Italian criminal law. Nevertheless, the national legislator has not always followed criteria of clarity and precision in drafting the relevant legislation.

§2. Law No. 68 of 22 May 2015

620. Law No. 68 of 2015 (provisions on environmental crimes), responds to the need to introduce an adequate response in the legal system to the criminal phenomena of large-scale pollution of the ecosystem, which has a general nature and is not limited to one or just a few sectors. Specifically, it creates two main new crimes (environmental pollution and environmental disaster), accompanied by other criminal provisions necessary for the overall success of the system and by rules on the relationship with the regime on the liability of legal entities. The law makes significant changes both to the Italian Criminal Code as well as to Legislative Decree No. 152/2006 (environmental provisions).

With respect to changes made to the Italian Criminal Code, the most significant is the introduction of a new section dedicated to environmental crimes, inserted in VI*bis*, immediately after the section on crimes against public safety. Five new crimes are introduced: in addition to environmental pollution (Article 452*bis*, aggravated in accordance with the following article when the pollution results in deaths or injuries) and environmental disaster (Article 452*quater*), which is also punishable based on negligence (Article 452*quinquies*), they are: the trafficking and abandonment of highly radioactive material (Article 432*sexies*), the prevention of controls (Article 452*septies*) and the failure to implement remedial measures (Article 452*terdecies*). Further, new aggravating circumstances have been introduced: the first (Article 452*octies*) relates to the associative offences referred to in Articles 416 and 416*bis*; while the other (Article 452*novies*, 'aggravating environmental circumstance'), is applicable when an act considered to be a criminal offence is committed for the purpose of committing one or more of the crimes provided for in the section. Article 452*decies* contains the regime on the 'voluntary payment of a penalty'; Article 452*undecies* introduces a new case of mandatory confiscation and equivalent measures; Article 452*duodecies* governs the compensatory measure of restoring damaged places to their original condition. The Italian Criminal Code, in addition to the new section, also contains provisions regarding the new crimes: the doubling of the terms of the statute of limitations (modification of Article 157, sixth paragraph, of the Italian Criminal Code); and the application of the ancillary penalty of the prohibition against negotiating contracts with the public administration (modification of Article 32*quater* of the Italian Criminal Code). It also provides for the application to environmental crimes of the regime on the liability deriving from crimes committed by legal entities, modifying Article 25*undecies* of Legislative Decree 231/2001.

Second, the law intervenes with respect to Legislative Decree No. 152 of 2006, adding a new part VI*bis* which contains the 'sanctions regime on administrative and criminal offences in the field of environmental protection'. The amendment introduces – for the offences already provided by the consolidated text related to the various areas of protection, and therefore not for the newly introduced offences which have the nature of a crime – the specific possibility of settling the offence when the requirements ordered by the competent supervisory bodies have been fulfilled. The new regime is modelled after the one on the settlement of offences regarding occupational safety contained in Articles 20 et seq. of Legislative Decree No. 281/2008.

§3. The Crime of Environmental Pollution

621. The first paragraph of the new Article 452*bis* of the Italian Criminal Code punishes with detention (ranging from two to six years) and a fine (ranging from

EUR 10,000 to EUR 100,000) anyone who wrongfully causes significant and measurable impairment or deterioration: (1) to water or air, or extensive or significant portions of soil or subsoil; (2) of an ecosystem, biodiversity – including agrarian, flora or fauna.

Different from the offences already in effect in the various areas of environmental protection, the provision does not follow the model of an offence based on polluting activity in the absence of authorization or the exceeding of limit values, but provides for a crime consisting of an event and damage, in which the damage consists of the significant and measurable impairment or deterioration of the above indicated environmental assets. The crime, which involves 'unrestricted conduct', can also be committed as an omission, i.e., the failure to prevent the event by whoever has specific obligations of prevention. The provision does not expressly refer to environmental pollution beyond its title, because it provides for a crime involving any conduct resulting in the occurrence of an event, i.e., the crime is not a specific act or omission but is the result of the act or omission. The conduct that causes the damage may therefore be different than the conduct deriving from the general definition of pollution set forth in Article 5 of Legislative Decree No. 152 of 2006, which refers to 'the direct or indirect introduction, following human activity, of substances, vibrations, heat or noise, or more generally of physical or chemical agents, in the air, water or soil which could harm human health or the quality of the environment, cause the deterioration of material goods, or damage or disturb the recreational value of the environment or other legitimate uses of it'.

With reference to the requirements of 'significance' and 'measurability', the first indicates clear evidence of pollution due to its scope, while the latter refers to the need for an objective possibility of quantification, both with reference to the environmental matrices that have been 'attacked' as well as the scientific parameters (biological, chemical, organic, naturalistic, etc.) of the alteration. The concept of 'significant' and 'measurable' impairment or deterioration reproduces the definition of environmental damage set forth in Article 300 of Legislative Decree No. 152 of 2006 ('any significant and measurable, direct or indirect, deterioration of a natural resource or of its usefulness') as well as the Community concept of 'environmental damage' established by Directive 2004/35/EC, which uses the expression 'measurable adverse change in a natural resource or measurable impairment of a natural resource service, which may occur directly or indirectly'. It follows that the criminal standard punishes polluting activities that do more than merely exceed risk thresholds or limit values, but which do not amount to those irreversible or particularly onerous modifications of the ecosystem that constitute the more serious crime of environmental disaster.

The object of the crime identified by the incriminating standard can be, severally: water, air, extensive or significant portions of the soil or subsoil, an ecosystem, or biodiversity. The provision does not contain a definition of 'ecosystem', so it is necessary to refer to the common meaning, according to which the ecosystem is 'the entirety of living organisms (community), the surrounding physical environment (habitat) and the biotic and chemical-physical relationships within a specific space of the biosphere'. It is significant that, to avoid interpretative uncertainties, the legislator referred to 'an ecosystem' and not to 'the ecosystem in general', with the result that the crime can also consist of aggression to an individual, isolated environment.

The major interpretative problems derive from the use of the adverb 'abusively', which outlines criminally liable conduct, excluding conduct not performed in breach of the legal provisions. While on the one hand the problem arises as to whether the crime exists in the case of the infringement not of specific provisions, but of general principles (e.g., those of precaution, prevention, etc., set forth in Article 3*ter* of Legislative Decree No. 152 of 2006), or of the requirements contained in administrative permits not strictly functional to environmental protection (but, for example, to protect landscape, health or urban planning). On the other hand, the measure can be interpreted to refer just to the case of unauthorized conduct in that it is *sine titulo*, with the exclusion, therefore, of all situations where it is possible to find a formal authorization to carry out the activity from which the significant environmental alteration derives. The latter interpretation, however, conflicts with the established case law of the Court of Cassation, which affirms that the abusive situation includes not only acts carried out in the absence of the prescribed authorizations or on the basis of expired authorizations, or which are blatantly unlawful or in any case which are clearly disproportionate to the type of activity required, but also those that violate State or regional laws – even if not strictly relevant to the environmental sector – or administrative requirements. Constitutional case law thus interprets the adverb 'abusively' as referring to all activities that do not comply with the precise standards in the sector of waste collection and disposal (Criminal Court of Cassation, section III, judgment No. 46170 of 21 of September 2016; judgment No. 15865 of 21 January 2017).

The second paragraph of Article 452*bis* provides an aggravating circumstance in the case of pollution of protected areas or damage to protected animal and vegetable species, which operates according to the general mechanism provided by Article 64 of the Italian Criminal Code, with an increase of the penalty by up to one-third. The generic reference to 'protected' species must be integrated with the specification provided by Annex IV to Directive 92/43/EC (on the conservation of natural and semi-natural habitats and of wild fauna and flora) and Annex 1 of Directive 2009/147/EC (on the conservation of wild birds), even though not expressly referred to by the criminal provision.

§4. The Crime of Death or Injury As an Unwanted Consequence of the Crime of Environmental Pollution

622. The new Article 452*ter* of the Italian Criminal Code regards the case of death or serious injury to one or more persons, deriving from the unwanted consequence of the crime of environmental pollution, modelled after Articles 586 and 589 of the Italian Criminal Code. The provision provides an articulated list of graduated penalties based on the seriousness of the consequences of the crime punished by the previous article, aiming, in substance, to increase the penalties for acts that in any case would be punishable as injuries or negligent homicide.

It is significant that the legislator has not provided an analogous provision with reference to the more serious crime of environmental disaster set forth in the following Article 452*quater* which has a greater potential for damage with respect to the physical safety of persons. Further – as will be discussed below – environmental disaster is in any case committed when the impairment or deterioration has reached such a level that it constitutes an 'offence to public safety due to the significance of the act based on the extension of the impairment or its harmful effects or due to the number of persons affected or exposed to danger'; with the result that Article 452*ter* is only applied in the case – which is very infrequent in practice – of pollution that has provoked death or injuries as an unwanted effect, without, however, its occurrence constituting at the least exposure to danger to public safety.

This crime is only committed if the adverse event resulting in death or injury is unwanted, even indirectly and without any malicious intent of the transgressor, because if he acts even though there is the concrete possibility of further consequences occurring as a result of such act and he nevertheless accepts the risk, he is responsible, based on complicity in participation in a crime, both for the main crime (environmental pollution) as well as for the crime committed as an intended consequence of the first (homicide or malicious personal injury).

§5. Environmental Disaster

623. Article 452*quater* of the Italian Criminal Code states that 'Other than the cases provided by Article 434, anyone who abusively causes an environmental disaster shall be punished by detention ranging from five to fifteen years. Environmental disaster alternatively consists of: 1) the irreversible alteration of the equilibrium of an ecosystem; 2) the alteration of the equilibrium of an ecosystem whose elimination is particularly burdensome or achievable only through exceptional measures; 3) the offence to public safety based on the significance of the act due to the extension of the impairment or its harmful effects or due to the number of persons affected or exposed to danger. The penalty is increased when the disaster is produced in a naturally protected area or an area subject to landscape, environmental, historic, artistic, architectural or archeological restriction, or harms protected animal or vegetable species'.

As with Article 452*bis*, Article 452*quater* also provides the requirement that the conduct be abusive, for which reference is made to the comments set forth in section 3 above.

The provision contains an exception with respect to the general case of 'disaster' set forth in Article 434 – which punishes by detention ranging from one to five years whoever commits an act aimed at causing the collapse of a construction or part of it or another disaster, if danger to public safety derives from the act – which, prior to entering into effect, also covered environmental issues. Specifically, Article 434 punishes a 'macro event', which includes not only major disastrous events that are immediately evident (collapse, shipwreck, derailment, etc.) which occur in a limited period of time, but also those events that are not immediately perceptible, which can occur over a very extended period of time, which also produce the impairment of safety characteristics, the protection of health and other values of the person and of society that support a finding of harm to public safety. In other words, the basis of the crime of environmental disaster is the expansive potential of the harm, together with its potential to collectively expose an indefinite number of persons to danger; with the consequence that, for purposes of determining whether it was committed, an extraordinarily serious and complex event is necessary, but which does not have to be exceptionally immense. In brief, therefore, in the prior regime, the crime of an 'unnamed' environmental disaster set forth in Article 434, first paragraph of the Italian Criminal Code was a crime involving the advance perpetration of an act that created danger, perfected by conduct that modified an area, as long as capable in practice of threatening the environment with exceptionally serious damage, even though with effects that were not necessarily irreversible (Constitutional Court, judgment No. 327 of 30 July 2008).

With the introduction of Article 452*quater* of the Italian Criminal Code, the 2015 legislator wanted to specify the concept of environmental disaster, providing an alternative definition: '1) the irreversible alteration of the equilibrium of an ecosystem; 2) the alteration of the equilibrium of an ecosystem whose elimination is particularly burdensome and achievable only through exceptional measures; 3) offence to public safety due to the significance of the act based on the extension of the impairment or its harmful effects or due to the number of persons affected or exposed to danger'. Different from in Article 434 of the Italian Criminal Code, in the new provision the 'dimensional' and 'offensive' elements of the act are not required jointly but severally. In any case, the definition of disaster faithfully reproduces the meaning of damage having the nature of irrepressible dissemination and expansiveness, which collectively exposes to danger an indefinite number of persons.

Article 452*quater* contains – as seen – a reservation clause, which limits its scope of application 'other than to the cases provided by Article 434'. The provision is unclear, because the overlapping between the two measures does not appear to be particularly problematic, and therefore the intent of the legislator could be that of repeating the intangible nature of the stages of environmental disaster already classified under Article 434 of the Italian Criminal Code, emphasizing in some manner its imperviousness to the new, more serious, regime (in this sense, Criminal Court of Cassation, section I, judgment No. 58023 of 17 May 2017).

§6. Pollution and Negligent Disaster

624. Article 452*quinquies*, first paragraph, of the Italian Criminal Code extends criminal liability for the crimes of environmental pollution and environmental disaster due to negligence, consequently reformulating the system of sanctions, with a lowering of the penalty by one-third to two-thirds. The second paragraph contemplates a further reduction of one-third of the penalty if the commission of the acts set forth in Articles 452*bis* and 452*quater* results in the danger of environmental pollution and environmental disaster. Even though it refers to cases of negligence, the provision set forth in the second paragraph must refer to the danger of pollution or disaster caused by negligence, as the cases of negligently causing danger are already covered by the attempt of defining a negligent offence (Article 56 of the Italian Criminal Code). The standard appears to be based on the concern of analytically covering all conduct that is potentially polluting or disastrous, in order to fully implement the European Directive on criminal protection of the environment (2008/99/EC of 19 November 2008) to the extent it requires the incrimination of conduct that is also dangerous. Problems are raised, however, in this context of interference between the new regime set forth in Article 452*quinquies*, second paragraph, and the offences that already exist, structured in terms of danger, such as, for example, those set forth in Article 257 of Legislative Decree No. 152 of 2006.

§7. The Trafficking and Abandonment of Highly Radioactive Material

625. The new Article 452*sexies* of the Italian Criminal Code condemns, unless the act constitutes a more serious crime, the conduct of whoever abusively sells, buys, receives, transports, imports, exports, procures for others, detains, transfers, abandons or unlawfully disposes of highly radioactive material, providing, in the second paragraph, for an increase of the penalty if the act results in danger of impairment or deterioration to water or air, or to extensive or significant portions of soil or subsoil or of an ecosystem, biodiversity, including agrarian, flora or fauna, and a further increase of the penalty, in the third paragraph, if the act results in danger to the life or safety of persons. The comments made in section 3 above apply to the prerequisite that the conduct must be wrongful, and precisely due to the presence of such prerequisite, the addition of the adverb 'unlawfully' just to the conduct of whoever 'disposes' of the material is illogical to the extent that it seems to be the result of a drafting error by the legislator.

The aggravating circumstances set forth in the second paragraph are modelled on the analogous provision of Article 452*bis* on environmental pollution: the criminal significance regards the danger of impairment or deterioration to water or air or to extensive or significant portions of the soil or subsoil, or to an ecosystem, with the additional reference to biodiversity, including agrarian. More generally, the entire system of aggravating circumstances appears to be inadequate with respect to the specific case, which is punished because it is intrinsically highly dangerous, and it is thus difficult to contemplate a crime that is not aggravated, at least in accordance with the second paragraph. Moreover, there is already a provision in the legal system – Article 3 of Law No. 704 of 7 August 1982 (Ratification and implementation of the Convention on the physical protection of nuclear material, with annexes, opened for signature at Vienna and New York on 3 March 1980) – according to which 'Anyone without authorization who receives, possesses, uses, transfers, alienates or disposes of nuclear material in a manner that causes death or serious personal injury to one or more persons or that results in the threat of such events, without prejudice to the provisions of Articles 589 and 590 of the Italian Criminal Code, shall be punished by detention of up to two years. If only property damage is caused that is particularly serious or which results in the threat of such event, the penalty of detention of up to one year shall be applied.' There is, therefore, a problem of coordination between the aggravating circumstance of the third paragraph of Article 452*sexies* of the Italian Criminal Code and Article 3 of Law No. 704/1982.

A further problem of interference appears in relation to the second paragraph of the following Article 452*quaterdecies*, which provides for the aggravated case of organized activity for the unlawful trafficking of highly radioactive waste: the specialty clause added to the new Article 452*sexies* suggests that if the basic elements are present (nature of the waste, organization, objective of unjust profit; substantial quantity), Article 452*quaterdecies* can absorb the new case, because it provides for greater penalties – ranging from three to eight years of detention – with respect to those provided in the basic case set forth in the first paragraph of the new crime.

§8. The Failure to Remediate

626. The new Article 452*terdecies* of the Italian Criminal Code punishes, unless the act constitutes a more serious offence, with detention ranging from 1 to 4 years and a fine ranging from EUR 20,000 to EUR 80,000, anyone who, being obligated to do so, does not carry out the remediation, restoration or recovery of the condition of the places involved. The obligation to take action can derive from the law, a court order or from a public authority. The new case does not raise issues of overlapping with respect to that of Article 257 of Legislative Decree No. 152 of 2006, which provides for a penalty (detention ranging from six months to one year or a fine ranging from EUR 2,600 to EUR 26,000) for anyone who causes pollution of the soil, subsoil, surface water or underground water exceeding the risk thresholds, if they do not provide for remediation. In fact, the reservation clause ('unless the act constitutes a more serious offence'), contained in Article 452*terdecies* of the Italian Criminal Code limits its application just to cases exceeding the risk thresholds that do not (at least) constitute pollution, or which have not caused the significant and measurable impairment or deterioration of the assets indicated in Article 452*bis*.

§9. Organized Activities for the Unlawful Trafficking of Waste

627. Article 3, paragraph 1, clause *a* of recent Legislative Decree No. 21 of 1 March 2018, aimed at rationalizing the criminal system (with the introduction of a 'code reservation'), transferred to the Italian Criminal Code Article 260 of Legislative Decree No. 152 of 2006, introducing the new Article 452*quaterdecies* (Organized activity for the unlawful trafficking of waste). The provision provides that: 'Anyone who, for the purpose of obtaining an unjust profit, through various acts and by providing the means and ongoing organized activities, sells, receives, transports, exports, imports, or in any case abusively manages large quantities of waste shall be punished by detention ranging from one to six years.'

If the waste is highly radioactive, the penalty of detention ranging from three to eight years is applied.

A conviction results in the accessory penalties set forth in Articles 28, 30, 32*bis* and 32*ter*, with the limitation set forth in Article 33.

The court, by means of a conviction or a judgment issued in accordance with Article 444 of the Italian Code of Criminal Procedure, orders the remediation of the condition of the place and can subject granting the conditional suspension of the penalty to the elimination of the damage or danger to the environment.

Confiscation of whatever served to commit the crime, or whatever constitutes the result or product of the crime, is always ordered, unless it belongs to persons extraneous to it. If this is not possible, the court identifies assets having an equivalent value available to the convicted transgressor, even indirectly or through third parties, and orders that they be confiscated.

The choice to introduce the crime of organized activity for the unlawful trafficking of waste in the Italian Criminal Code was explained in the government report due to the autonomy of the case and its components with respect to the administrative regime on waste contained in Legislative Decree No. 152 of 2006, as well as the application to such crime of many of the provisions contained in the new section VI*bis* on the voluntary payment of a fine, confiscation, accessory and ablative penalties, as well as the attribution of competence for the crime to the District Anti-Mafia and Anti-Terrorism Directorate.

The delegated legislator instead decided to maintain all of the remaining criminal provisions within sector legislation, on the grounds that 'the structure of environmental offences and their placement in uniform and tendentially exhaustive standards (except for technical integrations by secondary sources and administrative authorities) advise against separating the criminal penalties from the relevant administrative precepts, in line with the Italian legislative tradition and with a model that has by now been assimilated by the legal professions and the recipients of the legislation. The most frequently applied environmental crimes have for some time been inserted in uniform or "organic" laws, such as criminal law appendixes to complex administrative legislation, which establish the conditions and limits on the performance of specific activities (building construction, waste management, hunting, etc.)'.

The case law of the Court of Cassation has delineated the boundaries and characteristics of the crime of organized activities for the unlawful trafficking of waste (initially provided by Article 260 of Legislative Decree No. 152 of 3 April 2006), noting that it is a repetitive crime which is only perfected through the realization of different acts of the same kind, aimed at obtaining an unjust profit, with the necessary preparation of a professional organization of means and capital, even if rudimentary, that is capable of managing significant quantities of waste in an ongoing manner (Criminal Court of Cassation, section 3, judgment No. 46705 of 3 November 2009; section 3, judgment No. 52838 of 14 July 2016). The crime does not necessarily have a multi-person nature but requires the preparation of a structure aimed at achieving the illegal trafficking of waste, which can be committed even by just one person (Criminal Court of Cassation, section 3, judgment No. 15630 of 12 January 2011; section 3, judgment No. 36119 of 30 June 2016). For purposes of the commission of the crime, environmental damage or the serious threat of it is necessary, because the provision of environmental remediation contained in the fourth paragraph of the cited article only refers to the case in which the damage or danger is effectively verified and, therefore, cannot change the nature of the case from a crime of presumed danger to a crime involving damage (Criminal Court of Cassation, section 3, judgment No. 19018/2013 of 20 December 2012). For purposes of the existence of the specific intent required to commit the crime, it is necessary to demonstrate that whoever committed the act knew that they belonged to an unlawful organization in order to obtain an unjust profit, which can consist, among others, in revenue or even a personal benefit, such as the simple reduction of business costs or the reinforcement of the position of each defendant within the company (Criminal Court of Cassation, section 4, judgment No. 29627 of 21 April 2016; section 3, judgment No. 53136 of 28 June 2017). Case law has also clarified that the significant quantity of waste necessary to commit the crime must refer to the overall waste processed through the multitude of transactions that are carried out, even when, considered individually, they can be qualified as being of a modest entity (Criminal Court of Cassation, section 3, judgment No. 46950 of 11 October 2016).

The same as the previous Articles 452*bis*, 452*quater*, and 452*sexies*, Article 452*quaterdecies* of the Italian Criminal Code also requires the abusive nature of the conduct, to which the comments already made in section 3 apply. With respect, finally, to the aggravating circumstance provided for the trafficking of highly radioactive waste and to its relationship with the crime set forth in Article 452*sexies*, reference is made to what is indicated in section 7 *supra*.

§10. Aggravating Circumstances

628. Article 452*octies* of the Italian Criminal Code provides: that the penalties set forth in Article 416 (which punishes a criminal organization) be increased when the association is aimed, exclusively or concurrently, at committing one of the environmental crimes; that the penalties provided by Article 416*bis* of the Italian Criminal Code (which punishes a mafia-type criminal organization) are increased when the association is aimed at committing one of the crimes provided by this section or to acquire the management or in any case the control of economic activities, concessions, authorizations, contracts or public services in environmental matters; finally, that both penalties are further increased if public officials or persons entrusted with a public service who exercise functions or services in environmental matters are part of the criminal association. It is clearly a measure aimed at preventing the alarming phenomenon of organizations whose profits result in all or to a significant extent in environmental criminality.

Article 452*nonies* provides for an increase of the penalty when any other crime is committed for the purpose of committing one of the environmental crimes provided by the new section VI*bis* of the second book of the Italian Criminal Code, by Legislative Decree No. 152 of 2006 or by any other legal provision on environmental protection.

§11. Other Provisions

629. The new Article 452*septies* of the Italian Criminal Code, which was also introduced in 2015, provides that 'unless the act constitutes a more serious offence, anyone, by denying access, hindering or artificially changing the state of places, prevents, obstructs or eludes environmental supervision and control or occupational safety and hygiene, or compromises their results, shall be punished by detention ranging from six months to three years'. The provision introduces a specific case of a restricted intentional crime, aimed at avoiding the prevention of or in any case interference with controls. The reservation clause ('unless the act constitutes a more serious offence') could be operative if the act constitutes, for example, the more serious crimes set forth in Articles 336 and 337 of the Italian Criminal Code (violence, threats, resistance to public officials).

Article 452*decies* of the Italian Criminal Code provides a mitigating circumstance for anyone who tries to prevent the criminal act from having further consequences or, before declaring the initiation of the trial of first instance, concretely carries out safety interventions, remediation or, if possible, the restoration of the condition of the places involved, or anyone who concretely assists the police authority or judicial authority with the reconstruction of the act, or who identifies whoever committed it or removes significant resources used to commit the crimes.

In the case of conviction or plea bargain for the crimes set forth in Articles 452*bis*, 452*quater*, 452*sexies*, 452*septies* and 452*octies*, whatever constitutes the product or profit of the crime or which serves to commit the crime can be confiscated or, if this is not possible, the assets available to the convicted person, either indirectly or through a third person, can be confiscated as an equivalent (Article 452*undecies* of the Italian Criminal Code).

In the case of conviction or plea bargain for one of the new environmental crimes, the court can order the recovery and, if technically possible, the restoration of the state of the places, with the expenses for such activities to be borne by the convicted persons and legal entities obliged to pay the monetary fines in the case of the former's insolvency (Article 452*duodecies* of the Italian Criminal Code). Case law has clarified that the power to impose such obligations rests with the court and not with the public prosecutor during the preliminary investigation (Criminal Court of Cassation, section III, judgment No. 32365 of 9 May 2017).

Paragraph 8 of Article 1 of Law No. 68 of 2015 intervenes on Article 25*undecies* of Legislative Decree No. 231 of 2001, inserting environmental crimes in the list of offences that constitute grounds for the administrative liability of legal entities resulting from such crimes, with the application of monetary fines and disqualifying penalties. Paragraph 6 of Article 1 tightens the restrictive regime for the new crimes, whose terms are doubled with respect to the ordinary crimes provided by Article 157, sixth paragraph of the Italian Criminal Code, in order to render the new law effective.

Paragraph 9 of Article 1 instead modifies Legislative Decree No. 152 of 2006, introducing 'Part VI*bis*' containing the sanction regime on administrative and criminal offences in the field of environmental protection and consisting of seven new articles (Articles 318*bis* through 318*octies*). The new provisions, modelled on existing provisions on occupational safety, replicate the mechanism of the extinction of the offence upon compliance with the orders issued and payment of an amount calculated as a fine. Specifically, it provides that: (a) the transgressor is given orders by the supervisory body (or by the police authority), with a term for regularization and with the communication of notice of the offence to the public prosecutor (Article 318*ter*); (b) the verification of compliance and the imposition of the penalty follow specific terms and procedural phases (Article 318*quater*); (c) the public prosecutor who is informed of the offence by any means must notify the supervisory body or police authority in order to allow the order to be imposed (Article 318*quinquies*); (d) the offence is extinguished after compliance with the order and the payment of the administrative fine, and the proceedings are then archived by the public prosecutor (Article 318*septies*).

Part V. Juridical Actions of Individuals

by *Stefano Grassi*

§1. Introduction

630. The rights of citizens and associations in relation to property and environmental interests are protected by the principles established by the Constitution. Reference can be made, above all, to the principle that allows access to the courts in order to defend subjective rights and legitimate interests (Article 24, paragraph 1, Constitution). The Italian legal system distinguishes between 'subjective rights' (when the subjective position of the individual or association is directly and expressly recognized by law, as for example, in the case of real property rights such as rights of passage, rights of use, etc.) and 'legitimate interests' (when the position of the individual or association is only indirectly protected by law). An example of the protection of legitimate interests is the legal regulation of determined relationships in order to guarantee pursuit of public interests and purposes: the individual favoured by the proper pursuit of such public interests can enforce this position of advantage both by opposing the improper exercise of public powers (such as when regulations in favour of environmental or landscape protection are violated), and by insisting on adoption of necessary environmental protection regulations.

Article 24 of the Constitution does not specifically refer to the concepts of group interests or collective interests. 'Group interests' are a plurality of subjects entitled to juridical guarantee; 'collective interests' arise when that plurality of subjects becomes a more or less organized collective (society) for purposes that are related to the protection of those interests. Starting from the 1970s, however, constitutional case law has also affirmed the right to juridical protection in accordance with Article 24 of the Constitution with reference to subjective positions other than subjective rights and legitimate interests, thus, recognizing group and collective interests. Examples of this extension of constitutional protection are the rights relating to the protection of health and a healthy environment; television viewers; and consumer interests.

The Italian legislator has also recognized these interests, although in a less satisfactory manner, and it is significant to note that this first took place by reference to the protection of environmental interests: Article 18 of Law No. 349 of 1986 on environmental damage; Article 9 of Law No. 241 of 1990 which provides forms of protection of group interests in the context of administrative proceedings; as well as

Law No. 281 of 1998 on the rights of consumers and users (which was then repealed and replaced by the current Consumers' Code, Legislative Decree No. 206 of 6 September 2005).

Article 113 of the Constitution has clarified that the judicial protection of legitimate rights and interests can also be extended to the public administration, abrogating all of the norms that previously limited judicial supervision of the activity performed by public authorities (e.g., the non-appealable nature of political acts). Judicial protection cannot, in fact, be excluded or limited to particular means of opposition or appeal or determined categories of acts; whereas the law will determine the effects of judicial decisions on the illegitimate acts of the public administration (including the annulment of the same illegitimate acts). The protection of citizens with respect to the public administration can take place even before recourse to the courts and before issuance of administrative provisions, in accordance with the principle of the normal course and impartiality of the public administration sanctioned by Article 97 of the Constitution, coherently with the principle of equality guaranteed by Article 3 of the Constitution. Both the norms that guarantee the right to environmental information and the norms that guarantee the right to participate in environmental proceedings can be included in the implementation of these principles.

§2. The Right to Environmental Information and the Right of Participation

631. The right to environmental information is based both in the constitutional norms and legislative principles that, with respect to the public administration, give precedence to the principle of publicity and transparency of its acts and activity (Articles 3 and 97 Constitution) as well as to the norms of Community Treaties, which with particular reference to environmental protection identify in the right of environmental protection the corollary of the principles of precaution, prevention and correction at the source of the damage caused to the environment (Article 191 of the TFEU).

632. Community law affirms the principles of publicity and transparency of administrative action (such principles form the basis of all procedures relating to EIAs, in accordance with the regime set forth in the directives of the EC). Environmental information is at the basis of the creation of the European Environmental Protection Agency (Council Regulation 1210/90 of 9 May 1990), which is supposed to gather and manage environmental information. The Community explicitly implemented the principle of freedom of access to environmental material by means of Directive 90/313 (adopted at the same time as the regulation that created the European Agency, 7 June 1990), as well as by directives intended to guarantee active forms of collaboration in environmental protection operations (Regulation No. 66/2010 EC on ecolabels and No. 1221/2009 EC on ecoaudits, as well as Directive No. 75/2010 EU on the integrated control of pollution, implemented by Law No. 96 of 6 August 2013 and Legislative Decree No. 46 of 4 March 2014; but the major part of the Community directives and regulations regarding environmental protection contain specific norms aimed at identifying 'environmental information' and the manner of gathering it, as well as relative access to and diffusion of the same, in accordance with a policy that has been proposed on more than one occasion in all of the action programmes in this area.

633. Community Directive No. 90/313 was anticipated in the Italian legal system by Article 14 of Law 349 of 1986 (third paragraph), according to which:

> any citizen has a right of access to available information regarding the state of the environment from the offices of the public administration in accordance with the existing law, and can obtain a copy of the same upon reimbursement of reproduction expenses plus the actual office expenses; said amount is established by an act published by the interested administration.

This norm affirmed for the first time in the Italian legal system a principle which was subsequently confirmed by the general norms on administrative proceedings set forth in Law No. 241 of 1990 (Articles 22 et seq.); the norms of the Uniform Text on Local Entities (Article 10 of Legislative Decree No. 267 of 2000); and the numerous regional laws that have implemented the principle of the right to environmental information. This principle is now set forth in Article 3*sexies* of Legislative Decree No. 152 of 2006.

634. Community Directive No. 90/313/CEE was substituted by Directive No. 2003/4/EEC, which adjusted the regime on access to environmental information to the principles set forth in the Aahrus Convention of 25 June 1998 (ratified by Italy by means of Law No. 108 of 16 March 2001 and signed both by the EC and by the individual Member States). Directive No. 2003/35/EC was approved to implement the Aahrus Convention, with respect to public participation in the preparation of some environmental plans and programmes. Directive No. 2003/4/EEC was implemented by Legislative Decree No. 195 of 19 August 2005, which more clearly defines the concept of environmental information (Article 2), the regime on access and the relative judicial guarantees (*see* Article 7) and an exhaustive indication of the cases in which access can be denied (Article 5).

In practice, the most delicate problems arise in exercising the right of access to environmental information that private parties are required to provide to the public administration (e.g., companies required to comply with norms on major accident risks, in compliance with the 'Seveso' Directive; or all of the companies and individuals required to provide information necessary to create a waste registry: Article 189, Legislative Decree No. 152 of 2006), in view of guaranteeing confidentiality and trade secrets as opposed to the right of citizens to accurate and timely information.

Equally delicate are problems raised by laws that obligate private parties to directly inform the public of environmental risks, or the consequences that their projects and activities might produce in the environment: again, they regard manufacturing cycles that might generate major environmental risks, and obligations of the manufacturers of specific kinds of products to provide information to consumers on the collection and disposal of their products. These problems also involve the right of employers to obtain the information they need so that they can effectively control the application of rules on occupational diseases and all appropriate measures to protect the health and physical integrity of workers and the environment where they work.

635. Access to environmental information is denied, in accordance with the subsequent second paragraph, when the disclosure of information could cause damage to:

(a) privacy regarding the resolutions of public authorities in accordance with what is established by outstanding law;
(b) international relations, public order and public security, or national defence;
(c) judicial proceedings or the possibility for the public authority to carry out preliminary criminal investigations;
(d) commercial and industrial trade secrets, in accordance with what is established by outstanding law, to protect a legitimate economic and public interest, including statistical confidentiality and tax secrecy, as well as industrial property rights in accordance with Legislative Decree No. 30 of 10 February 2005;
(e) intellectual property rights;
(f) the privacy of personal data or regarding an individual, in the case they have not consented to the disclosure of information to the public, considering what is set forth in Legislative Decree No. 196 of 30 June 2003;
(g) interests or protection of anyone who has voluntarily offered information requested, who was not legally required to supply it, unless the interested party consented to the disclosure of the information in question;
(h) protection of the environment and landscape to which the information refers, as in the case of the location of rare species.

The provisions on public access to information must be applied *restrictively, weighing with respect to each request to access information the public interest to receive environmental information and the interest served by denying access* (Article 5, paragraph 3).

Case law has clarified that anyone, without the obligation to demonstrate the existence of a legally relevant interest, can have access to information on the state of the environment and the landscape in the national territory. The request for access must be formulated in a specific manner with reference to the environmental matrices or to the measures or factors referred to in paragraphs 2 and 3 of Article 2, Legislative Decree No. 195 (Council of State, V, judgment No. 6339/2009). The request for access can also consist of a generic request for information on a specific environmental context, provided that this context is specified (Council of State, VI, judgment No. 668/2007). The interest of widespread knowledge, the conditions of the constituent elements of the ecosystem and of man-made phenomena, requires the sharing of all scientific data relating to the physical, chemical and biological elements that determine its structure with stakeholders (T.A.R. Lazio-Rome, section II*Ter*, judgment No. 2141 of 27 February 2018). Indiscriminate access to all matters related to a specific sector of administrative activity is not allowed, however, because access cannot be transformed into a tool of systematic and generalized control of the management of all ongoing administrative procedures or, more generally, of all of the work of a public entity' (T.A.R. Lazio-Rome, section I*bis*, judgment No. 4800 of 2 May 2018; in the same sense *see* T.A.R. Sicily-Palermo, section I, judgment No. 289 of 2 February 2018).

636. The right to receive information (which, with respect to the public administration, is directly connected to 'administrative information', understood as a right having as its object a 'declaration of knowledge' by the public administration) as opposed to a mere right of access to information presents at least three different facets: the right to receive accurate and objective environmental information; the right to obtain the maximum amount of available information from subjects involved with the environment; and the right to the continuity of information in environmental matters (in particular, made available by the public administration).

637. The right to obtain accurate and objective information can be guaranteed with respect to the public administration by means of its obligation to have collections of data that are prepared and maintained by independent organisms. With respect to this issue, reference is made to regulation of the gathering of statistical data and the guarantee of independence of the organs entrusted with such compilation (*see*, in particular, Articles 2, 8, 12 and 14 of Law No. 322 of 1989), as well as the strategic functions which must be performed in this area by ISPRA which manages the National Network System for Environmental Protection (*Sistema nazionale a rete per la protezione dell'ambiente*) (*see* Articles 1 et seq., Law No. 132 of 28 June 2016).

638. A second group of guarantees are related to the presence of technical committees which gather and evaluate data relating to the environment. There are numerous laws providing for the utilization of such organs and technical consulting in order to guarantee the accuracy of environmental information. The functions of ISPRA should be strengthened in this area as well. An important principles has been indicated by Article 9 of Law No. 132 of 2016, which defined the (essential levels of technical environmental performance – *livelli essenziali delle prestazioni tecniche ambientali*), as the homogeneous minimum level for monitoring, control and technical support entrusted to the national network system, in order to ensure the objectives of collective prevention provided by the essential levels of health care (in the same direction *see* Article 34 of Legislative Decree No. 152/2006, as modified by Article 3 of Law No. 221 of 2015, with particular reference to technical standards).

639. A further guarantee is the possibility to control the data gathered by the public administration. Examples are the power of the Ministry of the Environment to control and perform technical verifications, including upon the request of individual citizens, and the possibility of such ministry to supply experts and technicians to control data gathering performed by other administrations. Analogous controls can be entrusted to the Environmental Protection Agency (now ISPRA).

640. The specific needs of environmental information, which loses its utility if it does not provide a broad and trustworthy basis for data and cognitive elements regarding the 'state of the environment', require indispensable guarantees that such data is gathered with continuity and in an objective manner. These guarantees can come, above all, from respect of some of the essential requirements of environmental information itself: the standardization of data and monitoring activity.

The accuracy and objectivity of information must be accompanied by an adequate translation in common, comprehensible language of officially gathered data, in order to permit diffused control and to render the right to receive such information effective.

641. The right to be informed allows the most complete valuation of the interests affected by works and renders the right to participate in the decision-making process effective.

This principle forms the basis of the necessity of an open information gathering process, capable of balancing the various interests involved in view of the information that has been obtained.

The above leads to the necessity of prior publication of works projects. The private parties who intend to carry out such works are responsible for the publication of the relative dates thereof. For example, *see* the provisions relating to EIAs; the specifications regarding the publication in newspapers of information relating to the works to be performed; as well as the same norms regarding the possibility of obtaining verifications and receiving technical opinions (already mentioned with respect to the principle of the accuracy of the relative information).

642. Public hearings regarding EIAs are of maximum importance in this area, which refer to consultations and opinion polls, referendums and cognitive investigations of organs with legislative functions. These procedures are added to the forms of publicizing the projects already provided for in the bureaucratic approval process of urban planning instruments.

643. The right to participate in the proceeding guaranteed by Article 9 of Law No. 241 of 1990 which establishes new norms with respect to administrative proceedings, is particularly important in the context of the protection of environmental interests. Persons and organizations protecting group interests such as the right to a healthy environment and the reduction of pollutants can also participate in the proceedings. Such principles allow control and social participation starting from the creation of administrative acts, forcing the administration to take into consideration memorandums and documents pertinent to the object of the proceedings in the valuation of the results of the information gathering process and in the selection of interests. The obligation to supply reasons for eventual decisions, with reference also to the data acquired in a proceeding open to the public in which all interested parties have participated, allows a subsequent penetrating control by the court allowing access to the subjects who participated in the proceeding.

On the basis of Article 40 of Legislative Decree No. 97 of 2016, the state, regional and local public administrations, autonomous and special companies, public entities and public service providers, as well as any individual or legal entity performing public functions related to environmental issues or that exercise administrative responsibility under the control of a public body, must publish available information and environmental reporting on their institutional websites for purposes of their institutional activities. This information must be highlighted in a specific section called 'Environmental Information' (except for cases of exclusion of the right of access to environmental information already indicated above).

Article 7 of Legislative Decree No. 192 of 2005, provides that, in the case of rejection of a request to access environmental information due to failure to respond within the statutory deadline, the applicant can file an appeal within thirty days in court or can request that the above decision be reviewed by the competent ombudsman based on territory (the review is performed by an ad hoc Access Commission for acts of State bodies). Failure to appeal the refusal, whether express or tacit, within the term does not allow the petition to be repeated nor the consequent appeal of the subsequent refusal, if it is merely confirmatory of the first (Council of State, section V, judgment No. 423 of 23 January 2018).

The regime in this sector provides specific rules to protect access to environmental information (*see* Article 14, paragraph 3 of Legislative Decree No. 152 of 3 April 2006 on EIA; Article 24, paragraph 4 and 27 of Legislative Decree No. 152 of 3 April 2006 on SEA; Article 29*decies*, paragraph 8 of Legislative Decree No. 152 of 3 April 2006 on IEA; Articles 178 and 179, paragraph 7 of Legislative Decree No. 152 of 3 April 2006 on waste management, Article 219, paragraph 2, clause *c* of Legislative Decree No. 152 of 3 April 2006 on the management of packaging waste, and Articles 23 and 24 of Legislative Decree No. 105 of 26 June 2015 on industrial activities at risk of being major accident hazards).

§3. Administrative Remedies

644. The Italian system traditionally provides administrative remedies and forms of control of the acts of the public administration which must or can precede court control. There are various kinds of appeals: opposition, hierarchical appeals and extraordinary appeals to the President of the Republic (DPR No. 1199 of 24 November 1971).

645. An opposition is directed to the same authority that issued the order being appealed and contains a specification of the reasons why the interested party requests the same administration to change its decision. It is a remedy of an exceptional nature that is expressly provided only in determined subject matters, among which those relating to environmental protection do not appear. Such form of appeal can, however, be utilized to permit re-examination by the same administration of acts that impact environmental resources or values.

646. A hierarchical appeal is directed to the authority that is hierarchically superior, regarding decisions and acts of the authority that is hierarchically inferior. The superior hierarchical authority is usually the ministry, but a hierarchical appeal can be proposed with respect to any organ hierarchically superior to the organ that issued the act. Numerous laws provide the possibility of presenting a hierarchical appeal that is also directed at an authority that in reality does not have a superior hierarchical relationship with respect to the organ that issued the order ('improper hierarchical appeals'). The hierarchical appeal must be presented within thirty days by the interested party.

Both oppositions and hierarchical appeals can be based either on constitutionality or the merits. Hierarchical appeals are, however, very often left undecided. In order to get around this practice, law and case law interpret the administration's silence as a rejection of the appeal (consequently allowing an immediate appeal to a court of law).

647. An extraordinary appeal to the President of the Republic is formally considered to be administrative, but it is very close to a judicial appeal. The appeal must be presented within 120 days from the issuance of the administrative act, by means of service of process analogous to that of judicial appeals, and is decided by a DPR after receiving an opinion regarding the appeal expressed by a section of the Council of State (the Government's consultative organ, which is also the top organ in administrative jurisdiction). An extraordinary appeal constitutes an alternate remedy with respect to a judicial appeal and, differently than opposition or a hierarchical appeal, can only contain a censure of legitimacy but cannot address the merits. These appeals, in which the competent ministries usually collect the documents that are necessary for the decision, are rarely utilized and are decided after lengthy delay (the parties can request precautionary measures while waiting for a decision on the appeal).

§4. Judicial Remedies

648. Citizens, associations and public entities can seek the protection of environmental interests that may have been damaged by the behaviour, activity, or acts of private parties or the public administration, before all of the courts that are provided for within the Italian legal system. As is seen, in fact, environmental interests are entitled to direct protection by the law and are indirectly connected with the protection of other interests (such as the right to property and other real property rights) that interested parties can have enforced by the courts.

It is, therefore, possible for individual citizens to appeal to an administrative court of law unlawful administrative acts that regard the environment. So that the action in front of an administrative court is not transformed into a class action that can be initiated by any class member, case law requires that the petitioner demonstrate that it is in a position (e.g., that he or she lives in a particular neighbourhood) to claim that the administrative act being appealed has caused concrete damage (e.g., a reduction to the economic value of an asset, such as real property or health).

649. Article 313, paragraph 7, of Legislative Decree No. 152 of 3 April 2006, provides that in any case, parties damaged by an event that damages the environment, their health or assets that they own have the right to take legal action against the parties responsible for protecting the rights and interests that have been harmed.

In view of the need to comply with constitutional principles (Article 24 of the Constitution), the law, thus, specifies that each individual maintains the right to the compensation of damages for harm to individual assets. Competence usually rests with the civil court.

650. The criminal court adjudicates accusations of crimes arising from behaviour that contrasts with environmental protection. Injured parties can constitute themselves as civil parties in criminal proceedings. In such sense, public entities that represent the interests of the State community (central State), regional community (regions) and provincial or local communities (municipalities and provinces) have standing to appear; as well as public entities to whom the law attributes the protection of environmental interests (e.g., the entities managing the natural parks), as well as recognized environmental organizations when they claim that harm has been caused to interests that they aim to safeguard on the basis of their constitutions, who can enforce, at every stage and level of judicial proceedings, the rights and powers attributed to the person that is the victim of the crime (most recently, *see* Criminal Court of Cassation, section IV, judgment No. 22022 of 22 February 2018, which refers to Criminal Court of Cassation, section III, judgment No. 34220 of 22 September 2010), as well as individual citizens or associations directly harmed by the criminal behaviour. The association is entitled to exercise, 'at every stage and level of the proceedings, the rights and powers attributed to the party harmed by the environmental crime' (Criminal Court of Cassation, section IV, judgment No. 22022 of 22 February 2018), 'The standing of entities representing collective interests in legal proceedings presumes recognition of the ontological correspondence of the interests protected by the entity with those protected from the crime that is the object of the proceedings, to be assessed strictly in view of the structure and nature of the criminal behaviour' (Criminal Court of Cassation, section IV, judgment No. 22022 of 22 February 2018).

651. The Court of Auditors (an organ created by the Constitution to control the legitimacy of acts that involve expenses by the government and the State's balance sheet, as well as adjudicate accounting responsibilities and damage caused by public employees to the State treasury due to illegitimate behaviour) performs an indirect control of behaviour damaging environmental interests, by making directors and administrators responsible for illegitimate acts that cause damage to environmental resources or factors, the landscape or elements of historic and artistic interest. This court has first level regional sections and central sections having a second level of jurisdiction. Its united central sections can be requested to decide matters of principle.

652. Administrative courts (consisting of regional administrative tribunals provided by Article 125, II paragraph, Constitution), which adjudicate at the first level, and the Council of State, in its juridical sections, at the second level decide appeals regarding legitimacy (violation of law, lack of competence, excess of power) which are proposed by citizens, by associations or by the same interested public entities by means of the ordinances and behaviour of the public administration (*see* Legislative Decree No. 104 of 2 July 2010). The review is limited to defects of legitimacy which implies, in environmental matters, the difficulty of an administrative court to guarantee effective protection in fields in which decisions (and, therefore, the damage of interests) depend on technical valuations. Administrative courts cannot adjudicate the exercise of powers of technical discretion, except when they are clearly erroneous and when illogical solutions have been adopted.

653. With respect to the protection of environmental values, the normal rules distinguishing between the jurisdiction of ordinary courts of law and administrative courts prevail: ordinary courts of law are only able to adjudicate subjective rights, whereas administrative courts are competent to adjudicate matters regarding legitimate interests. Two exceptions have recently been made to this distinction: in fact, matters exist in which it is not possible to correctly identify and distinguish the positions directly protected by the legislator in the form of subjective law and those that are considered due protection of positions of legitimate interest (traditionally, these relate to the employment relationship of public employees, but also controversies related to acts, measures or conduct of public administration with respect to urban planning and building construction – *see* Article 133, Legislative Decree No. 104 of 2 July 2010). This implies a more efficient protection of many sectors of the environmental regime, because in its exercise of exclusive jurisdiction, the administrative court can order the acquisition of evidence, including by means of technical consultants, as well as compensation of damage including reintegration in a specific form.

§5. The Standing of Environmental Associations

654. An 'environmental' resource is a public asset, whose protection can also be enforced by associations that have been confirmed to be representative of the common interests of the community to which they belong. The Court of Justice has clarified – on the basis of Article 9, paragraph 3, of the Aarhus Convention of 25 June 1998 and Article 47 of the Charter of Fundamental Rights of the EU – that a duly constituted environmental protection organization operating in accordance with the requirements provided by national law is entitled to challenge before a court a decision authorizing a project which could harm environmental interests protected by European standards (ECJ, second section, 20 December 2017, in case 664/15).

Case law has specified some connection factors as factors that entitle associations able to protect public interests (territorial location, statutory objectives and the effective representation of entities and associations with respect to the interest that is the cause of action: *see* Plenary Session of the Council of State No. 24 of 19 October 1979).

655. Article 13 of Law No. 349 of 1986 provides that:

national environmental protection associations and those located in at least five regions are identified by decree of the Minister of the Environment on the basis of the programmatic objectives and the democratic internal system provided for by statute, as well as on the continuity of their activity and its external significance, upon the opinion of the National Council for the Environment, which must be issued within 90 days of the request.

From 1987 to 2018, seventy-six associations were identified, even though in practice only four associations enforced their right of action provided by Article 13 (WWF, Italia Nostra, FAI and Legambiente).

Case law has found that the lack of inclusion of an environmental association in the list prepared by the ministerial decree does not automatically exclude their right of action. The verification of their prerequisites is, therefore, done on a case-to-case basis with reference to the specific interest that is the cause of action.

656. The role of environmental associations and the powers granted to them were recognized for the first time by Article 18, paragraphs 4 and 5 of Law No. 349 of 1986 which attributes them with a power to make a claim, the power to participate in civil and criminal actions and the power to file appeals in administrative courts seeking the repeal of unlawful acts.

Case law has specified that 'environmental associations are entitled to appeal any administrative act, but the special nature of their standing to appeal is preliminarily conditioned by the objectives they pursue and only allows them to make claims that are functional to satisfying environmental interests, instead prohibiting claims related to other kinds of violations' (T.A.R. Emilia-Romagna Bologna, section II, judgment No. 346 of 19 April 2018); *see also* Council of State, judgment No. 991 of 2013; T.A.R. Liguria, section I, judgment No. 941 of 2017).

Environmental interests can also be protected through the appeal of general administrative urban planning acts of a planning and programming nature if they have a negative impact on environmental aspects' (Council of State, section V, judgment No. 3109 of 24 May 2018; *see also* Council of State, section IV, judgment No. 2329 of 14 April 2011; T.A.R. Lombardy Milan section II, judgment No. 2336 of 22 October 2013; Council of State, section IV, judgment No. 839 of 19-02-2015). This is due to the comingling of environmental issues with urban planning issues (Council of State, section V, judgment No. 3711 of 28-07-2015; T.A.R. Campania-Naples, section VII, judgments No. 2964 and No. 2965 of 3 May 2018).

Recognized associations also have the power to be a party to legal actions in the place of the municipality or province in whose territory is located the resource that is the object of the damaging act, or in *substitution* of entities that are institutionally entitled to claim compensation for environmental damage (Article 9, paragraph 3, Legislative Decree No. 267 of 2000).

657. By means of Legislative Decree No. 152 of 3 April 2006, the right of action to seek compensation for environmental damage was granted to the Ministry of the Environment, and, thus, the role of environmental associations was reduced.

Specifically, Article 318 of Legislative Decree No. 152 of 3 April 2006 repealed Article 18 of Law No. 349/86, with the exception of the power to participate in proceedings regarding environmental damage and the power of recourse to the administrative court against unlawful acts (in order to comply with the international principles of the Aahrus Convention, which requires encouraging information, participation and the right of action of the interested public in environmental matters).

Standing to appear as a civil party in proceedings for environmental crimes regarding acts committed after 29 April 2006 rests exclusively with the State, specifically the Ministry of the Environment. The Environmental Minister can request compensation for environmental damage of a public nature, considered to be harm of the public interest to the integrity and health of the environment. The regions, public and private entities can appear as civil parties in criminal proceedings in accordance with Article 2043 of the Italian Civil Code only to obtain compensation of economic and non-economic damage deriving from the same detrimental conduct, but consequent to the harm of their rights other than the public interest to environmental protection (Criminal Court of Cassation, section III, judgment No. 6727 of 12 February 2018; *see also* section III, judgment No. 24677 of 09/07/2014, Busolin e altri, Rv. 264114; section III, judgment No. 633 of 29/11/2011, Stigliani, Rv. 251906; as well as Fundarò, Rv. 252907; section IV, judgment No. 24619 of 27/05/2014, Salte Rv. 259153; Criminal Court of Cassation, section III, judgment No. 20150 of 16 May 2016).

The substitute power provided by Article 9, paragraph 3 of the Uniform Text on the Organization of Local Entities (No. 267 of 2000) of associations and the public to seek compensation for environmental damage was also repealed, and, thus, only the Ministry of the Environment can initiate an action seeking compensation for environmental damage.

The new Article 309 of Legislative Decree No. 152 expressly grants non-governmental organizations that promote environmental protection in accordance with Article 13 of Law No. 349 of 1986 the *power to file claims* and make observations, supported by documents and information, on any case of environmental damage or imminent threat of environmental damage, and to request State intervention for environmental protection.

It is also possible for recognized environmental associations and territorial entities (municipalities, provinces and regions) to initiate legal actions in the case of the ministry's failure to act (based on the formula silence amounting to non-compliance) after a request made in accordance with Article 309 of cited Legislative Decree No. 152 (Council of State, section VI, judgment No. 2318 of 2007; T.A.R. Lazio-Rome, section II*bis*, judgment No. 367 of 12 January 2018). The Ministry of the Environment is required to assess requests for intervention and observations regarding cases 'of environmental damage or the threat of environmental damage' made by non-governmental organizations. The ministry must initiate the procedure and provide information on the initiatives and measures that are taken (T.A.R. Campania-Naples, section I, judgment No. 5913 of 15 December 2017).

Article 310 of such decree confirms *that associations have a right of action to seek the annulment* of acts and measures approved in violation of cleanup obligations or obligations to compensate environmental damage, as well as against the silence amounting to non-compliance of the Ministry of the Environment and to seek compensation for damages suffered resulting from the ministry's delay in adopting precautionary, prevention or containment measures to combat environmental damage.

Selected Bibliography

General Legislation

Amirante, D. *Diritto ambientale italiano e comparato (Princìpi).* Naples: Jovene, 2003.
Amirante, D. *La forza normativa dei princìpi.* Padoa: Cedam, 2006.
Andronio, A. *Le ordinanze di necessità e urgenza per la tutela dell'ambiente.* Milan: Giuffrè, 2004.
Antonini, L. (ed.). 'L'imposizione ambientale nel quadro del federalismo fiscale'. in *Studi sul federalismo fiscale* diretti da Mario Bertolissi. Naples: Jovene, 2010.
Barile, P., E. Cheli & S. Grassi. *Istituzioni di diritto pubblico.* XVI ed. Padua: Cedam, 2017.
Benacci E. *Compendio di Diritto dell'Ambiente.* X ed. Naples: Edizioni Simone, 2018.
Benozzo, M., et al. *Commento al codice dell'ambiente.* Turin: G. Giappichelli, 2013.
Blasizza E. (ed.). *Ambiente 2018. Manuale normo-tecnico.* XII ed. Milan: IPSOA, 2018.
Butti, L. 'L'utilizzo della scienza nel diritto ambientale'. *Riv. giur. amb.* (2014): 129.
Cafagno, M. *Principi e strumenti di tutela dell'ambiente. Come sistema complesso, adattativo, comune.* Turin: Giappichelli, 2007.
Capaccioli, E. & F. Dal Piaz. 'Ambiente (tutela dell'): parte generale e diritto amministrativo'. in *Novissimo Digesto Italiano.* Appendice, vol. I. Turin: UTET, 1980.
Caravita, B, A. Morrone & L. Cassetti. *Diritto dell'ambiente.* Bologna: Il Mulino, 2016.
Carbone L., G. Napoletano & A. Zoppini (eds). *La disciplina della gestione dei rifiuti tra ambiente e mercato.* Bologna: Il Mulino, 2018.
Carli, B. *L'uomo e il clima.* Bologna: Il Mulino, 2017.
Cavallaro, M.C. 'Il principio di integrazione come strumento di tutela dell'ambiente'. *Rivista italiana di diritto pubblico comunitario* (2007): 467.
Cecchetti, M. *Principi costituzionali per la tutela dell'ambiente.* Milan: Giuffrè, 2000.
Chiti, M.P. & Ursi R. (ed.). *Studi sul codice dell'ambiente.* Turin: Giappichelli, 2009.
Clarich, M. 'La tutela dell'ambiente attraverso il mercato'. *Dir.pubbl.* (2007): 219.
Conti L. *Lineamenti di diritto dell'ambiente.* Rome: Edizioni Nuova Cultura, 2017.

Selected Bibliography

Cordini G. *Diritto ambientale comparato*. Padua: Cedam, 2002.

Cordini G., P. Fois & S. Marchisio. *Diritto ambientale. Profili internazionali europei e comparati*. Turin: Giappichelli, 2017.

Cornacchia L. & N. Pisani. *Il nuovo diritto penale dell'ambiente*. Bologna: Zanichelli, 2018.

Costato, L. & F. Pellizzer. *Commentario breve al Codice dell'Ambiente*. Padua: Cedam, 2012.

Crosetti A., et al. *Introduzione al diritto dell'ambiente*. Bari – Rome: Laterza, 2018.

Dani, A. *Le risorse naturali come beni comuni*. Grosseto: C&P Adver Effigi, 2013.

De Leonardis, F. 'La disciplina dell'ambiente tra Unione Europea e WTO'. *Dir.amm.* (2004): 513.

Dell'Anno P. *Diritto dell'ambiente*. V ed. Padua: Cedam, 2018.

Dell'Anno, P. *Princìpi di diritto ambientale europeo e nazionale*. Milan: Giuffrè, 2004.

Dell'Anno P. & E. Picozza. (eds). *Trattato di diritto dell'ambiente, Vol. I: Princìpi generali*. Padua: Cedam, 2012.

Dell'Anno P. & E. Picozza. (eds). *Trattato di diritto dell'ambiente, Vol. II: Discipline ambientali di settore*. Padua: Cedam, 2013.

Dell'Anno P. & E. Picozza. (eds). *Trattato di diritto dell'ambiente, Vol. III: Tutele parallele. Norme processuali*. Padua: Cedam, 2015.

Di Benedetto, D. *La disciplina degli organismi geneticamente modificati tra precauzione e responsabilità*. Naples: Edizioni Scientifiche Italiane, 2011.

Di Benedetto S. *Sovranità dello Stato sulle risorse naturali e tutela degli equilibri ecologici nel diritto internazionale generale*. Turin: G. Giappichelli, 2018.

Di Plinio, G. *Diritto pubblico dell'ambiente e aree naturali protette. Il dualismo giuridico dell'ambiente fra tutela comparativa e protezione integrale*. Turin: Utet, 1994.

Di Plinio, G. & P. Fimiani (eds). *Principi di diritto ambientale*. II ed. Milan: Giuffrè, 2008.

Di Tullio D'Elisiis A. *I nuovi reati ambientali e le strategie difensive*. Rimini: Maggioli, 2016.

Esposito, G.M. *Tutela dell'ambiente e attività dei pubblici poteri*. Turin: Giappichelli, 2008.

Ferrara, R. (ed.). *La tutela dell'ambiente*. Milan: Giuffrè, 2006.

Ferrara, R., M.A. Sandulli & C.E. Gallo. (eds). *Trattato di diritto dell'ambiente, Vol. I: Le politiche ambientali, lo sviluppo sostenibile e il danno*. Milan: Giuffrè, 2014.

Ferrara, R., M.A. Sandulli & S. Grassi. (eds). *Trattato di diritto dell'ambiente, Vol. II: I procedimenti amministrativi per la tutela dell'ambiente*. Milan: Giuffrè, 2014.

Ferrara, R., M.A. Sandulli & A. Crosetti. (eds). *Trattato di diritto dell'ambiente, Vol. III: La tutela della natura e del paesaggio*. Milan: Giuffrè, 2014.

Feola M. *Ambiente e democrazia, Il ruolo dei cittadini nella governance ambientale*. Turin: Giappichelli, 2016.

Fodella, A. & L. Pineschi. *La protezione dell'ambiente nel diritto internazionale*. Turin: Giappichelli, 2010.

Fonderico, F. 'Ambiente'. *Encicl. Giur. Treccani*, 2007.

Fracchia, F. *Introduzione allo studio del diritto dell'ambiente.* Naples: Editoriale Scientifica, 2013.
Fracchia, F. *Lo sviluppo sostenibile.* Naples: Editoriale scientifica, 2010.
Fracchia F. 'Sulla configurazione giuridica unitaria dell'ambiente: art. 2 Cost.e doveri di solidarietà ambientale'. *Dir. Econ.* (2002): 215.
Fracchia, F. & M. Occhiena. *I sistemi di certificazione tra qualità e certezza.* Milan: Egea, 2006.
Germanò, A., et al. *Commento al Codice dell'ambiente.* Turin: Giappichelli, 2013.
Giannini, M.S. '"Ambiente": saggio sui diversi suoi aspetti giuridici'. *Riv.trim.dir-.pubbl.* (1973): 15.
Giannini, M.S. 'Difesa dell'ambiente e del patrimonio naturale e culturale'. *Riv. trim. dir. pubbl.* (1971): 1122.
Giuffrida R. & F. Amabili. (eds). *La tutela dell'ambiente nel diritto internazionale ed europeo.* Turin: Giappichelli, 2018.
Grassi S. 'Ambiente e Costituzione'. *Riv. Quadr. di Diritto dell'Ambiente* (2017): 113.
Grassi, S. 'Tutela dell'ambiente (diritto amministrativo)'. *Enc. Dir., Annali,* I. Milan: Giuffrè, 2007, 1114.
Grassi S. *Problemi di diritto costituzionale dell'ambiente,* Osservatorio sulla legislazione a tutela dell'ambiente. Milan: Giuffrè, 2012.
Grassi, S., M. Cecchetti & A. Andronio (eds). *Ambiente e Diritto.* Florence: Leo S. Olschki, 1999.
Greco, N. *La costituzione dell'ambiente: sistema e ordinamenti.* Bologna: Il Mulino, 1996.
Greco R. *Codice dell'ambiente.* Turin: Ed. Nel Diritto, 2011.
Groppi T. 'Sostenibilità e costituzioni: lo Stato costituzionale alla prova del futuro'. *Dir. Pubbl. Comun. ed Eur.* (2016): 1, 43.
Izzo, S. *Il principio di integrazione ambientale nel diritto comunitario.* Naples: Editoriale Scientifica, 2006.
Kramer, L. *Manuale di diritto comunitario per l'ambiente.* Milan: Giuffrè, 2002.
Lombardi Vallauri, L. (ed.). *Il meritevole di tutela. Studi per una ricerca.* Milan: Giuffrè, 1990.
Lugaresi, N. *Diritto dell'ambiente.* Padua: Cedam, 2015.
Macrillò A. *I nuovi reati ambientali. Le risposte giurisprudenziali alla l. 22 maggio 2015, n. 68.* Rome: Dike Giuridica Editrice, 2017.
Maddalena, P. 'La giurisprudenza della Corte Costituzionale in materia di tutela e fruizione dell'ambiente'. *Riv. giur. amb.* (2010): 5.
Maglia, S. *Diritto ambientale.* Milan: Ipsoa, 2011.
Maglia S. *Codice dell'ambiente.* Piacenza: Ed. La Tribuna, 2018.
Marcatajo G. *Il danno ambientale.* Naples: Ed. Scientifiche Italiane, 2016.
Marzanati, A. & R. Pupilella. 'Ambiente: il sistema organizzativo ed i principi fondamentali'. in *Trattato di diritto amministrativo europeo,* Parte Speciale, t. 1, edited by M.P. Chiti & G. Greco. Milan: Giuffrè, 2007, 157.
Massera A. (eds). *Diritto amministrativo e ambiente.* Naples: Editoriale Scientifica, 2011.
Mastragostino, F. (eds). *Gli strumenti economici e consensuali del diritto dell'ambiente.* Naples: Editoriale Scientifica, 2011.

Selected Bibliography

Mezzetti, L. *I diritti della natura. Paradigmi di giuridificazione dell'ambiente nel diritto pubblico comparato.* Padua: Cedam, 1997.

Montini, M. *La necessità ambientale nel diritto internazionale e comunitario.* Padua: Cedam, 2001.

Morbidelli, G. 'Il regime amministrativo speciale dell'ambiente'. in *Scritti in onore di Alberto Predieri.* Milan: Giuffrè, 1996.

Morano G. *Pubbliche amministrazioni e nuovi istituti Green.* Rome: Aracne, 2016.

Murgia, C. (ed.). *L'ambiente e la sua protezione,* (Atti del convegno di studi giuridici, Cagliari, 19–20-21 aprile 1989). Milan: Giuffrè, 1991.

Nascimbene, B. & L. Garofalo. *Studi su ambiente e diritto. Il diritto dell'Unione europea.* Bari: Cacucci, 2012.

Nespor, S. & A.L. De Cesaris. *Codice dell'ambiente.* III ed. Milan: Giuffrè, 2009.

Pardi, L. *Gli strumenti di mercato a tutela dell'ambiente.* Naples: Editoriale Scientifica, 2012.

Pennasilico, M. (eds). *Manuale di diritto civile dell'ambiente.* Naples: Edizioni Scientifiche Italiane, 2014.

Perfetti L. 'Premesse alle nozioni giuridiche di ambiente e paesaggio. Cose, beni, diritti e simboli'. *Riv. giur. amb.* (2009): 1.

Pericu, G. 'Ambiente (tutela dell')'. in *Digesto disc. pubbl.* Turin: UTET, 1987.

Petrocchi M. *Compendio di Diritto dell'Ambiente.* Rome: Nel Diritto Editore, 2018.

Picozza E. (eds). *Nozioni fondamentali di diritto dell'ambiente.* Rome: Aracne, 2016.

Pierobon A. (eds). *Nuovo manuale di diritto e gestione dell'ambiente.* Rimini: Maggioli, 2012.

Police, A. (ed.). *Ambiente, attività amministrativa e codificazione: atti del primo colloquio di diritto dell'ambiente.* Milan: Giuffrè 2006.

Porena, D. *La protezione dell'ambiente tra Costituzione italiana e "Costituzione globale".* Turin: Giappichelli, 2009.

Porporato A. *Misure ripristinatorie, Governo del Territorio, Ambiente, Beni Culturali e Paesaggio.* Turin: Giappichelli, 2018.

Postiglione A. 'Ambiente: suo significato giuridico unitario'. *Riv. trim. dir. pubbl.* (1985): 44.

Postiglione A. *Diritto internazionale dell'ambiente.* Rome: Aracne, 2013.

Pozzo, B. (ed.). *Green economy e leve normative.* Milan: Giuffrè, 2013.

Pozzo, B. 'Tutela dell'ambiente (diritto internazionale)'. *Enc. dir., Annali,* Vol. III. Milan: Giuffrè, 2010, 1158.

Predieri, A. *Urbanistica, tutela del paesaggio, espropriazione. Saggi.* Milan: Giuffrè, 1969.

Renna, M. *I* 'princìpi in materia di tutela dell'ambiente'. *Riv. quadr. dir. amb.* (2012): 1–2, 62.

Rossi, G. *Diritto dell'ambiente.* Turin: Giappichelli, 2017.

Rota, R. (eds). *Lezioni di diritto dell'ambiente.* Rome: Aracne, 2018.

Roversi Monaco M. *La tutela dell'ambiente nella giurisprudenza amministrativa. Profili ricostruttivi.* Bari: Cacucci, 2018.

Santoloci M. & A. Santoloci. *Diritto all'ambiente.* Terni: Diritto all'ambiente edizioni, 2017.

Sassone S. *Vademecum dell'ambiente: guida pratica agli adempimenti, obblighi e autorizzazioni per le imprese.* Rome: EPC, 2018.

Scoca, F.G. 'Tutela dell'ambiente: impostazione del problema dal punto di vista giuridico'. *Quad. reg.* (1989): 533.

Spantigati, F. *Valutazione giuridica dell'ambiente.* Padua: Cedam, 2002.

Sturloni G. *La comunicazione del rischio per la salute e per l'ambiente.* Milan: Mondadori, 2018.

Sunstein, C.R. *Il diritto della paura. Oltre il principio di precauzione.* Bologna: Il Mulino, 2010.

Tallacchini, M.C. *Diritto per la natura. Ecologia e filosofia del diritto.* Turin: Giappichelli, 1996.

Telesca M. *La tutela penale dell'ambiente.* Turin: Giappichelli, 2016.

Environmental Impact

Benozzo, M. & F. Bruno. *La valutazione di incidenza. La tutela della biodiversità tra diritto comunitario, nazionale e regionale.* Milan: Giuffrè, 2009.

Ferrara, R. (ed.). *La valutazione di impatto ambientale.* Padua: Cedam, 2000.

Filippucci, L. *La valutazione di impatto ambientale e la valutazione strategica, alla luce delle modifiche introdotte dal dlgs. 4/2008.* Milan: Edizioni Ambiente, 2009.

Fracchia, F. & F. Mattassoglio. 'Lo sviluppo sostenibile alla prova: la disciplina di VIA e VAS alla luce del d.lgs. n. 152 del 2006'. *Rivista trimestrale di diritto pubblico* (2008): 121.

Giuliani B. 'Valutazione ambientale strategica, valutazione d'impatto ambientale e autorizzazione integrata ambientale'. in *Trattato di diritto del Territorio*, edited by G.F. Scoca, P. Stella Richter & P. Urbani, vol. 2. Turin: Giappichelli, 2018, 1067.

Greco, R. 'Le procedure di valutazione di impatto ambientale per le grandi opere'. in *I Contratti di appalto pubblico*, edited by C. Franchini. Turin: UTET, 2010.

La Camera, F. *Misurare il valore dell'ambiente: con le procedure per la valutazione ambientale in Italia.* Milan: Edizioni Ambiente, 2009.

Labarile, M.A. 'Autorizzazione integrata ambientale, come cambia il ruolo delle BAT (Best Available Techniques)'. *Riv. giur. amb.* (2013): 1.

Landi, G. *Guida alle procedure di autorizzazione ambientale.* Turin: UTET, 2009.

Monte M. & V. Torretta. *Valutazione e impatto ambientale, manuale tecnico-operativo per l'elaborazione di studi di impatto ambientale.* Milan: Hoepli, 2016.

Musone, R. (ed.). *La conferenza di servizi in materia ambientale.* Rome: Aracne, 2013.

Environmental Information

Cammelli, A. & E. Fameli. *Informatica, diritto ambiente. Tecnologie dell'informazione e diritto dell'ambiente.* Naples: Edizioni Scientifiche Italiane, 1998.

Garzia, G. *Il diritto all'informazione ambientale. Tra situazioni soggettive e interessi pubblici.* Rimini: Maggioli, 1998.

Deliperi, S. 'Diritto all'informazione ambientale, un importante strumento per la difesa dell'ambiente'. *Riv. giur. amb.* (2007): 594.

Fioravanti S. *Guida alla informazione ambientale.* Bologna: Irnerio, 2010.

Fonderico, F. 'Il diritto d'accesso all'informazione ambientale'. *Giorn. dir. amm.* (2006): 675.
Parola, G. 'L'accesso all'informazione ambientale: il diritto internazionale'. *Giur. it.* (2007): 2314.
Recchia, G. (ed.). *Informazione ambientale e diritto di accesso.* Padua: Cedam, 2007.
Sau, A. 'Profili giuridici dell'informazione ambientale e territoriale'. *Dir. amm.* (2009): 131.

Environmental Damage

Accinni, G.P. *Disastro ambientale. Dall'horror vacui all'horror pleni.* Milan: Giuffrè, 2018.
Alberton, M. *La quantificazione e la riparazione del danno ambientale nel diritto internazionale e dell'Unione europea.* Milan: Giuffrè, 2011.
Anile, F. *Danno ambientale: le nuove norme.* Milan: Edizioni Ambiente, 2007.
Barbierato, D. 'La tutela risarcitoria del danno ambientale'. *Resp. Civile* (2009): 1412.
Bianco M., R. Bordi & E. Gallo. 'Il risarcimento del danno all'ambiente: il caso Pieve Vergonte'. *Amb. & Svil.* 12 (2018): 803.
Camilletti, F. 'Danno ambientale'. in *AA. VV., Ambiente inquinamento responsabilità, Enciclopedia degli Enti Locali,* vol. IV. Milan: Giuffrè, 2009, 337.
Caterini M. *Effettività e tecniche di tutela nel diritto penale dell'ambiente.* Naples: Edizioni Scientifiche, 2017.
Cutrera, A., G. Pastorelli & B. Pozzo. (eds). *Seveso trent'anni dopo: la gestione del rischio industriale.* Milan: Giuffrè, 2006.
De Lia, A. 'Ambiente, diritto penale e principi costituzionali nella "beautiful countries": osservazioni rapsodiche'. in *Federalismi.it.*, 7 Nov. 2018.
Di Landro, A.R. *La responsabilità per l'attività autorizzata nei settori dell'ambiente e del territorio. Strumenti penali ed extrapenali di tutela.* Turin: Giappichelli, 2018.
Fimiani, P. *Le nuove norme sul danno ambientale.* Milan: Il Sole 24 ore, 2006.
Fimiani, P. *La tutela penale dell'ambiente.* Milan: Giuffrè, 2015.
Francario, L. *Danni ambientali e tutela civile.* Naples: Jovene, 1990.
Giampietro, F. *La responsabilità per danno all'ambiente.* Milan: Giuffré, 2006.
Giulietti, W. *Danno ambientale e azione amministrativa.* Naples: Editoriale Scientifica, 2012.
Iannone, R.F. *L'illecito ambientale.* Milan: Giuffrè, 2018.
Izzo, S. *La precauzione nella responsabilità civile.* Padua: Cedam, 2004.
Lemme F. & F.E. Salomone. 'Gli illeciti penali ai danni del territorio'. in *Trattato di Diritto del Territorio,* edited by Scoca G.F. P. Stella Richter & P. Urbani, vol. 2. Turin: Giappichelli, 2018, 1257.
Maddalena, P. *Danno pubblico ambientale.* Rimini: Maggioli, 1990.
Moscheta G. & A.M. Citrigno. *Tutela dell'ambiente e principio 'chi inquina paga'.* Milan: Giuffrè, 2014.
Nicotra, I. & U. Salanitro. (eds). *Il danno ambientale tra prevenzione e riparazione.* Turin: Giappichelli, 2010.

Paone, V. 'I reati contro ambiente e paesaggio nei dati delle Procure: l'Istat fa il punto sugli ultimi dieci anni'. *Amb. & Svil.* 10 (2018): 633.
Paone, R. 'La particolare tenuità del fatto e i reati ambientali'. *Amb. & Svil.* 11 (2018): 729.
Patti, S. 'La quantificazione del danno ambientale'. *Resp. Civ.* 7 (2010): 485.
Perulli, G. (ed.). *Il danno ambientale.* Turin: Giappichelli, 2012.
Pozzo, B. *Danno ambientale e imputazione della responsabilità. Esperienze giuridiche a confronto.* Milan: Giuffrè, 1996.
Pozzo, B. 'La Direttiva 2004/35/CE e il suo recepimento in Italia'. *Riv. giur. amb.* 1 (2010).
Pozzo, B. *La responsabilità ambientale.* Milan: Giuffrè, 2005.
Prati, L. *Il danno ambientale e la bonifica dei siti inquinati: la nuova disciplina dopo il d. lgs. 152/2006 e la sua riforma.* Milan: Ipsoa, 2008.
Ronchi, E. (eds). *La riforma dei rifiuti a 20 anni dal D.Lgs. 22/97 e alla vigilia delle nuove direttive rifiuti-circular economy.* Milan: Edizioni Ambiente, 2017.
Rotolo G. *Riconoscibilità del precetto penale e modelli innovativi di tutela. Analisi critica del diritto penale dell'ambiente.* Turin: Giappichelli, 2018.
Salanitro, U. 'La nuova disciplina della responsabilità per danno all'ambiente'. *Responsabilità Civile e Previdenza* (2006): 678.
Salanitro U. 'Il danno ambientale tra interessi collettivi e interessi individuali'. *Riv. Dir. Civ.* 1 (2018): 246.
Taddei, G. 'La responsabilità per danno ambientale'. *Gazzetta Ambiente* (2008): 87.
Villani, L. 'Il danno ambientale e le recenti modifiche del codice dell'ambiente (d. leg. N. 152 del 3 aprile 2006) nel sistema della responsabilità civile'. *Resp. Civ.* (2008): 2173.

Environmental Associations

Caianiello, V. 'La tutela degli interessi individuali e delle formazioni sociali nella materia ambientale'. in *Localizzazione degli impianti energetici e tutela dell'ambiente e della salute*, edited by G. De Vergottini. Rimini: Maggioli, 1988.
Cortese, F. 'La partecipazione procedimentale e la legittimazione processuale in materia ambientale'. *Giorn. dir. amm.* 5 (2010): 498.
Neri, V. 'Tutela degli interessi ambientali e legittimazione all'azione: spunti di riflessione (commento al Tar Toscana, sezione II, n. 1505 del 6 ottobre 2009)'. *Corriere Merito* 1 (2010): 93.

Water Pollution

Conti, D. 'Telerilevamento Ambientale: le Nuove Tecnologie a disposizione per la tutela dell'Ambiente marino ed il monitoraggio costiero'. in *Createspace Independent Pub* (2017).
Garzia, G. 'Inquinamento acque'. in AA. VV., *Ambiente inquinamento responsabilità, Enciclopedia degli Enti Locali*, vol. IV. Milan: Giuffrè, 2009, 493.
Maglia, S., & A. Labarile. 'Tutela delle acque sotterranee: le nuove disposizioni del D. Lgs. n. 30/2009'. *Ambiente e Sviluppo* 6 (2009): 523.
Prati, L. *Scarichi e inquinamento idrico dopo il T.U. ambientale.* Milan: Ipsoa, 2006.

Selected Bibliography

Prati, L. & G. Galotto. *Scarichi, inquinamento idrico e difesa del suolo: la nuova disciplina dopo il d. lgs. 152/2006 e la sua riforma.* Milan: Ipsoa, 2008.
Staiano S. (eds). *Acqua. Bene pubblico, risorsa non riproducibile, fattore di sviluppo.* Naples: Jovene, 2017.

Air Pollution

Borzì, A. 'Inquinamento atmosferico'. in AA. VV., *Ambiente inquinamento responsabilità, Enciclopedia degli Enti Locali*, vol. IV. Milan: Giuffrè, 2009, 543.
Cartei, G.F. (eds). *Cambiamento climatico e sviluppo sostenibile.* Turin: Giappichelli, 2013.
Midiri, F. 'La disciplina delle emissioni in atmosfera nel testo unico ambiente'. *Riv. giur. amb.* (2010): 249.
Nespor, S. 'Inquinamento atmosferico'. *Riv. giur. amb.* (2011): 289.
Patrono, P. 'La disciplina penale dell'inquinamento idrico e atmosferico dopo il c.d. testo unico ambientale: problemi vecchi e nuovi'. *Riv. Trim. Dir. Pen. Economia,* 2008, 703.

Waste

Various Authors. *Codice dei rifiuti commentato.* Rimini: Maggioli, 2017.
Various Authors. *La disciplina dei rifiuti tra ambiente e mercato.* Bologna: Il Mulino, 2018.
Bottino, G. & R. Federici. 'Rifiuti'. in *Trattato di diritto amministrativo europeo*, edited by M.P. Chiti & G. Greco, Parte Speciale, t. 1. Milan: Giuffrè, 2007, 1679.
Bovino C. '2019, addio al Sistri'. *Amb. & Svil.* 11 (2018): 711.
Busà M. & P. Costantino. *La disciplina dei rifiuti. Prontuario tecnico-giuridico.* Rimini: Maggioli, 2012.
Calligaris, L. et al., *Biotecnologie sanitarie e ambientali.* Milan: Hoepli, 2016.
Cimellaro A. & M. Busa. *Recupero dei rifiuti e procedure semplificate.* Rimini: Maggioli, 2014.
Cinquina, P. *Rifiuti. Manuale tecnico-amministrativo.* Naples: Sistemi Editoriali, 2010.
Connett P. *Rifiuti Zero, una rivoluzione in corso.* Lucca: Dissensi, 2012.
Ficco, P. (ed.). *Gestire i rifiuti tra legge e tecnica.* Milan, Edizioni Ambiente, 2018.
Fodella, A. *Il movimento transfrontaliero di rifiuti pericolosi nel diritto internazionale.* Turin: Giappichelli, 2004.
Giampietro, F. (ed.). *Commento alla direttiva 2008/98/CE sui rifiuti: quali modifiche al codice dell'ambiente?.* Milan: Ipsoa, 2009.
Giampietro, P. *La nuova gestione dei rifiuti.* Milan: Il Sole 24 ore, 2009.
Gubello, R. 'La Regione non può decidere quando un rifiuto non è più un rifiuto, nota a Cons. Stato, Sez. IV, 28 February 2018, no. 1229'. *Riv. giur. amb.* (2018): 374.
Maggiora, E. 'Rifiuti'. in AA. VV., *Ambiente inquinamento responsabilità, Enciclopedia degli Enti Locali*, IV. Milan: Giuffrè, 2009, 747.
Maschietto, E. 'Il Consiglio di Stato prende l'abbrivio dalla Corte di Giustizia'. *Riv. giur. amb.* (2018): 178.
Muratori, A. 'La riformata direttiva quadro sui rifiuti'. *Amb. & Svil.* 8–9 (2018): 519.

Muratori A. 'Le nuove BAT per gli impianti di trattamento dei rifiuti'. *Amb. & Svil.* 10 (2018): 613.

Land Reclamation

Butti, L. & F. Peres. 'Siti inquinati (bonifica)'. in AA. VV., *Ambiente inquinamento responsabilità, Enciclopedia degli Enti Locali*, IV. Milan: Giuffrè, 2009, 999.
Camici, D. et al., *Bonifica dei siti contaminati. I diversi profili giuridici amministrativi-penale-civili*. Rimini: Maggioli, 2012.
Cenini, M.S. *La proprietà della terra inquinata*. Milan: Giuffrè, 2017.
Chilosi, M. (ed.). *Siti contaminati: disciplina delle bonifiche e responsabilità ambientale*. Milan: Il Sole 24 ore, 2008.
Cingano, V. *Bonifica e responsabilità per danno all'ambiente nel diritto amministrativo*. Padua: Cedam, 2013.
Di Landro A.R. 'I problemi relativi al delitto di omessa bonifica-ripristino'. *Riv. Trim. Dir. Pen.* 1–2 (2018): 355.
Fonderico, F. 'Alla ricerca della "pietra filosofale": bonifica, danno ambientale e transazioni globali'. *Giorn.dir.amm.* (2009): 918.
Prati, L. 'Imputabilità dell'inquinamento e nesso causale tra giurisprudenza nazionale e comunitaria'. *Riv. giur. amb.* (2012): 89.
Siclari, D. *La bonifica dei siti inquinati tra tutela dell'ambiente e giustiziabilità delle pretese*. Naples: Editoriale Scientifica, 2017, 136.
Taddei, G. 'Il rapporto tra bonifica e risarcimento del danno ambientale'. *Ambiente* (2009): 417.

Noise Pollution

Bitetto Murgolo, A.L. 'Nuisance e danni non patrimoniali'. *Danno e Resp.* 4 (2018): 478.
De Mauro, A. 'La disciplina delle immissioni tra indennizzo e risarcimento'. *Danno e Resp.* 3 (2018): 291.
Fracchia, F. *L'inquinamento acustico*. Padua: Cedam, 2001.
Manca, V. 'Inquinamento acustico: la giurisprudenza di legittimità si consolida'. *Amb. & Svil.* 12 (2018): 811.
Muratori, A. 'Due decreti legislativi adeguano la disciplina italiana sul rumore agli "standard" europei: o almeno ci provano, ma deludono'. *Amb. & Svil.* 5 (2017): 321.
Zucchetti, A. 'Inquinamento acustico'. in AA.VV., *Ambiente inquinamento responsabilità, Enciclopedia degli Enti Locali*, IV. Milan: Giuffrè, 2009, 515.

Radiation

Cocco, G. (ed.). *Inquinamento da campi elettromagnetici e normativa di tutela*. Turin: Giappichelli, 2001.
Gizzi, L. 'La tutela penale dall'inquinamento elettromagnetico'. *Riv. nel diritto* (2009): 44.
Maglia, S. & M.A. Labarile. 'Inquinamento elettromagnetico: il punto a 10 anni dalla legge quadro'. *Ambiente e Sviluppo* 6 (2010): 531.
Olivetti Rason, N. (ed.). *Inquinamento da campi elettromagnetici*. Padua: Cedam, 2002.

Picozza, E. & S.M. Sambri. (eds). *Il diritto dell'energia*. Padua: Cedam, 2015.
Quadri, S. *Energia sostenibile. Diritto internazionale, dell'Unione europea e interno*. Turin: Giappichelli, 2012.
Tumbiolo, R. *L'inquinamento elettromagnetico*. Milan: Giuffrè, 2001.

Landscape

Abrami, A. *Legislazione e amministrazione del paesaggio*. Rome: Aracne, 2018.
Amorosino, S. *Introduzione al diritto del paesaggio*. Rome-Bari: Laterza, 2010.
Angrilli, M. *Piano progetto paesaggio: urbanistica e recupero del bene comune*. Milan: Franco Angeli, 2018
Cammelli, M. (ed.). *Il Codice dei beni culturali e del paesaggio*. Bologna: Il Mulino, 2007.
Cangelosi, G. *Tutela dell'ambiente e territorialità dell'azione ambientale*. Milan: Giuffrè, 2009.
Carpentieri P. 'Il ruolo del paesaggio e del suo governo nello sviluppo organizzativo e funzionale del Ministero e delle sue relazioni inter-istituzionali'. *Aedon* 2 (2018): 1127.
Cartei, G.F. (ed.). *Convenzione europea del paesaggio e governo del territorio*. Bologna: Il Mulino, 2007.
Cartei, F. *La disciplina del paesaggio tra conservazione e fruizione programmata*. Turin: Giappichelli, 1995.
Ciccarese, T. 'La Corte costituzionale torna a pronunciarsi sul riparto di competenze tra Stato e Regioni in tema di tutela ambientale e paesaggistica'. *Riv. giur. amb.* (2018): 339.
Crosetti, A. *La tutela ambientale dei beni culturali*. Padua: Cedam, 2001.
Crosetti, A. & E. Vaiano. *Beni culturali e paesaggistici*, V ed. Turin: Giappichelli, 2018.
Famiglietti, G. & N. Pignatelli. *Codice dei Beni Culturali e del Paesaggio*, II ed. Rome: Nel Diritto Editore, 2018.
Granara, D. (ed.). *Tutela paesistica e paesaggio agrario*. Turin: Giappichelli, 2018.
Immordino, M. 'Paesaggio (tutela del)'. in *Digesto delle discipline pubblicistiche*, vol. X. Turin: UTET, 1995.
Predieri, A. 'Paesaggio'. in *Encicl. Dir.*, XXXI. Milan: Giuffrè, 1981.
Spuntarelli, S. 'Le Regioni alla prova della tutela del paesaggio'. *Giur. Cost.* 656: 2018.
Vettori, N. 'Il piano paesaggistico alla prova. I modelli della Toscana e della Puglia'. *Aedon* 1 (2017): 1127.

Nature Conservation

Abrami, A. *Il regime giuridico delle aree protette*. Turin: Giappichelli, 2000.
Amirante, D. (ed.). *La conservazione della natura in Europa*. Milan: F. Angeli, 2003.
Antonio G. *Ambiente versus paesaggio. Il <bene universale> paesaggio tra sviluppo e protezione sostenibile*. Rome: Aracne, 2017.
Crosetti, A. 'Aree naturali protette'. in *Dig. disc. pubbl.*, aggiornamento, vol. I. Turin: UTET, 2008, 10.

Crosetti, A. N. Ferrucci. *Manuale di diritto forestale e ambientale*. Milan: Giuffrè, 2008.
Di Plinio, G. & P. Fimiani (ed.). *Aree naturali protette*. Milan: Giuffrè, 2008.
Ferrucci, N. *Diritto forestale e ambientale. Profili di diritto nazionale ed europeo*. Turin: Giappichelli, 2018.
Passaglia, P. & F. Raia. (eds). *La protezione dell'ambiente nella disciplina delle aree protette*. Turin: Giappichelli, 2006.
Simoncini, A. *Ambiente e protezione della natura*. Padua: Cedam, 1996.

Water Resource Management and Soil Protection

Di Benedetto, S. *Sovranità dello Stato sulle risorse naturali e tutela degli equilibri ecologici nel diritto internazionale generale*. Turin: Giappichelli, 2018.
Lugaresi, N. & F. Mastragostino. *La disciplina giuridica delle risorse idriche*. Rimini: Maggioli, 2003.
Prati, L. *Inquinamento idrico. Autorizzazioni, controlli, responsabilità*. Milan: Ipsoa, 2001.
Urbani, P. *La difesa del suolo*. Rome: Edizioni delle Autonomie, 1993.

Mining

Chianale, A. *Il diritto minerario nella giurisprudenza*. Turin: Giappichelli, 2017.
Del Gaudio, A. *Attività estrattive: cave, recuperi, pianificazione*. Naples: Liguori, 2007.
Francario, F. *Il regime giuridico di cave e torbiere*. Milan: Giuffrè, 1997.
Gisotti, G. *Le cave: recupero e pianificazione ambientale*. Palermo: Flaccovio, 2008.
Iacoviello A. 'Il riparto della competenza legislativa tra lo Stato e le Regioni in materia di beni minerari'. in *Riv. giur. ed.*, 2018, part 2, 153.
Sertorio, M. *Miniere e cave tra disciplina nazionale e regionale*. Milan: Il Sole 24 ore, 2003.
Vaccarella, M. *La disciplina delle attività estrattive nell'amministrazione del territorio*. Turin: Giappichelli, 2010.

Selected Bibliography

Index

The numbers here refer to paragraph numbers.

Index

Made in the USA
Monee, IL
18 October 2026

66041375R10234